Alien Policy in Belgium, 1840–1940

ALIEN POLICY IN BELGIUM, 1840–1940

The Creation of Guest Workers, Refugees and Illegal Aliens

FRANK CAESTECKER

Berghahn Books
New York • Oxford

First published in 2000 by **Berghahn Books**

www.BerghahnBooks.com

Library of Congress Cataloging-in-Publication Data

Caestecker, Frank.
Alien policy in Belgium, 1840–1940 : the creation of guest workers, refugees and illegal immigrants / Frank Caestecker.
p. cm.
Includes bibliographical references.
ISBN 1-57181-986-X (alk. paper)
1. Alien labor--Belgium. 2. Immigrants--Belgium--Social conditions. 3. Belgium--Emigration and immigration--Economic aspects. I. Title.

HD8508.5.A2 C336 2000
331.6'2'09493--dc21

99-085996

British Library Cataloguing in Publication Data
A catalogue record for this book is available
from the British Library.

Printed in the United States on acid-free paper.

ISBN 1-57181-986-X (hardback)

Contents

Tables and Graphs

Foreword

This is a book about the origins of contemporary alien policy. Dealing mainly with Belgium, it is a case study of a development to be seen in all countries of Western Europe. An analysis of the history of alien policy can yield important insights. Western European alien policy finally took its definitive shape during the interwar period, but to trace the origins of contemporary policies one has to go back to the nineteenth century.

By 1940 a pattern of alien policy had been created in Belgium which was a radical rupture with the past. This new alien policy aimed at attracting additional labor when it was considered beneficial for the economy, while excluding these labor migrants from society. This so-called guest-worker system, which is well-documented in Belgium for the post-World War II period by the study of the labor sociologist, A. Martens (1975), attempted to funnel immigrants into undervalued segments of the labor market by means of work permits. It was especially beneficial and until the middle of the 1950s almost exclusively restricted to the mining sector. The quasi-monopoly held by the mining sector in the employment of aliens in the 1940s and 1950s was the result of a historical process in which the socio-economic alternatives for aliens were being dismantled. Until the 1920s immigrants were able, without any intervention by the authorities, to occupy a place in the Belgian socio-economic structure; in the 1940s and 1950s they were directed towards the mining sector. In the 1960s and 1970s the range of economic sectors confronted by labor shortage extended beyond heavy industry, and the occupational opportunities of foreign workers were expanded, but the state still attempted through a system of work permits to restrict the immigrants' access to the labor market to those jobs which Belgian labor shied away from. A similar development is to be observed in the other countries of Europe. In the post industrial society of the 1980s and 1990s labor shortages were replaced by labor surpluses. Globalization and the concomitant automation of industry caused high unemployment among low-skilled workers. The Western European states, including Belgium, called a stop to all labor migration in the 1970s. At the same time globalization and the political transformations in its wake gave impetus to new patterns of migration. This new migration to Western Europe gave rise to an underclass of undocumented workers, but most of these immigrants could, at least temporarily, legalize their stay by taking advantage of provisions for asylum seekers. The asylum crisis and the rise of the extreme right caused a hardening of immigration policy in the 1990s. The pattern of alien policy set by 1940 remains, however, the framework of contemporary policy in Belgium. Also in other countries the definition of desirable and undesirable immigrants established during the interwar period remained largely unchanged.

As this book demonstrates, the constraints in the implementation of contemporary alien policy were already noticeable at the moment of its inception. The increasing criticism nowadays over tightening immigration policy finds its strength in the defense of the individual against an all powerful state. Liberal states cannot directly attune alien policy to market forces and to the interests of labor, business, and the state itself. Alien policy has to take into account the precarious relationship between the individual and the state. Whether articulated by institutions or not, ideological checks come into play. Belgium, as one of the first liberal states on the continent, has a long history in its alien policy in which a balance had to be struck between liberal ideas of respect for the individual and the collective interests of the nation for which the state stands. Since the nineteenth century these normative constraints have limited the ability of the Belgian state to control migration. The most conspicuous example of these constraints is the constant presence of the refugee as a category within Belgian alien policy. Another constraint in contemporary alien policy, but seemingly of much less impact nowadays, is of a diplomatic nature. Sending countries can defend the interests of their nationals abroad and in this manner influence the alien policy of the host country. Belgium as an open economy and, to a lesser extent as a player in international relations, can be susceptible to such pressures. In the past Belgium was even more susceptible to diplomatic pressures on its alien policy as the large number of Belgians abroad gave foreign policy considerations considerable weight within alien policy making.

This book illustrates, over the long time span covered, the slow process of transformation of alien policy. The interaction between social actors including business, labor, state agencies, middle classes, foreign governments, and the immigrants themselves gave alien policy its specific mold. The careful analysis presented by Caestecker points to the different interests involved in alien policy and addresses the question of how economic, legal, ideological, and political forces interact.

Klaus J. Bade
Institute for Migration Research and Intercultural Studies (IMIS)
University of Osnabrueck, FRG

Dedication

This book is largely the result of a four-year stay at the European University Institute (EUI) in Florence and is a throughly reworked version of a thesis defended at that institute in 1994. This research has benefitted from the close attention of several scholars at the EUI and elsewhere. They are too many to enumerate, but I want to mention in particular Prof. H.G. Haupt and Prof. K. Bade. Professor H.G. Haupt was for four years a motivating, yet critical supervisor and has continued to support my work since then. Prof. K. Bade was most stimulating during the reworking of the manuscript. A grant by the Humboldt Foundation even made it possible for me to join him in 1996 and 1997 at the Institut für Migrationsforschung und Interkulturelle Studien der Universität Osnabrück. The hospitality which I received there made it possible for me to rework the manuscript. Also the support of my Belgian tutors, Prof. H. Balthazar, Prof. E. Witte and Prof. P. Janssens should be mentioned. Of course the research of other historians, jurists, and social scientists as indicated by the bibliography has also been used extensively to further my understanding of the very different topics addressed in this study. I am also grateful to the staff of Berghahn Books and to an anonymous reviewer for their help in the last stages of making the manuscript fit for publication. I owe special thanks to the people who made my English into standard English. Especially Bonnie, but also John Hartman have taken up this ungrateful task. This book would not have been possible if Lynne, who came to visit me in Italy in 1990, had not prolonged her visit and shared my migratory life since then.

Introduction

This book deals with the transformation of Belgian alien policy between 1840 and 1940. A transformation by which the nineteenth century alien regime was exchanged for the regime of the twentieth century. By 1940 the new pattern in alien policy was established, excluding all aliens, including long-established resident aliens from participating in social and economic life on the same terms as nationals. The main thrust of this book is that the transformation of alien policy reflects a fundamental change in the functioning of the political system. The transformation of alien policy is not a result of increasing migration to Belgium. As table 1 illustrates the percentage of aliens within the total population of Belgium, according to population censuses, did not increase that spectacularly in the interwar period to warrant a reversal of policy.

We argue that it is not change in immigration to Belgium, but the change of the Belgian polity which has to be credited with the transformation in alien policy. The change from a liberal, parliamentary political system to a corporate system in which "national" interests were extended to include the private interests of more social groups caused the change in alien policy. The influence of these private interests on state policy caused

Table 1 *Percentage of Aliens Within the Total Population*

	Number of aliens	*Percentage*
1890	171, 438	2.8
1900	212,474	3.1
1910	254,547	3.4
1930	319,230	3.9
1938	339,799	4.1

the alien policy to be radically reshaped whereby the rights of aliens were severely curtailed. Immigrants, although performing work essential to the functioning of the economic system, were set apart. The political response to international migration has to be seen within the global changes of Belgian society and its polity. Alien policy is not a marginal phenomena, it provides us with a central theme around which the analysis of nineteenth and twentieth century society can be structured in order to arrive at a more complete understanding of the process of global historical change. A changing historical reality which is highlighted by the long time span being covered: a century. As starting point we take 1840; by that date the Belgian state had settled the issues of its borders and thus of its inhabitants. Also the administrative apparatus of the new state was functioning adequately by that time. For example, statistics were collected by 1839. Using May 1940 as an endpoint is more controversial, as the Second World War was not really a caesura in Belgian alien policy. The alien policy immediately after the Second World War followed the current of the 1930s. Taking 1952 as an end date would have taken into account the new alien law of 1952. This alien law did away with the last vestiges of nineteenth century alien policy, while at the same time firmly establishing a refugee policy, based on the international refugee regime in the Geneva Convention (Caestecker 1992:63ff.). It was the final stage in the evolution of Belgian alien policy. We chose not to include the postwar period because the transformation of alien policy had been largely finalized by 1940. The first decade after the Second World War was the heyday of the new alien policy; including this decade would have illustrated the implementation of the policy rather than analyzing new developments.

International migration is a social, cultural, economic, and political phenomenon. In theories of international migration, economic factors tend to prevail and far too little attention is paid to the role of the politics. This book argues that politics decides, to a certain extent, the direction, volume, and composition of international migration. This political history embedded in a broad and changing economic, social, cultural, and political reality, highlights the influence of political decisions on migration flows. Politics also influences the manner in which we name the people involved in the process of geographical mobility: emigrants, immigrants, and migrants. In general one, has to be cautious about the use of labels to designate people as they have strong ideological overtones. In this introduction we will clarify each of the labels being used and what these words exactly stand for. "Emigrant" and "immigrant" refer to the point of view of, respectively, the sending region (state) and the receiving region (state), whereby the definite directional character of the migration is underlined. The term migrants reflects much better the migration experience in the sense of its directionality and stability over time. The migratory experience is a series of displacements, depending on the shifting locations of opportunities and the use people want to make of these opportunities. Therefore we have a preference for migrants and so speak of migrant communities. The terms "emigrants" or "immigrants" we use as political constructions, i.e. if we refer to migrants within a context of states (or regions) which respectively receive or send migrants. The label "migrants" disregards the international dimension in the migration process and puts international migration on the same footing as internal migration. This distinction is a political and not a social one, however; as this study focuses on the political dimension of migration to Belgium the use of the word migrant refers here mostly to migrants crossing borders.

The central focus of this book is not on international migration, but on the decision-making process in alien policy. Such an analysis is meant to disentangle the interaction of economic, legal, ideological, cultural, and political forces. Analyzing alien policy, one covers very diverse fields. One of the first topics to address is the concept of "alien". Aliens only exist by virtue of the existence of nationals. The issue of the development of citizenship as a legal institution regulating membership is addressed in this study. We are particularly indebted to Brubaker (1992) for giving insights to the issue of codification and rationalization of state membership. The changing criteria for access to membership in the Belgian state are addressed, but besides this technical and political issue, the focus is mainly on the changing implications of this membership of the nation, i.e. the process of nationalization of society. This pervasive process has very eloquently been outlined in the seminal books on France by Weber (1976) and Noiriel (1991). Both authors contributed greatly to my understanding of this process. The label "alien" is being used here to refer to the legal status of immigrants, i.e. those of foreign nationality. It does not denote any subjective content. In French, *l'étranger* opposes national; so too the English pair alien/citizen. Both refer to a legal status. In English, there are two ways to designate l'étranger: "foreigner" designates a person originating from another country, while the stranger is he who is foreign to a certain place, independent of his legal status. In French, the subtlety of foreignness is completely lost, only the legal term is left over. In Dutch, the foreigner can be labeled as *buitenlander*, only denoting the legal status. This label is and certainly was hardly used. Mostly the term *vreemdeling* which refers to the legal status as well as to the foreignness of the person is used. One has to bear in mind that alien when it is used in quotes is the English translation of *étranger* or *vreemdeling*. The label "alien" does not necessarily connotate otherness; even in legal terms, aliens can be equal to nationals. For this legal emancipation of aliens we use, following Hammar (1990: 14-17) the label "denizens". "Denizen" was the intermediary category in old English law between alien and citizen. "Denizen" was used in England up to the 1840s for those privileged aliens who were not citizens. The concept "denizen" is used for those aliens whose residency status was fully guaranteed and who had full access, on equal terms with the national, to the labor market, business, social welfare, education etc. It is a status that permits aliens to remain indefinitely in the host country and to participate in social and economic, but not political life on the same terms as nationals.

The changing status of aliens within the host society is a central element in alien policy. Aliens can be put on a continuum where the denizens (and the naturalized aliens) are at one extreme, and at the other extreme are the expellees, the deportees. This book analyzes the shifting location of aliens on this continuum in Belgium. In order to make these shifts in location more legible we distinguish two components within alien policy. We shall call the regulation and control of the entry of aliens "immigration policy" and legislation and activities dealing with the social, economic, cultural, legal, and political integration of aliens residing in the country "immigrant policy". Immigration policy is more than just border policy; it also refers to the policy to tolerate or to expel immigrants who are already in the country. Within immigration control, we therefore distinguish between external control, control as immigrants entered the country, and internal control, control once immigrants gained entry. Aliens residing in the country can be subject to internal immigration policy as well as immigrant policy. As a rule immigration policy keeps aliens under the arbitrary power of the state. Within immigration policy, the executive power has the unrestrained legal capacity to reduce the number of immigrants by enforcing remigration. The intensity of immigration control as well as the duration during which immigrants remain subject to arbitrary immigration policy after their arrival is at the discretion of the state and changes throughout history. Immigration policy is mostly slowly extinguishing by the gradual granting of exemptions from arbitrary state power, fragments of which can remain valid until the alien is a denizen or a national. The gradual attenuation of the migrant's subjection to internal immigration control coincides with them becoming subject of immigrant policy.

The main argument of this book is that immigration policy extended its grip over aliens throughout the time period investigated in this book. Therefore we speak of the creation of the guest worker. The term *Gastarbeiter* was coined in German governmental circles at the end of the 1950s and has a strong ideological overtone. It was used in public speech in opposition to foreign labor *(Fremdarbeiter)*, which was reminiscent of the Nazi regime, although this latter term occasionally appeared in early intragovernmental papers (Steinert 1995). It was also generally used in Dutch during the 1970s to denote foreign workers performing menial labor. The label underlines the temporary nature of the presence of aliens on the labor market and in the receiving society in general and is used only by the extreme-right in their proposals for the expulsion of non-European Union migrants. "Guest workers" or workers temporarily abroad, is therefore a very recent term. We use it to designate the function attributed to aliens not only just entering Belgium, but also during their stay in the country, i.e. a subservient workers' group. The alien policy designed in the 1930s made all "recently" immigrated aliens subject to an immigration policy which would make them into guest workers. This analysis of the evolution of the state's alien policy was stimulated by historical research about the German and the French case. Respectively, Bade (1984 and 1987) and Cross (1983) have provided me with stimulating insights. Not only labor and business, but also the state itself and the labor-exporting countries each had their strategies to mold international migration to their benefit. To advance their interests these groups lobbied to influence alien policy, but at the same time they developed their autonomous schemes. The analysis of these private alien policies has been stimulated by the studies by Noiriel (1984, 1988) and Sabel (1982) which point out the pervasive influence of politics on the labor market.

Aliens are not only subject to alien policy as economic actors, but also as political actors. The internal politics of the migrant communities has received considerable attention in historical research (Caestecker 2000). Historical research in the field of migration is a recent phenomenon, not only in Belgium, but also in other Western European immigration countries. European historians only discovered this dimension of the national past in the eighties. This sudden interest was connected with the rise of an intellectual elite within the migrant communities themselves and with political developments which made the migrant issue a national concern. Historical research in the field of Jewish immigration was the forerunner in this area. Its turbulent war history, together with a large intellectual group within the Jewish community, focused attention on the Jewish community's past. It was initially American researchers - in connection with the internal evolution in American historiography - who investigated the Jewish migrant communities in France and Germany. In Belgium, this migrant community also was given the most attention. Schreiber (1995-1996) has studied the internal evolution of the Jewish population in the nineteenth century and the influence of migration on the Jewish communities. Van Doorslaer (1996) has explored the Left, particularly the Communist-organized Jewish migrants in the interwar period. The Italian migrant community in Belgium also received attention in historical research. Morelli, in line with the French school around Milza, has focused on the political organization of the Italian community in the interwar period, in which she analyzed at length the fight between fascist and anti-fascist emigrants. With the anti-fascist Italians in interwar Belgium we are confronted with a specific group of emigrants, the refugees.

Refugees are people forced to leave their country of origin for political reasons. Although we acknowledge that there is no sharp line to draw between refugees and (economic) migrants, we consider the distinction between politically and economically induced migrations an important reality within population movements. Refugees are also migrants, but for the sake of convenience we denote economic migrants as migrants in contrast to refugees. The labels "migrants" and "refugees" refer to this different sociological reality of migration. Corresponding with this distinction, we can distinguish within alien policy between refugee policy and immigration/immigrant policy. The causes of emigration of refugees are distinct from those of migrants, but refugees are also economic actors and as such evoke within the receiving society similar concerns. The dichotomy in international migration is justified only to a certain extent. How refugees obtained a distinct treatment within alien policy is yet another focus of this book. The only publication dealing with Belgian alien policy before 1940 is an analysis of the reception of refugees from Nazi Germany by Garfinkels (1974). She describes the refugee policy of the 1930s as a harmonious linear process, in which the rights of the refugees were increasingly strengthened. The subtitle -"the problem of refugees"- does not seem fitting. The refugees did not pose any problem in this book. For Garfinkels the interests of the refugees did not collide with the political and economic interest of the host country to any great extent; on the contrary, in a harmonious symbiosis their differing interests were brought together. The interpretation presented here refutes this depoliticized perspective, as it shows that developing a distinct policy for refugees was subject to intense political struggle and that Belgian refugee policy, not only in the 1930s but also before, remained, from a sociological point of view, an incomplete policy. The political and sociological reality of refugees did not always correspond. In this study the political category "refugee" is in quotation marks indicating that these refugees were acknowledged as such by the authorities (recognized as eligible for the status of refugee). "Refugee" has hence no pejorative meaning; it refers only to the political confirmation of their status of refugee. The "refugee" policy can cover the sociological reality of refugees, but does not do so by definition.

The last category of aliens discussed in this book is the undocumented alien, in common parlance the illegal alien. The latter term is another example of the strong ideological overtone a label can have. "Illegal alien" is a political category, which strongly accentuates these aliens' non-obedience to the law. It is a category with a built-in repressive notion. In order to circumvent this dimension, migrants who are put in an "illegal" category are labeled undocumented aliens. We consider that (im)migration can be illegal, (im)migrants not.

We have mentioned four categories within alien policy: denizens, guest workers, the refugees, and the illegal aliens. Aliens were bestowed or deprived of rights depending on the category in which they were placed and for each category an appropriate policy was developed, i.e. immigration/immigrant, refugee, and expulsion policy. The labels "guest worker", "illegal aliens", "refugees" and "denizen" are used in this book to make clearer the pervasive changes occurring in the period under investigation. To describe a long-term process, a changing reality, we cannot borrow from the terminology of one era, but must impose our own unifying concepts. The use of these labels has the advantage of uniting some epochally-restricted categories which had a similar effect (for denizen: *domicilié* until 1876, aliens with residence status until 1936, and after 1936 privileged aliens; for illegal alien: expellees and vagrants of foreign nationality for most of the nineteenth century, undocumented aliens in the interwar period).

The Structure of this Book

A historical analysis of immigration and the policies it engendered has to be seen in its proper political and socio-economic context. The transformation of Belgian society is outlined in the introduction of each of the chapters. It is within this context that the changes in the alien policy have to be situated. An outline of nineteenth century alien policy is presented in the first two chapters. In chapters three to five we give a overview of the meaning of the migration for Belgian industry in the 1920s, and we designate the forces shaping this immigration, including the role of the state. The state's alien policy remained virtually unchanged during the whole decade, but it did not remain unchallenged. In chapters three and four we elaborate, at length, on the proposals put forward by different interest groups to change the alien policy and the causes of the failure to implement any of those changes. In chapter five we analyze an alternative way of economic insertion of immigrants; migrants who set up their own businesses and perhaps give employment opportunities to some of their co-migrants. The last four chapters analyze migration to Belgium and the changes in alien policy in the period 1928-1939 following a strictly chronological pattern.

This book is "limited" to an analysis of a strictly Belgian subject, but changes in alien policy in neighboring countries are outlined in so far as they affected Belgian alien policy. This influence should not be underestimated. First of all, during the whole period investigated, Belgian alien policy took the interests of the large number of Belgians abroad into account. How changes in alien policy in the neighboring countries affected the Belgian emigrants will be analyzed in order to indicate to what extent alien policy in Belgium was influenced by Belgian emigration policy.

Secondly, changes in Belgian alien policy were sometimes adjustments to or even imitations of policy in neighboring countries. A systematic overview of French, German, and Dutch alien policy during the period investigated will be briefly presented in the concluding chapter. The conclusions show that the transformation of Belgian alien policy has certain Belgian peculiarities, but that the changes which occurred in Belgian alien policy conform to a general picture of a Western European development.

The sources being used

This analysis of alien policy is founded mainly on my own primary research. The scanty literature on the topic has already been mentioned. In the book, references are mainly to be found to the archival collections used for this research. The archives of agencies of the Belgian state were crucial for this dissertation; the extensive archival collection of the Ministry of Justice and the Ministry of Foreign Affairs were particularly useful for analyzing alien policy. The archives of the Ministry of Labor and of the Ministry of Economic Affairs were a disappointment. Lacunae in their source material caused many aspects of our problem to be inadequately addressed, especially for the period after 1935 when these ministries had an important voice in alien policy. Luckily, the vast archive of the Mine Administration in the National Archives and the smaller collections at its regional offices, together with the archives of the National Labor Exchange Office gave us extensive material on foreign labor. The papers of the Council of Ministers, of poor quality, give some information on key decisions. My research in Dutch, German, French, Polish, Hungarian, Swiss, and Czechoslovakian archives also yielded important material. Especially the archival collections of the Ministries of Foreign Affairs of these countries were very useful for our analysis. In Poland we could also consult the material of some local labor exchange offices that took part in recruitment for Belgian industry. The collection of the Polish Catholic Mission in Belgium, kept at the Archives of the Archbishopric in Gniezno, was another valuable source of material.

Another source of information was the ethnic press. Especially the Polish daily newspapers, *Narodowiec* and *Wiarus Polski* and, for only a short period, *Dziennik Ludowy,* were especially useful in providing interesting information. Archives linked to the mining industry and, to a much lesser extent, the metallurgic industry were the third axis of our archival collection. Most of these archives were linked to the employers, however, some material on the unions was also collected. The archives of the Fedechar and three of its constituent members (the associations of mining companies of the basin of Charleroi, Mons, and Limburg) constituted the bulk of our material concerning the mining industry. Archives of some individual mines have provided some additional information. For the attitude of the middle classes we had, unfortunately, only fragmentary information at our disposal. The Chambers of Commerce and various middle-class organizations did not keep their archives. For an analysis of the background of their interventions, we were then forced to rely mainly on the press. For this, we utilized the few publications we found of the organizations involved, along with a number of national daily newspapers. We also consulted a number of rich archival collections of diverse actors. José Gotovitch put the microfilms of the archives of the Belgian Communist Party, which were kept in the Institute for Marxism-Leninism in Moscow, at our disposal. During a visit to New York, we were able to consult the archives of the Joint, we also looked through the "Belgian collection" (the papers David Trocki) of the YIVO. For the Social-Democratic stance we relied on the microfilms of the Bureau of the Belgian Workers Party and the papers of Emile Vandervelde and his wife Jeanne, who in her office of secretary of the Belgian League of Human Rights had compiled an absorbing collection on issues related to our research. The Red Cross Archive, The Royal Archive, and the archive of the archbishopric in Mechelen and the bishopric of Liège provided us with additional material. We also conducted some interviews in Poland, Czechoslovakia, and Belgium between 1986 and 1990 with (children of) migrants who had worked in interwar Belgium. These interviews gave a direct experience of how it was to be an immigrant in those years.

A thorny issue for a researcher on Belgium is of course the linguistic aspect. For names of organizations we have in general, if no English equivalent was available used the French name. In the interwar period, French was still the dominant working language, hence both for this reason and for reasons of consistency French has been the only non-English language used. In place names, English is used if an equivalent was available, otherwise the Dutch variant is used for Flemish and French for Walloon names. This book is an abridged version of a Ph.D.thesis defended at the European University Institute in Florence. For the professional historian who is interested in more detailed references for sources being used, I refer to the original manuscript which is available in WP6.0 under my name at the following Internet address: http://www.imis.uni-osnabrueck.de (Gäste).

Chapter 1

A Brutal Alien Policy, 1840–1861

The Belgian revolution against Dutch rule in 1830 is to be situated within the global transformation of the agrarian *Ancien Régime* to industrial-bourgeois society, of a feudal society to a society based on individual freedom. The conflict between old and new, which this transformation engendered is also to be found within the forces which led to the Belgian revolution. The revolution against the Dutch regime – a regime which, in an authoritarian way, strove for the modernization of society, including changing the economic structures towards industrial capitalism – was the result of a coalition between the progressive and the conservative forces. On the one hand, there were those members of the middle classes (professionals) who were striving for greater political participation by the citizens. On the other hand, there were the agrarian and clerical forces who wanted to restore the old order. Both these forces found each other in a coalition "Unionism" which made use of deep social discontent among the lower social classes to establish a new regime. The features of the new regime were a compromise between the two factions. The conservative forces (the Catholic current) succeeded in limiting democratization with, among other measures, ungenerous suffrage provisions which required a minimum direct-tax contribution. In 1848, in order to prevent a democratic revolution, suffrage was extended to its constitutional limits whereby the middle class was co-opted in the regime. As such, the voting right was limited to one in eight male citizens older than twenty-five .The progressive forces (the liberal current) succeeded in establishing a liberal state based on a constitution which guaranteed freedom of speech, press, assembly, association, and religion. The political system was dominated by liberal and Catholic notables and the political locus of the new regime was Parliament. The Belgian Constitution of February 1831 established the equality before the law of all inhabitants of the kingdom. This was in accordance with the liberal spirit of the new regime.

The new Belgian state was highly supportive of industry. The creation of the new regime disrupted the economic balance of emergent industry by the loss of the Dutch markets. An aggressive policy by the new state sustained the young industry. The highly protective tariff of 1834 kept away any fierce foreign competition (Mokyr 1976). Belgium was the first country after Great Britain to industrialize and in the middle of the nineteenth century was one of the most industrialized areas of Europe. The agrarian sector still dominated the Belgian economy in these years, but 32 percent of the Belgian labor force was already active in the secondary sector (De Brabander 1983:46). The most important industrial branches were cotton, flax, wool, coal mining, and metallurgy. The backbone of Belgian industrial development was the mining industry. In the first half of the nineteenth century Belgium was the largest coal producer on the Continent. The Belgian mine basins, Liège in the east, Borinage in the west and in between the basins of Centre, Charleroi and Namur were part of the great Western European group of coal fields stretching from the Pas de Calais in France to the Ruhr in Germany. The Belgian mining basins supported the metallurgical industry. Belgium rivaled Britain as the world's most modern iron and steel producer. The most important financial institution in the country, the *Société Générale de Belgique* had considerable interests in heavy industry. Shortly after the Belgian revolution the *Société Générale* invested in heavy industry in Hainaut. In the second half of the nineteenth century the *Société Générale* expanded greatly its industrial interests and in particular in the coal industry where it controlled between one-third and one-fourth of the coal production. The holding not only financed these firms, but also had considerable influence on management.

The shift from an agrarian economy to an industrial one did not occur without social disruptions. Especially in Flanders, the restructuring of the labor market brought social dislocation on a massive scale. Linen textiles produced by a labor intensive industry in rural Flanders – the source of the Flemish prosperity in the eighteenth century – was in the first half of the nineteenth century replaced by machine-made cotton and linen. In the Flemish proto-industrial regions the eviction of labor from this old economic activity did not follow the pace of the creation of new industrial jobs. This structural factor, together with an economic depression, potato blight, poor grain harvests, and epidemics devastated Flanders in the 1840s. The Belgian liberal regime did not impede entry or exit from the country. On the contrary, between 1848 and 1855, due to the desperate economic situation, emigration of the surplus population was even strongly stimulated by local as well as central authorities (Schepens 1973:94ff.). The economic disaster in Flanders triggered a large scale emigration mainly to the French industrial department of the Nord. The population explosion of French industrial towns in the Nord such as Roubaix, Lille, Tourcoing was mainly to be attributed to Flemish immigration. Between 1851 and 1861 the number of Belgians in France nearly doubled, from 128,000 to 204,000. The advent of the industrial revolution in Belgium did not cause such an abrupt social change all over Belgium. The transformation of the labor market during the first three quarters of the nineteenth century formed a set of incremental shifts towards the new reality. Heavy industry exclusively located in Wallonia offered a steady livelihood to an ever-increasing share of the newly proletarianized peasants in that area.

The attraction of foreign workers by Belgian industry seems to have been limited. Local sources of labor were sufficient to still the hunger for manpower of the new industries. It is not yet feasible to assess adequately the importance of international migration to mid-nineteenth century Belgium. Hardly any studies have been made, statistics are lacking and the few figures available are hardly reliable. The only source available over a certain time period is the number of files created by the Department of Aliens upon registration of every new immigrant of foreign nationality. This figure is, however, also a function of administrative centralization. In the nineteenth century, numerous aliens were only registered after living for years in Belgium. Graph 21 indicates that there was a slow, incremental increase in migration to Belgium. This migration was mainly a migration of qualified labor, of artists, intellectuals, white-collar workers, and businessmen. These immigrants were not the underprivileged; most of them were qualified urban-based people who hoped for increased opportunities in the growing Belgian cities (De Schaepdrijver 1990; Lis 1986:58). This picture of skilled migration does not cover the international migration to Belgium in its totality. International migration to the Belgian cities resulted, to a minor degree, also from the pull of a regional center whose range of attraction broadened to include regions beyond the national borders. This "incidental" crossing of the borders was especially the case for the southern Dutch migrants in Antwerp and Brussels. They occupied those positions in which the migrants from the Belgian countryside were also to be found. They worked in lowly qualified trades and in household services (Lis 1986:45; De Schaepdrijver 1990). A strict distinction between international and internal migration is inappropriate for this period. We should distinguish rather between long-distance, international migration which was largely an urban-to-urban movement, and regional migration, which covered rather short distances, but could be also from abroad. The aim of both streams of migrants was radically different: the former was a migration in search of better opportunities, and the latter was a mere survival strategy to satisfy minimal needs.

Immigration Policy as Border Control

The liberal current of the Belgian revolution had succeeded in imposing a decentralized structure on the state. In the domain of immigration policy, control was also decentralized. The local authorities in the border towns granted immigrants access to the country on the basis of their passports. Only in doubtful cases did they ask for the advice of the central authorities. In these turbulent times in which revolution and reaction followed upon each other, geographic mobility was suspicious. Hence state control over migration, be it internal or international, was considered necessary for preserving public order. In principle all immigrants were required to carry a valid passport with a Belgian visa, but this regulation had a class bias (Soignie 1858:103; ARMJ 34). Foreign workers were exempt from this obligation as they were already controlled as workers. Labor independent of nationality was seen as an element to be controlled. The control was subcontracted to the employers. The mobility of labor had been restricted by Napoleonic legislation requiring that workers carry a workbook *(livret)* signed by their employer, which reported their employment history. This obligation was canceled in Belgium in 1830. It was one of the concessions to labor during the Belgian revolution. From 1841 onwards, due to the insistence of the mining companies, workers were required to carry a workbook. This implied the obligation of informing the employer of one's departure and hence respecting an advance notice requirement (Leboutte 1988). Foreign laborers looking for work in Belgium were not obliged to carry a passport upon immigration; a workbook was sufficient.

During the 1830s, those who wanted to increase the power of the central state attacked local autonomy. This campaign for a strong state was successful in the issue of border control. By 1839 the admission of immigrants had become the exclusive competence of the central authorities. Fixed border posts were established and special personnel, on the payroll of the central authorities, were in charge of border control (Foutre 1985:126ff.). The agitation of the Sûreté, an intelligence service founded in 1832 was particularly instrumental. The Sûreté was formally dependent on the Ministry of Justice, but in practice was largely autonomous. This intelligence service had to inform the authorities about any danger which threatened the young kingdom. A threat from the north was manifest since the Dutch King Willem I had not yet recognized the new kingdom. This central police agency survived the stabilization of the new kingdom with the peace agreement with the Netherlands in 1839.

The Belgian Constitution of February 1831 established the equality before the law of all inhabitants of the kingdom. Aliens, however, quickly became a target of special interest to the state. The Sûreté centralized all matters concerning aliens, including, since 1839, decisions on the admission of aliens in the country. The control of the borders under the authority of the Sûreté meant that each year several hundred aliens were refused access to Belgium (Graph 14). Among those aliens who were *refoulé* (refused access to Belgium) were quite a number of "refugees". These "refugees" of the first half of the nineteenth century – political activists fleeing persecution – were a socially exclusive lot. They were mostly from the upper class and although they found it difficult to make both ends meet in exile, their lifestyle remained bourgeois. Their cause, overthrowing their repressive governments, seemed sympathetic to Belgian liberals. They were ideologically and socially close to the Belgian national elite. But even though the Belgian authorities were quite sympathetic to them and their cause, the policy towards them was restrictive. The Belgian authorities wanted to keep "refugees" out of the country. Embassies were ordered not to grant them visas. The border guards received instructions not to let these political activists enter Belgian territory (Reiter 1992:117f. and 211). "Refugees," as political actors par excellence, could jeopardize the precarious diplomatic balance by which the new state was able to exist. Within Restoration Europe, the liberal kingdom of Belgium was only tolerated and could not risk giving its neighbors any pretext to intervene. "Refugees" who succeeded in entering the country were, however, not sent back to their country of origin. *Non refoulement* was the only concession to "refugees" by liberal Belgium. The authorities first looked into each case to see if a genuine refugee was being dealt with. If the authorities considered that to be the case, those who had the means for their upkeep were granted temporary residence while their less affluent colleagues had to leave the country. For those destitute "refugees" who agreed to leave Belgium, the Belgian authorities financed their voyage to Great Britain. Not only destitute "refugees", but also "refugees" whose convictions were considered subversive (Republicans, Socialists, etc.) or where diplomatic pressure was exerted for their expulsion, were escorted to the port of Ostend (Saint-Ferréol 1870:1, 44ff.; ARMJ 247).

In the beginning of the 1840s the aim of the immigration policy was not only political, but also social in nature. The collapse of the Flemish flax and linen industry had caused great distress. The authorities felt that local labor had to receive the minimal protection of not increasing competition in the already extremely slack labor market. They therefore declared a strict freeze on immigration in 1840. In subsequent years the authorities only tried to enforce an immigration freeze during the winter, as the Minister of Justice considered that labor was then at its most needy and that the government had to give them a hand by stopping the immigration of foreign labor (ARMJ 34). Consideration of the interests of labor in immigration policy in the early 1840s was mainly meant to preserve the political status-quo. This same preoccupation with public order, together with agrarian interests, caused the state not to contribute to the uprooting of the rural population in order to provide industry with a larger supply of labor. Conservative forces influential within the government aimed at stabilizing the rural population in the countryside. The new poor law of 1845 (local authorities were required to assist a pauper only after eight years of residence, previously it had been four years) was enacted to diminish the mobility of the poor (Van Damme 1990). Industrial interests were still secondary to agrarian interests in the formulation of the policy of the Belgian state. The restriction on immigration of foreign labor in the early 1840s was, however, not directed against industry. It was clearly stated that the regulation of the mobility of alien laborers was not to thwart the labor needs of the Belgian industry in any way. Aliens whom the industrialists had called upon for specific tasks were exempted in particular (ARMJ 34).

Stringent administrative control at the borders was canceled altogether in 1842 (Graph 14). As international railway connections increased, Belgian border guards were no longer able rapidly to check all the passports of train passengers. The railway companies complained that the border guards delayed their trains. The government decided to shift the control of passports and means tests of aliens to the interior of the country. Thus, local authorities again became responsible for the implementation of immigration policy. Initially, local authorities of the border towns bore the main brunt. They had to check the passports and means of livelihood of those aliens who had entered Belgian territory by other means of transport than the train. If the means of livelihood of these aliens, who had mostly arrived on foot, were insufficient, they were to be refused access to the country. For all others and for those who had reached the interior of the country by train or by slipping through the border, the Sûreté had to be consulted. If they had regular papers and means of making a living they were, in principle, allowed to stay. By 1850 most immigrants crossed the borders without being noticed by the local authorities of the border towns (Table 2 based on *Exposé de la situation du Royaume* 1841-1850:503). Local authorities in the interior of Belgium became largely responsible for the implementation of immigration policy.

The change in immigration control was preceded by the introduction in 1846 of the obligatory registration of all inhabitants in the population reg-

Table 2 *The Implementation of Immigration Policy, 1848-1850*

	1848	*1849*	*1850*
Aliens declaring themselves at the border	54,661	36,252	25,181
Aliens declaring themselves in towns	47,849	48,030	44,625

isters. Although no historical research has been done on this spectacular decision – at that time unique for a European state – it is highly likely that besides being better informed about society, a desire to control the population also played a role. Anyway, it is likely that control over immigrants in the interior of the country became more effective. The unregistered stay of immigrants was easier to check. All persons arriving in a community from abroad, whether they were Belgians or not, had to present their passports to the municipal authorities in order to be registered in the population register. The Sûreté had to be notified of the aliens' arrival and final consent to their stay remained the competence of this central office. Pending the decision of Sûreté, undocumented or destitute aliens were to be placed in custody. While, in general, the alien who had the necessary papers and a source of income was granted permission to remain in Belgium, other aliens, in particular those without a source of income, were mostly expelled (Soignie 1858:102ff.). The expense created by the arrest of destitute or undocumented aliens pending decision of the Sûreté caused rose sharply. Because the central authorities mostly decided to expel them anyway, the Sûreté ordered local authorities in 1850 to expel alien vagrants without prior notification (Soignie 1873:172f.). As Graph 15 indicates, the number of people removed from Belgian territory because they were either destitute or lacked papers oscillated around eight hundred annually in the 1850s. From 1850 onwards, refugees and military deserters who were to leave the country were explicitly granted a choice of border crossing. By offering this choice to these unwanted aliens the liberal Belgian regime made sure that its expulsion policy did not turn into a disguised extradition policy. Extradition was a sensitive issue for a liberal regime surrounded by regimes which were much less concerned about human rights. In 1852 this facility was extended to all foreign vagrants, they all could choose to which border they would be brought to. The strong liberal values of the Belgian regime (and the small size of the country) meant that the individual liberty, even of its unwanted guests, had significance.

The conclusion should not be drawn from this overview that there was a stringent control over immigration in the period between 1840 and 1860. The ambition of immigration policy to control human mobility was, without fingerprints or photographic identification, largely illusory (Saint-Férreol 1870:2, 35). Migrants could cross frontiers with little difficulty and reside virtually without problem once they had arrived. The lack of an efficient central administrative apparatus – the Sûreté was totally dependent on the cooperation of the local authorities because it was badly staffed – weakened the grip of the central authorities on migration. Not only weak administrative capacities, but also economic interests impeded the stringent control of immigration. The effectiveness of immigration control was deliberately limited in order to foster the development of the port of Antwerp. In the first half of the nineteenth century, the port became an important transit place for emigration overseas and there was strong pressure to make it easier for the mostly German emigrants to pass through Belgium (Kurgan and Spelkens 1976:68f.). Implementation of the alien legislation was therefore rather lax.

Only with the sudden upsurge in politically-sensitive refugee migration after 1848 did the central authorities try to impose a strict border control and implement a restrictive policy. The failed liberal revolutions of 1848 created a stream of refugees. In 1850 about eighty foreigners (Poles, French, Italians, Germans, and Hungarians) in Belgium were considered to be refugees (ARMJ 250). The number of "refugees" rose spectacularly in the following years. In total 2,400 aliens obtained asylum between 1848 and 1853. The number of asylum seekers increased sharply after the French coup d'état of Louis Napoleon in December, 1851; not less than 1,572 French refugees obtained asylum. Although the number of asylum seekers in these years was probably greater, the large number of expulsions immediately after the coup, as indicated by Graph 14 is a testimony of the refusal to accept more refugees. All refugees without valid papers were either sent over to Great Britain or were returned to the French-Belgian border (Saint-Ferréol 1870:1, 45). That notwithstanding this restrictive policy so many Frenchmen were granted asylum was probably linked to the deliberate policy of the new French regime to expel the notorious members of the opposition with a passport valid for Belgium (Reiter 1992:215). Their immigration into Belgium therefore was not illegal. All the refugees of December 1851 who had immigrated legally had to hand over their passports and papers upon arrival in Belgium and had to declare their source of income. Very soon afterwards, depending on their financial means and their political activities, orders of either internment or expulsion followed. Those who were allowed to remain in Belgium were interned, mostly in small towns under the strict supervision of the local police (Reiter 1992:211; Saint-Ferréol 1870:1, 76 and 61ff.). The Belgian authorities quickly took additional measures to prevent a further influx. Not only a passport, but also a valid visa was required. Those refugees who immigrated illegally were refused asylum. They were immediately expelled, even if they had just left French prisons (Payne 1966:48; Saint-Ferréol 1870:2, 35ff.; Wouters 1963:1038). Because massive, politically-induced migration was no longer directed to the Belgian border in the years that followed, prohibition of aliens from entering Belgium was soon considered obsolete. Protection of the labor market was also judged inappropriate, free migration was an obvious corollary of free trade and its benefits could not be doubted. Supply and demand had to be given full liberty. Free trade alliances were signed with numerous countries in which the free mobility of citizens of the contracting partners was also stated. In

1861 all passport regulations were annulled. As Graph 14 indicates, in the period after 1861, immigrants were no longer refused access due to lack of appropriate identity papers.

Immigrant Policy in an Autonomous Society

In the 1830s the central authorities had far-reaching ambitions to control immigration to Belgium. The Sûreté in Brussels had to be notified of the arrival of any alien in Belgium and would subsequently decide if those aliens would be allowed to remain in the country. Not only was movement into Belgium to be controlled, but also every alien, independent of his length of residence in Belgium, had to register with the central alien administration. The knowledge of their whereabouts would enable the authorities to order any alien who was no longer considered desirable to leave the country. The increasing number of political refugees in particular, were considered by the Belgian authorities to be a threat to the diplomatic position of Belgium. The Sûreté was to see that aliens, whether they were refugees or not, did not undertake any undesirable political activities. The Sûreté took this task to heart and summoned all local administrations, as well as the judiciary and the army to provide them with any information concerning aliens residing in Belgium. In this way the biography of every alien was constantly updated. The data, together with information on political activities gathered by spying on them, were used to decide on expulsions (Keunings 1980). A central control over aliens turned out not to be so easy to establish. This tiny central bureaucracy had hardly any support from the local authorities who stood firm on their autonomy. The municipal authorities did not consider it worthwhile to report to the Sûreté about aliens who had been living in their community for years. The central authorities were not always even notified of new immigrants (ARMJ 34). When the central authorities were notified of the presence of aliens in a municipality, not only did they decide if they could remain in the country, they also wanted to decide which status was to be attributed to them. Three different types of alien status emerged out of the Alien Law of 1835: aliens without residency status, those with, and the *domiciliés*. This law was prolonged by Parliament for only three years at a time out of concern not to grant the executive too much power over aliens. The triennial prolongation of the law was dependent on a report on the use the government had made of its power over aliens.

The first category of aliens, those without residency status, was only tolerated. They were given a precarious entitlement to stay; the Sûreté could decide arbitrarily to expel them (*renvoyer*). A second category of aliens was aliens with residency status. No legal provisions were provided concerning the granting of this status, it was totally dependent on administrative practice. The Sûreté made the granting of residency status contingent on formally approved domicile. Residence as such did not grant this status, only if an alien was registered by the Sûreté and this central administration agreed upon his stay in Belgium could an alien acquire residency status. It seems that a considerable number of immigrants never obtained residency status. Foreign labor in particular was refused the advantage of this status. The authorities wanted to retain their hold on them and granting them residency status would prevent the authorities from taking any action against them in the future. Thus only temporary residence permits were granted (ARMJ 34). For "refugees" this was also considered the most appropriate strategy. Those "refugees" who were tolerated in Belgium not only had to be able to support themselves, but were also called on to abandon politics. Strict police control over these "refugees" was to guarantee that they adhered to this condition of stay. If it was discovered that a refugee was politically active, expulsion followed. In order to enable the administration to expel "refugees" whenever they did not respect the conditions on which they were accepted, hardly any "refugees" were granted residency status, but given only a tenuous right of abode (ARMJ 250 and 902; AFAB Correspondance réfugiés: II,7).

Aliens with residency status could only be expelled if they were considered dangerous. This meant that they disturbed public order or had been convicted of criminal offenses. Among the latter, destitute aliens who had been convicted of vagrancy were included. The Poor Law of 3 April 1848 even stipulated explicitly – the verdict in the Jones affair (see below) had just been given – that the authorities had to expel aliens with residency status after being convicted of vagrancy. A royal decree (*expulsion*) was necessary for the expulsion of aliens with residency status to legally take effect. An alien, who after having been *expulsé,* returned to Belgium could be brought before the court and be punished with a prison term of fifteen days to six months because of *rupture de ban.*

The famous Jones affair put the administrative power which the Sûreté exerted over aliens into a dubious legal position. Jones, an English woman who had been expelled (*renvoyée*) in 1845 because of lack of means of support contested this administrative decision. She claimed that her expulsion was illegal since she had been living in Antwerp since September 1840 and that no royal decree of expulsion was promulgated. The Sûreté, in line with its administrative practice, contested her claim of residency status since they had never formally approved of her stay. The judiciary found for Jones, stating that the Aliens Law of 1835 did not qualify the type of domicile needed for residency status and that therefore de facto domicile had to be taken into consideration (Cuvelier 1939; ARMJ 851; PHK 1846:550). This reasoning put most of the power which the

Sûreté had been exerting over aliens into jeopardy. According to the Sûreté, this unacceptable verdict implied that it would be to the alien's advantage to elude the police. By staying some months in Belgium without declaring oneself to the authorities, an alien would acquire legal protection. This could not have been the aim of the legislature. Without fundamentally changing its practice, the Sûreté became more cautious. Temporary residency permits continued to be issued, but only in exceptional cases. "Refugees" in particular were granted this precarious legal status. Grudgingly, the Sûreté had to consider de facto domicile in some cases and to limit its administrative power over these aliens (ARMJ 902). But as a rule, aliens who declared their arrival to the municipal authorities and could prove their identity acquired residency status (ARMJ 864 and 234). Notwithstanding these proposals, the administrative practice of the Sûreté was never legally consecrated. The law of 1835, which was vague concerning the granting of residency status, continued to be prolonged without any significant changes, and the central authorities arbitrarily used the competence that was granted to them (Godding 1970:316ff.).

The third category of aliens were those with a status of *domicilié*. These aliens were legally equal to the nationals, except in political rights. They could not be expelled. They even had some rights and duties (to serve in the militia) reserved for nationals (PHS 1848:1521f.; PHK 1848:1269f.). Unlike all other aliens, they were not to be excluded from municipal welfare as stipulated in the Poor Law of 1845.The status of *domicilié* was a truly denizen status. To become a *domicilié* was an exceptional favor granted to very few aliens, most of them bourgeoisie. In the first two decades after the foundation of the Belgian state, 338 aliens were attributed this status (Graph 18). Although we do not have any figures for the next decade, it seems the status of *domicilié* was an exceptional favor for an increasing number of well-to-do aliens (*La Belgique Judiciaire* 1850:365; *Exposé de la situation du Royaume* 1852:504).

The authorities did not wield their power over aliens residing in Belgium in the interests of national labor. If an alien had the means to assure his subsistence he could remain in Belgium, even if this meant replacing national labor. That the presence of aliens was not to be dependent on the (subjective) interests of the popular classes was illustrated by the events of 1848. In that year Belgian labor was dismissed en masse in France. The political revolution of 1848 had made French workers audacious and they pressured employers to fire their foreign workers. The French authorities had no immediate input in this xenophobic campaign, although in many towns local authorities failed to provide foreign labor and, in particular, Belgians the necessary protection against street violence. Belgian emigrants could only turn to the French authorities for financial aid for repatriation (Chatelain 1977:863; Lentacker 1974:199ff.). The anti-Belgian policy in France created a strong popular outcry in Belgium. Belgians wanted to retaliate against the French in Belgium. Given the economic downturn, the returnees and the unemployed local workers wanted to profit from the eventual dismissal of French immigrants in Belgium. This popular pressure had very little perceptible influence on the Belgian authorities. The traditional policy was maintained (Wouters 1963:603ff.). As Graph 14 indicates, in that year there was simply an increase in the number of people rejected at the border, but no increase in the number of aliens expelled. The former had little to do with social considerations, but rather with the authorities concern over dangerous political immigration.

Social considerations did, however, play a role in the policy towards destitute aliens. In 1845 aliens, except the *domiciliés* were excluded from locally organized social assistance. Only the central authorities were authorized to grant social assistance to aliens. As Belgium was rather an emigration than an immigration country it was considered that a generous treatment of its immigrants by the central authorities could have beneficial effects on the treatment of Belgians abroad. In the interest of Belgians abroad, bilateral agreements with other states had to be reached to arrange for the reciprocal reimbursement of the cost of social assistance to destitute emigrants. Such treaties had been concluded with the Netherlands (1841 and 1849) and Luxembourg (1843), but because of the limited results and the administrative complications both these treaties were canceled by 31 May 1849 (*Exposé de la situation du Royaume* 1865: II, 100). In the absence of bilateral agreements concerning social assistance all aliens were totally dependent on the goodwill of the Belgian central authorities. The granting of social assistance to aliens was based on a principle which challenged legal provisions. In 1853, Minister of Justice C. Faider categorically stated that it was not only the explicit legal bond as was expressed by nationality, but also birth in Belgium which decided whether a person came under the responsibility of the Belgian government. Aliens born in Belgium, could, even if they remained of foreign nationality count on the benevolence of the authorities and receive welfare (ARMJ 702). It does not seem that the Belgian authorities flatly refused welfare to all other immigrants who applied for support as Belgians abroad in general were also supported if in need. In France, the favorite destination of Belgian emigrants, there was no institutionalized discrimination at all of Belgian immigrants. In the domain of social policy, the French central state only provided the overall framework whereby discrimination based on nationality was refuted. Belgian immigrants could profit from the provisions of the mutual assistance law of 1850 as well as from the law of 1851 on access to hospitals or hospices on the same terms as the French. In France public assistance to the needy, also to immigrants be they of foreign nationality was a matter for the communal authorities. The communal welfare bureaus treated Belgians very much like the local population.

Private initiatives which continued to have a very important role in social assistance in France also ignored the nationality criterion in giving out aid. In France social assistance was still largely granted in the Catholic tradition of charity, within which the poor as God's creatures did not have a homeland (Houzé de l'Aulnoit 1885). In Prussia, the destination for only few Belgian emigrants, the central authorities did play a more important role in social policy. The Prussian welfare laws of the middle of the century stipulated explicitly that local authorities were required to assist any pauper. Although not formally regulated by bilateral agreements, aliens in France and Germany were not excluded from locally organized welfare. The situation in Belgium where welfare for aliens was not locally, but centrally, organized was thus exceptional and brought considerable expenses for the state. The cost of social assistance for aliens in Belgium charged to the central authorities soared. While in 1833 assistance to sick, destitute and insane aliens caused an expense of 11,630 francs, this rose to 145,827 francs in 1860 (*Exposé de la situation du Royaume* 1885: II 486f.).

Besides protecting Belgians abroad, alien policy aimed also at keeping out or removing the "undeserving" poor of foreign nationality. The Poor Law of 3 April 1848 stipulated that the authorities had to expel, after a conviction for vagrancy, even aliens with residency status. The dynamic of alien policy had in this manner a link with the business cycle. Immigrants who already had a livelihood in Belgium were not disturbed, but unemployed and destitute aliens became a target for state action. Notwithstanding the legal provision to expel convicted vagrants of foreign nationality this does not seem to have been executed in practice without consideration of their links with Belgium. Some of these vagrants were treated with mercy by the Belgian authorities, because of the length of their stay in Belgium and because of the lack of possibilities to return to their country of origin. Due to humanitarian considerations as well as to considerations of efficiency, i.e., these aliens would return to Belgium anyway, numerous other destitute aliens also received financial support from the Belgian authorities (ARMJ 865).

Another state interest, besides that of preventing "undeserving" aliens from becoming a burden on public welfare and protecting Belgians abroad, which alien policy had to serve was preserving public order. This implied the removal of those aliens who disturbed public order, i.e., criminals or political activists. The number of expulsions of aliens with residency status for political reasons remained minimal. Between 1833 and 1860 only seventy-four aliens, mostly "refugees", were officially expelled for this reason (Reiter 1992:211; Bartier 1981). The most notorious of them was Karl Marx. The Belgian refugee policy in this period was largely determined by diplomatic considerations. Notwithstanding the liberal persuasion of most of the refugees – a political conviction which was shared by a large part of the Belgian elite – the practice of the Belgian liberal state in granting asylum was restrictive. The neighboring countries, for the most part with conservative regimes, accepted the independence of Belgium on the condition that it did not intervene in any manner in their affairs. "Refugees" had to refrain from being politically active. Diplomatic pressure from Prussia, Russia, Austria, and later also from France assured that exceptions to this rule were hardly ever made (Reiter 1992:263f.; Ronin 1992:52ff.). The experience of Switzerland, which had been threatened with a military invasion by its neighbors because of its too liberal refugee policy, was a clear warning for the Belgian authorities. Belgium did not want to provoke its neighbors in any way (Garsou 1939:57; ARMJ 250). As Reiter (1992:215) in his study of German refugees in the 1840s concluded, the Belgian authorities remained loyal to their asylum tradition within the principles that they had laid down for the "refugees". Requests by foreign powers to expel "refugees" who respected the Belgian conditions of asylum were mostly denied. This adherence to a restricted asylum tradition was largely a result of the pressure of the liberal fraction within the national elite (Reiter 1992:215; Saint-Ferréol 1870:1, 50ff.)

One can categorize the Belgian alien policy during the period envisaged here as brutal in its legal provisions, by refusing aliens access to welfare provisions, independent of the length of their residence in Belgium. Also expelling destitute, politically active or any other unwanted aliens at will can be categorized as brutal. This assessment has to be nuanced. We have already mentioned that the authorities did not fully exercise the arbitrary power they wielded over aliens. Asylum continued to be granted. Residency status limited administrative power over aliens, numerous aliens received welfare, and the expulsion policy was pragmatic. Even more important for the assessment of the alien policy was the contemporary ambiguity of the distinction between Belgian and alien. A public official, Jules de Soignie, even found it necessary to publish a study entitled "The Distinction between Belgians and Aliens" in 1858. He legitimized his booklet by referring to aliens who posed as Belgians and Belgians who were sometimes considered aliens. De Soignie considered that the difference between Belgians and aliens was for most people too blurred to make a clear-cut distinction; his study on nationality legislation aimed to rectify that (Soignie 1858:4f.). It was, however, not the absence of knowledge of the principles of nationality law as De Soignie claimed, but the lack of societal interest in the idea of the national which explains why alien was a nebulous category. The category of nationals had very little relevance even for the authorities. This is illustrated by the absence of data on nationality in nineteenth-century statistics (see also PHK 1848:1263ff.; PHS 1848: 1521ff.). Only the place of birth was deemed important for classification, the authorities did not consider it worthwhile to collect information on the nationality of the inhabitants of Belgium.

Administrative practice in the field of nationality law also indicate that the nationality of a person had very little relevance in nineteenth-century society. Belgian nationality legislation was based on the Napoleonic codification of state membership and combined the principles of birthplace, descent, and domicile. The basic principle of Belgian nationality law was *jus sanguinis*, that Belgian nationality was transmitted by descent, from a father to his children, regardless of birthplace. This principle of descent was complemented with the possibility of choosing Belgian nationality for those who had been born in Belgium from foreign parents. The children born in Belgium of foreign parents were not attributed Belgian nationality, but were able to claim Belgian citizenship upon reaching the age of majority. An alien was also able to obtain Belgian nationality via naturalization. Ordinary naturalization gave aliens the same rights as Belgians with the exception of the right to take part in national political life. To be able to file a request for naturalization, the applicant had to have lived in Belgium for a minimum of five years. A request for naturalization had to go through a rather long procedure, part of which involved the Parliament passing a judgement on this petition. A naturalization request was also quite expensive. Ordinary naturalization produced citizens who were unable to act politically. Complete political rights were only awarded through *la grande naturalisation*. Foreigners could only receive the latter on the initiative of the Belgian executive or legislative power and only because of special services these foreigners had rendered to Belgium. Granting of nationality was, in contrast with the claiming of nationality not a right, but a favor. The state retained total discretionary powers in this field. When all formal conditions for ordinary naturalization were fulfilled Parliament could still judge whether or not to grant citizenship (Caestecker 1997b).

Most of the aliens qualified to claim or receive Belgian nationality, i.e., either they had been born in Belgium or had been residing in Belgium, a minimum of five years, showed little interest in becoming Belgian. In the period between 1830 and 1872, out of 1,569 adjudgements of nationality 870, or 55 percent, were granted to aliens for whom Belgian nationality was necessary for their professional career. Article 7 of the Belgian Constitution stipulated that Belgian nationality was required to perform a public function (from holding public office to being a member of a jury). Throughout the nineteenth century the public service developed only rudimentarily and the number of jobs for officials was limited. Moreover aliens were admitted to administrative government functions, only the personnel with official responsibilities had to be Belgians (Soignie 1873:118). Servicemen, civil servants, shipping captains, and teachers had every reason to become Belgian (Stengers 1976:77; Schreiber 1995:218). But professionally most immigrants, whether they were workers, entrepreneurs, or tradesmen had little or no reason to become Belgian. Another advantage of becoming Belgian was that one could enjoy political rights. Political rights were, however, not only contingent on Belgian nationality, but until far into the nineteenth century, also on the possession of a certain amount of capital. Given the limited advantages it is of no surprise that only a select group of immigrants aspired to membership of the Belgian nation. In particular, laborers who had immigrated to Belgium rarely claimed Belgian nationality, let alone applied for Belgian nationality. It was of little or no importance to them as being an alien in nineteenth century Belgium involved hardly any disadvantages. Certainly for aliens born in Belgium there was hardly any difference between the treatment of those who claimed Belgian nationality and those who retained their original nationality. Although legislation on Belgian nationality did not honor a radical *jus soli,* within administrative pratice this was the central principle with which Belgian subjects were demarcated. The absence of statistics concerning those aliens who claimed Belgian nationality before 1871 displays the lack of interest in the formal bond of nationality. These declarations of indigenousness were not conscientiously filed by the local authorities since being born in Belgium entitled the claimants, at least in practice, to treatment as a Belgian subject. The local authorities also glossed over their duty to inform the Sûreté of every claim of Belgian nationality. Registration by the Department of Aliens was therefore imperfect. This administrative neglect is a clear indication that nineteenth century Belgium was not at all nationalistic in its social reality.

The Belgian state had great difficulties imposing on an autonomous society an immigrant policy involving state-led intervention against a certain category of inhabitants. "Belgian" society assimilated immigrants, notwithstanding their lack of Belgian nationality. By their assimilation these aliens were exempt from the brutal treatment which the state had formally reserved for all aliens. Even the central authorities took this spontaneous process of assimilation into account when they implemented their immigrant policy.

Conclusion

Alien policy throughout the period 1840-1861 can be seen as brutal as the legal provisions stipulated, at least in the interpretation of the executive authorities that aliens could be treated at will by the authorities. Aliens were provided hardly any protection against an all powerful state. Only those few aliens who acquired the status of *domicilié* were protected against administrative discretion. The aim of alien policy was to expel immigrants if they harmed the national interest, economically or politically. The concerns of alien policy were threefold: protecting Belgians abroad, safeguarding public order, and limiting public expenses. Within the national interest, which alien policy pretended to defend, the interests of the popular classes in Belgium were totally ignored. Only in the famine years of the 1840s was protecting the position of nationals in the labor market evoked. The executive power took into account within their alien policy these social considerations mainly to preserve the political status-quo.

Refugee policy was particularly restrictive as political refugees – the political actors par excellence – potentially brought a high risk for domestic security and tranquillity. They could even endanger good diplomatic relations with their countries of origin. On the other hand, the Belgian liberal regime was ideologically constrained in its handling of refugees. Refugee policy had thus a particular dynamic. Sometimes barriers were erected – passport regulations and stricter border controls – to prevent political refugees from entering. Once refugees had entered and were considered genuine refugees, the Belgian liberal regime imposed constraints upon the manner in which these people could be treated. They could not be sent back to their country of persecution. What happened depended on economic factors. "Refugees" could either be granted residence, or if they did not have sufficient financial means at their disposal, they could be sent to Great Britain.

The liberal values to which the Belgian regime adhered attenuated in fact very diverse elements of the brutal alien policy. Not only "refugees", but all unwanted aliens could choose the border by which they had to leave Belgium. Liberal Belgium still retained a highly symbolic respect for individual liberty. Much more important was that the judiciary limited administrative power over aliens by restricting the scope of immigration policy. The legislative power, Parliament, also constrained the powers of the executive branch of the state over aliens by dooming the Sûreté to remain a relatively weak institution and by enacting the alien law only for short periods. The effectiveness of alien policy was not only limited by liberal values, but also by technical problems, lack of resources, and economic interests. Probably the most important reservation about the brutal alien policy is its lack of actual influence on social reality. Long established aliens – independent of the provisions of nationality acquisition – were treated as nationals in social life. Although legally still aliens, they were able to claim the same rights as Belgians. Analyzing alien policy in the nineteenth century is thus a delicate issue. The dichotomy "alien" and "national" was not yet clearly established. There was also no need for a clear delineation as the majority of the population had no direct relationship with the central state whatsoever. State administration was not very dense, political rights were for the happy few, and social rights were scarce.

Chapter 2

ALIEN POLICY IN THE HEYDAY OF LIBERALISM, 1861-1914

In the second half of the nineteenth century the policy of the Belgian state definitely turned to liberalism. This liberal policy was no longer questioned by the Catholics as the traditional elites became more and more integrated in the new economic order by investments in industry and by the integration of capitalist principles in agriculture as well. The big landowners were no longer interested in the prices of agrarian commodities and hence protectionism, as their profit was made by the higher rents for farmers. Their interest was in preserving a large demand for land in the agrarian sector. During this period Belgium remained one of the most industrialized areas of Europe. The "long depression" in the years 1873-1896 changed little in this respect. The backbone of Belgian industrial development remained the mining industry. The favorable economic conditions for the European mining industry in the three decades before the First World War acted as a stimulus for the Belgian mining industry, but the weakness of the Belgian coal industry became manifest. The Belgian coal deposits were smaller, narrower, and more curved than those elsewhere in Western Europe and only by means of increased mechanization could the Belgian coal companies compete on the international markets. The Belgian mining basins supported the metallurgical industry. The position of the Belgian iron and steel industry, located in Liège and Charleroi, weakened. By the end of the century new investments, which assured the supply of the necessary raw materials at competitive prices, together with the use of technological innovations and a new business organization, made it possible for the Belgian iron and steel industry to catch up with international competitors. As a consequence of these developments a new boom ensued (Bruwier 1981; Strikwerda 1991).

At the same time new industries also expanded in Belgium (chemical and non-ferrous industries). The main problem for Belgian industrial production was an unstable demand. Fluctuating demand is characteristic for a capitalist economy, but in the Belgian case this was magnified by the lack of a large domestic market. Its dependency on external demand made it difficult to realize the economies of scale necessary to modern techniques. The open nature of the Belgian economy meant that fluctuations on the international market were immediately felt.

The rural economy underwent a much less brutal transformation than that of industry. There was, on the one hand, the persistence of subsistence farming with little contact with the market. At most the subsistence farmers provided some foodstuffs to neighboring small towns. On the other hand, there was also a growing sector of medium and large-sized farms which sold their products in the national and international markets. This was the part of the agrarian sector which went on to become an industry (De Belder 1981). The agrarian industrial economy saw a distinct trend away from cereal production and towards activities such as livestock, dairy farming, and market gardening. An influx of cheap overseas grains caused this shift in production. The industrialization of Belgian agriculture was checked by the dominance of small-scale plots. Agriculture predominantly targeted the domestic market which absorbed about 90 percent of the total production.

Industry definitely took the upper hand in the Belgian economy. This was obvious on the labor market. While in 1846 55 percent of the Belgian labor force was active in the agricultural sector, this decreased to 31 percent in 1896 and to only 22 percent in 1910 (De Brabander 1983:46). The outflow from agriculture was mainly to industry. Heavy industry particularly was labor hungry. The transition of economic activity to industry was facilitated by the introduction of cheap train tickets. From 1869 onwards the government offered cheap workingmen's tickets on the national railroads which allowed workers to remain in the countryside and till the land and at the same time to work in the cities and the industrial basins. While in 1869 these cheap tickets were only granted to those commuting within a radius of 25 km, this was extended to 100 km in 1892 and became unlimited in 1896. These train tickets made it possible for commuters to combine industrial work with their traditional agrarian occupation. Industrial labor no longer implied the definitive emigration of rural inhabitants. A daily or weekly displacement was now possible (Mahaim 1910).

The introduction of workingmen's tickets balanced the interests of the agrarian elites and their concern to keep demand for land high with the increasing demand for industrial labor. It had also a political objective to keep the newly proletarianized peasants away from the subversive Socialists.

The emergence of the labor movement challenged the political monopoly of the elites. This movement aimed first, because of the lack of initiative by the state and the employers in the social domain, at a material improvement in the lot of labor. The cooperatives and, to a lesser extent, the sickness funds were the cradle of the labor movement which grew into a truly socialist subculture. The labor unions and their *Maisons du Peuple* became the center of labor's social life. In 1885 a Socialist labor party was created, the Belgian Workers' Party (POB). It was an umbrella-organization for cooperatives, trade-unions, and mutual benefit societies. The demand for the vote was the central feature of working-class politics. The state responded to this call for the democratization of society with sheer repression. The growing discontent among labor about its socio-economic and political exclusion resulted in some violent outbursts (1886, 1889) and in an organizational drive among labor. The violent riots of 1886 and 1889 challenged the regime. The middle and upper classes of society suddenly realized the threat that the popular classes posed to their well-being.

The traumatic experience of 1886 was the impetus for political democratization as well as for state intervention in the socio-economic domain. Increasingly, the government sought to treat labor's claims as legitimate interest-group grievances, not class attacks. The authorities realized that it was not sufficient to reprimand protest; to preserve the regime labor protests had to be neutralized. It was expected that this could be achieved by an organizational dominance of the lower social classes by the traditional parties. The Liberal and especially the Catholic organizations followed the pattern set by the Socialists and tried to mobilize the middle classes and labor around their immediate economic and psychological needs. A myriad of organizations were set up which became part of a "modern" Catholic subculture in these Flemish regions where proletarianization was taking place (Craeybeckx 1973-1974). Similar Liberal initiatives to find popular support met with much less success. This organization of labor by the traditional parties coincided with the gradual enlargement of the franchise. The first step was the introduction of universal male suffrage with plural voting in 1893. This was the end of the political system dominated by Liberal and Catholic notables. It was replaced by a mass party system in which three political families – the Liberal, Catholic and Socialist parties – competed for votes. In order to stop the progress of Socialist electoral support and also to resist the secularization of newly proletarianized workers, the progressive wing in the Catholic party obtained more influence in the decision-making process. These so-called Christian Democrats also received important organizational autonomy.[1] The Socialists only became an integral part of the political system with the First World War, when they were coopted in a government of national union to form a united front to repel the German invader.

In the field of industrial relations a similar evolution is to be seen. Trade unions were only slowly recognized as collective actors. In the wake of the industrial revolt of 1886 the interests of labor were given greater consideration. Unions actively sought government mediation in the settlement of strikes, a clear indication of labor's changing relationship to the state. For social as well as economic reasons, industry started organizing. Finance capitalism, in particular the *Société Générale de Belgique* and to a lesser extent the *Banque de Bruxelles* promoted industrial cooperation. Employers in the glass, metallurgic and mining industries were the first to organize. In 1895 they founded the *Comité Central du Travail Industriel.* A nationwide mining employers' organization was founded in 1908, the *Fédération des Associations Charbonnières de Belgique* (FEDECHAR). By 1910 the *Comité Central du Travail Industriel* had expanded its membership by accepting the membership of the employers' organizations of the textile and metal construction industries. In 1913 this employers' organization changed its name into *Comité Central Industriel* (CCI). The CCI was particularly strongly represented in the traditional heavy industries (mining, glass, metallurgic, etc.). During the first two decades of the twentieth century the employers and their organizations strenuously resisted all attempts by workers to infringe on their prerogatives. In fact, the employers felt betrayed by the public authorities, who clearly felt the threat of the labor movement and who seemed to give the labor organizations more support than they gave the industrialists. Therefore, it was not so much the increased financial costs due to higher wages and social legislation that put them on the defensive, but the fact that they felt they had lost control, not only of the state, but even of their own private enterprises.

State intervention resulting from the new political constellation remained extremely modest. A Ministry of Labor and Industry was set up in 1895. Labor legislation was slow to develop. In 1889 the labor of women and children was regulated; in 1892 underground mine work for women under twenty-one and in 1911 any mine labor for women and children was prohibited. The work week was limited by law to six days in 1905. Underground mine labor was restricted to a maximum of nine hours a day in 1909. That labor legislation was not strictly implemented because of a large number of loopholes, but it was a clear break with liberalism. Legislation was also enacted to stimulate workers to save to become owners of their own houses. Home ownership was considered a means to integrate the proletariate into the larger society. The state also intervened in the domain of insurance in case of sickness, old age, and disability. The first social security legislation dates from this period. Previously, employers had provided voluntary private health and old-age schemes as a means to retain labor. Organized labor had set up mutual insurance funds on a voluntary basis which took care of members in case of sickness. There were strong demands on the state not so much to provide welfare provisions, but rather to play a supportive role for the already existing welfare schemes. Not only the Catholics, but also the Socialists took a firm stance on the autonomy of their institutions. In 1894, the state accorded grants for the administration of these mutual insurance funds and by 1900 the state even co-financed the benefits accorded the members of those funds. A new qualitative step was taken in 1903 when employers were obliged to pay premiums for accident insurance. In 1912 mandatory pension insurance was introduced in the mines, a scheme financed by the miners, the employers, and the state. A system of public intervention in case of unemployment was also introduced in those years. This arrangement was not made on the national level, but at the municipal level. It took the form of a supplement to trade union unemployment funds (Vanthemse 1989). Another element of the new state policy was that in 1914 elementary education was made compulsory. Employers were longtime opponents of the introduction of compulsory primary education as it would eradicate all child labor from the labor market. Certainly as important was the opposition of the Catholics, who associated compulsory school attendance with the development of secular state education (Gubin and Lefèvre 1985). The Belgian Parliament settled the ideological struggle around the educational issue by guaranteeing parents the effective right to educate their children according to their world view. This implied that not only the public authorities, but any private body – in fact mostly Catholic clergy – could found a school for children who were of age. These schools were given broad leeway in setting up their curriculum. Any of these private schools could receive financial support from the Belgian authorities.

The new policy which the state embarked upon after 1886 was not meant only to alleviate misery and mollify labor's anger. Not only were social welfare measures introduced, the means at the disposal of the state to quell any revolt were also extended. It was a mix of carrots and sticks. The year 1886 brought not only an awareness of a social problem, but also of a social danger. The social state took it upon itself to protect the popular classes, while at the same time the power of the police state was strengthened by increasing the number of gendarmes and by expanding the domain in which the state could repress against dangerous individuals, the so-called ringleaders of the revolt (Dupont-Bouchat 1986, Deneckere 1997:250).

The extension of state-powers had but one aim, the survival of the regime, and different means were implemented to this end which all expanded the powers of the state. The spectacular growth of Belgian capitalism led to a crucial transformation in the manner in which society functioned. This transformation not only had important repercussions in the economic sphere but also in the social and political domain. This process – a bundle of concomitant changes – occurred at the end of the nineteenth and the beginning of the twentieth century, individual competition was superseded by collective organization and concerted action. Labor organizations and employers' associations were the carriers of this development. Because the autonomous collective effort of entrepreneurs and labor was unable to solve the conflicts which capitalism engendered, the state intervened. This intervention, in comparison with that of other European states occurred quite late. Indeed, until the First World War Belgium was economically very "modern", but its politics were "archaic". The change in the nature of the Belgian state occurred in a piecemeal fashion. The expansion of the intervention of the state was initiated in the 1890s, brisk change would only occur after the First World War.

From an Emigration to an Immigration Country

In the second half of the nineteenth century Belgium continued to be an emigration country. Rural poverty in Flanders in particular drove thousands of laborers out of the country. This Belgian emigration was mainly, if not exclusively, directed towards France. In 1861, 204,900 Belgians had been counted in France; their number would more than double in twenty years time. In 1886 the French population census listed 489,000 Belgians. Two-thirds of these Belgians were living and working in the Nord, the French department bordering on Belgian Flanders. The Nord's explosive industrial growth was unique by French standards. The labor force provided by Belgium helped to make it the premier industrial area in France.

At the end of the nineteenth century, due to the economic depression, French laborers whose livelihood was threatened protested against the competition of Belgian immigrants. Just as in 1848, street violence forced hundreds of Belgians, who in some cases had lived in France for years, to return to Belgium. This xenophobic campaign met with a strong response among the authorities of the Third Republic. It was not that the French state was involved in forcing Belgians out, but rather that the intervention of the French state in social reality was starting to be restructured. Until the 1880s the French state had rejected discrimination based on nationality, but formal membership of the French state now became a necessary qualification to benefit from the incipient welfare state. The accident insurance law enacted in 1898 and the 1905 law for the aged and infirm were reserved for French nationals. Local authorities started to interpret legislation along nationalist lines so that hospitals and hospices, for example, became increasingly a privilege of the French nationals. Belgians were also discriminated against because of their nationality by local welfare bureaus (AFAB 3289 and 3286). Legislation was introduced to ensure that preference was given to French workers on the labor market. The law of

1893 declared that all foreigners coming to France to look for work had to declare themselves to the local authorities. This measure was designed by Parliament as a disguised protectionist measure. The declaration of residence or arrival entailed a payment. For French legislators this payment was the crux of the new legislation: control over foreign labor was seen mainly as a variant of tariffs to protect national labor (Noiriel 1988:74ff.).

The Republicans were willing to make the state intervene to protect French labor's interests in order to enlarge the social base of the regime. Foreign labor's privileges also had to be eliminated. Belgians established in France were able to escape French military service by invoking their Belgian citizenship. French labor argued that employers gave preference to young workers of foreign nationality who did not run the risk of being sent to the barracks. This discrimination in favor of Belgian labor was abolished by the extension of *jus soli*. Second-generation immigrants were defined as French in 1889. This caused a considerable decline in the number of Belgians in France. Paired with this was an increase in requests for naturalization and claims of French nationality. Becoming French was seen as a safeguard against discrimination, street violence, dismissal, and expulsion. As a consequence, the number of Belgians in France dropped from 482,300 in 1886 to 278,100 in 1911. The number of Belgian nationals in France also declined because the character of Belgian labor migration to France had changed. The two decades before the First World War saw a huge increase in the number of commuters as well as seasonal migrants from Belgium in France. French agrarian and industrial protectionism after 1892 caused the cost of living in Belgium to be considerably lower than in France. By working in France, but living in Belgium, these migrant workers could take advantage of high French wages but avoid high French prices. About fifty thousand Belgians left each spring for seasonal work in agriculture or brick making, while the same number commuted daily or weekly to work in industry in the Nord. The cheap workmen's tickets in Belgium helped to maximize the profits of these migrant workers (Strikwerda 1993).

A few thousand Belgians emigrated in this period to the German Reich and the Americas. The number of migrants involved was marginal in comparison to those who left for France. The Belgian emigrants in Germany were confronted with the state much earlier than their counterparts in France. Since the early nineteenth century, Belgian emigrants in Prussia, just like any other foreigner, had to declare their arrival to the local police and present documents to prove their identity (Jackson 1997:350). At the end of the nineteenth century, immigrants not only had to prove their identity, but also their citizenship. The documents issued to Belgian emigrants by Belgian local authorities made no mention of their citizenship and in 1896 new documents were designed for emigrants to Germany which stipulated the Belgian citizenship of the bearer. In contrast to France interests proper to the state (conscription and limiting public expenses), rather than social considerations explain this new administrative demand. In 1909 German alien policy took a change of course. From that year onwards, the explicit authorization of the German authorities was necessary before foreigners were able to engage in wage labor in Germany. Belgian workers, just as any foreign worker in Germany, had to apply for an *Inlandslegitimationskarte.* This authorization was only valid for one employer, as the employer of the foreign workers was listed on this residence and work permit. The workers were tied to their employer. Only with the agreement of this employer could a foreign worker change jobs; a foreigner at work without this identity card would be expelled (Caestecker 1999). In contrast to France, this was not a social protection measure assuring preference of national workers on the labor market. Reducing the immigration of foreign labor was also not the objective. This institutionalized discrimination against foreign labor was introduced to prevent labor turnover. The authorities intended to discipline the foreign labor force by curtailing their mobility.

The social protectionism of the democratic French state and the economic interventionism of the authoritarian German *Kaiserreich* did not provoke a change in Belgian emigration policy. The Belgian liberal regime considered emigration a matter of individual liberty which the rules of supply and demand would regulate. The state had to limit itself to providing general protection to its citizens abroad. The Belgian ambassador in Berlin did not consider the measures of economic control in the German Empire to be seriously detrimental to the interests of the Belgian workers in that country. The French measures of social protection on the other hand were seriously investigated. The Belgian authorities offered the French a bilateral agreement in order to grant each other's citizens welfare on the same footing as nationals. The French authorities were not interested in such an agreement. The small French community in Belgium certainly did not outweigh the Belgian community in France. The Belgian authorities insisted upon the fair treatment of their nationals in France, but they were not willing to influence the French in any other way. It was not considered the state's role to stimulate or stifle emigration (AFAB 3286 and 3293).

While at the end of the nineteenth century, France had lost some of its attraction for Belgian labor, Belgium seemed to exercise a greater pull than before. It is not clear when the scales tipped or if Belgium had already become an immigration country before the First World War. The statistics on new arrivals are not very reliable. Only after 1880 did the Department of Aliens register a yearly increase of more than fifteen thousand new immigrants. After 1899 the number of files clearly ballooned (Graph 21). This gives no indication, however, of the length of residence of the immigrants. One has to consider as well that these figures are also a function of the degree of administrative centralization. Clear quantitative figures for the extent of the foreign community in Belgium are only available after 1890, when nationality data was requested for the first time in the population census. The previous census do not give data on nationality, but only on place of birth. We can, therefore, only draw serious conclusions for the evolution in immigration from the turn of the century onwards. While in 1890, 171,000 aliens were counted, their number rose to 206,000 in 1900 and to 254,000 in 1910. Not only the number, but also the economic position of aliens in nineteenth century Belgium is difficult to establish. The problem is that only scattered data is available. The first overview of the occupational position of foreigners in Belgium is to be found in the population census of 1910. Table 3 presents the distribution of the aliens and the Belgians among the three occupational sectors in that year.

We see that aliens were hardly represented in the primary sector to the advantage of the tertiary sector. A closer look at the secondary and tertiary sectors gives us the more salient features of the occupational position of aliens. Aliens were active throughout the tertiary sector, so it is difficult to discern a distinct economic profile. They were even represented among public officials, military personnel, and liberal professions. The only concentration of foreigners in the tertiary sector is to be found in the sector of domestic servants (22 percent). This scattered presence of aliens is also true for the secondary sector, but here we can point out some occupational groups. Heavy industry employed about 20 percent of the aliens active in the secondary sector, mostly in the mines. The production of clothing employed another 14 percent of the aliens in the secondary sector, while 7 percent of the foreigners made their livelihood in the diamond industry. The latter were mostly Eastern European Jews who integrated this expanding, traditionally Jewish industry. In the last quarter of the nineteenth century, the Antwerp diamond industry attracted workers from Galicia and entrepreneurs from Odessa and Bialystock (Schreiber 1996:260ff.). This concentration in one sector was an exception. Aliens had no distinct occupational profile in Belgium in 1910.

The picture which emerges from the scarce additional data on the economic position of foreigners in nineteenth-century Belgium is that of a migration of qualified manual and non-manual labor, of artists, intellectuals, white-collar workers, and skilled journeymen. The international migra-

Table 3 *Distribution of Aliens and Belgians Among the Three Economic Sectors in 1910*

	Alien	*Belgian*
Primary sector	6	22
Secondary sector	41	47
Tertiary sector	53	31

tion to cities such as Charleroi, Antwerp, Brussels, and Liège was a result of the new opportunities which those expanding cities offered. These immigrants were not the underprivileged; most of them were qualified urban-based people who hoped for increased opportunities in the growing Belgian cities. Businessmen found new markets in Belgium. German merchants and bankers in particular set up businesses in Antwerp and Brussels. These banking-houses and commercial firms created a demand for white-collar workers. German clerks found jobs in the growing number of Antwerp- and Brussels-based German businesses. Artisans also saw opportunities in the Belgian cities and at times even succeeded in conquering specific branches of production. In the residual group of those immigrants without professions, students were mentioned. Belgium offered hospitality to a large foreign student population of Eastern European origin mainly preparing themselves for technical (engineering) and commercial professions. On the eve of the First World War, foreign students at the University of Liège or the Higher Institute of Commerce in Antwerp even constituted more than half of the student body. Most of these students left Belgium after they finished their studies (Ronin 1993:171-191). The opening of the Belgian Institutes of Higher Education to foreign students was a deliberate policy of the academic authorities to enhance the prestige of their institutions. Also the Belgian authorities were eager to attract foreign students as these people would be among the future elite of their countries. Foreign students were considered agents for the promotion of the economic and political interests of Belgium.

The population census of December 1910 ignores the seasonal migrants among whom there was also highly skilled labor. Thus, the largely foreign personnel of the Palace Hotels at the seaside were, among others, not included in this statistic. These luxurious hotels were only open during the summer, hence the foreign cooks, receptionists, and waiters had already left by the time the census took place. Ostend, along with some other resorts at the Belgian seaside and in the Ardennes (Spa), were the places where cosmopolitan high society spent its holidays during the summer. The personnel in contact with the clientele not only had to speak the three main European languages (German, French, and English) fluently, but also had to be able to serve the exclusive tastes of these clientele. A maximum of comfort was provided in those *Palaces,* the service was also at the highest level. Local labor was only used for menial tasks where contact with the clientele was minimal: chambermaids, coachmen, dishwashers, etc. (Billiet 1987). The *directeur d'hôtel*, the *chef de cuisine*, the *maitres d'hôtel* and the *chefs de rang* were all of foreign nationality and moved along with the wealthy. At the end of the summer, they left the Belgian seaside for other exclusive meeting places of the international haute bourgeoisie of the Belle Epoque (San Remo, Menton, Nice..).

This picture of skilled labor migration does not cover international migration to Belgium in its totality. Not all migrants were drawn by the high quality of the opportunities offered in Belgium. International migration to Belgium also resulted from the pull of a regional center whose range of attraction broadened to include regions beyond the national borders. In particular in the industrial basins, international migration corresponded to this pattern of migration. The large number of German nationals who were employed in the mines and metallurgic firms at the East of the Liège basin are a case in point.

The radius within which labor was attracted to heavy industry in Wallonia expanded considerably at the end of the long nineteenth century. This was due to a fundamental change within the miners' communities in Wallonia which occurred in the last quarter of the nineteenth century. Since the beginning of that century, the miners' profession was passed from generation to generation. A new demographic pattern came into existence with the long depression of the years 1873-1896. This crisis created a deep fear of falling back into poverty. Before, miners had large families as children were a safeguard for the future. They could not only be sent out to work at a very early age, but they also assured that there would be a source of income when the parents became old or infirm. In the second half of the nineteenth century, demographic behavior started to change. There had been a period of full-employment between 1850 and 1873 during which the standard of living had risen steadily. The great economic downturn between 1873 and 1896 endangered this new feeling of security and hope for improvement provided by the industrial world. The less skilled, women, and children were especially hard hit. Skill and education came now to be seen as safeguards against deprivation. In order to protect their recently acquired well-being, the birth of children was restricted. Miners and metal workers were the vanguard of this demographic transition in Wallonia (Leboutte 1987). Children were no longer seen as mere producers; they also had to bring social prestige by obtaining a well-paid and stable job. Education was the means of providing this (Vandervelde 1903:89). The broadening of occupational choices and the improved living standards at the end of the nineteenth century meant that the possibility of a better life appeared to be within everyone's reach. This transformation expressed a changing world view of the Walloon miners' families. Satisfaction with their traditional lot was exchanged for a more aspiring vision of their future. For Walloon heavy industry this break in tradition caused an important recruitment problem. The social disposition of Walloon labor towards heavy industry clearly became negative. Local labor could no longer be rejuvenated.

Meanwhile state intervention in the labor market, i.e, limitation on working hours and restrictions on the use of child and female labor, was diminishing the labor supply. Just before the First World War, decisions were taken with important repercussions for labor recruitment in Belgian heavy industry. Obligatory school attendance until fourteen years of age, enacted in 1914, caused the erosion of the foundation of the recruitment strategy of heavy industry. Military service, made obligatory for all men in 1913, also pulled young men away from industry. Only by making the character of work in heavy industry less arduous, dirty, and unhealthy, or by compensating for these defects by increasing the workers' pay, could more Walloons be induced to stay in heavy industry. It is likely that to pursue such a strategy would have been economically unviable, certainly for the Belgian mine industry which already at that time was hardly profitable. Heavy industry developed another strategy; they expanded their recruitment beyond Wallonia. Flanders, as a densely populated region with small land holdings, was able to provide abundant labor for industry. At that time, the development of transport (steamship and railways) together with the abolition of agrarian protectionism forced the local agrarian economy to open to the market. The drop in grain prices, together with the collapse of cottage industries due to the second industrial revolution, dealt a blow to the traditional agrarian economy. This meant that the small landholders of Flanders had to look for new sources of income. In Flanders itself there were very few opportunities. The demographic dualism of Belgium, together with the changes in the agrarian economy meant that the large supply of labor in Flanders could be tapped by labor-hungry industry in Wallonia. The Walloon attraction for Flemish labor was facilitated by the introduction of workers' daily or weekly train tickets. The commuting of Flemish laborers provided a solution to the labor shortage problem in the Walloon industrial basins. Local recruitment was extended to national recruitment. Belgium became one unified labor market (Mahaim 1911). By the turn of the century the Belgian labor market alone could not satisfy the labor-hungry mining industry. Migrants from Eastern and Southern Europe supplemented the labor force. This immigration from Eastern and Southern Europe no longer had the characteristics of a long-distance migration in search of better opportunities.

The distinction between long-distance, international migration which was largely an urban-to-urban movement, and regional migration, which covered rather short distances, but could be also from abroad started to wane in the very beginning of the twentieth century when an expanded and more homogeneous industrial labor market could no longer satisfy its unskilled labor needs within the regional space. Thus long-distance migration became rather more survival strategy to satisfy minimal needs and had as such the characteristics of the regional migration of the previous period (Ronin 1992:99f.). It was the prelude to the massive twentieth century international migration, which would encompass ever longer distances.

Towards a Firm Internal Immigration Control

After 1861 all people in Western Europe were guaranteed the right of free travel; border control and passport regulations were totally abandoned. This did not mean that control over aliens arriving in Belgium had been abolished. All newly immigrated aliens had to be registered in the population registers by the local authorities, but first the Sûreté had to be notified of their arrival by a form which provided full information about the alien: civil data, last address abroad, date of arrival in Belgium, source of income, occupation. If the alien had any kind of identifying document, he could be recorded shortly afterwards in the population registers, that is if the Sûreté had no negative information on his antecedents. If no documents were submitted, the alien was given a period of time in which to prove his identity. For aliens who had no source of income – vagrants and beggars – the Sûreté had ordered in 1850 that local authorities could expel them without prior notification.

The abolishment of passport regulations meant that aliens did not have to ask for permission to immigrate to Belgium. The offence of illegal immigration could no longer be used against the political activists par excellence, the refugees. There was also much less need for it, since the refugee problem had become much less of a priority in international relations. The crushing and lasting defeat of the revolutions of 1848 caused the conservative regimes to regain confidence. Stability returned to Europe and hardly any new dissidents were forced to leave their countries of origin. The fate of the older "refugees" was eased as one government after another offered amnesty to the former rebels forced to live abroad. Until 1860, the pressure of foreign powers explained Belgium's restrictive asylum practice to a large degree. After 1860, the Belgian authorities considered the emerging Socialist movement a serious threat to the Belgian regime. Any strengthening of Socialism, if by activists who had been forced to flee their country of origin, had to be prevented. These revolutionaries were not considered "refugees" (Destatte 1991:276). This was obvious in the reception of the refugees who fled Paris in 1871, after the defeat of the Commune. They were considered criminals, not refugees. To hinder their immigration, passport requirements for French citizens were re-introduced. In May 1871, not only a passport, but also a valid visa became obligatory. As the fear of the refugees of the Commune diminished and as the closing of the border was unsuccessful anyway, the regulations were relaxed in November 1871. These immigrants, although not considered refugees, could remain legally in Belgium if they registered, kept away from politics, and found a way of supporting themselves (Devreese 1972; Keunings 1980:143).

Besides this momentary political intervention, which had had little effect anyway, the fluctuations in the number of expellees were largely a result of the business cycle. Poor immigrants could, when there was a large labor demand, easily be absorbed by industry and agriculture. An oversupply of labor was, however, considered to be a danger to public order. Particularly after 1871, during the recession of the last quarter of the nineteenth century, there was an increasing oversupply of labor. This recession, throughout the whole of Europe, forced more and more people to find new livelihoods. These mostly uprooted peasants – the recession was primarily an agrarian depression – caused the number of wandering poor to increase. Belgian immigration regulations did not stop the German and French poor from looking for a livelihood by crossing the Belgian border. The immediate response of the authorities was to expel thousands of destitute immigrants. Graph 14 illustrates the dramatic increase in the number of expulsions at the end of the nineteenth century. The continuous expulsion of alien vagrants did not seem to stop the flood, on the contrary the number of undesirable immigrants seemed to rise each year. Harsher repression was called for. The Sûreté proposed that the Minister of Justice provide sanctions to prevent the unauthorized return of unwanted aliens. If an alien who had residency status was expelled from Belgian territory (*expulser*) this so-called dangerous alien risked a prison sentence of fifteen days to six months upon his return for *rupture de ban*, while the alien without residency status who was expelled ran upon return no risk of punishment by a prison sentence. The Sûreté wanted this anomaly changed; the latter's return should also be punished by a prison sentence (ARMJ 865). This provision did not become law, but an alternative with the same outcome was found.

In 1878 the Minister of Justice J. Bara decided to consider aliens without residency status who were indicted for misdemeanors dangerous aliens. They were to be expelled by royal decree (ARMJ 861). Extending this possibility beyond the provisions of the law, which only provided for expulsion by royal decree of aliens with residency status was of dubious legality, but no conflicts with the judiciary rose (Bekaert 1934:117f). In 1881 some aliens without residency status in Belgium were also expelled by royal decree for the mere fact of vagrancy or begging. These migrants had been *renvoyé* numerous times, but each time they had returned to Belgium. They were now considered dangerous aliens and expelled by royal decree. This enabled the authorities to punish a subsequent return. While in the beginning of the 1880s, few aliens – the most notorious of the foreign vagrants and beggars – had been *expulsé* in this manner, at the turn of the decade their number rose to more than a hundred annually (Graph 16 and PDK 1874-1896). Some of the latter had already been expelled by royal decree after having been brought to the border twice. Repression created its own dynamic; expulsion by royal decree became less selective. A total of 391 persons of foreign nationality without residency status were expelled by royal decree between 1881 and 1891 for the mere fact of begging or vagrancy. The threat of imprisonment in Belgium did not necessarily stop these migrants from returning to Belgium and most were subsequently condemned several times for *rupture de ban* (Graph 17).

In a random sample of sixty-two aliens who had never acquired residency status but were expelled by royal decree anyway only eighteen were not recorded in the following years as having returned to Belgium. The forty-four others returned to Belgium and were expelled repeatedly; if the Sûreté could catch them in time they were brought before the court.[2] On average these aliens were condemned four times for *rupture de ban.* Marcel Bastiaans, an one-armed cowman, in the decade after his *expulsion* on 31 March 1883 was brought before court for *rupture de ban* twenty-seven times. He was also expelled several times after 1883 without being brought to the court. This handicapped Dutchmen spend thirty-eight months in Belgian prisons or penal colonies for illegal stays in Belgium. He was never indicted for any other crime. In 1905 – at age seventy-two – he died in a Belgian prison. Jean-Pierre Euffles, a 47-year-old Luxembourg national who alleged to have been a volunteer in the French Foreigners' Legion in Africa, was arrested the first time in 1889 for vagrancy and immediately *renvoyé.* He was removed from Belgian territory as a vagrant six times in the following years until he was finally deemed a dangerous alien and expelled by royal decree in May 1891. Afterwards, Jean-Pierre Euffles was brought before the courts eleven times because of *rupture de ban,* and he had to spend eleven months in prison. As we will see further on, he also became a regular of the Belgian vagrant colonies. He was to spend four years of his life in these colonies. In 1901 at age 59, after being expelled twenty-two times, he decided that Belgium was too hazardous to his freedom and he did not return, at least not under this identity.

The judiciary did not mechanically follow the repressive logic of the executive. In most cases the minimum sentence of fifteen-days imprisonment was meted out. In a sample of 216 judgements, aliens were punished with a prison sentence above one month only sixty-eight times, and only four times did a magistrate mete out the maximum sentence of six-months imprisonment. This lenient treatment of returned expellees was due to the courts being responsive to the notion of equal treatment. The judges considered this breach of the law inoffensive. At the beginning of the 1890s, the administrator of the Sûreté did not judge the experiment very positively. Prison did not cure these hardcore vagrants of their passion for vagabondage. Repression hardly seemed to have any effect on them at all (ARMJ 603).

In 1892 the repressive strategy towards the wandering poor was re-oriented. While previously all able-bodied vagrants were to be imprisoned, the vagrancy law of 1891 made a distinction between the deserving and the non-deserving poor among them. This law stipulated a distinct treatment for the victims of economic misfortune. The authorities considered that not only the sick or invalid but even able-bodied vagrants could be deserving; they could have become destitute through no fault of their own. Unemployment was no longer seen only as a moral problem. Deserving vagrants were to be taken care of in so-called *maisons de refuge* with very liberal supervision. Non-deserving vagrants were brought before a police court, and if this court of summary jurisdiction ascertained that they were without a means of support by their own doing, by "asocial" behavior, they were confined to the penal colony in Merksplas for several months, sometimes even for up to two years. For recidivists, the law fixed the term at up to seven years. This colony was run as a prison and the inmates had to work. Vagrancy was also more effectively managed by the creation of the *casier de vagabondage et mendicité*, similar to the police record for criminals (Meeuwissen 1981). This aimed at preventing asocial vagrants from perverting the deserving poor and from further destabilizing the social order. Separating these non-deserving poor was the main objective, but a heavy-handed approach to re-education could possibly provide for social reintegration. As mentioned, the expansion of the role of the state after 1886 (of which this policy was a direct expression), was a highly ambiguous process. The vagrancy law of 1891 diversified state intervention by providing for assistance to deserving vagrants, but it also strengthened the state in its repressive role. The authorities obtained more extended powers and resources to combat the non-deserving vagrants.

While Belgian vagrants were arrested and possibly sentenced to forced labor, the policy towards the alien poor did not change immediately after the enactment of the new poor law of 1891. Vagrants and beggars of foreign nationality did not have to appear before the police court: they were "only" forced to leave the country. The re-education of these "asocial" persons was not the duty of the Belgian government. As a consequence, in 1891 questioning over nationality was inserted into the interrogation protocol of the police and the gendarmerie. While only information on place of birth had been requested earlier, now nationality suddenly became important (ARMJ 619).

The Governor of Limburg – the province bordering Prussia and the Netherlands – had been criticizing what he called the lax policy towards alien vagrants. In 1891 he stepped up his criticism. He considered the mere expulsion of these vagrants discrimination against Belgians. Belgian vagrants were convicted, while aliens did not have to serve a sentence. In addition, and more importantly for the Governor, this expulsion policy was totally ineffective. It certainly did not stop aliens from coming to Belgium, even those immigrants who had been expelled returned the same day and the authorities were powerless to stop them. They could only take them back to the border. The governor of Limburg called for harsher repressive measures. He deemed the detention of these alien vagrants to be necessary to deter their return. He also considered a few exemplary convictions sufficient to keep poor aliens away from Belgium. His plea was supported by personalities from other border regions (ARMJ 601 and 603; PHK 1887:228 and 1890:474). The head of the Sûreté was opposed to a repressive policy. According to him, the experience with those foreign vagrants who had been expelled by royal decree had shown sufficiently that a more repressive policy would not yield positive results. On the contrary, imprisonment would create a bureaucratic burden and increased expenditure for the Belgian treasury. The dissuasive influence of the example would, according to the administrator of the Sûreté, be minimal because the foreign poor were a highly mobile and amorphous group of people. The detention of a few of these aliens would therefore, be unknown to the others, and the foreign poor, totally ignorant of the dangers awaiting him, would still immigrate to Belgium (ARMJ 603).

The Minister of Justice, J. Lejeune, accepted the point of view of the administrator of the Sûreté that convicting all poor immigrants was not feasible, but he felt that action had to be taken against the "recidivists". It was unacceptable that aliens who had already been expelled simply returned. In January 1892 he ordered the immediate expulsion of poor immigrants to continue, but he backed the Governor of Limburg by adding that all those aliens who had already been expelled once should also be convicted before expulsion. If a poor alien dared to come back to Belgium for a third time – after first a condemnation and a second expulsion – an imprisonment of two years would follow. Repression should stop them from returning to Belgium (ARMJ 658 and 638; Halot 1900:200f.). Already in April 1892 this strategy was modified. Belgian vagrants realized very quickly that their non-Belgian companions in misfortune were not brought before the court and thus by pretending to be alien they could also avoid long-term imprisonment. The authorities were convinced that a large number of Belgian vagrants posed as aliens in order to avoid a conviction. To prevent this, a first condemnation for vagrancy led, regardless of nationality, to a minimum term of four-months imprisonment. During these four months, the authorities hoped to filter out the pseudo-aliens who had – just as the other Belgians in Merksplas – to serve longer prison sentences. The aliens who were residing in Belgium were also not set free after four months. Their expulsion would be to no avail as they would return anyway, thus they were treated in the same manner as Belgians. If an expelled alien vagrant after a four-month sojourn in the penal colony dared to return to Belgium he was to be sentenced to an eight-month term. The alien inmates of the penal colonies turned out to be a troublesome lot. In contrast to the Belgians, they used every opportunity to escape. Most of the aliens were, therefore, confined in security barracks under close supervision. When, in July 1892, four hundred aliens started a hunger strike to protest against overpopulation of their barracks and bad treatment the authorities curtailed the prison terms for aliens by half. A first condemnation brought two months in the penal colony, a second one four months, etc.(ARMJ 635; Halot 1900:200).

In 1892, 1,010 aliens were convicted, sent to a vagrant colony, and after serving their sentence expelled. In the same year the number of *renvoi* dropped from about eight thousand to less than three thousand (Graph 14; PDK 1896-1897:207). The forces of law and order called the new strategy towards the wandering poor an unexpected great success: migration was being mastered. Minister of Justice Lejeune also evaluated the tough policy positively. It was, in his opinion, the only way to stop the rising "incursion of the scum of the population from neighboring countries". During the following years immigrants continued to be convicted and locked up in the vagrant colonies. In 1893, 641 aliens entered the penal colonies, this rose to 857 in 1894 and 960 in 1895. The winter of 1895 witnessed a spectacular rise in immigration of poor aliens. Only very few of them were sent to the *maison de refuge*. The penal colony saw a sharp rise in foreign inmates (ARMJ 647 and 650). The worrying element for the authorities was that a hard core of vagrants had been convicted to ever longer prison terms in the penal colony. Marcel Bastiaans was one of them, he was joined by several others of the hardcore foreign poor who had been expelled by royal decree in the 1880s. In total, Bastiaans was convicted for vagrancy three times; in September 1895 he had to serve a sentence of eight months. His colleague in misfortune Jean-Pierre Euffles was confined for the first time in the vagrant colony in April 1892. In June 1895 Euffles was arrested for the fifth time and had to stay a whole year in the colony. Between April 1892 and February 1896 he had only been a free man for ten months.

Graph 1 illustrates this repressive experiment. The repression seemingly had hardly any effect on these old offenders. The penal colony became overcrowded. As the administrator of the Sûreté had predicted, the bureaucratic burden rose and the costs for the Belgian treasury jumped sharply, while the return in the sense of controlling migration seemed to be limited. In March 1896, the Minister of Justice returned to the old policy of expelling destitute aliens, if necessary, several times. The vagrant colonies were allowed to release all their inmates of foreign nationality. The Gendarmerie received instructions to no longer bring foreign vagrants to the police courts to convict them, but instead to transport them immediately to the border without even informing the Sûreté. That Belgian vagrants would again pretend to be of foreign nationality so as not to be interned was a side-effect the authorities could hardly control. The Gendarmerie

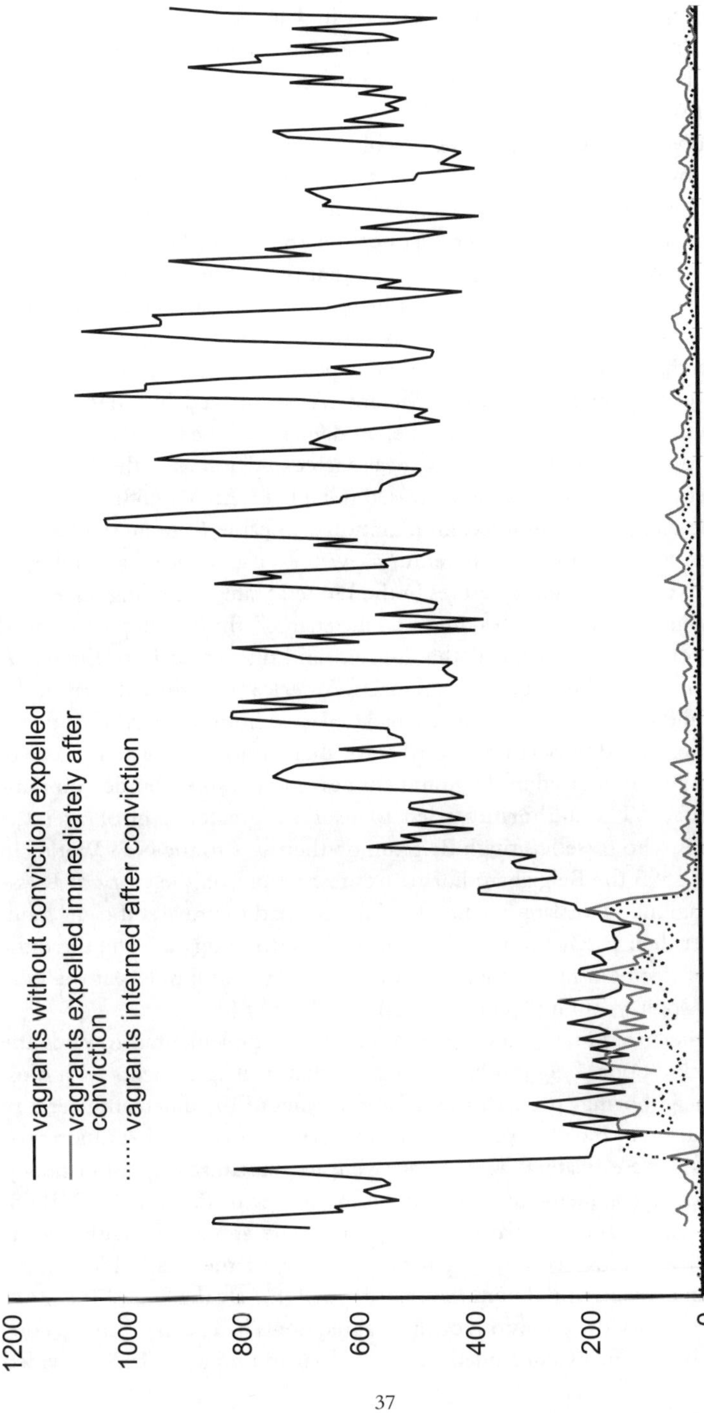

Graph 1 *Aliens Expelled, Convicted, and Interned for Begging and Vagrancy, 1890-1909 (monthly figures)*

was called upon to be extremely vigilant in that respect (ARMJ 658; Halot 1900:209f.). The experiment of imprisoning foreign vagrants was short-lived. Notwithstanding the surplus in the supply of labor until the First World War, it was not repeated. The whole procedure was considered too expensive and too burdensome. Expulsion once again remained – as illustrated by Graph 14 – the main sanction against undesirable immigrants. The expulsion of foreign vagrants by royal decree remained exceptional; it was still agreed that the experiences of the 1880s had shown that this had no effect whatsoever on the hardcore vagrants. By the turn of the century it seems the memory of the lesson of the 1880s began to fade away. The Minister of Justice, J. Van den Heuvel, decided, on the instigation of the Sûreté, that repeat offenders would be expelled by royal decree in order to make expulsion policy more efficient. As illustrated by Graph 16 an increasing number of vagrants were, on demand of the Sûreté, considered dangerous aliens and expelled by royal decree and, just as in the 1880s, the convictions for *rupture de ban* increased (Graph 17; ARMJ 638).

The danger of unwanted immigration also came from an unexpected quarter. The late nineteenth century saw the enactment of a number of restrictive immigration measures in the United States, including the exclusion of anyone "likely to become a public charge", those with pre-arranged work contracts, the criminal, the diseased, and the political undesirable. A rising number of European emigrants to America were turned away at the shore, and those among them who had departed from the port of Antwerp were repatriated to Belgium, regardless of their country of origin. Some of those migrants arrived in Belgium penniless and became a burden on public welfare. The authorities tried to exercise greater control over the migrants who passed through Belgium on their way to the New World. In August 1893 the Belgian authorities set restrictions on the entry of Russian emigrants. Russians heading for America had to prove sufficient funds to cover their passage to their homeland. Due to smuggling and the difficulty of distinguishing emigrants from other Russian travelers at the border, this policy had little effect (Ronin 1993: 222ff.).

In the meantime, a new strategy had been implemented towards the wandering poor. Belgium had signed international agreements with most of its neighboring countries in the later decades of the nineteenth century as a solution to the most pressing humanitarian issues of the expulsion procedures. These bilateral agreements were to humanize expulsion policy. Initially these agreements, for example the one with Bavaria (21/2/1868) were only meant to repatriate the insane. The agreement with Prussia (3/12/1868) provided not only for repatriation of the insane, but also for Prussian orphans in Belgium (Soignie 1873: 24f.). By the end of the nineteenth century the provisions of these agreements had been extended considerably. The treaty concluded with the German Empire in 1877 provided for the organized repatriation of destitute Germans who due to poor health or old age were no longer able to support themselves. While previously, at most, the very young and insane aliens had been repatriated, now a larger group profited from this less cruel treatment. Instead of dumping elderly or disabled aliens at the border, Belgium and the German Reich now officially agreed to receive their unfortunate subjects and to provide some (minimal) assistance when they returned. These bilateral agreements curtailed the states' expulsion powers since the nationality of the destitute person had to be decided upon unambiguously before one could proceed to expel. During the sometimes long diplomatic negotiations preceding the expulsion, the person remained a charge of the state who wanted to expel him. This was clearly a humanization of the expulsion procedure, but only for a very small minority of the expellees (ARMJ 377).

All other undesirable aliens were still dumped at the borders. By 1886 the question of which border, however, was no longer a matter of choice by the expellee. The expulsion procedure was in this sense radically modified in the last quarter of the nineteenth century. The Sûreté had been advocating the abolishment of the free border choice for vagrants since the beginning of the 1880s. The administrators of the Sûreté had consistently argued that all other strategies to combat unwanted immigration were doomed to fail. They only reluctantly supported the repressive option of 1892 and they also rejected tightening border control or control of the aliens already in the country. This lukewarm attitude to these strategies to combat unwanted immigration was motivated by their belief in what they considered as the only valuable weapon against foreign vagrants: to return them to "their" country. The administrators argued that a victory in the battle with international vagrancy was only possible if every country disciplined its own vagrants. The only solution to the plague of vagrancy was a national one and expulsion policy should be rationalized in this sense. Undesirable aliens had to be sent back to their country of origin. If they did not originate from an adjacent country, they had to be expelled in the direction of that country. The Minister of Justice, J. Bara, and the Minister of Foreign Affairs, G. Rolin Jacquemijns, in the Frère Orban-Van Humbeeck Cabinet, the last Liberal government of the nineteenth century, were strongly opposed to a break with a long tradition of free border choice for the expellees. Since the middle of the nineteenth century this Belgian tradition had been defended against all proposals, in particular by Prussian (later German) authorities, to "rationalize" the expulsion policy on the basis of state membership of the expellees. The freedom of the individual to choose where to go to was to be respected.

In 1884 the German authorities decided unilaterally to stop the "chaos" at their Western border. Only German expellees were granted access to German territory, while all third country expellees the German authorities could get hold of at the border were returned to Belgium. Only those third country nationals who could document that they had to pass through the German Empire to return to their country and had money for the transit fare were not returned to Belgium. The Belgian authorities indignantly refused to pay for the repatriation of able-bodied foreign vagrants and identifying the nationality of the vagrants was also considered too onerous a task. About the same time, the Dutch authorities returned any Spanish, French or Italian penniless migrant which the Belgian authorities had brought to the Dutch border. The Belgian authorities realized it was senseless to let the vagrants of these nationalities decide themselves to be brought to the eastern border. In this way Belgium would never get rid of them. From 1885 onwards they were expelled at the French border. The French retaliated in 1886 by sending all expellees from Belgium, except Frenchmen back to Belgium. In April 1886 the Sûreté ordered that only French citizens be brought to the French border. The removal of undesirable aliens from Belgium reached a stalemate. It quickly turned out that the French border remained open to nationalities other than the French. The short-lasting closing of the border to other than French nationals had more to do with the industrial unrest in Belgium (the revolt of 1886) than with retaliation for Belgium's decision to expel vagrants even against their wish to France. By 1886, the Sûreté had abolished free choice for undesirable aliens as which border would be the place of their expulsion. This radical rupture with the traditional practice of free border choice for expellees was the result of a new, national logic in expulsion practice. For most of the nineteenth century the Belgian state had expelled the poor or otherwise undesirable immigrants at will. The radical change in expulsion policy had not been a conscious decision of the Belgian authorities, but rather forced upon them. The attitude of the neighboring countries played into the hands of the Sûreté. This administration had cunningly used the nationalistic border control of the neighboring countries to further its own goal. Although France revoked its decision of April 1886 very shortly afterwards, the Sûreté did not change its instructions to the Gendarmerie. This administration considered the free choice of border for the expellees a facility which promoted international vagrancy (ARMJ 600, 659, 668 and 703; ANMI 12586; Halot 1900:204ff.).

Due to the fact that most undesirable aliens were no longer randomly expelled, but were sent back to their country of origin, special provisions had to be provided for refugees. Returning refugees to their country of origin usually meant extraditing them to their country of persecution. The Belgian authorities considered that unacceptable as the Belgian tradition of hospitality for the politically persecuted had to be preserved. In 1885, a special status for refugees was installed. All destitute aliens who were to be expelled had to be questioned as to whether they were pursued for political reasons. The allegations of those who claimed to be refugees had to be verified and genuine refugees were to be tolerated in the country (ARMJ 345; Halot 1900:205f.; PHS 1888:179). While in 1850 in the circular letter of the Sûreté to the Gendarmerie concerning the expulsion of foreign vagrants, refugees, and military deserters were mentioned as one and the same category of expellees who explicitly deserved the free choice of border, in 1885 deserters (and draft evaders) were no longer granted special rights in expulsion policy. Although desertion and draft evasion were not catalogued under the crimes listed for which extradition could be applied, the Belgian authorities refused to grant these vagrants residency. The number of military deserters fleeing penniless to Belgium was too high and their allegations would be too difficult to verify. They had to be returned, independent of the consequences which awaited them (PHK 1901:1783; PHS 1888:179; ARMJ 703). While until the 1880s free border choice was daily procedure, by the end of that decade it was the exception. Destitute deserters in particular could profit from this possibility. Sometimes local authorities, contrary to the instructions of the central authorities, escorted destitute deserters to the border of a third country. But even at the level of the central authorities, free border choice was used as a loophole to avoid disguised extradition. In fact, only the expulsion of French vagrants constituted a real danger of unlawful extradition since, except for the short period in 1886, expelled vagrants, independent of nationality, could still enter France. Unwanted French immigrants were all returned to their country, independent of their antecedents, as no alternatives were available. The central authorities tried to legitimize the repatriations of French deserters: the risk of them being brought before a French court were minimal, these young men were a danger to Belgium as they were prone to criminal behavior and would overburden social assistance, etc. The authorities went to great pains to avoid being accused of extraditing deserters. Special transports of French deserters to be expelled were organized independently of the regular transport of undesirable aliens to the French border. These irregular transports were to enable the expellees to outwit the French border police in order to prevent extradition (ARMJ 498, 661,663, 703, 709 and 910).

The effort to rationalize the removal of undesirable aliens on a national basis was sealed with diplomatic agreements. A bilateral agreement with the Netherlands in 1888 stipulated that the Dutch authorities agreed to the transit through their territory of Scandinavians and Northern Germans (ARMJ 709). A French-Belgian agreement was reached in 1896 and in the same year the German Empire also concluded an agreement with Belgium. In 1897 a British-Belgian agreement was reached. These treaties stipulated that every country had to accept its own poor nationals who had emigrated or give free passage to those who had to pass through their territory (De Boeck 1927:581). Expulsions were no longer a unilateral affair. Constraints were imposed by the neighboring countries. When from the first of October 1900 the German *Staatspolizei* established a control post at the German-Belgian border in Herbesthal to control everyone entering the German Reich many more third-country expellees were returned to Belgium. In 1908 the Dutch rescinded on the agreement of 1888 and only accepted their own nationals. This was due to the difficulties the Netherlands had in getting rid of undocumented and destitute Scandinavians and Northern Germans expelled to the Netherlands by Belgium. The German authorities demanded, following the German-Dutch treaty of 1904, documentary proof of the nationality and if applicable, the funding for the transit through Germany. The pressure on the Belgian-German border rose. The German authorities only tolerated the immigration of third country nationals if their nationality was documented and in addition, except for the citizens of Austria-Hungary, they had to have the funds for the transit through the German Reich. Very often third-country nationals expelled by Belgium were sent back and forth at the border. This inhuman situation in which unwanted aliens, because they were not able (or willing) to document their nationality or because they had the "wrong" nationality, got trapped at the Belgian-German border repeated itself time and again until the outbreak of the First World War (Herder 1913; AFAG R 70433). The old practice of bringing aliens secretly to the border without notifying foreign officials was still part of expulsion policy. Expulsion procedures were still not that rational, and anarchy still existed at the borders.

Immigrant Policy becomes Operative

The alien law of 1835 had numerous successors, in which the original provisions were only slightly modified. Finally in 1897, the alien law became a statute law. Aliens were still classified according to the three types of alien status which the alien law of 1835 had established: aliens without residency status, those with, and the *domiciliés*. Aliens who had declared their arrival with the municipal authorities and their stay approved by the Sûreté, acquired, at least in the view of the Sûreté, residency status and were protected against arbitrary expulsion. They could only be expelled by royal decree. This administrative practice of granting residency status continued to be based on a vague article in the alien law. Until 1897 the administrator of the Sûreté proposed numerous times that the Minister of Justice institutionalize the administrative practice, i.e., insert unambiguously in the alien law that de facto domicile did not grant any protection, and that only after an officially approved stay could residency status be acquired. The Sûreté was even ready to submit its power to a strict time schedule. The administrator of the Sûreté proposed in 1876 that only one month after the alien declared his arrival at a commune, he was to be registered in the population register through which he acquired residency status. He deemed that one month was necessary for his office to check their antecedents (ARMJ 865).

The insistence of the administration on legalization of the administrative procedure was to no avail, the alien law of 1897 copied the formulation of the law of 1835 and remained vague on the conditions of acquiring residency status. The then Minister of Justice, the Catholic V. Begerem, refused to clarify the vague wording of the conditions by which residency status was acquired as this would pin the authorities down to a clear procedure, a procedure which by a liberal intervention of Parliament could put all immigrants, even if they were undesirable, under the rule of law. Immigration policy would be strongly curtailed if administrative power over aliens were to be largely abolished (PHK 1897:383ff.: ARMJ 851). The Sûreté in order to prevent a repetition of the famous Jones affair probably restrained itself so that no conflicts between the judiciary and the executive branch of the state would arise.[3]

The power which the Sûreté wielded over aliens was used in a manner similar to that of the previous period. Aliens who disturbed public order, i.e. criminals and political activists were removed from the territory. The expulsion of political activists was still an important task to which the Sûreté had dedicated itself. This was no longer to deflect any external threat, but to safeguard the regime. The authorities considered that the country was now endangered by social radicalism linked to an international revolutionary movement. Immigrants of "revolutionary" persuasion, whether they were refugees or not, had to be thwarted in their attempts to undermine the regime. About 280 aliens were expelled by royal decree for political reasons between 1875 and the outbreak of the First World War (Graph 16). In fact many more activists were expelled. For example in the 1890s aliens who had been convicted of restricting freedom of labor due to participation in strikes were as a rule expelled (ARMJ 861). The competition which foreigners caused on the labor market or in the general economy was not an issue within alien policy. The Sûreté did not take into account the interests of the popular classes when implementing alien policy. The authorities considered the hiring of foreign labor a private affair of the employers. The state had no business in this (Delrée 1981). This implied that employers could freely use foreign labor as strike breakers. Employers called on Germans during a port strike in 1907 in Antwerp, and on Italians during a strike in the quarries of Ecaussines in 1899, for example.

Besides political activists and criminals, aliens residing in Belgium who had become unemployed and destitute were another target for expulsion.

The exclusion of aliens from locally organized public welfare since 1845 had been greatly mitigated. The poor law of 14 March 1876 stipulated that the status of *domicilié* was no longer necessary to obtain a *domicile de secours* by which one could receive locally organized public welfare. After five years of residence, aliens who became destitute were no longer dependant on the central authorities for receiving welfare. While up until 1876 the central authorities had assumed full financial responsibility for the support of destitute aliens, this responsibility was largely transferred to the local authorities. In 1860 the central authorities had spent 145,827 francs supporting destitute aliens; in 1875 this had risen to 237,319 francs (*Exposé de la situation du Royaume* 1885: II, 486f.). In 1891 the bill had risen to 254,844 francs, but when the reform in that year dropped the period of residence necessary for a domicile de secours to three years, the bill was halved (*Exposé de la situation du Royaume* 1900: 788). The successive reform of the poor law was to alleviate the state treasury, but at the same time the lot of the settled aliens who fell into poverty was improved. All settled aliens were treated in the same manner as Belgians and became members of the welfare community. Only recent immigrants were still totally dependant on the goodwill of the central authorities if they became needy. A provision in the law of 1876 enabled the central authorities to expel any destitute aliens, but as far as the spirit of the law was concerned settled aliens were not to be removed (PHK 1875:118; ARMJ 374). The leeway which the state retained was to induce other states to reach bilateral agreements with Belgium to assure social assistance to Belgian emigrants. Especially in the second half of the 1890s international cooperation became successful. Belgium concluded agreements with Germany, Italy, and Switzerland which provided for social assistance for their emigrants in Belgium under the condition of reciprocity (Edgar 1899:6ff.).

Whether expulsion was for political, criminal or economic reasons, the Belgian liberal state favored the voluntary departure of aliens with residency status expelled by royal decree. These unwanted aliens were to be given a certain amount of time to leave the country. Only after this period elapsed could they be escorted to the border. The Sûreté considered this facility of voluntary departure a nuisance as those unwanted aliens could only be condemned for *rupture de ban* if it could be proven that they had left the country. Aliens who, notwithstanding an expulsion by royal decree, remained in Belgium or who refused to depart could not be condemned. They could, however, be brought to the border after the period of voluntary departure had elapsed, and if they returned a condemnation for *rupture de ban* was possible. The Sûreté, however, did not consider it an important problem since it involved only a few cases. The administrator of the Sûreté considered that an increase of such unpunishable expellees was not to be feared as life in Belgium was too difficult for these aliens for many of them to risk remaining (ARMJ 883).

The most favorable status an alien could acquire in Belgium was still that of *domicilié;* these aliens were put on par, except for political rights, with Belgians. This denizen status remained an exceptional favor, but only for well-to-do aliens. In the 1880s, 370 aliens received this status, in the next two decades their number declined considerably; two hundred in the 1890s and only 160 in the decade thereafter (Graph 18). Several categories of aliens became entitled to the status of *domicilié* by force of law. Aliens married to Belgian women who had recognized her child born during their stay in Belgium were added as a category of denizens in the alien law from 1865 onwards. From 1880 onwards this category was extended to foreign husbands of Belgian women who had resided in Belgium at least five years. In 1874 the legislature had inserted a third category of denizens in the alien law: aliens born in Belgium residing in the country until the period had passed in which they could claim Belgian nationality (at age twenty-three). The administrators of the Sûreté did not appreciate that the law enumerated four denizens categories. They considered it a nuisance since it limited the power their office wielded over aliens. Although the status of *domicilié* lost some of its prerogatives (this status was no longer necessary to be eligible for locally organized public welfare), it still protected the alien against expulsion. The legislative power did not take the objections of the Sûreté into account, and when the law of 1897 finally made the alien law a statute law, those four categories of denizens were enumerated in the law (Godding 1970: 308ff.; ARMJ 865).

The 1880s were a transitional decade in which the aspirations of the settled aliens to improve their legal status was radically altered. Before the 1880s settled aliens rarely felt the need to change their legal status. After the 1880s Belgian nationality became a mass aspiration for settled aliens. This change was not because the brutal immigrant policy as it was legally designed, but hardly implemented in the period 1840-1860, became fully operative and forced immigrants to seek protection in Belgian nationality. On the contrary, the most severe discrimination in immigrant policy was toned down. As already mentioned, the settled alien became member of the Belgian welfare community. In 1876 aliens, just as any Belgian who had lived for at least five years in one municipality, became eligible for locally organized public welfare. The residence requirement was formally diminished to three years in 1891. The reasons for the new and sudden interest in the nationality of the host country were more fundamental. In the last quarter of the nineteenth century, the state increased its penetration of society. Universal suffrage democratized politics. Conscription became more generalized. Occupational opportunities in the service of the state became manifold. The first steps towards a welfare state were also taken in those years. The expansion of the intervention of the state brought an increasing interest in formal membership in the state as it identified the bearer of the duties and rights to which the expanding state had given rise. The abstract, legal tie between the state and the individual acquired a growing importance in societal life.

This breakthrough of the principle of nationality is illustrated by the sudden appearance of data on nationality at the end of the nineteenth century. Only in 1880 were the local authorities required to ask for the nationality of an alien arriving in their municipality (Van Mighem 1882: 25). It was not until 1890 that a column was reserved in the population register for nationality. It was also in that year that the population census counted the population of Belgium by nationality for the first time. Before, only the place of birth was deemed important for classification. The change of classification of the population, now on the basis of nationality, is the crystallization point of the state putting a new, national order into society. This was expressed most spectacularly in the political realm: all male Belgians got the right to vote. The political democratization at the end of the nineteenth century caused the status of Belgian to gain importance. The abstract tie between the state and the individual which had little or no importance in the previous period now became the gateway to participation in society.

The increasing importance of state membership ran parallel to changes in the legislation governing nationality, changes which articulated the political will to assimilate settled aliens. In contrast to the autonomous process of assimilation which was dominant in the previous period, from the 1880s onwards assimilation demanded also a formal decision of the state to consider aliens members of the national community. Four times the legislature provided the possibility of amnesty for those Belgium-born aliens who had neglected to claim Belgian nationality by a declaration of indigenousness at age of majority. Not only was access to Belgian nationality more readily available to aliens born in Belgium, this was also the case for immigrants born abroad. The Law of 6 August 1881 drastically liberalized the procedure of *grande naturalisation*. The conflict between the material and political interests of these aliens had to be superseded as contrary to the country's interests. Aliens who had settled in Belgium were to be integrated politically. In addition, the application fee for either of the two types of naturalization was halved. An indication of the importance of the status of Belgian is the increasing number of aliens that claimed Belgian nationality by a declaration of indigenousness. That twelve thousand aliens born in Belgium, who had exceeded the age of majority, made use of the amnesties and that the number of naturalizations, in particular of the *grande naturalisation,* increased considerably are also clear signs of the increasing importance of nationality (Graph 19 and 20; Caestecker 1997b).

In the last quarter of the nineteenth century disputes over the status of Belgian rose sharply as an expression of the increasing importance of nationality. The democratization of the political system made clear that the local authorities did not apply the determination of nationality in a very conscious manner. The accounts of the declarations of indigenousness were particularly disorderly. Belgians of foreign origin whose predecessors had claimed Belgian nationality could have quite a bit of difficulty obtaining proof of their being Belgian. Residence in Belgium, even if it stretched over generations, was no guarantee of Belgian nationality. In 1909 the ambiguity concerning the verification of Belgian nationality was cleared away: all persons born in Belgium and who, in 1909, had been residing in Belgium at least six years and whose father was also born in Belgium, were declared Belgians. The Law of 1909 modified the acquisition of Belgian nationality by aliens born in Belgium from a declaration of indigenousness to an automatic bestowing of the nationality. This liberalization of nationality legislation was a clear cut expression of the political will to assimilate settled aliens, at the same time the Belgian nation was defined unambiguously. Uncertainty as to whether one was Belgian or not became a matter of the past. Notwithstanding the growing impact of the national category in social life, the mere presence of aliens was scarcely a matter of public preoccupation. When in 1902 the Central Commission for Statistics proposed composing a distinct table concerning the aliens in Belgium within their publication of the population census of 1900, the proposal was rejected. It was considered inopportune (Ronin 1993:259). Aliens residing in Belgium were not considered a problem. In order to prevent the nationalization of Belgian society from excluding them from the advantages for which they as settled aliens were considered eligible, the authorities promoted the inclusion of settled aliens in the national community.

At the same time some powerful industries advocated an organized recruitment of foreign labor. In contrast to the public authorities, these employers did not want to assimilate these immigrants. They aimed at segregating these foreign workers from Belgian society. The goal of the recruitment of immigrants was to make subservient workers out of them. The mining industry confronted with a labor shortage, looked for ways of increasing its intake of unqualified migrants after 1910. The Belgian labor supply was not sufficient. In order to have enough ancillary workers (haulers, etc.) management started to think about the systematic recruitment of aliens. Recruitment from the neighboring countries, Germany and the Netherlands, increased in those years. In 1911 Galician workers were recruited through the Krakow-based emigration organization *Polskie Towarzystwo Emigracyjne*. Italy was also considered a source of manpower. The number of aliens employed in the mines remained small, at most 5 percent of the miners were non-Belgians. It was, however, a novelty that heralded the growing dependence of the Belgian mines on foreign labor. The future exploitation of the newly discovered coal deposits of Limburg (Flanders) would especially necessitate an intake of foreign labor. It would be impossible to fulfill the expected need for twenty to thirty thousand miners in this basin with Belgians alone, and the mining companies counted on the future recruitment of about five thousand foreigners, probably Italians or Poles (*Recueil du Conseil Supérieur d'hygiène publique* 1912:457).

The miners' union, however, opposed the recruitment of aliens. The solution to the shortage of labor for the mines they advocated was the improvement of working conditions and wage increases. Technological investment to increase productivity was also part of their solution. The Socialist miners' union did realize, however, that at least for the exploitation of the new Limburg coal basin immigrants would be necessary. Organizing these immigrants in the unions would be necessary, but the union realized that this would be a difficult task (*L'ouvrier mineur* 1913). This official position of the miners' union should not make us think that the recruitment of foreign labor was merely imposed on local labor. On the contrary, in some mines where aliens were recruited, it seemed to be a corporate solution rather than a employers' strategy to divide and weaken labor. Although corporatism only became a genuine feature of Belgian political economy after the Second World War, even at the end of the nineteenth century there were already some isolated attempts to accommodate labor. In Mariemont-Bascoup, a large mine of the Centre basin, management invited labor to discuss most aspects of the mine's labor policy. Raoul Warocqué, the "enlightened" director of this mine had, after a general strike of "his" miners in 1875-76, reflected about the possibilities for preventing further conflicts with his labor force. Shortly thereafter he introduced *chambres d'explication* and in 1888 a *conseil de conciliation*. In this harbinger of modern industrial relations, in 1911, labor representatives were asked what they thought of the prospect of recruitment of foreign labor. Raoul Warocqué proposed recruiting aliens, Chinese or Polish, for the ancillary tasks, "aliens who one could consider of lower order, who would never be skilled workers". Management proposed limiting the occupational mobility of these aliens so that they could never become competitors with local labor. This proposition was endorsed by the workers. The shortage of menial laborers in the mines also caused discontent among the local miners. They were forced to do the menial tasks so that their wages fell. The recruitment of aliens would enable them to stick to their better paid work and the fact that in the long run no competition by those immigrants was to be feared pleased them in particular. There had already been some conflicts among laborers when Flemish migrants were promoted to higher levels; this had been resented by local labor. The recruitment of these aliens would at least prevent such disputes (Musée Mariemont, Warocqué).

Conclusions

The aim of alien policy remained largely the same as in the previous period, i.e., immigrants were tolerated if they did not harm the national interests, economically or politically. Within the national interests, which alien policy pretended to defend, the interests of the popular classes were totally ignored. Social considerations were totally absent in the decision-making process. If an employer wanted to recruit aliens, even if they replaced national labor – whether or not they were strikebreakers – the state did not intervene. Any alien could establish a business in Belgium, even if this new competitor forced a Belgian to go out of business. The exclusion from political and social power of the majority of society meant that the majority's private interests were not taken into account.

After 1860 control at the borders was abolished. External control was exchanged for internal control. Administrative discretion was safeguarded to a large extent in alien policy. Immigration control was meant to remove aliens who were considered unable to support themselves or who were a threat to public order. The effectiveness of internal immigration control was limited due to technical problems, lack of resources, and economic interests. The interests of transportation companies also constrained immigration policy as did liberal values. In the domain of expulsion policy, the practice of free border choice reflected the liberal political culture of nineteenth-century Belgium. Free border choice of expellees expressed the importance attached to individual liberty in the political culture of liberal Belgium. The susceptibilities in the field of disguised extradition also reveal that liberal values, even in relation to foreign vagrants, had considerable weight within the Belgian polity. This political culture restrained those, in particular the administrators of the Sûreté, who wanted to "nationalize" expulsion policy by returning all Belgium's unwanted guests to "their" country. The advocates of a "nationalized" expulsion policy praised their strategy as highly efficient. That all unwanted guests, even the totally harmless, would in this way be treated like extradited foreign criminals was not acceptable to the Belgian political elite. At the end of the nineteenth century, forces which favored a more heavy-handed approach to unwanted immigration gained momentum. The free border choice Belgium granted to its expellees was rejected by the German authorities as it imposed too much of a financial burden on them. Making use of Germany's and in its wake also Dutch opposition against free border choice, the Sûreté, as the main force to fight for the abolishment of this favor for unwanted immigrants, was able to get its way. Free border choice was abolished.

Other strategies to combat unwanted immigration were less controversial. Until 1879 unwanted immigrants were merely dumped at the border of choice. From that year onwards unwanted aliens who had been *renvoyé* numerous times were singled out on a case-by-case basis and expelled by royal decree, so that this hard core of foreign vagrants could be condemned for *rupture de ban*. Outright repression had to make expulsion policy more efficient. This repression radicalized to become a collective sanction against unwanted immigration between 1892 and 1896. The high cost of this heavy-handed approach to immigration control, exacerbated by resistance by the immigrants themselves meant that the policy finally had little effect and the experiment was aborted. To punish and deter poor immigrants was no longer an issue; sending them over the border again and again remained the strategy for combating unwanted immigration. By 1900 the most stubborn vagrants were again selected on a case-by-case basis to be expelled by royal decree. The hope which the administration put in the criminal prosecution of aliens was only partly met by the courts. The courts hardly ever meted out severe sentences for *rupture de ban*. The judiciary considered these vagrants much less of a danger than its habitual clientele and embodied in its lenient treatment of the vagrants the notion of equal treatment before the law.

Before 1885 there was no need felt for special provisions for refugees as *non refoulement* was assured by the principle of the free choice of border. Only in 1885, as a result of the abolition of free choice of border due to the "nationalization" of the expulsion procedure did the status of refugee regain prominence. Even destitute "refugees" found a safe haven in Belgium. The distinction between "refugees" and immigrants remained blurry. The treatment of the Commune refugees and Socialist refugees in general is revealing for the ideological construct that the notion of refugee was. A "refugee" is not so much an emigrant forced to flee his country, but an emigrant recognized as such by the host state. That Belgium was, at least in the last quarter of the nineteenth century, a politically reactionary country explains the implementation of a politically, restrictive definition of "refugee". The denial of provisions within expulsion policy for military deserters after 1885 shows that liberal values and/or humanitarianism clearly had their limits. At least in the official expulsion policy after 1885 deserters were treated as any other vagrants, i.e., returned to their country of origin. The large number of destitute deserters was considered a threat to the "national" interests and special arrangements were denied to those previously deserving cases.

While immigration policy definitely tightened, the evolution of immigrant policy was a mixed blessing. There was also a strengthening of policy. In 1897 Parliament no longer constrained the powers of the executive branch of the state over the aliens. The alien law entered the statute book, the triennial prolongation of the law which had a restraining effect on the aliens police was no longer deemed useful. The conditions by which residency status was acquired remained vague in the alien law as the authorities did not want to be pinned down to a clear procedure, a procedure which by a liberal intervention of Parliament could put all immigrants, even if they were undesirable, under the rule of law. Immigration policy would be strongly curtailed as administrative power over aliens would be largely abolished. This did not imply that the administration abused its power. Residency status was granted after a few months of registered stay. The most brutal legal provisions of the previous period were, also, attenuated. Parliament granted several categories of aliens denizens status – the status of *domicilié* – by which they were exempted from the exclusionary powers which the state wielded over aliens. The poor law of 1873 did not require that an alien had to be a *domicilié* to be eligible for municipal welfare. Formally, the poor laws of 1873 and 1891 made a distinction between Belgians and aliens, between bearers of the right to welfare and non-bearers of this right, but in practice settled aliens were granted the same privileges as Belgians after an ever shorter period of residence in Belgium. In addition, assistance to needy aliens became less a matter of charity as it grew out of international obligations embodied in bilateral agreements reached with some countries. The executive branch of government was also constrained in its policy by liberal values strengthened by the attitude of the judiciary, diplomatic considerations, and the interests of the Belgian community abroad. The alien police aspired to sweeping exclusionary power over aliens, but due to these counter forces settled aliens were mostly unaffected.

The most important new feature of this period is that those who were subject to migrant policy were clearly defined. The legal reality of citizenship became a social reality. In contrast to the previous period, state membership acquired an importance for all with political democratization and the increasing intervention of the state in social reality. The state needed a clear-cut category to ascertain membership status precisely and thus it grafted the category of nationality onto social reality. The dichotomy "alien" and "national" became a distinction between bearer and non-bearer of specific rights and obligations. The breakthrough of this nationality principle is illustrated by the sudden appearance of data on nationality in the censuses, by the differentiation among Belgians and aliens in social and criminal policy (the vagrants), and by a new expulsion policy which abolished the free choice of border and returned undesirable aliens to "their country". Also the sudden upsurge of publications in the very beginning of the twentieth century on nationality legislation and alien policy (Halot, Edgar and Van Mighem) expressed the sudden importance of the national category in social life. This increasing significance of being alien, if not the creation of the status of alien, caused the inhabitants of foreign nationality to be subject to a discriminatory policy. Steps were taken for the formal assimilation of aliens in the national community by liberalizing access to Belgian nationality. The law of 1909 meant a breakthrough in this expansion of the nation.

The definition of the two categories of alien policy – desirable and undesirable – was still very rudimentary: the desirable alien was the self-supporting (im)migrant and the undesirable alien was the destitute (im)migrant. Only at the very end of this period, just before the First World War, would the definition of desirable and undesirable become a bone of contention. The willingness which appeared to mold immigration into an intake of manpower "beneficial" not only for industry, but also for national labor in the first decade of the twentieth century was radically new. This was a prelude of discussions to come. That aliens became an issue in international relations and that bilateral cooperation was attributed increasing importance to manage migration were also definitely new phenomena. These new features of alien policy would become dominant over the following decades.

Notes

1. For those members of the Catholic Party who were not part of the Christian Democratic section of that party we will use the label Catholic politician. It refers therefore mostly to politicians issued out of the traditional establishment and loosely organized in the *Fédération des Associations et Cercles Catholiques*
2. The analysis of the sample of 62 vagrants indicates that the statistics on expulsion were more a function of repression by the state than of the reality of the immigration of the poor. The vagrants of our sample alone accounted for slightly more than a thousand expulsions in the 1880s. As 391 vagrants were expelled by royal decree in the 1880s, we can assume that about 6,400 expulsions were to be attributed to this group alone. Therefore, 391 aliens were responsible for nearly 10 percent of the total of 70,000 expulsions in the period 1882-1892.
3. Before the First World War residency status was granted after four months of registered stay. Administrative practice in this matter still has to be more closely scrutinized in order to date this practice.

Chapter 3

Inchoate Regulation of Immigration into Belgium, 1919-1924

During the German occupation of Belgium, the mining installations had hardly been damaged. The Belgian mining industry could profit from the dire coal shortages of the immediate post-war years. Shortly after the war, coal was extracted at full capacity. Because of the introduction of the eight-hour day in 1919, labor shortages soon occurred. Most companies in Wallonia hoped to attract more Flemish workers. They would be the easiest to settle in these industries. Partial or even complete reimbursement of train tickets, the provision of quicker transport by bus by the employers, and the offer of better living conditions close to the factory or mine were different means of attracting Flemish labor. Due to the start of the exploitation of rich veins of soft coal in Limburg, competition for Flemish workers increased. The reconstruction effort in the war zones of the northwest of Flanders gave a considerable number of Flemish workers work at home. Also France called upon Flemish workers for reconstruction.

Of the Flemish workers who decided to work in Belgian heavy industry most preferred to commute daily to these industrial basins, instead of settling there. The eight-hour working day, together with very low transportation costs made it feasible for most Flemish workers to do so. Flemish peasant workers were not inclined to link their fate with heavy industry. They continued to reside in their villages and, if heavy industry provided the only or easiest additional income available they would commute to the industrial basins (Caestecker 1998b). Labor shortages continued to be felt, even after the reconstruction effort of the immediate post-war years was over. This was partly due to the political changes occurring after the First World War.

The loyal cooperation of the Socialists during the war years and the social turmoil which threatened liberated Belgium in 1918-19 precipitated the introduction of an electoral system based on one-man, one-vote in 1918. The political recognition of workers as full-fledged citizens strengthened the position of the Socialists in the political sphere. The balance of power within society also shifted fundamentally as a result of the explosion of trade-union membership: from approximately 130,000 members before the First World War, Socialist membership skyrocketed to 689,000 in 1921. In those years the Socialists were at the height of their strength and could, by their participation in the government, walk away with important concessions: e.g., the eight-hour work day. The democratization of political life provided a favorable breeding ground for an active social policy. The emergent Belgian social state was distinct in that it subcontracted to private organizations many of its new interventions in the socio-economic sphere. Health insurance is a case in point. The state continued, just as before the First World War to subcontract the concrete implementation of health insurance to private bodies, but with extended state subsidies. The Socialist and Christian Democratic funds remained the most important agencies for this component of social insurance, but employers also had their own funds. This was not only the case with health insurance but also with unemployment insurance. As we mentioned earlier a system of voluntary unemployment insurance had been introduced at a local level at the end of the 1890s. Immediately after the First World War the central government stepped in. J. Wauters, the Socialist Minister of Labor[1] in the three governments of national union (1918-1921), re-introduced the prewar system but with financial subsidies from the central state. Not only union funds could count on state support, but in practice unemployment insurance remained a quasi-monopoly of the unions. The other, non-union-affiliated unemployment funds were public-sector insurance funds set up by municipalities and employers' unemployment funds, but both remained marginally within the administration of unemployment insurance. While, in principle, the employers had rejected unemployment insurance, after the First World War they had to cooperate with the new political reality. Their main concern now was to have an influence on the actual form unemployment insurance took. They were even willing to contribute financially to the scheme, in order to have control over the unemployment funds (Vanthemse 1989). The enfranchisement of labor after the First World War coincided with its being recognized as a collective actor in the private sector. A system of direct bargaining between employers' and workers' organization took shape in various industrial branches, initiatives which were strongly promoted by the post-war cabinets of national union. These joint commissions recognized the trade unions as the official partners of the employers.

Social legislation, in particular unemployment insurance, led to a more rigid functioning of the labor market. Trade union pressure and state intervention led to an increasing homogenization of the conditions in the labor market. It became increasingly difficult to play upon wage levels and working hours in order to steer the labor market. Other factors such as the increase in laborers' home ownership – the result of legislative measures promoting home ownership among the lower social classes enacted by the conservative forces in the wake of the social revolt of the 1886 – also diminished the flexibility of the labor market. These political interventions meant that the labor supply would be less easily adjusted to the demands on the labor market. The labor shortages in heavy industry occurring after the First World War were not just a phenomena caused by the reconstruction effort. Not only political, but also social changes mentioned in the previous chapter expressed themselves in shortages in certain segments of the labor market. Insufficient supply, in heavy industry in particular, would turn out to be a lasting characteristic of the Belgian labor market.

After the war capital reorganized. In 1914, two important industrialists – Raoul Warocqué and Evence Coppée – entered into an association with the *Banque de Bruxelles* and this new holding with considerable industrial interests made that interwar Belgium had two powerful financial groups in which bank and industrial activities were concentrated. The *Société Générale de Belgique*, although now in competition with another important holding, was still the backbone of the Belgian economy. By 1940 the SGB alone controlled about 40 percent of Belgian industrial infrastructure and had direct or indirect control over 800 companies.

A Restrictionist Backlash of the War

After the liberation of Belgium, immigration was immediately regulated. Passports were required and visa-requirements were introduced, in particular for subjects of former enemy countries. The neighboring countries did the same. In France, the regulation of immigration was put on an entirely new footing. During the war, France had renounced its prewar commitment to a free labor market. Because of the labor needs of the war economy, colonial and Chinese workers had been recruited en masse. To assure their efficient allocation, the state monitored and controlled the occupational mobility of these immigrants by means of work permits. Given the huge post-war labor shortages in construction, heavy industry, and agriculture, this control was extended into peace time. In 1920 about 200,000 Belgians were working in France reconstructing war-damaged regions. These Belgian workers were recruited at frontier hiring offices where they were provided an identity card which specified their work assignment. This administrative regulation was also applicable for those 45,000 Belgians who took up the prewar tradition and commuted, now mostly daily to industry in the Nord or migrated in spring for seasonal work in French agriculture (Cross 1983:55f.). The French regulation of migration was not to hinder immigration; on the contrary, immigration was stimulated by the authorities. The French authorities, in agreement with the employers, even proposed to several countries, including Belgium, a bilateral immigration treaty to assure a steady flow of foreign labor. Through its administrative control of foreign labor, the French state aimed to protect the investments of the labor-recruiting industries against those industries who wished to procure foreign labor free of charge. The identity card for all immigrants also enabled the state to control the population of foreign nationality, mainly to separate the wheat from the chaff (i.e. criminals, former enemies, and Bolsheviks). By 1923 the fear for a revolution had abated and regulations for the entrance of aliens were liberalized. Belgian commuters were exempted from administrative control of immigration; they no longer needed an identity card (Lentacker, 1974:277; AFAB 2642bis I).

In Belgium immediately after the war the regulation of immigration was politically, not economically motivated. The country would be protected against undesirable guests not only by means of passports and visa requirements, but also identity cards (Council of Ministers, 1.8.1919). Immediately after the war, all inhabitants of Belgium had to apply for an identity card. While for Belgians this was a mere administrative formality, for aliens the granting of an identity card following registration in the population register was dependent on the Sûreté's decision to give consent to their stay in the country. The granting of an identity card was preceded by a detailed investigation which would assure that Germans and aliens with a criminal record would not receive an identity card. The Sûreté could decide autonomously to expel (*renvoyer*) those who just arrived in the country. After four months of residence immigrants were registered in the population register. At this time they received an identity card which implied that they were granted residency status. These aliens could only be expelled by royal decree for disturbing public order or conviction of criminal offences.

The democratization of the electorate and the participation of Socialists (and Christian Democrats) in the government, concomitant with recognizing a role for trade unions in industrial relations and the expansion of social legislation, changed the nature of the Belgian state. The interest of labor not to increase the competition in the labor market was, however, only slowly taken into consideration. In January 1921 the Minister of Foreign Affairs, H. Jaspar, ordered the embassies to take social considerations into account whenever a blue- or white-collar worker applied for a visa (AFAB 2642bis I). Immigration control remained largely fictitious, as most immigrants did not have to carry a visa upon entry; even the visa requirement for the citizens of former enemy countries, except Germans, was not strictly adhered to. Illegal immigration as such, without passport and eventually visa, was not considered a reason to deny residence (AFAB 9538).

Labor needs for the reconstruction effort chiefly explain this liberal immigration policy. The changing nature of the Belgian state did not affect emigration policy either. Emigration was still considered a matter of individual liberty which the rules of demand and supply would regulate. The terms of the discussion were, however, different from the prewar period. The earlier labor surpluses had run down to dangerously low levels, even in Flanders. Emigration seemed to entail a loss of manpower needed for the national economy. The Catholic and Liberal members of the government considered curtailing all labor migration to France by refusing to give passports to potential emigrants. The advocates of a liberal emigration policy were the Socialists. They considered impeding emigration unfeasible; they even argued that emigration was beneficial to labor. Emigration would make the Belgian labor market tight and entice employers to increase wages (Council of Ministers, 1.3.1920). The outcome of these discussions was that emigration was only modestly combated. Passports were no longer handed over free of charge. The small fee, even for those who were destitute would hamper emigration to France. The French proposal for a bilateral immigration treaty was rebuffed and the Belgian authorities refused any cooperation in directing Belgian labor to France. An official press campaign was launched to inform potential emigrants of the occupational opportunities in Belgium itself (AFAB, 2641bis and 2642bis).

Only at the very end of this period, when emigration to France had slowed down and the labor shortages in certain segments of the Belgian labor market had become less acute was Belgian emigration policy reorientated. The individual liberty to work abroad was no longer hampered; on the contrary, the protection of Belgian workers in France became a priority in Belgian emigration policy (ARA, Theunis, yellow-6). Guaranteeing Belgian workers in France a minimal income in case of sickness or unemployment had been a demand since the end of the nineteenth century. Given the labor needs of the French economy in the early 1920s, the French authorities had signed labor treaties with labor-exporting countries such as Poland and Italy which stipulated that French welfare provisions were accessible to their emigrants. A similar French-Belgian labor treaty was agreed upon on 24 December 1924 which required local authorities to give destitute Belgians aid on the same terms as they gave to the French.

Thus, notwithstanding the Belgian policy, emigration to France increased in comparison to the prewar situation. Immigration to Belgium was also on the rise. Shortly after the war, thousands of foreign builders and navvies were employed in Belgium to help reconstruct the country, which had been heavily damaged by the war. During 1919 and 1920, nearly twenty thousand Dutch laborers immigrated to Belgium to help with rebuilding those parts of Belgium which had been ravaged by the war (Swierenga 1993). Most likely they were also joined by North Africans who had been forcibly deported to France during the war, either as civilian workers or as soldiers. After the war, when they were ordered to return to Algeria, some of them "deserted" to Belgium (Stora 1985). A more important number of laborers came from Italy. This labor emigration from Italy reached a peak, according to the Italian figures, in the spring of 1922. By the summer of 1922 demand for foreign workers had fallen sharply as the reconstruction of the devastated regions had largely been completed and because the program of public works had been cut off to reduce the spending deficit by the Belgian State.

Alien policy, including expulsion policy, continued as before the war. The Belgian authorities still expelled foreign vagrants, 5,135 expulsions of vagrants were executed in 1921. A few hundred criminals, a very few subversive aliens, and some other unwanted aliens were also removed from Belgian territory (Graphs 15 and 16). The Netherlands accepted only its own nationals, while the aliens originating from Southern Europe were dumped at the borders with France and Luxembourg. East and Central Europeans were brought to the German border. Before the First World War, German authorities had made access to their country dependent on unambiguous proof of the nationality of the expellees and, if applicable, the necessary funds for their transit through Germany. Immediately after the Great War, German authorities were unable to attach any condition to the acceptance of unwanted aliens expelled by the Belgian authorities. The vanquished Germany was dependent on the goodwill of the Belgian authorities, also in expulsion policy. In the period 1920 to 1922 about a thousand aliens – some Germans, but mostly Poles – were escorted into occupied Germany by Belgian police and handed over to the German police who brought them further eastwards.

The German occupation of Belgium during the war had repercussions not only on expulsion policy, but also on nationality legislation. After the war all Belgians of German extraction were banished from their new nation. All Belgians were not equal before the law. "New" Belgians of German descent were collectively punished for collaboration. For the first time in Belgian history, a fundamental difference was made between Belgians by birth (or naturalization) and Belgians by descent. The so-called shaken faith in the Belgians of foreign origin caused the liberal nationality legislation of 1909 to be revised substantially. The royal decree of 15 May 1922 did away with the automatic bestowing of Belgian nationality on Belgium-born aliens. One no longer became Belgian just by residing in Belgium; being Belgian became more subjectively shaded. The candidate Belgian had to show an affective bond with Belgium. He had to publicly declare this by choosing Belgian nationality upon reaching the age of majority. The criteria for being able to choose Belgian nationality were also tightened. At least a six-year period of residence was necessary for Belgium-born aliens to become Belgians. Every candidate for Belgian nationality also had to give up his former nationality. Dual citizenship was no longer tolerated. In addition, the judiciary received a discretionary authority over the acquisition of nationality. Magistrates had to determine whether the candidate for Belgian nationality could be counted on by the Belgian nation. The court, as sentinel to the entryway to Belgian nationality, was to have access to all relevant information about these candidates. The proper publicity also had to be given to their claiming of Belgian nationality: it had to be posted in the newspaper, on the wall of the city hall, and outside the residence of the candidate for Belgian nationality. Anyone who thought that this Belgium-born alien who aspired to become Belgian could be accused of a lack of loyalty with regard to his future home could inform the court (Pasinomie 1922:102ff.). As a result of these amendments, the number of acquisitions of Belgian nationality fell (Graph 20). The naturalization procedure was also amended by the law of 1922. The criteria for *grande naturalisation* became more lax and their number skyrocketed. The criteria for application for ordinary naturalization was hardly changed and the number of aliens who became politically impotent Belgians in this manner only increased to a limited degree (Graph 19).

Non-Regulated Immigration

The hope which Belgian heavy industry had put in Flemish labor surpluses to alleviate the labor shortages in the south of the country were not met. Flemish commuters were only loosely bound to heavy industry; some only turned up during winter while others offered their services when the economy declined. Only when heavy industry provided the only jobs available could the companies be sure of all their Flemish commuters, but unemployment benefits tended to undermine the "beneficial" effects of economic downturns (Caestecker 1998b). Flemish immigration thus offered only a partial solution to the desertion of the Walloon workers. Hiring foreign labor was the only recourse the companies had.

In 1923-1924 we observe a massive increase in foreign labor. A sprinkling of nationalities, dominated by Dutch, Italians, and North Africans immigrated to Belgium. The mines in particular took in a large number of foreign workers. While in September 1922, only 3 percent of the miners were of foreign nationality, by November 1923 their numbers had increased to 10 percent; 17,020 aliens were then working in the mining sector. In the spring of 1924 their numbers decreased slowly and in May of that year only 15,543 foreigners were left. Not only the mines, but many other industries and even agriculture made use of aliens. This migration was largely a spontaneous process, a process whereby supply and demand of the international labor market found each other. In fact the most interested industrial group, mining, was not satisfied with this spontaneous migration process. They wanted to have greater control over migration.

In 1924 a powerful representative of the mining companies, Habets, looked upon the French employers as the best example of how to proceed. He argued that a central immigration organization of all the employers, not limited to the mining industry, should organize the intake of foreign labor. This organization should regulate all aspects of labor immigration. Not only their recruitment, but also their wages, housing, and even pastoral care and the education of their children had to be planned by this organization. This employers' organization was to become the immigration office for the whole of Belgium (ACCA 25.6.1924). Very little of this ambitious plan materialized during these years. In this chapter we will see that the employers had much less control over the immigrants than Habets would have liked.

In particular in 1922 and 1923 employers had hardly any control over foreign labor. Several thousand North-Africans, Poles, and Italians offered their services spontaneously to Belgian heavy industry. Most of the Poles and North Africans came indirectly to Belgium, they first had spent some time in France. The North Africans had been forced to help France in the war effort and were not willing to return home once the war was over. The Poles who had been recruited by French employers for reconstruction, mining, and agriculture, but were dissatisfied with conditions in France hoped that in Belgium they would be treated better (Ponty 1988:123-134; AFAP 9538). Some Poles came directly from the Ruhr, the German mining region which had a thriving Polish community. Unemployment and inflation made them look for a new place of abode. Among the Italians there was a considerable number of political refugees who had fled Italy after Mussolini took over power. These immigrants mostly had come to Belgium illegally, either on their own initiative or brought by a "smuggler". Generally they had no passports, let alone Belgian visas. Notwithstanding their illegal arrival, they were, just like most other aliens, tolerated by the Belgian authorities. The acute need for labor meant that any labor offer, North African or other, refugees or those deserting their employers in France, was eagerly accepted. Even Poles, who employers mostly equated with bolsheviks, were hired (AAN, *Ambasada w Londynie,* 51) . Not only the mining industry, also the metallurgic and chemical industries used these immigrants to alleviate their labor shortages. Employers could not be very selective as the increasing labor shortage forced them to accept anyone.

By 1924 the employers had developed a conscious recruitment strategy to alleviate their labor shortage. The balance between demand and supply tipped in favor of the employers. Among those foreign workers who had offered their services spontaneously, Italian refugees and North Africans were largely dismissed. An important factor in the exclusion of North African labor once they were no longer essential was without any doubt racism. In 1923 the hiring of North African labor had provoked a backlash from local labor, including a four-day strike in which two thousand Belgian miners in several mines participated and demanded the dismissal of all North Africans. Employers were now able to comply with the local demand to remove these most resented immigrants (*L'ouvrier mineur* 1924:1,2). In the following years hardly any North Africans immigrated to Belgium. In the summer of 1924 the French colonial authorities had, under pressure from the large agrarian estates in Algeria which were anxious not to lose their agrarian manpower, introduced emigration restrictions (Stora 1985:72; Nouschi 1984:42).

Organized recruitment in the Netherlands and Italy

After 1920 Dutch authorities were alarmed by the large number of their citizens who became unemployed due to the economic downturn. The deprivation of the unemployed was alleviated by the dole or public work, which constituted a considerable burden on the national budget. The Dutch Ministry of Labor wanted to promote the emigration of unemployed Dutchmen through a labor exchange program with Belgium in order to diminish public expenditures. Immediately after the First World War, Belgian authorities wanted to be able to influence the functioning of the labor market. Public labor-exchange offices were set up. They were administrated jointly by trade unions, employers, and public officials. The employers considered these corporate agencies as trade-union dominated institutions. Without the cooperation of the employers these labor exchanges offices could only play a marginal role in the labor market. In addition, these public labor-exchange offices had to confront competition from private, mostly Christian-Democratic, labor-exchange offices which also were subsidized by the state. As a result the public network of labor-exchange offices hardly expanded. Most importantly, it had no centralized direction and became totally inefficient (Vanthemse 1989).

The lack of a central labor office in Belgium impeded Dutch-Belgian coordination at the central level. But the Brussels labor office became the semi-official partner of the Dutch central labor office. The public labor exchange office in Brussels mediated vacancies, initially only for Brussels but, by the end of 1922, its services had extended beyond to include the industrial basin of Charleroi. The public labor office in Hasselt (Limburg) also cooperated in this endeavor. The crucial problem was that very few unemployed Dutch were eager to respond to the needs of the Belgian labor market. Among the Dutch unemployed, hardly any had professional experience in mining or in the iron and steel industry. Most could only be employed as unskilled labor in these sectors. Although these emigrants were guaranteed the same wages as Belgians, these wages were insufficient to support their families who remained in the Netherlands. Because of the exchange rate, the Belgian franc stood very low. Taking the family to Belgium was not easy as there was a severe house shortage in Belgium. The Dutch authorities soon concluded that emigration to Belgium was only feasible for unemployed single men. In the Netherlands several municipal labor exchange offices, stimulated by the central authorities, tried to force some of their unemployed single men to accept work in Belgium. The unemployed did not succumb to these pressures that easily. Protest by the unemployed, sometimes backed up by the trade unions or the Social-Democratic party, meant that in the end only very few Dutch were in this way forced to leave for Belgium. The threat of being disqualified from unemployment aid was soon revoked, because in the immediate post-war period, the unemployed were able to mobilize enough political power to legitimize their claim for labor within the national realm. Although there was a surplus of labor, Dutch labor was, just as Belgian labor, no longer so tractable that it could be forced to respond quickly to labor market needs. During 1922 and 1923, a few thousand Dutch went to work in Belgium partly through this scheme, mostly in the building trades, but also in the mines and in the iron and steel industry (ARDH 180-182; *Rapport de la Bourse officiele du Travail*, Bruxelles 1922-1923).

A similar semi-official bilateral structure was set up in the spring of 1922 to channel Italian workers into the Belgian labor market. The Brussels labor exchange office signed an agreement with the Italian *Uffici di collocamento* to send masons and other skilled construction workers to Brussels. Following this agreement, 630 skilled Italian builders were recruited between May 1922 and December 1924 to work in construction. In the beginning of 1923, the labor office of Brussels erroneously obtained a number of unqualified Italian workers through its arrangement for skilled builders with the Italian labor offices. The labor office contacted with the mine companies in Charleroi, who were very eager to receive these Italians. This spontaneously established pattern of recruitment was endorsed by the Italian authorities, as the mediation of an official institution offered more guaranties, especially in avoiding the recruitment of Italians by industries where the labor force was on strike. The labor office of Brussels had to advise on all demands for Italian labor. The office's guideline was that national labor had absolute priority, but the recruitment of foreign labor was deemed necessary due to the shortage of manpower in certain labor market segments. The Italian authorities, through the central emigration agency, the *Commissariato Generale dell Emigrazione* (CGE), felt that they were in a strong bargaining position, because the demand for labor was high and alternatives for recruiting labor were few. Strict conditions for the recruitment of Italian labor were set. All the costs linked to the administrative procedure (including passports) were at the expense of the employer. The employer also had to offer a full year's contract. If the migrant was dismissed before the end of the contract because of lack of work or sickness, the employer had to repatriate this employee. The Italian authorities also kept an eye on the working and living conditions offered. Employers were compelled to specify wages and to guarantee decent housing and food. Employers who tried to abuse the Italian migrants were blacklisted and could no longer apply for Italian labor (*Rapport de la Bourse officiele du Travail,* Bruxelles 1922:14ff.). Some employers tried to circumvent these expensive conditions and the slow bureaucratic procedure by recruiting Italian labor autonomously. Especially the mining sector, which was badly in need of labor, tried to bypass the CGE and set up their own recruitment scheme in Italy. These prospective employers had to deal, however, with an Italian state which considered recruitment in Italy as coming under its competence. The Belgian mines could not bypass the Italian state in this endeavor (Caestecker 1993d). A main disadvantage in this Italian immigrant scheme was that the employers had no hold over the migrants. Although the recruitment of Italian labor was an investment in time and in money, the return was not at all sure. Many of the Italians used the Belgium scheme only to get permission to leave Italy and to enter France. Even if the Italians arrived at the mine, for the most part they did not intend to stay there. Many Italians had no experience of underground mine work, since they were only familiar with open-air mining. Once they realized that mining in Belgium was very different from what they had expected, quite a few of them looked for another occupation. The spill-over of Italian migrants recruited for the mining industry to other industrial sectors was considerable. The iron and steel industry was particularly eager to recruit the Italian mine deserters. Several thousand Italians were working in this industry by 1924, although these companies had rarely applied to the Italian authorities for labor. Construction, the quarries, and the chemical industry were other important outlets for the Italian migrants who preferred not to stay in the mines. The mining companies felt defenseless. They considered it impossible to reach an agreement with other industries, especially with the iron and steel industry, to prevent them from poaching the Italians the mining industry had sent for. The interests of both industries in this field were too different to find any agreement (BdL 181).

The Catholic Minister of Labor, R. Moyersoen, did not appreciate the initiatives of the public labor exchange offices in the field of labor recruitment abroad. Probably he resented the monopoly of these institutions, which threatened the expansion of the Christian Democratic labor exchange offices. In October 1923 the director of the labor office in Hasselt was fired because he exceeded his authority by making an arrangement directly with the Dutch authorities. The labor office in Brussels was also told that it had to limit its mediation to Brussels. Control of the Italian recruitments by the labor office of Brussels was taken over by the Ministry of Labor. The previous ad hoc arrangement was replaced by an official agreement between the two states. The Belgian authorities felt that the Italian authorities should offer more guarantees to Belgian industry. The Belgian authorities also wanted to promote their own interests. The Catholic Minister of Labor, R. Moyersoen, in particular wanted to protect the national labor market. Italian labor should not take jobs for which Belgians were available. The Belgian authorities negotiated with the Italians to have an official say in the recruitment of Italians for Belgian industry. The strengthening of the position of the employers vis-à-vis the migrants was one aim. Not so much the interests of the employers, but rather the proper interests of the Belgian state prevailed in the arrangement finally concluded with the Italian authorities. The Italian authorities, who already in 1922 had been interested in official guarantees for their emigrant labor, were to consult the Ministry of Labor about the state of the labor market. In principle, only when there was an officially sanctioned need on the Belgian side to recruit Italian labor would the Italian authorities act. The protection of the national labor market was ensured (BdL 181; AFAB 2647bis; *Arbeidsblad* 1923:2199ff.).

With the Dutch authorities, no agreement was reached. The absence of such an agreement is striking, given the evident advantages which Dutch labor offered for the implementation of the new immigration regulations of April 1923. This was probably due to a lack of pressure from powerful employers. The mining companies did not consider Dutch immigrant labor very diligent. The urban laborers who were sent out by the Dutch labor offices in particular were even considered to be rebellious. The lack of an institutional framework to coordinate this labor exchange at a central level meant that the Dutch authorities had very little leeway for pressuring their local labor offices to send their clients to Belgium. The employment of Dutch in Belgium decreased considerably (BdL 582 and 259; ARDH 180).

By 1924 the recruitment scheme which the Italian authorities had set up was considered the best available solution to the labor shortage problem in the Belgium mining sector. The employers considered that it at least gave some guarantees concerning the morality of these migrants. The employers became aware of the potentially politicized nature of Italian labor. The refugees who offered their services spontaneously were not considered useful labor, while those recruited directly in Italy were felt to be more valuable. By 1923, Italian immigration to Belgium was largely destined for the mines. On 31 of August 1923, there were already 3,824 Italians working in the mines; this increased to 5,611 on November 1, and to 6,150 by the end of 1923. In total, nearly 6,000 Italians were recruited for the mines through this official scheme between 1922 and 1924. Construction, the quarries, and the metallurgic industry recruited only 2,000 Italian workers. The mining industry was the only one still to call upon Italian labor during the economic downturn of 1925 (*La lutte contre le chômage* 1925:65ff.; *Le notizie sull'emigrazione a sul lavoro* 1922:32/7; *Rapport de la bourse officielle de travail Bruxelles*, 1922-1923). Notwithstanding the fact that the shortage of labor had shifted by then to an oversupply of labor in the Belgian labor market, the mines still needed manpower.

The Recruitment of Polish Labor

As mentioned before, Polish labor had been recruited in Galicia already in the 1910s. In the beginning of the 1920s, heavy industry was not satisfied with the foreign labor they were hiring and hoped that recruitment in Poland would yield better workers. The Polish authorities knew that their labor surpluses were in high demand and that they could impose strict conditions on any recruitment in their country. Recruitment and travel costs were made an expense of the companies, which also had to assure the workers a job for one year. Prior to recruitment, Poland required an official labor treaty which would stipulate the equal treatment of Polish and local labor, including receipt of health care and unemployment benefits. In this way the receiving state would assure that the employers kept to the terms of their contract and that the Polish consulates would not have to repatriate sick or unemployed Polish migrants. In exchange, the Polish authorities guaranteed suitable immigrants, who would be politically and technically selected by the Polish authorities. Therefore, it would no longer be necessary to employ illegally immigrated Poles who were not well qualified and among whom there were quite a few undesirable individuals (AFAP 9538, AFAB 2652bis).

Heavy industry pressed the authorities to start negotiations with the Polish authorities to assure labor from Poland for them. The employers in heavy industry preferred, however, direct recruitment without any state involvement. Although they considered labor recruiting a prerogative of management and resented any state intervention in this field, they were forced to call upon the Belgian authorities to clear the way for them.

Agrarian interests also were in favor of a Polish-Belgian labor treaty. The Minister of Agriculture, A. Ruzette, strongly insisted on such a treaty in order to secure the necessary Polish farmhands. A few hundred workers were recruited in Poland between 1923 and 1924 for agriculture and mining. The Polish authorities hoped by this experiment to increase the pressure on the Belgian authorities. A carefully selected group of Polish workers should improve the rather negative opinion the Belgian employers had of Polish migrants. The Polish authorities reasoned that Belgian employers, after receiving a batch of outstanding workers would be eager to recruit more hard-working Poles. In this way they would put pressure on the Belgian authorities to yield to the Polish demand for a labor treaty (AFAP 9538).

The Belgian authorities, however, were not prepared to sign a labor treaty. The Minister of Foreign Affairs, H. Jaspar, was not eager to encourage any migration to Belgium. He considered the need for foreign labor as strictly temporary due to emigration to France. After reconstruction, the Belgian workers would return. No engagements should be made as very soon foreign workers would no longer be needed. A labor treaty with Poland was also strongly rejected as it would cause unilateral expenses for the Belgian treasury, because equal rights to social security would be advantageous only for the Poles since no Belgians were working in Poland. A negative side-effect was that even unwanted Jewish immigration from Poland would profit from this arrangement. Polish Jews found a livelihood in Belgium not in heavy industry or agriculture, but in sectors such as the leather and garment industries where there was no shortage of labor (see chapter 5). On the contrary, unemployment among Belgian labor in these sectors was not uncommon and the Polish Jews only aggravated this surplus of labor. A labor treaty with Poland would mean that those Polish Jews, whom Belgian industry did not need at all, would be even more attracted to Belgium (AFAB 2652bis). Jaspar even rejected the very principle of a treaty between states in the field of immigration. He argued that the recruitment of labor and especially the conditions of its employment were a private affair between employers and employees and was not the affair of the state. The role of the state should be limited, Jaspar claimed, to a moral and medical control of immigration (AFAP 9538-9539; PHK 1923: 2038). Top officials within the Ministry of Industry and Labor also were opposed to a Polish-Belgium labor treaty. Polish immigration could only be encouraged if it could be directed to those segments of the labor market with a labor shortage. Only after a new alien law had established the rights and duties of foreign labor to assure this could a labor treaty with Poland be envisaged.

By 1923 the Polish authorities wanted to hasten the negotiations with the Belgian authorities as the need for a labor treaty was pressing. Political reasons prompted the Polish authorities to increase pressure on the Belgian authorities. An alternative had to be found for those Poles who had worked in the German Ruhr for generations, as they were being threatened with expulsion. By 1914 Polish-speaking miners recruited from the eastern provinces of Prussia formed about a third of the labor force in the Ruhr mining region. When, in 1918, the Poles obtained their own independent state, very few of the Ruhr Poles left for the new state. The dim socio-economic prospects in the new Polish state, as well as a continuing struggle with regard to its external boundaries meant that most of the Ruhr Poles remained in Germany. When the process of opting for German or Polish nationality, which had been provided for in the Treaty of Versailles, came into operation in 1921-1922, many Ruhr Poles decided to adopt German nationality. Only a small number opted in favor of Poland. This expression of a strong Polish national loyalty was a risky choice for those who remained in the Ruhr. Job prospects in Poland were slim and the choice of Poland was strongly resented in Germany. Anti-Polish resentment in the Ruhr strengthened during the Belgian-French occupation of the Ruhr in 1923. The Poles were seen as collaborators because of the friendly diplomatic relations between France and Poland. This poisoned the climate between Ruhr Poles and Germans in the Ruhr district and caused those Ruhr Poles who had opted for Poland to realize that it would be better for them to depart. The economic downturn that had erupted with the stabilization of the German mark caused the Ruhr mines to cut manpower drastically. Many Ruhr Poles who had been hesitant to leave Germany after they had opted for the Polish nationality were now forced to make their living elsewhere (Kleßmann 1978 and 1986).

By the end of 1923, the Polish authorities were pleading with the Belgian government to open Belgium's borders to their nationals in the Ruhr. France could not take them all and returning to Poland was not a realistic option. The Polish authorities revoked the demand for a labor treaty because of the emergency situation. They were disposed to giving their full support to the transplanting of Ruhr Poles to Belgium. The Minister of Foreign Affairs, H. Jaspar, remained strongly opposed to the immigration of the Ruhr Poles. The Ruhr Poles would come to stay, while, according to Jaspar, the Belgian economy only needed foreign manpower to alleviate a temporary labor shortage. The political creed of these Ruhr Poles was, according to Jaspar, also dangerous. The Ministers of Labor and Justice were less intransigent. Rather than employing North Africans, the recruitment of these Poles would be a preferable solution to the structural shortage of labor in the mining industry. These Ruhr Poles were fully integrated into industrial society, they were even qualified miners, so they offered a definite advantage, argued both Ministers, in terms of stability and productivity. Even the Italian immigrants did not score that high (ARMA bC1C16D/59). According to the Polish embassador the advice of the head of the Sûreté, Gonne was decisive in the whole issue (AFAP 9538). Gonne pointed out the needs of the industry and put forward the linguistic affinity (German speakers) and even cultural closeness as reasons for opposing the over-cautious Minister of Foreign Affairs. Gonne stated clearly that he did not consider the immigration of Ruhr Poles as posing any danger to public order. Jaspar's fear for this Polish immigration was, in his opinion, unjustified, since the Ruhr Poles were qualified miners and had nothing to do with the Jewish artisans who pretended to be industrial workers, but in fact were tailors, hatmakers, or leatherworkers (AAD 12).

Jaspar was clearly isolated in his opposition to the immigration of the Ruhr Poles. His decision to oppose their immigration was overturned by the Council of Ministers on 12 December 1923. His colleagues considered the need for foreign labor in the mines as structural. The recruitment of Ruhr Poles would enable the employers to make a positive selection from among the manpower available. In 1924 a few thousand Polish qualified miners were recruited in the Ruhr. By 1925 about five thousand Polish workers were making a living in Belgium. Poles were already competing with Italians to become the most important group of foreigners in Belgium's heavy industry. Only a limited number of Ruhr Poles recruited by the mining companies left for other industries. This was due to the large number of professional miners among these Polish migrants. Employers were eager to retain them.

Not only the qualifications of these immigrants, but also the hope among the employers that they would be apolitical meant that the mining companies would make an additional effort to retain them. The Winterslag mine in the Limburg basin was the most outspoken in its intention to create provisions for all its Polish miners. The mine director wanted to attract several thousand Poles and the company would pursue a multicultural strategy to make these workers feel at home. The company was ready to strongly support their cultural heritage. A Polish school, a Polish priest, and ethnic organizations, all strongly subsidized by the mine, would cater to all the needs of the Polish community (AAG III.1; KADOC, Broekx, 14.5.6). By 1925, very little had materialized out of the objective to create a Polish subculture. The constraints on a multicultural strategy would turn out to be multiple. Only the Catholic Church had taken some steps to implement one dimension of this multicultural strategy, that of Polish pastoral care. The motivation of the Church was of course different from the employers' goal of stabilizing the Polish mine community. The Church aimed at preserving the Catholic faith within the Polish migrant communities. The threat of Socialist propaganda in the heavily secularized Walloon mining communities had to be countered. In order to have any success it was considered essential, because of language difficulties, to call upon Polish priests. A permanent Polish mission was necessary. The calling for Polish priests was not only a matter of clerical assistance, it also brought more secular concerns. Where would the newly arrived priests be lodged and on what financial means would they live? The Archbishopric contacted the employers of the Polish workers. Some of them had already voiced concern that their Polish workers were without pastoral care. The response of the mining companies in every basin which employed Polish workers was generous. Even mine directors who were known for their non-religious convictions were eager to support the Polish priests financially. Housing would be made available and a financial subsidy was also promptly promised (AAB, Dessain, IV). The Polish Archbishop was officially requested by the Belgian Church to provide some priests. The Polish Ministry of Foreign Affairs joined the Belgian request as the presence of a permanent Polish mission would prevent the "denationalization" of the Polish community in Belgium. All these pressures were to no avail. The Polish Archbishop felt that he needed all his priests in Poland itself; the vocations in Poland were too few to permit any of them to leave for a mission among the small Polish community in Belgium (AAB, Mercier, XXII-100; AAG III 1). The multicultural strategy of employers and the Church alike remained largely limited to intentions in the first half of the 1920s. Only later, in the second half of the 1920s would the efforts of the Catholic Church yield results. Some mining companies would also then invest heavily in the multicultural endeavor.

Russian Refugees, a Politically Safe Immigrant

The Russian refugees – about one million people – were subjects of the former Russian empire who fled abroad in the years immediately after the Russian Civil War. They were the first group of refugees for which the international community catered. In June 1921, a High Commissioner for Russian refugees, the Norwegian polar explorer Fridtjof Nansen, was appointed. All the members of the League of Nations saw repatriation as the solution for this refugee problem. The Soviet authorities were not at all eager to permit a massive, unrestricted return. The Soviet decrees of November and December 1921, reinforced in 1924, deprived anti-Bolshevik Russians of their Russian citizenship. Now the refugees were officially stateless. The High Commissioner had to change his strategy and now advocated the resettlement of Russian refugees outside the Soviet Union.[2] The Belgian authorities were asked to take their share of refugees. Political considerations – the international sympathy for these refugees and the expected role these refugees would play once "legality" was restored in Russia – meant that Russian refugees were granted visas for Belgium (AFAB 12,178). Increasingly labor market considerations pleaded in favor migration of Russian refugees. About 30,000 Russian fugitives asylum in Bulgaria, shortly after the end of the Civil War. Many re occupied as ancillary workers in the mines near Pernik, Bulgaria. The economic backwardness of Bulgaria, together with political developments (the recognition of the Soviet Union and rising nationalism) meant that most Russian refugees were looking for another asylum country. Belgium was one of these alternatives. Crucial for their immigration was the role of a charity organization – with sympathies for the political cause of these refugees – which provided housing and jobs. The Belgian authorities were willing to grant visas as they knew this charity organization would assure the reception of these refugees. Since this organization had branches only in Belgium's urban centers (Antwerp and Brussels), all refugees were settled in those cities and most were employed as domestic labor (governesses, cooks, gardeners, maids, etc.). Domestic servants were in short supply in these years and the urban bourgeoisie was very willing to take in some of this refugee labor (AUNO R1748). In 1924 the charity organization contacted some mining companies because they saw considerable job opportunities in this industry for their protégés. Some mining companies were eager to recruit what they considered to be politically safe labor. As these potential immigrants had worked in the Bulgarian mines, they hoped to recruit not only an order-loving, but also a qualified labor force (BdL 259). In 1925 only, about 700 visas were requested by the mining industry in order to recruit Russian refugee labor. The Belgian authorities granted them willingly (AAD 12). The travel costs were paid either by the charity organization or by the International Labor Organization. The refugees had to reimburse at least a part of these costs. The mines had to pay a quarter of the costs if the refugee-labor remained in the mine for four months. Probably only half of the requested refugees arrived in Belgium. Competition with French recruitment among refugees in Bulgaria and the opportunity to settle in culturally closer communities meant that the enthusiasm for emigration to Belgium turned out to be rather limited. In particular, the unattractive job offer, mining, and the fact that the refugees had to pay their voyage at least partly themselves meant that the number of candidates for the Belgian mines remained limited (AAD 12). As we will see in the next chapter, the interest in Russian refugee labor diminished considerably in the following years.

The State Attempts Immigration Control

Labor immigration in the first half of the 1920s has to be positioned in a volatile political climate. Shortly after the war, the regulation of immigration as a means of protecting national labor became a central preoccupation of the authorities. Labor, however, quickly lost its political clout. The Socialists, with about 35 percent of the electorate behind them, were excluded from the government in 1921. The Catholic-Liberal government of G. Theunis took over power. This government had no interest in expanding social benefits for labor. Monetary preoccupations came to the fore. Immediately after the war the Belgian government had initiated a large scale program of reconstruction. The Belgian authorities embarked on this operation because they thought that financing was assured by German reparations. Their reliance on German reparation payments proved to be an error. The government outlays were financed, to a great extent, by the creation of money, which led to inflationary pressure. Budget deficits ran high. The Theunis governments (1921-1925) had the balancing of the state budget as their aim, but they barely succeeded in putting a halt to inflation. In the social domain, concessions to labor were halted by 1922. No more joint commissions in which unions were recognized as partners of employers were founded. Union recognition in the years immediately after the war had been forced upon the employers only by the specific circumstances of those years. The employers also organized. Big agrarian interests in Wallonia founded their own organization, the *Fédération Nationale Belges des Unions Professionelles Agricoles,* to represent their interests (Van Molle 1990). The employers, especially those in heavy industry organized by the *Comité Central Industriel*, with the large resources at their disposal battled the newly acquired power of labor, which was still particularly strongly represented in the traditional heavy industries. In 1921 the metallurgical firm Ougrée-Marihaye refused to negotiate with the Socialist metalworkers union and succeeded in keeping its workforce out of the union for the next decade by presenting a firm stance during a nine-month strike. It was the start of a general offensive by employers to reconquer "their" labor force. Employers continued to see the unions, not so much as "social partners" but as class enemies. The employers' support of militant anti-Communist and anti-Socialist organizations such as *Union Civique* and SEPES (*Société d'Etudes Politiques, Economiques et Sociales*) were illustrative (Gotovitch 1996; Balace 1987:589ff.). The increasing activity of employers in the domain of social policy was another expression of their anti-union offensive. Industrial firms created or expanded sickness funds and unemployment insurance. Company unions were also founded (Vanthemse 1987: 269).

As mentioned before, in 1922 there was an unprecedented upsurge in immigration. The Catholic Minister of Foreign Affairs, H. Jaspar, saw these migrants as a dangerous lot. His virulent anti-communism meant that he saw most of the migrants as bolsheviks. In addition, his Germanophobia meant that he considered all emigrants from Central Europe or even Northern Italy as Germanophiles (AAD 12). Certainly just as important was his perception of this immigration as a social danger. Most of these immigrants, argued Jaspar, responded to labor market shortages which were only of a temporary nature. Belgian labor was attracted by the higher salaries paid in the reconstruction projects in the North of France and after reconstruction those workers would return to Belgium. The presence of a considerable number of foreign laborers would ultimately cause unemployment. This would, in turn, increase government expenses (unemployment benefits) and could even create social disorder. Foreign labor should be channeled to those segments of the labor market where there was a temporary labor shortage, but as soon as Belgians returned aliens should be removed. Jaspar convinced the government that the state should acquire a new role: the protection of the national labor market. The Catholic Minister of Agriculture, A. Ruzette succeeded in exempting the agrarian labor market from this developing state policy. The demarcation line which was drawn between the agrarian and industrial labor market was partly the result of the exceptionally tense conditions on the agrarian labor market. More important was the absence of organizations of agrarian workers. The adherence to nineteenth-century liberalism, for which agrarian interests strongly lobbied, was not challenged (ARMA BC1C6D/59). The three above-mentioned considerations (public order, safeguarding of the industrial labor market for nationals and curtailing public expenditure) led to the introduction of a restrictive immigration policy for industrial labor from April 1923 onwards.

The procedure of this policy was as follows: every alien who wanted to work in Belgian industry had to apply for a residence permit either at the embassy if he needed a visa to immigrate, or with the provincial authorities if he was already in the country or did not have to carry a visa upon immigration. If the Sûreté, by a routine search of the criminal record, determined that the immigrant posed no danger to public order and if the Ministry of Labor concluded on the bases of the labor contract that the immigrant responded to a labor market need, then the immigrant was granted a short-term residence permit (valid for three or six months). Every extension of this residence permit depended on the above-mentioned considerations. This procedure would enable the authorities to react quickly to changes in the labor market, and, in particular, to prevent aliens from entering segments of the labor market where there were no labor shortages. Only labor contracts with a repatriation clause were considered valid for granting a temporary residence permit. This would guarantee that foreign labor would leave as soon as the state of the labor market deteriorated. A certificate of nationality would make sure that the country to which the migrant would return was clearly established.

The latter provided the reasoning behind the Belgian authorities opposition to the immigration of Ruhr Poles in 1923. Given the labor shortages at the beginning of the 1920s in France and Belgium, there was considerable interest in recruiting these qualified miners. In 1922 the French mining companies set up a recruitment office in Duisburg in agreement with the Polish authorities. In this way, fifty thousand Ruhr Poles set off for France (Ponty 1988). The FEDECHAR also tried to set up a recruitment office in Bochum, but due to the opposition of the Belgian authorities, no Ruhr Poles could be recruited in that year. The Belgian authorities wanted to ensure the possibility of repatriating foreign labor if they were no longer necessary. Those who had assumed German nationality were not welcome in Belgium, those who had opted for Polish nationality had to go through the whole procedure so that their nationality was settled definitively. Since a definitive agreement between Poland and Germany was only signed in August 1924 this condition proved to be an insurmountable barrier for recruiting these qualified miners. The large pool of labor in the Ruhr could therefore, not be tapped by the Belgian mine industry in 1923. For the Ruhr Poles, only a spontaneous and illegal immigration to Belgium was possible in that year (AFAB 2652bis; BdL 181).

Largely for diplomatic reasons, the probationary period during which every extension of the immigrant's residence permit depended on labor market considerations was limited to two years, then these labor migrants acquired residency status. This new immigration policy was short-lived, but 4,037 migrants who worked or wanted to work in Belgian industry filed for temporary residence permits between 22 March 1923 and 3 February 1924. On the advice of the labor-exchange offices and the Sûreté, 80 percent of the applicants were granted a permit (*La lutte contre le chômage* 1925: 63f.). The number of applicants fell sharply by the middle of 1923 and in March 1924 the regulation of industrial foreign labor was revoked.

The revocation of this new immigration policy was the result of the strong opposition it encountered. First of all, heavy industry was strongly opposed to this new regulation of immigration. Although the employers agreed on the need for state control over immigration, this regulation, they argued, should only aim at eliminating politically dangerous elements. They disapproved of any consideration of protection of domestic labor. Immigration was necessary for a smooth functioning of the economy. In addition, regulation based on the state of the labor market would only increase the power of the trade unions, as they controlled the public labor exchange offices which evaluated the needs of the labor market. The mining companies especially criticized the obligation to guarantee the repatriation of the aliens they called upon. The mining industry hired a large number of aliens, who considered the mines as only a stepping stone to other occupations. The mining companies could not finance the repatriation of all these temporary miners. They argued that this spill-over to other industrial sectors was no problem, as the industries where these foreign workers ultimately found their livelihood also had a shortage of labor. The crux of the argument of the mining industry was that their recruitment campaigns were beneficial to the global Belgian economy as the attraction of foreign labor alleviated tensions on the overall labor market (Fedechar 4/5.1923;AAD 12). The Minister of Foreign Affairs, H. Jaspar, tried to rebut these points by pointing out that the mining companies could make the immigrants pay for their repatriation. A regular deduction from the immigrants' salary would soon yield the sum of money necessary for a return ticket. And if immigrants left for other industries, the new employer became responsible for their repatriation. The new state policy was designed, close to the French model, to limit this spill-over, by promoting a selective recruitment of labor abroad. Only labor which was apt (and willing) to do the specific jobs which the Belgians had deserted was to be called upon. Jaspar promised the full support of the public authorities for such selective recruitment. The quality of labor recruited in this way would, according to Jaspar, outweigh the limited liability the new state policy imposed on the employers (ARMA bC1C16D/59;AFAB 2652bis). The mining companies did not share his opinion, they sometimes overtly refused to submit to the new regulations (BdL 181; PHK 1923: 2038).

Of equal importance is the fact that Jaspar could not count on the diligent cooperation of the communes. Municipal authorities had to order the foreign workers residing in their communes to apply for a residence permit with the provincial authorities. Initially some communes did so, but soon it turned out that the procedure for obtaining a residence permit was a time-consuming one. It took weeks, even months for the Sûreté, the labor-exchange offices, and the Ministry of Labor to process the applications. By the time a decision was made, a large number of applicants – foreign labor was a extremely mobile group – had already left the commune. Some even moved on purpose to avoid a refusal. By the beginning of 1924 most communes no longer bothered to require residence permits. It seemed to be a waste of time, even those aliens whose application for a residence permit had been refused were not bothered by the authorities. While in the middle of 1923, foreign workers still spontaneously left the country when they were refused a residence permit, this was not the case in 1924 when it became clear that the threat of forced expulsion would not be carried out (*La lutte contre le chômage* 1924: 47 and 1925:63f.; AAD 12). This absence of the ultimate sanction, expulsion, was the death-blow to the new immigration policy. Although, according to H. Jaspar, the Minister of Justice had the discretionary power to expel any alien who had not yet obtained residency status, the Sûreté declared itself unable to do so. The Sûreté adhered strictly to its traditional interpretation of the alien law of 1897 whereby immigrants acquired residency status after four months of registered stay in Belgium. The refusal of the Sûreté to cooperate in the execution of the regulation of April 1923 was not only based on a legal argument, it was also grounded in the Sûreté's denial of any need of protection for the national labor market (AAD 12 and 1B6). The "sabotage" of Jaspar's policy by the Sûreté led to the bizarre situation whereby only those who, before their emigration, asked for a visa in a Belgian embassy still fell under the strict application of the regulation of April 1923, while those aliens who immigrated illegally or did not need a visa were not affected. Already by the summer of 1923, the Catholic Minister of Labor, R. Moyersoen, who, together with H. Jaspar, had been the architect of the new immigration policy, became alarmed about the unfavorable turn that their policy had taken. He underscored the industries' need for foreign labor and pointed out that the actual implementation of their policy discriminated in favor of illegal immigration. Labor recruitment in the emigration countries – a recruitment which could bring selected manpower adapted to the specific needs of the labor market into the country – was hindered by the measures of April 1923. Moyersoen increasingly insisted on the need for foreign labor and minimized the dangers resulting from the intake of foreign labor. In his plea for a return to a liberal immigration policy, the insight that the labor needs of industry were perhaps structural shone through (AFAB 2652bis).

In addition to internal opposition, diplomats of allied countries put pressure on Jaspar to exempt their citizens from this new policy. The Dutch authorities were especially concerned about restrictions on the mobility of their citizens towards Belgium. They insisted that Dutch emigrants should be a privileged category (ARDH 180-181). At the same time, the governor of Antwerp petitioned for a restrictive alien policy. He argued that not only unemployment, but also housing shortages and crime were aggravated by the growing immigration. His demand was endorsed by labor organizations in Flanders who, because of increasing unemployment in this region, insisted upon an effective restrictive immigration policy. The Minister of Foreign Affairs, H. Jaspar, probably because of the representations received from the Dutch authorities wanted to accord Dutch immigrants a more favorable treatment. The Minister of Labor, R. Moyersoen, was strongly opposed: the Dutch were the main group of immigrants in unemployment stricken Flanders and the complaints of the governor of Antwerp and the local labor organizations could not be totally ignored. Jaspar could not satisfy the contradictory pressures put on his immigration policy and he decided to withdraw the Ministry of Foreign Affairs from any involvement in alien policy (AAD 12 and 1B6). In February 1924 the Liberal Minister of Justice, F. Masson, obtained total jurisdiction over immigration policy; even the decision to grant visas was handed over to this ministry. The regulations of April 1923 were immediately revoked and Masson returned to the traditional alien policy.

Expulsion policy in 1923 and 1924 continued along the same lines as in the very beginning of the 1920s. The number of expellees involved was considerably higher. In 1923, there were 3,853 expulsions of foreign vagrants and a few hundred aliens were expelled by royal decree (Graphs 15 and 16). Most of them were expelled to Germany. The Belgian position of power over the Germans, while the Belgian troops occupied the Ruhr meant that the German authorities had to accept any alien expelled by Belgium.

Conclusion

Labor immigration into Belgium during the first half of the 1920s was not a haphazard result of "push" and "pull" factors. Immigration to Belgium in that period was not only the spontaneous response of a labor surplus in the peripheral countries to the needs of the Belgian labor market. While economic factors explain the broad trend, the political dimension is crucial to the understanding of the details of this process. Labor migration to Belgium, to a large extent, was a result of deliberate policy decisions. Although we find a sprinkling of nationalities working in Belgium, their distribution and the changes over time were not random, but the result of a complex political process. The authorities of the emigration countries, the Belgian state, employers, and the migrants themselves influenced the actual ethnic and social composition of foreign labor working in Belgium.

In the period 1922-1923, the unpreparedness of the employers and the fairly inflexible attitude of the Belgian authorities, especially the Minister of Foreign Affairs, H. Jaspar, was responsible for the limited labor offer from abroad. The decidedly unpragmatic attitude of the authorities was reflected in the short-lived regulation of immigration of industrial labor in April 1923. This regulation was put into place because of an erroneous evaluation of the nature of the needs of the labor market and the perception of the immigrants as a political danger. The former consideration – ensuring that national labor would be hired when they returned from lucrative jobs in the reconstruction of France – was new for the state. By that time labor had already lost most of its political clout. The hallmarks of this short-lived change of liberal alien policy were a priority for Belgian labor and the funneling of foreign workers into labor-short sectors. This innovation, albeit without lasting consequences for migration to Belgium, was a prelude to the state policies to come. In contrast to the nineteenth century, the state's interests were now more directly at stake when foreigners caused unemployment among national labor. Given the increasing power of parties and unions acting in behalf of labor, the political and social consequences of foreign labor displacing national labor could be far-reaching. Foreign labor could also entail state subsidies for unemployed Belgian workers. Hence, the authorities wanted to ensure that foreign labor was employed only in those jobs for which no Belgians were available and that these immigrants would not stay longer than they were strictly needed. These interests would be ensured by controlling immigration during the initial two years' settlement in Belgium. The leading protagonist of this policy to regulate labor immigration was the Catholic Minister of Foreign Affairs, H. Jaspar. He was much more concerned with immigrants as political actors than as economic actors. He feared that these immigrants would import the revolutionary upheavals which the emigration countries had known, upheavals which until then Belgium had been spared. This preoccupation aligned him with those acting on behalf of national labor who worried much more about the immigrants as economic actors, threatening to displace national labor. This restrictive regulation was not considered acceptable by the whole state apparatus. The Liberal Minister of Justice, F. Masson, refused to implement the restrictive measures. None of the undesirable foreign workers (undesirable according to the new restrictive philosophy) were expelled. Masson stated that legal constraints made it impossible for him to do so. Just as important was the opposition of powerful economic interests (heavy industry) to this state endeavor. These economic, political and legal constraints sharply limited the implementation of the restrictive measures and led to their quick revocation. Free immigration was officially restored in 1924.

Initially, in 1922 and 1923, the employers were hiring all labor that was offered. North Africans, Italian refugees, Poles who had deserted their jobs in France, with or without required documents, they all were hired. By 1924 the mining industry was in the position of recruiting workers abroad and therefore, selecting which workers would be hired. The recruitment campaigns sought out the ideal mine worker: hard-working, qualified for the job and disciplined. The desertion of Walloon workers from heavy industry called for the immigration of a settler population, a body of experienced and loyal workers. One of the first targets was the large number of unemployed in the Netherlands. It quickly became evident that Dutch labor would not be able to meet the structural needs of the Belgian labor market. The economic situation of the Netherlands, together with the political power of Dutch labor in the Dutch polity meant that few Dutch workers, even if unemployed, were desperate enough to take the jobs in the mines the Belgians shunned. Those Dutch who remained willing to work in Belgium were mostly qualified workers who had come on account of the better opportunities. Unskilled Dutch workers also tried their luck in Belgium, mostly in construction. These seasonal jobs were worth pursuing, given the geographic proximity; these workers, however, had no intention of staying in Belgium. They only came for a short stint of work, to return home a few months later with their savings. For linguistic and geographical reasons both these groups worked mostly in Flanders and competed, due to the economic dualism of Belgium, directly with local labor. Not so much Dutch, but rather Italian and Polish labor, was recruited in the following years. Throughout the whole interwar period they remained the dominant nationalities within foreign labor. The employers who developed a more conscious recruitment strategy to alleviate their labor shortage were able to dismiss their North African labor which had provoked the ire of their racist Belgian workers. The leeway of the employers in the international labor market was, however, curtailed by the authorities of the countries where a labor surplus was available. Given the large demand for labor, France was also in dire need of labor, the emigration states could pose certain conditions on recruitment in their country. Some states made recruitment conditional on the active involvement of the Belgian state, to the annoyance of Belgian employers. Although foreign labor's access to the Belgian labor market was officially restored in 1924, the Belgian state was able to retain some control over organized immigration to Belgium due to the insistence of the emigration countries upon having some state guarantees for their emigrants. International migration to Belgium was definitely politicized. Belgian industry was not able to recruit autonomously in the international labor market, political controls could not be bypassed. Italy and the Ruhr in particular offered a pool of cheaply available labor. The mining companies had to invest very little in the recruitment of foreign labor. With little cost, the quantity of labor available ceased to be a problem, even if quality did not.

The overall evaluation of foreign labor by the employers was not that positive. Foreign labor was necessary for alleviating the labor shortages in the mines, but migrants hired were characterized by a lack of qualifications and low productivity. Even their "discipline" was not especially outstanding. Occupational opportunities in other industrial sectors and returns to the country of origin meant that a significant number of immigrants did not remain in the mines. The need for a foreign labor supply that was constantly being replenished and the impossibility of training the transients caused some mining companies to be willing to invest in these newcomers. These companies were eager to enhance work performance and also the loyalty of the immigrants. Some plans to exert influence over foreign labor were developed, but they rarely led to any practical implementations.

Notes

1. Throughout the whole interwar period, the Minister of Labor also had other duties, namely oversight of social welfare and before 1934 even industry.

2. The League of Nations had only advocated a special institution for those refugees in order to organize their repatriation. As it turned out that this was impossible, most countries within the League of Nations wanted to put an end to this international refugee organization. Refugees were not considered an international, but a domestic problem. Each asylum country had to decide on its own what to do with the refugees on its territory. Nansen received little financial support from public authorities. His office was to be of a purely charitable nature and financed only by private donations. In order to be able to continue more constructive work for the refugees, Nansen collaborated with the International Labor Organization. The ILO, with more financial means than the Nansen office, looked for resettlement and employment of the Russian refugees. The most important innovation in those years was the issuing of the Nansen passport to all Russians claiming refugee status. This document certified the holder's identity and category of statelessness and enabled Russian refugees to travel. It was the first facility ever granted to refugees by the international community (Raeff 1990; Johnstone 1988).

Chapter 4

Liberal Alien Policy under Severe Strain, 1925-1928

As mentioned in the previous chapter, from February 1924 onwards the liberal alien policy was again in force. Upon arrival, immigrants had to notify the communal authorities of their presence. Four months after their arrival, these aliens were registered in the population register. Registration implied that the immigrant received an identity card (equivalent to residency status) analogous to the identity card for Belgians. This was only possible after the payment of a residence tax to the provincial authorities. Even those immigrants who had no valid passport or a required visa were inscribed in the population register and obtained residency status four months after their arrival. The Sûreté was confident that they would quickly put order in the, by then, chaotic alien administration. All immigrants would be registered and those who were deemed undesirable by this administration would, if necessary, be forcibly removed. It turned out, however, that an efficient alien administration was not so easy to establish. A lot of aliens shirked the obligation to register because of the residence tax and the rather complicated administrative formalities. The Sûreté estimated that at least a quarter of all aliens in Belgium were unknown to its administration. The need to know the whereabouts of all aliens in Belgium – a necessity made especially acute when an increasing number of crimes were committed by aliens – led the Sûreté to propose the creation of a separate administration for aliens. A special identity card for aliens renewable every two years would guarantee a more strict observance of the regulations. The Sûreté did not want to curtail the residency status of immigrants, but only to know their whereabouts (AAD 1B6). Although in October 1925 the Council of Ministers agreed to the Sûreté's proposal to introduce a special identity card for aliens, this reform was not implemented.

In fact this limited reform proposal triggered discussion on a more sweeping reform of the alien policy. Until then the Sûreté had succeeded in opposing any in-depth discussion of alien policy. In June 1924 the Christian Democratic Minister of Labor P. Tschoffen had proposed setting up a commission to discuss immigration policy shortly after the revocation of the regulation of April 1923. The Sûreté had just obtained exclusive responsibility for alien administration and strongly opposed this proposition. The Sûreté was convinced that they could carry out their new duties with great competence. A well-directed alien policy along traditional lines should be perfectly able to put an end to all complaints. The situation had already improved considerably, so why should any other department prevent them from finishing this job? If, however, alien policy were to take up a radical new aim – the protection of the national labor market – then new legislation would have to be introduced. According to the Sûreté, the law of 1897 did not create a mandate for expelling aliens who merely competed with national labor. One could not consider aliens undesirable just for that reason. The Minister of Justice could not take sole responsibility for a new orientation in alien policy. Only after a decision by the legislators to place a new alien law, this time not a police law, but a social law, into the statute book could such a radical change be implemented. The Sûreté, however, considered such a change unnecessary. The suggestion of Minister of Labor, P. Tschoffen, was rebuffed. The political representation of labor in the Theunis cabinet (1921-1925) was marginal. This government had the balancing of the state budget as their aim and social considerations were clearly not a priority. When nearly a year later the French authorities asked if they could send their redundant North African labor over to Belgium, the absence of any way to stop such a flood of colonial labor from France was the occasion for Tschoffen to push through his idea of an interdepartmental commission to discuss Belgium's immigration policy. The commission met only once when Theunis was heading the cabinet, in February 1925. The Ministry of Labor had to wait for a new cabinet to call the commission again.

The elections of April 1925 saw a landslide victory of the Socialists. The Socialists obtained even more votes than the Catholic party. This gave them important leverage in the newly formed cabinet. The Liberal party refused to participate in any cabinet, because of its serious defeat. The conservative Catholics launched a virulent campaign against a government with Socialist ministers, although there was no alternative to Socialist participation. Thus only Socialists, together with the Christian Democrats and the Flemish wing of the Catholic party were left to form a new cabinet. An autonomous Catholic labor movement developed very slowly in the first decades of the twentieth century and was taken into account only because of its support by the episcopacy and its link to the Catholic party.

The competition for labor support with the much stronger Socialist movement necessitated a radicalization of the Catholic labor movement. Only then was the paternalistic interference of the other social classes within the Catholic world turned back. In order to accommodate the democratic wing of the Catholic party, which threatened to set up an independent party, the episcopacy gave its blessing to a cabinet with the Socialists (Gerard 1985). The "democratic" cabinet of Poullet-Vandervelde thus had a strong political representation of labor.

The "democratic" cabinet seems to have been more interested in implementing fundamental changes in alien policy, and the interdepartmental commission met regularly until it submitted a bill to the Council of Ministers in February 1926. This commission, composed of experts and senior civil servants of the relevant departments (Labor, Foreign Affairs and Justice) had no clear-cut political mandate. It was more a meeting of technical experts. The legitimacy of intervention by the state on the labor market – politically the most controversial issue – was taken for granted by most of these officials. Only the manner by which the state would intervene was at stake in their debates. The discussions of the commission were basically to refine a bill drafted by the Director General of the Ministry of Labor Vercruysse. This bill proposed to introduce a dual criteria for granting aliens residence. Not only public order, but also social considerations should decide about the authorization granted to an alien to stay in Belgium. Therefore the Minister of Justice would have to share responsibility for alien policy with the Minister of Labor. The alien's residence permit would be linked to a specific occupation and every change of occupational status would necessitate a new authorization. In order to perpetuate control over occupational status, it would become impossible for aliens to achieve residency status. The diplomatic reasons evoked in April 1923 to limit the control over labor migrants to a period of two years no longer appeared to be valid. Until their naturalization, aliens would remain under the arbitrary jurisdiction of the authorities. Whenever the presence of an alien was no longer economically justified, the authorities would be able to expel him. According to Vercruysse, this legislation had to encompass all aliens since foreign labor could otherwise circumvent the restrictions by making use of a professional status other than wage labor. In the final draft submitted to the Council of Ministers, a flexible definition of employee would enable the authorities to track down all foreign labor independent of the professional status they took up. That "genuine" foreign businessmen would have to register each change of economic activity – an undesirable side effect of the original bill – therefore became obsolete. The new policy would necessitate that the state be equipped with instruments to adequately evaluate the state of the labor market. a national labor-exchange office would have to be created together with a committee composed of representatives of employers and labor organizations to advise the Minister of Labor.

The commission argued that the bill would enable the authorities to cope with the new social and political reality of international migration. To introduce a strict state control over the aliens was necessary, first of all, to curtail the power of the emigration countries. Only an enlargement of the power of the Belgian state would enable Belgian industry to recruit foreign labor without having to concede to all conditions impose by the authorities of the emigration countries. Secondly, new legislation was necessary to protect the country against uninvited immigrants. The danger of undesirable immigration had increased considerably, and in most other European immigration countries (France, Germany, Great Britain), the state had obtained far-reaching powers for removal of aliens. An overall economic downturn would increase the number of foreigners in Belgium due to their expulsion from the neighboring countries. Without any legislation, Belgium would be left unarmed. A third reason for intervention was more controversial. The commission asserted that unregulated immigration had a devastating impact on unemployment and therefore also on public finance. This, they argued, had already been proven during the slight economic downturn of the mid-twenties. They argued that in construction the presence of Italian and Dutch builders had increased unemployment among Belgians, while Polish leather workers had threatened the livelihood of their Belgian colleagues. In the Borinage basin, Belgian miners had been laid off while aliens remained on the job. The task of the state in the new alien policy would be two-fold. Firstly, the state, in collaboration with representatives of labor and employers' organizations, would streamline access to the national labor market by deciding how many immigrants were necessary to alleviate specific shortages in the labor market and by facilitating the recruitment of this manpower. Secondly, the state had to prevent foreign labor from working outside of the sectors which suffered labor shortages. The Vercruysse bill got strong support from the trade unions. The Socialist union, in particular, espoused Vercruysse's ideas, especially his proposal for the corporate regulation of immigration. This support was not sufficient to bring about the sweeping reform in alien legislation that the passing of the Vercruysse bill would have caused.

The bill remained largely an intellectual exercise for senior civil servants. It was heavily criticized. Especially Gonne, the administrator of the Sûreté, considered it a highly unrealistic proposal because of its radical scope. To abolish residency status would, he argued, definitely encounter severe opposition within both legislative bodies. Liberal elements in Parliament would certainly try to prevent passage of the bill, because it would put all aliens under the discretionary powers of the administration. Parliament did not have a chance to voice their opposition to this bill; it was never put before them. The bill was, however, presented to representatives of heavy industry and their criticism was probably an important element in its silent death. They strongly contested the bill, because of the power it would give the executive. Their vehement opposition aimed at nipping the potential for political arbitrariness in the bud. Heavy industry feared that extensive state power to regulate immigration would potentially be used against their interests. Vercruysse did his utmost to show industry that the legislation would yield important advantages for industry in terms of a stronger bargaining power with the emigration countries. He insisted that there was no danger that the legislation would infringe on their right to recruit foreign labor to alleviate shortages in the labor market. The Director General of the Ministry of Labor did not want to alienate the powerful employers of heavy industry. For this reason, an even tighter control over foreign labor by imposing a government authorization on industry for every alien they wanted to employ was not envisaged, Vercruysse said, because it would charge the state with too much responsibility. He realized that an all-encompassing control over foreign labor, including a control over the employers would rationalize the control over foreign workers, but he knew too that was too radical a proposal. Vercruysse did not convince heavy industry. Industry did not want any intervention by the state in the labor market. The whole endeavor would limit the freedom which industry needed. Having to work through the labor exchange offices and the central authorities would only create more bureaucratic hurdles. In order to produce the best results, the labor market, as the market for goods, should not be regulated. The employers disapproved, just as in 1923, of any protection of the national labor market. State control over immigration should be limited to eliminating politically undesirable aliens. The basic assumptions of the interdepartmental commission were too controversial, the bill was shelved.

Soon afterwards the cabinet of Poullet-Vandervelde was forced to resign. In May 1926, notwithstanding a clear majority in Parliament, the cabinet stepped down, due to opposition from conservative Catholics and Liberals representing banks and business interests. This powerful opposition was especially clear in the first and abortive attempt to stabilize the franc. The resistance of the local banks to this "leftist" cabinet was the particular cause of the abdication of this government (Vanthemse 1978). A government of national unity was formed. That industrial and financial interests held a paramount position was symbolized by the key personality in the new government: Emile Francqui, the vice-governor of the *Société Générale*. His plan to stabilize the franc succeeded. In November 1927 the Socialists left the government and for the next eight years Belgium was ruled by Conservative-Liberal coalitions. During these years alien policy remained essentially a nineteenth-century laisser faire policy.

Even a limited modification such as the introduction of a special identity card for aliens was not implemented (AAD 1B6; ARA, mijnadministratie-oud fonds, 972.3; ARA, Theunis, 32).

The Controversial Fortunes of Immigration

Although the Theunis cabinet (1921-1925) had the balancing of the state budget as its aim, it barely succeeded in putting a halt to inflation. In 1925 the Belgian franc became overvalued. Largely due to monetary difficulties, the economy went into a downturn from 1925 onwards. Capital left the country and industrial production and exports stagnated. The shortages in the labor market diminished, the shrinking job opportunities and the diminishing value of the Belgian franc caused more and more immigrants to leave Belgium. Only the mining sector continued to absorb newcomers. The alien policy did not change. Economically useful immigrants were still tolerated, even if they had crossed the border illegally and had no valid identity papers. Large-scale recruitment of manpower was no longer deemed necessary. The mining companies were again able to recruit enough Belgian manpower since the massive postwar exodus to reconstruct France was over. For economic reasons Belgian emigration slowed down considerably. By 1928 a political will appeared in France to stop Belgian immigration as the state of the French economy declined drastically. The regulations for Belgians working in France who commuted daily as well as for those who left each spring to work in French agriculture had been liberalized in 1923. In 1928 all Belgian workers in France were again placed under administrative control. Every Belgian commuter or seasonal worker had to carry a commuters' card, which was delivered by the mayor of the Belgian municipality where they resided, and had to be approved by the French labor exchange office, depending on the situation on the local labor market. Only in the 1930s would the effect of this political decision be felt.

The Belgian mining industry, because of increased international competition went into a downturn. This shifting of power in the labor market was especially acute in the Borinage where it led to wage cuts, unemployment among Belgian miners, and a two month strike. The basin of the Borinage, because of its geological conditions (it contained only high-grade coal for industrial use in very uneven seams which inhibited mechanization) was very vulnerable to international competition. The crisis caused the closing of some of its most unproductive pits. The unemployed Belgian miners in this basin were enraged when they saw that a number of foreign miners, albeit a very small number, were kept on the job. Although the employers promised not to recruit new foreign labor, they refused to give Belgians principal priority over aliens. They declared that the selection of their personnel was based on professional and not on national criteria. The miners' unions, Socialist and Christian Democratic alike, voiced the anger of the local miners in a call for an immediate dismissal of all aliens in the basin. Even more, the trade unions pleaded for the dismissal of all foreign miners in Belgium, as this would enable a redistribution of the national manpower to eradicate unemployment. The Flemish miners in Charleroi should go to the Limburg basin, and the unemployed miners of the Borinage could take the vacant places in the other basins of Hainaut, caused by the departure of their foreign and Flemish colleagues. The Minister of Labor, J. Wauters, supported this trade union proposal and urged employers to fire their foreign labor. Although there was a relative decline in foreign manpower being used, the employers refused to yield to the demand of the trade unions. The specific tasks which foreign labor performed in the industry, together with the lack of flexibility of the Belgian miners, made the proposed solution, according to them, illusory (CMBo; CNMM; ACCA).

This dispute reflected a profound dissatisfaction within the trade unions about the alien policy because it largely ignored the socio-economic dimension of migration. The Christian Democrat and Socialist unions alike favored an alien policy which would take into account the implications of international migration on the labor market. For them, foreign labor could only be a supplemental labor force for those segments of the labor market where manpower shortages were being felt. The evaluation of these shortages should be left to a joint employer-trade union commission. Although the conflict over foreign labor in the mining industry remained largely of a local nature (the Borinage), it made the authorities reluctant to continue granting the mining industry permission to recruit. In any case, there was no urgent need for manpower. Production slowed down, and local labor and informal immigration could fulfill the need for manpower. The economic downturn even caused an oversupply of immigrants. More and more immigrants were not able to find a means of making a living. These destitute aliens were forcibly removed from Belgian territory. In 1925, 4,203 expulsions of foreign vagrants were carried out (Graph 15), about half of them to occupied Germany.

The Dawes plan and the Treaty of Locarno (1925) re-admitted Germany in the community of states. German sovereignty over its western border region was re-established in the summer of 1925, but the staff necessary to implement border control still had to be agreed upon by the allied forces. In August 1926 the *Rheinlandkommission* agreed to the creation of a border police unit at the Belgian-German border. On 1 November 1926 a *Grenzkommissariat* (border commission) was established. German protests against the Belgian expulsion policy, which intruded upon the national sovereignty of Germany, were heeded and in November 1926 Belgium agreed to no longer randomly expel undesirable third country nationals to Germany. Belgium could only force unwanted Germans to enter German territory. Other Central and Eastern European nationals could only be forced over the Belgian-German border if the German authorities consented to their arrival on German territory (a German visa) and if the Belgian authorities financed transit through Germany for the destitute among them (AFAG R70433; AAD 76C2/I; HStAD, Regierung Aachen, 22.891).

For those aliens originating from Eastern and Central Europe who had no clearly established nationality, the Sûreté realized that documenting their nationality, especially of those who refused to disclose their identity, could be very difficult and time-consuming. In order to identify the nationality of undocumented aliens the Belgian authorities wanted to expel, their internment would be necessary. On the basis of the 1892 vagrancy law, the authorities could intern all destitute aliens; the largest category of unwanted aliens. The Minister of Justice decided to retain in the vagrant colonies destitute aliens who lacked the necessary documents to legally return to their country of origin. They were only released after they had earned twenty-five francs; about four months labor. If, in the meantime, the papers necessary for a return to their country of origin could be arranged fine, if not they still had to leave Belgium. The results were to be felt immediately. In January 1927 nearly two hundred foreigners were detained in the vagrant colonies. Most of them were Poles. The managers of these colonies were not at all satisfied with these newcomers. These migrants were different from the habitual clientele of these institutions. While the Belgian vagrants were social outcasts, the aliens were ambitious people. They were eager to work. They had left their country with the intention of looking for a well-paid job and then to return with their savings to their country of origin. The economic downturn had undermined these plans and they did not even succeed in saving money to pay for their trip back home. Many had come to Belgium on their way home, hoping to find work in Belgium. The management of the colonies realized immediately that these people would not accommodate themselves easily to the regime of the colony. Forced labor in the vagrant colonies for a miserable wage was not their cup of tea (AAD 12 and 75C20).

The frustration of the migrants about their forced internment quickly exploded. In January 1927 a strike broke out, about fifty eastern Europeans in Wortel refused to continue working. They demanded their immediate release from the colony. In agreement with the consuls of Czechoslovakia and Poland a solution was found in the transfer of these vagrants to the Limburg mine-basin. This solution would be repeated in the following months, but there always remained a group of aliens in the vagrant colonies (AAD 75C 29). During the next two years the colonies constantly had between a hundred and two hundred foreign guests. Either no work was found for them, or the Sûreté considered them unwanted (subversive and criminal migrants). These aliens had to stay in the colony until they had earned twenty-five francs and were then expelled (Graph 22). The German authorities had hoped that the Belgian authorities would organize and finance the return of the unwanted Eastern and Central Europeans to their country of origin. The Belgian authorities never considered taking charge of their repatriation and only accepted the principle that free passage for third country nationals was dependent on the documentation of the nationality of the expellee. This was the only condition the French and Luxembourg authorities attached for giving expellees from Belgium access to their country. The Belgian authorities agreed that the German authorities had the right to refuse these third country nationals access to their country as forcing unwanted aliens without German visa on German territory was intruding on the national sovereignty of Germany and was contrary to international law. From November 1926 onwards the expellees were no longer brought to the immediate German-Belgian border, but were escorted by the police to the train station in Verviers, the last Belgian town before the Belgian-German border. In Verviers these aliens received an order to leave the country within six, twelve, or forty-eight hours. The Sûreté hoped that the threat of a second imprisonment in a vagrant colony would persuade the foreign vagrants to cross the German border voluntary. a problem occurred for those who had been expelled by royal decree. Until 1926 these so-called dangerous aliens, if they returned, were condemned for *rupture de ban* with a prison term of up to six months. To condemn these returnees became much more difficult from November 1926 onwards, as the public prosecutor could not document the effective departure from the country, a necessary condition for a conviction for *rupture de ban* (AAD 76 C2/I; AFAG R70433).

In 1926, labor immigration saw a short-lived upsurge. During a strike in the iron and steel industry of Charleroi in the winter of 1925/1926, the employers planned to recruit qualified metal workers in Germany. This old use of immigrants as strikebreakers was, however, thwarted by the decision of the Socialist Minister of Foreign Affairs, E. Vandervelde not to grant visas to these metal workers (Council of Ministers 1.2.1926). Even recruiting foreign labor to supplement more economically determined shortages in the labor market was an issue for the Socialist ministers in the "democratic" cabinet. In 1926, when because of the long-lasting miners' strike in Britain, the Belgian mining industry revived, management again looked beyond the borders to find the necessary manpower. Italians, Poles, North Africans, and also Russian refugees were again called upon by the mining companies to supplement the labor force. For the last three groups the authorities could regulate their immigration through the visa requirement. The Ministry of Justice asked each visa applicant to submit a medical certificate and a certificate of good conduct. That only medical and moral guarantees were asked for was resented by the Socialist ministers both in the "left" Poullet-Vandervelde cabinet and the cabinet of National Unity. They pressed hard for guarantees to make sure that the immigrants would work in the mines. They also wanted a labor contract which assured that equal treatment to Belgian labor was asked for in order to prevent undercutting local wages. The Socialist ministers went even further. They insisted on developing means to assure that this foreign labor once having entered Belgium would stick to mining and would not compete with local labor in other industries. The Director General of the Ministry of Labor,Vercruysse, did not consider legal innovations necessary to make foreign labor recruited for the mines stick to mining. The alien law of 1897 gave the authorities the right to expel those aliens who did not respect the law. That aliens recruited for the mines did not respect their original engagement to work in the mines was reason enough to expel them. The Liberal Minister of Justice , P. Hymans, contested that the law authorized the expulsion of mine deserters. As soon as foreigners had acquired residency status, their removal from the country was very difficult. More importantly, Heyman considered the susceptibilities of the Socialists exaggerated. The Sûreté did not even consider it necessary to consult the Ministry of Labor when employers applied for visas for foreign labor. The Minister of Justice argued that industry would not call upon foreign labor if the need had not been clearly established and anyway there were no problems with these immigrants (AAD 12).

When a few months later, by the fall of 1926, British miners resumed working, the Belgian mining industry again slackened. Britain succeeded in conquering its old markets without any problem. The Socialist Minister of Labor, J. Wauters, reacted immediately and decided in October 1926 – when there was still a slight shortage of labor – to oppose granting visas to labor for the mining industry. Wauters supported this opposition by pointing to the one-year contracts under which foreign labor was recruited. He predicted that the mining industry would find itself with huge stocks again, as the cause of the mining industry revival was artificial. The employers would have to reduce their workforce soon, but they would not be able to fire the newly recruited aliens until their contracts expired. This would make the Belgian miners the first to be dismissed (AAD 12). The decision of Wauters to put a halt to immigration was viciously attacked by the employers-friendly press on grounds that a shortage of labor would cause increasing unemployment in other industrial sectors because of a lack of coal. Coal shortages would make the winter for all Belgian citizens a very cold one. This violent press campaign was only directed against the Socialist ministers. It was, however, not only a party struggle. What was at stake was the right of the state to autonomously regulate the labor market. The influential *Echo de la Bourse* (28.11.1926) formulated this criticism in a clear manner:

> The Minister of Labor claims the right to regulate the labor market for the government... If only everyone would mind his own business! The directors of our mining companies know theirs. If they hire foreign labor, they know what they are doing. It is unacceptable that the state says to this industry "You have too many workers" and to another one "You do not have enough of them" What does it know about this? What kind of civil servant or minister is so presumptuous as to teach our heads of industry a lesson!

It is likely that after October 1926 the Minister of Justice no longer granted visas to foreign workers, but the official guideline of the Sûreté prohibiting the consulates to grant foreign labor visas was only dispatched to the embassies in February 1927. Only a little more than a year later, in April 1928, did the then Christian Democratic Minister of Labor, H. Heyman, agree to lift the ban on visas for foreign labor (AAD 12). In the short economic downturn between October 1926 and April 1928, the dismissal of foreign labor to save national labor from unemployment was again discussed. State officials, supported by the miners' trade unions proposed the replacement of unqualified foreigners by local unemployed labor. If it were necessary to find jobs for qualified miners who were unemployed, then qualified foreign workers had to be fired. Their dismissal would only mean a transfer to Limburg, as this new basin could still absorb skilled miners. When data were collected to analyze the results of the eventual dismissal of the foreigners, it turned out that about 50 percent of the foreign labor in the Walloon basins was qualified labor, while hardly any skilled Belgian miners were unemployed. The government officials realized that pushing for the dismissal of the foreigners was no longer possible; the Walloon basin was dependent on the skills of these immigrants. Unemployment outside the mining sector could hardly be solved by intervening in the labor market of the mining industry (ARA, Theunis, 30). This strategy would have encountered strong resistance by the mining industry anyway. The FEDECHAR had already defined its strategy, when the removal of foreign labor was first formulated. No outside intervention, be it from the state or the trade unions, could be accepted. All of its foreign labor was essential. Political and economic reasons intertwined in the employers' radical opposition to outside intervention. They even refused to dismiss unqualified foreigners as they doubted whether they would find unemployed Belgians willing to replace the immigrants. In addition, unqualified foreign labor was cheaper than local labor. Not so much because the wages being paid to foreign labor were lower, but because the immigrants were mostly single and the mines only had to provide a minimum of benefits to them. A last argument was more political; foreign labor could be used as a way to break the monopoly of the trade unions in the labor market (Committee Fedechar 27.12.1927).

The Employers Decide about the Profile of "Their" Immigrants

As mentioned before, the presence of foreign labor in Belgium had increased spectacularly in 1923. In particular the mining industry attracted a large number of aliens. In November 1923, 17,020 workers or 10 percent of the labor force in the mining industry was of foreign nationality. The number of aliens working in the mines declined in the following years. By May 1925, only 13,909 aliens were still employed in the mining industry. Because of the long strike in Britain the numbers of foreign labor jumped in 1926. By the end of 1926, this artificial revival of the mining industry was brought to a halt. On 15 November 1927, there were 16,633 foreign miners in the Belgian mine industry, 9 percent of the total labor force of this industry. By 1928, there was again a greater demand for coal and the local supply of manpower was again supplemented with labor from abroad. This fluctuating number of alien miners closely linked to the economic development of the mining industry hides the political dimension within this immigration to the mining industry. The changing national composition of the foreign workforce in the mines is an indication of the role of politics in this process. While in the first half of the 1920s three quarters of the aliens in the mining industry were from Italy, North Africa, or neighboring countries, their share diminished to half by 1927. By then 35 percent of the foreigners were Poles. The Italians and North Africans, the two main groups which alleviated the labor shortages in the first half of the 1920s, were hardly called upon between 1925 and 1928.

Very few unqualified laborers were still requested since unemployed Belgians offered their services for those jobs. The mining industry and to a lesser extent the quarries continued to apply for foreign labor, but mainly for workers with experience. Recruiting in North Africa became out of the question because of emigration restrictions and a racist Belgian administration who refused to give their agreement to labor recruitment in North Africa. The Sûreté saw North African labor as provoking racial prejudice and thus likely to cause problems of law and order. Out of a racist conviction, the administration simply refused to grant visas (AAD 12). In Italy only a few Italian stone men for the mines and stone cutters for the quarries were recruited. The number of North African miners dropped in this period nearly by half and at the same time North African labor was also, to a large degree, pushed out of other industrial sectors. Italian labor in Belgium remained scattered among different sectors. During those years the bulk of the Italian workers were employed in heavy industry. Mining was not as dominant an occupation among Italians as it was among other nationalities such as Poles and North Africans. Between three and four thousand Italians were working in the mines. At most a quarter of them were qualified miners, mostly stone men. The iron and steel industry also employed a few thousand Italians. Nearly all of them were working as ancillary workers particular in the blast furnaces. About five hundred Italians found a livelihood in the quarries, mainly qualified stone cutters. Construction remained the domain par excellence of the Italian migrants. Their number is, however, difficult to establish, but probably ran in the thousands. Dutch labor was still recruited and performed skilled jobs in different industries, including mining on a seasonal or one-time basis.

The Poles became the favorites of the mining industry. In 1925 the Polish authorities still prohibited recruitment in Poland itself. Only when all the demands of the Polish authorities were met, including the signing of a labor treaty, in which the full equality of Polish with Belgian labor was assured, would Polish labor be available for Belgian industry and agriculture (AAN 9538). The Belgian labor market continued to absorb unemployed and dissatisfied Polish migrants who mostly arrived illegally from the north of France and the Ruhr. The Polish authorities feared that the low professional and political quality of these Poles could jeopardize the future of Belgium as an immigration country for Poles. This anxiety turned out to be unjustified. When the British miners' strike of 1926 caused a sudden revival of the Belgian mining industry, mine management turned to the Polish authorities for additional manpower. Recruitment in Poland remained out of the question, but the recruitment of Poles residing in Germany was organized, in agreement with the Polish and Belgian authorities (AAN, Ambasada RP w Berlinie, 2229; AAD 12). By August 1926 the Polish authorities agreed to recruitment in Poland itself as some Belgian mines were ready to invest in Polish labor. These mines agreed to reimburse the travel costs of the Poles they wanted to recruit and even to co-finance Polish schools for the children of their workers. This willingness was due to the availability of qualified miners in Poland. In addition, the negative evaluation of the intake of Italian and North African labor caused the mining companies to look for more promising foreign labor. The Polish authorities promised clear guarantees that the investment in Polish labor would not be a loss. They gave medical and professional guarantees that the recruited labor was suited to mine work. Although some costs were involved in the recruitment of Poles (mainly transport costs), they only had to be paid if the Poles actually worked for the company which recruited them. The Polish authorities advanced all transport and visa costs. The mining companies agreed to reimburse these costs in quarterly installments until all costs were repaid to the Polish authorities after one year. This reimbursement by the mines was conditional upon the immigrant fulfilling the full terms of his one-year labor contract. This scheme was similar to the one adopted by the Italian authorities in August 1925. It was more advantageous for the employers than the Polish contracts of 1923 by virtue of the fact that in the earlier period the mine had to pay the transport costs to Belgium independently of the work performance.

The Polish agreement to lay open its vast labor reservoir arose from an overall improved diplomatic relations between Belgium and Poland. Although no results had yet been obtained, there definitely were less gloomy prospects for some kind of labor treaty. The Poullet-Vandervelde cabinet was more interested in labor affairs. While the Belgian authorities proposed discussing the terms of a labor treaty limited to the Polish miners, the Polish authorities wanted a general treaty which would put all labor from Poland on an equal footing with their Belgian colleagues, for old age pensions as well as for disability, sickness, and unemployment benefits. The Belgian authorities did not want the benefits conferred to be bestowed upon a vaguely defined group of people, in quantity as well as in quality, who were the Polish citizens in Belgium. This would imply a burden for the Belgian treasury without compensation by Poland. Only if new alien legislation came in effect allowing immigrants to be selected according to their economic utility could a more general labor treaty be envisaged (AAN 9539; AAD 12).

About five hundred miners were recruited in Poland in the summer of 1926. The mining companies were quite satisfied with the Poles (AAD 12). The spill-over of Polish migrants recruited for the mining industry was relatively limited. As in the first half of the 1920s, a small number of Polish immigrants worked in other industries, but their number increased only slightly and this notwithstanding the spectacular rise in the number of Poles in the mining industry. Not only Polish, but also Russian manpower was called upon in 1926, now not only from Bulgaria but also from the Baltic republics and from Germany. The International Labor Office wanted to find a permanent solution for Russian refugees whose livelihood in the first asylum country was not yet assured. The ILO representative in Belgium, M. Gottschalk, tried to make the Russian refugees more attractive for labor recruiters. He offered not only moral guaranties, but also assurances on their qualification and physical condition. Belgian mines applied for about two hundred visas in 1926. The Ministry of Justice considered it no problem to grant them visas, but the Socialist ministers considered this a far too liberal a policy. They vehemently criticized these authorizations as examples of the policy of the Ministry of Justice to automatically grant visas whenever companies asked. J. Wauters, the Socialist Minister of Labor, argued that the Russian refugees who still had not succeeded in settling could not be very useful manpower. He also pointed out that one had to be especially prudent with the Russians, as their refugee status meant that they came to stay. The pressure from the Socialists ministers meant that a gesture had to be made. When a visa was granted to a refugee, the embassies had to state clearly that the authorization to immigrate to Belgium was only granted on the condition that they would work in the mines. The Sûreté was, however, conscious that they had no legal means whatsoever to enforce this (AAD 12).

Notwithstanding the attitude of the Sûreté, the enthusiasm of the mining companies for the Russian refugees was beginning to wane. An important bone of contention was the travel costs: about four hundred francs per worker. In the beginning of 1926 it was proposed that the mining companies advance half of the travel costs, this sum could be deducted from the refugees' salary during the first six months of mine-labor. If the mine wanted to recover the costs, the refugee had to stay at least six months in the mine. This risky arrangement was not very popular among mining companies. In the second half of 1926 the mining companies were already able to recruit Russian refugees without any financial risk. The terms were even better than in 1924; the mines did not have to invest a penny in the recruitment. The ILO paid all travel costs and the refugees had to reimburse this sum directly to the ILO in six months time. Only about hundred Russian refugees were recruited through this scheme. When a group of Russian refugees recruited for Belgium in Germany did not even work one day in the mines, the ILO retreated totally from any involvement in the financing of the travel costs. The companies would have to pay for the whole trip themselves if they were interested in recruiting refugee labor. As a result, hardly any Russian refugees were recruited for Belgian mines after 1926 (AUNO Geneva C1241 and 1312). The advantage of a politically safe migrant did not outweigh the costs. Crucial in the decision not to pay the travel costs was that by 1926 the occupational loyalty of refugee labor was strongly distrusted. One was not at all sure that the refugees, who were recruited at a high cost, would stay in the mines. Other industrial sectors seemed to be more attractive to them. Probably even more important was their move towards the cities. The urban background of most of the Russian refugees meant that they looked in the cities, especially Brussels, for an alternative livelihood. Russian taxi-drivers, white collar workers, etc., became a common phenomena in the capital.

Trade Unions between Labor and National Interests

In 1926, at the instigation of the Socialist miners' union, a national congress of Socialist unions was held to devise a strategy towards foreign labor in the Belgian labor market. This congress pleaded for the creation of a national immigration council, a council in which trade unions and employers' associations together with the public authorities would decide the number of immigrants to be admitted to alleviate shortages on the labor market. The basic assumption of this council was that immigrants were a supplementary source of labor, only to be tapped when local labor could not meet the demand. Foreign labor was to be employed on equal terms with local labor. Regional branches of the immigration council would supervise their working conditions. The organization of foreign labor by the unions would also assure that they did not endanger the working conditions of Belgian labor (*Arbeidsblad* 1925:1344). This proposal was repeated over and over until the onset of the Depression. The Christian Democratic union paid much less attention to this issue. The need for a well-developed strategy was much less pressing, as Flanders, the main base of support for this union, was largely free of foreign labor.

During the 1920s foreign labor was hardly unionized. Only in the Limburg basin did the Socialist miners' union enjoy considerable support, especially among the Italians, Hungarians, and to a lesser extent the Poles. In fact, the membership of the Socialist miners' union in Limburg became dominated by foreign labor. The generally low unionization rate among immigrants was, according to the unions the result of the so-called backwardness of foreign labor. The large number of first generation industrial workers among the immigrants were not inclined to join a union. They were only interested in earning money and returning to their country. This was, however, not the whole picture. The relation between the two parts of the trade unions' strategy – the restrictive policy towards immigration on the one hand and the need to organize foreign labor once they were in the country on the other hand – was not an easy one. The protectionist attitude of the Belgian unions during the slight economic downturns, in 1925 and 1927, had alienated foreign labor. It was, however, not only this tension within the trade union strategy which undermined their unionization. Notwithstanding a verbal commitment to their unionization, the attitude towards foreign labor was not at all fraternal. The official policy of the trade unions was to unite the native and immigrant workers. At the grassroots, however, anti-foreign sentiments were powerful and thwarted the union policy to organize immigrants. The unions did little or nothing to mold the opinion of Belgian labor towards a more fraternal attitude, on the contrary they even exacerbated the alleged dangers which were attributed to foreign labor. The unions also did little to promote their strategy of a united front. The trade unions were unwilling to launch a unionization campaign among foreign labor and they never adequately financed the propaganda needed to organize foreign labor (Caestecker 1997:57ff.).

The unions also pursued only half-heartedly the particular interests of the immigrants. That only national labor was covered by social legislation was never frontally attacked. The trade unions pressured the Belgian authorities to reach bilateral agreements on social security legislation to include foreign labor, but removing nationality-based discrimination was not on the agenda. The unions wanted only to adapt social security legislation to what they considered the national interests (*Belgische Vakbeweging* 1926:388; *Le Franc-Mineur* 1931: 7/3). The union strategy in the field of pension legislation is a case in point. Foreign labor was excluded from receiving the generous benefits of old age insurance. The unions deemed it of no interest to revise pension law to give all foreign labor working in Belgium full benefits, only those foreigners working in the mines were deemed worthy of a pension. This limitation corresponded to the principle of foreign labor as supplemental labor. The unions considered foreign labor in the mines a necessity and strongly promoted a Polish-Belgian miners' pension agreement. Such an agreement was reached on November 7, 1931. The power of the unions was too weak to push the agreement to effective legislation. The agreement was never put before the Belgian Parliament. The government argued that this agreement would imply an annual expenditure for the Belgian government of two million francs and such an agreement could be accepted only with serious concessions by the Poles in other fields. This line of reasoning that foreign workers, who paid in deductions from their wages, did not qualify to receive old age benefits, because these were strictly tied to citizenship, had the upper hand within the government. The more generous, but certainly not internationalist attitude of the unions tasted defeat (*Le Franc Mineur* 1932: 2/4; AFAP 11,565 and 11,566). The voluntary insurance against unemployment is another example of the ambiguous attitude of the unions. The unions accepted the national bias in unemployment insurance legislation i.e., a foreign worker could only obtain the same benefits when unemployed as his Belgian colleague if there was a bilateral agreement with his country of origin. By 1932 such bilateral agreements had been reached with several countries including Poland and Czechoslovakia. The trade unions were in favor of reaching bilateral agreements with all emigration countries to deflect unemployed foreign labor from accepting poor working conditions. As the union was the main agent in the unemployment insurance system, unemployment insurance was also a powerful incentive to unionize foreign labor (AFAB 2656bis).

The last reason and not the least important for the low rate of unionization among foreign labor was the dominance of the Communist current within the politicized migrant communities in Belgium. The Belgian Communist Party was a marginal political group founded in 1922 which remained isolated throughout the 1920s and did not succeed in attracting a following of any importance among Belgian labor. Within the migrant communities the appeal of communism was, however, much greater. Ideological purity played a role. The Communists professed an integral internationalism, no distinction between workers on the basis of nationality was to be made. The Communists' attitude towards foreign labor, in opposition to that of the Socialists, was not discriminatory; any limitation on immigration to defend the Belgian working class was rejected. This unrestricted internationalism meant that political work among foreign labor was not compromised by giving priority to national labor. The appeal of communism was, however, largely the result of the fact that some immigrants came from countries (Italy, France) where the Communists organized an significant portion of labor. Communist refugees fleeing persecution in their home country or having been expelled from France, their first country of asylum, were also important in organizing the immigrants. If the Belgian trade unions wanted to attract a large following from the ranks of foreign labor they had to come to terms with the very different ideological composition of this labor force. Early on, the Communist refugees realized that in order to reach out to the largely unpoliticized labor migrants from their country the use of the Socialist organizations could be extremely helpful. They launched campaigns to organize their countrymen in the Socialist unions. The Communists concealed ideological differences for strategic reasons, but by the end of 1928 the Communist International had laid out a new strategy and had broken all ties with the Socialists unions. This Communist class-versus-class tactic meant that the Communists had to be organized independently or that work within the reformist unions only made sense if it led to separate groups splitting away from the Socialists, who were characterized as Social-Fascists. The Socialists unions had to be shunned; only the small *Chevaliers du Travail*, later the *Central Révolutionaire des Mineurs*, were considered genuine labor unions. The radicalization in Communist strategy after 1928 was not limited to an attack on the Socialists. A close front of the Communists meant that the immigrants also had to be integrated fully within the Belgian Communist Party. Until 1927 the Communist refugees and migrants were only responsible to their party of origin and they had a very loose relation to the PCB. As a consequence of the new strategy, the Communist immigrants were now considered an integral part of the PCB. This injection of militants of foreign nationality was crucial for the PCB. In 1930 the party had eight hundred members; half of them were aliens, and the party wanted to make full use of them. The immigrants had to compensate for the lack of local militants. The Italian Communists were the most important national section, but there were also important sections among the Jewish and Polish migrants. The radicalization of the Communist strategy in 1928 and the subsequent integration of the Communists of foreign nationality into Belgian party work was spectacularly illustrated by the participation of immigrants in independent Communist demonstrations, by strikes called by foreign Communists, and by the founding of independent Communist unions (Morelli 1983 and 1985:720ff.; Van Doorslaer 1996; Caestecker 1997:58ff.; APCB and Polish Communist press).

Conclusion

This chapter demonstrates that the liberal alien policy, which was restored in 1924 and was still in force in 1928, was under severe attack. The fact that many immigrants were no longer citizens of neighboring countries already put constraints on the traditional design. Undesirable immigrants could no longer be easily expelled. The most crucial challenge to the liberal alien policy was Belgium's shifting political reality. A new interest resulting from the democratization of political life – the protection of national labor – became an issue in alien policy. To let employers decide whether they would recruit alien labor caused conflict with the indigenous labor force, a labor force which was now strongly organized and had political leverage. That this was still an ambiguous issue became visible when the traditional elites and industry violently resisted the innovations which the "democratic" Poullet-Vandervelde government (June 1925-May 1926) wanted to introduce. Controversies arose in particular in conjunction with the Vercruysse bill, but this was not an isolated example. The "premature" ban on labor migration in October 1926, the pressure to dismiss, by preference, foreign labor in 1924 and 1925, repeated in 1927, and the priorities proposed by the Socialist ministers in recruitment also provoked considerable controversy. The Liberal Minister of Justice and the Sûreté opposed any restriction imposed by the state on the freedom of the employers to recruit immigrants. They argued that immigrants were needed to supplement or just to improve the quality of the labor force. The Belgian economy needed them, and the mere fact that the employers went out of their way to recruit them established this need clearly. In general, the right of an autonomous state policy was contested in this domain. The idea that the state, let alone the unions, could be allowed to infringe on the prerogatives of employers in personnel policy was strongly rejected.

The continued hiring of foreign labor in the mid-twenties was in response to a different kind of labor shortage than in the early twenties during which the labor market was tight. The economic downturn which started in 1925 caused an oversupply of labor. Immigration no longer mainly fed the global need for unskilled labor; it served specific labor shortages, in particular of qualified miners. Since the necessary labor was much more difficult to find and the recourse to supplier states implied some cost, more and more mines agreed to invest in recruitment, even if only by paying the travel costs of foreign labor. The Belgian state scarcely intervened in the recruitment. As in the nineteenth century, its role was limited to expelling superfluous immigrants. There were, however, indications that a re-orientation of the role of the state was to be foreseen. The pressure of the countries providing labor to attribute to the Belgian state a role in the immigration of their citizens is one element in the change. Another element was the insistence of the trade unions that the state play a more active role in alien policy. In Chapter six, dealing with the intake of immigrants during the last years of the 1920s, we will see that the employers, quite surprisingly given their hostility to state intervention in this domain, will also call upon the state to regulate immigration into Belgium.

Chapter 5

MIGRANT ENTREPRENEURS IN BELGIUM DURING THE 1920S

By the 1920s the economic structure of Belgium was clearly modern. Industry was characterized by centralized and mechanized production units. Some decentralized production was, however, retained. These "archaic" production units were even an essential part of the modernization of the economy. Accelerated concentration and the expansion of "sweatshops" were two faces of one and the same reality. They all adapted to the demands of their times. The small scale industries saw an increasing division of labor and specialization in order to survive. Some decentralized industries even underwent an expansion because of the specific characteristics of the commodities they were producing: commodities which were as yet difficult to standardize and whose demand was heavily dependent on the business cycle. Production for the emerging and still very unstable mass consumption market in particular required a flexibility which large scale and heavily mechanized industries found difficult to provide (Vanhaute 1994). Opportunities for small business were also found in trade and retailing. Some immigrants set up businesses. Some were ethnic and catered to the distinct needs of their co-ethnics. Two migrants' groups – the Italians and especially the Jews – succeeded, however, in establishing businesses which reached a clientele beyond their ethnic group.

Ethnic enterprises

Foreign butchers and bakers responded to the migrants' demand for culinary products of the homeland. Migrants who ran retail shops knew of the tastes of their co-ethnics and found a niche in their migrant community. More general ethnic products such as newspapers and movies were also provided by ethnic entrepreneurs. Little local competition was to be expected, as it demanded a profound knowledge of the migrants' country of origin. Most of these businesses were very small and employed only the immediate family members. Many were the source of a second income. In quite a few cases, especially in retail trade, the husband worked in the mines, while their spouses ran the business (*Wychodzca* 1938: 6/10f.).

These ethnic enterprises were viable within a large residential concentration of co-ethnics. Ethnic business opportunities were plentiful in the mining districts. In the 1920s the Limburg mine basin was particularly fertile ground for ethnic entrepreneurs. Two examples can testify to this. A Pole, Bissiorek, came from a well-off rural family, but had to flee from Poland as he had been implicated in a horse-smuggling affair. Starting in the mines, first in France and then in Belgium, he quickly turned to business. By 1929, he was running a bakery in Waterschei employing two bakers and four drivers. He had one car and four carts. He had a virtual monopoly of Polish bread in the Limburg mine region. An Italian entrepreneur, Ivan Misle, had four employees of different ethnic origin in his butcher's shop in Eisden and a branch in Waterschei. He built a picture theater in Eisden and also ran a retail shop and a wine bar. By the end of the 1920s he had four cars. Their success did not last. The main problem for these entrepreneurs was lack of capital. In 1932, when wages of the miners dropped and more of the Poles returned to Poland, Bissiorek went bankrupt. He had to return to the mines. Ivan Misle had borrowed half a million to expand his business at the end of the 1920s when prospects were bright, but the Depression came too soon for him. The failure of his picture theater – he had used cheap building materials and the rain ruined the roof – caused his "business-empire" to fall apart.

During the Depression in Limburg, no migrants would expand their businesses as had been done in the 1920s. Butchers and bakers would mostly serve only one mine community and employ no one else but kin and some apprentices. Bankruptcies remained high; being self-employed remained a risky choice. Failed would-be businessmen returned to the mines. Others sold their businesses after a few years and returned to their home country. Along with retail shops, bakeries and butchers' shops, an important number of restaurants and hostels were run by migrants. The cost barriers were limited. The hostels were, in general, property of the mines and managers of different origins were chosen by mine management. Breweries were ready to co-finance the establishment of a bar by a migrant, in exchange for the monopoly for their brand in that bar.

Ethnic businesses served the needs of their fellow countrymen also in Wallonia. Here a Polish entrepreneur, Felix Hetman, a pharmacist by profession, succeeded in building up a business which monopolized the demand for Polish bread and meat among the scattered Central European communities in Wallonia. He started out as a Polish-French translator for the Hasard mine in Cheratte. He won the confidence of the Polish miners and set up a savings bank with their money. This money enabled him to set up his own business. By 1930 he was running a retail shop for an exclusively Polish clientele. During the 1930s he expanded his business to become the Polish baker and butcher for Wallonia. By 1938, when he had to close down his business due to poor health, he employed at least four bakers and two butchers and had several apprentices. The bread and meat was distributed daily all over Wallonia with five trucks. The hostel sector was an important domain for ethnic entrepreneurs in Wallonia. While in Limburg private initiatives in this field were limited, this was not the case in Wallonia. Mines and factories provided many fewer hostels and, especially in the basin of Liège, there were great opportunities for private initiatives in this field. These foreign businessmen, just as the managers of the hostels run by the companies, provided not only lodging, but also necessary social services for newcomers. They wrote and translated letters, gave advice, held money, brokered jobs and arranged the necessary documents for their inexperienced fellow countrymen (Interviews; *Narodowiec* 28.2.1930).

The composition of this middle-class stratum among the foreign population remained highly fluid. There was a constant flow of migrants between entrepreneurship and industrial labor. Most, but not all ethnic entrepreneurs had either worked in industry before they started their businesses or they did so after an unsuccessful entrepreneurial undertaking. Very few of the migrants who tried their hands at these small businesses directed at their ethnic community had a worker or peasant background. Most of the qualified bakers and butchers were submerged within the labor migration. Only when the opportunity presented itself for them to exercise their "real" profession, did they become visible. A lot of those craftsmen came at the end of the 1920s, together with other migrants from the French mines. For them it was probably not so much the call of the Belgian mines which made them move to Belgium, but rather the possibility of escaping the mines. Only a few had enough money to establish their own business, some of them were also able to start working for an ethnic entrepreneur or as an assistant for a co-ethnic baker or butcher. Others ultimately had to work in the mines and hope for better times. The need for capital and for a large residential concentration of co-ethnics meant that the opportunities for ethnic businesses were limited. Self-employment in these sectors was also no protection against a radically declining living standard during the Depression. The number of potential customers declined considerably in the less prosperous years as a large number of the immigrants returned to their country of origin.

Italian Enterprises Serve Wider Markets

The Italians also had businesses which catered to the ethnic niche. Italian retail shops sold pasta almost exclusively to their co-ethnics. Italian construction enterprises provided for a wider market. An Italian speciality, mosaic flooring, became increasingly popular in the interwar period. This gave these Italian workers a strong position for setting up their own firms. Another Italian speciality, cement production, increased the chances of the Italians in the building trade. Another branch where Italian entrepreneurs were active was in the production and selling of ice-cream. The *gelatieri* were a very distinct group of migrants. In the 1890s Italians from the village Atina in the province of Caserte in Southern Italy had come to Liège. They sold ice cream during the summer and during winter they earned their living by playing music or by vending roasted chestnuts. Some of these *gelatieri* went back to Italy in winter, only to return to Liège the following summer. Thirty years later, by the end of the 1920s, the people of this village were still in Liège selling their ice cream, the number of Italians had increased and some had established real ice-cream parlors (*Bollettino del'R.Ministero degli Affari Esteri* 1928:521f.). In Ghent, in 1923 an ice-cream parlor was set up by natives of Cadore in the province of Belluno (Bovenkerke 1983:16). Very soon more people from Cadore departed for Ghent. By 1930 about thirty Italians were working as ice-cream venders in that town (Interview). The case of the Italian ice-cream vendors is a good example of a distinct path of migration, very different from that of the group of migrants on whom we have focused in the previous chapters. Those migrants did not answer to any specific demand on the Belgian labor market, but used the opportunities created by the unfolding buying power of the urban working class. These migrants used the first openings to a mass consumer market to offer their own product. The success of this product led to a chain migration, a self-sustaining process whereby successful emigrants attracted kith and kin to join them. This explains the remarkable specificity of the migrants' point of origin. It made these migrants a category of their own, set apart from the larger flow of migrant labor. This pattern, where migrants did not respond to specific shortages on the labor market but took advantage of an expanding market, is particularly noticeable in the case of Jewish migrants.

The "Jewish" Economy

Most foreign workers were employed in heavy industry. Industrial workers were, however, a minority within the Jewish migration to Belgium. Jewish migrants settled mainly in Antwerp and Brussels. Both cities were economic attraction poles for Jewish migrants: Antwerp for its diamond industry and Brussels for its leather industry. The dynamic of the migration to both cities was different, but by the late 1920s and certainly in the 1930s we can discern an increasing convergence of the lot of Jewish migrants in both cities.

Antwerp was an important port of embarkation for East European Jews leaving for the New World. Immediately after the First World War, the number of Polish and Russian Jews who emigrated through the port of Antwerp to the United States increased spectacularly. In 1920 and 1921 emigration proceeded easily, but in 1922, further emigration was restricted by American regulations. More and more Jews were forced to turn their temporary stopover into their final destination. The Antwerp diamond industry which had attracted East European Jews since the 1880s formed an outlet for these stranded migrants. After the war, the Dutch diamond industry which was largely controlled by Jews was transplanted to Antwerp. The Dutch Jewish entrepreneurs also brought their skilled diamond workers along. There were about two thousand Dutch Jews, working as highly skilled cleavers in Antwerp in 1923. They gave a first working of the smaller diamond stones. The larger stones were sawed by machines which were operated by Belgians who worked in large workshops. There was, however, a shortage of diamond cutters. This final operation was the least interesting skill within the diamond industry and easy to learn. The stranded Jewish migrants were among those enrolled in special schools set up to prepare personnel for diamond cutting *(De Diamantwerker* 1927:8,2). In 1923 there were about 13,500 diamond workers in Belgium. By 1926 their number had increased to twenty thousand, of which about two thousand were diamond cutters from Poland. These Polish Jews called upon their kin to join them and the new arrivals were initiated into diamond cutting. In 1928 and 1929 the total number of diamond workers rose to 25,000 of which the Polish Jews had an increasing share (Liberman 1935: 15; Michielsen 1953: 136; *Wychodzca* 1926:6,11).

In Brussels, it was the leather industry which attracted Jewish migrants from Eastern Europe. The migrants stood at the very source of a new branch in the leather industry, the production of women's handbags. Throughout the interwar period it would remain an exclusively Jewish branch of production. It was begun by Jewish migrants from Warsaw where an important leather industry was troubled by serious economic difficulties immediately after the First World War. The leather artisans searching for new venues settled in particular in Paris and Brussels, where they quickly detected the gap in the local leather industry. As well as their craftsmanship, these qualified artisans from Poland brought experience in business with them. They were soon able to make a niche for themselves in the Belgian economy. In order to open up a new market for their handbags, they were initially forced to be satisfied with low profit margins. Small family businesses played a key role. The leather workers usually brought their families along with them and everyone was put to work to make the initiative succeed. Sometimes not only the immediate nuclear family, but also kith and kin worked in these enterprises. Chain migration meant that young impoverished or unqualified Jews found their way to these small leather works. The distribution of these handbags was also monopolized by the Jewish migrants. Jewish peddlers and market vendors could offer these products for low prices, thanks to the sacrifices of the entire Jewish migrant community in this sector. These low prices also enabled less affluent women to follow the fashion in leather handbags.

This sector was never able to take control of an established share of the market; such a stability, which would make higher profit margins possible, was thwarted by a demand strongly linked to the state of the economy. Already in 1922 and 1923, this young industrial branch was confronted by a recession which laid bare a structural weakness. The demand for luxury products, such as leather handbags was elastic and could taper off spectacularly with the slightest decline in the business cycle. This industry was not only heavily dependent on the state of the economy, it had also to follow the whims of fashion. The yearly refurbishing of the production line in order to answer to the demands of quickly changing fashion made the production of fashionable handbags subject to enormous pressures. Fashion itself made peaceful long-term planning impossible. Flexibility was an absolute necessity in order to survive. Heavy investments scarcely made sense, since in order to respond to the market, a continuous renovation of production was necessary. Large units of production could not survive. Small enterprises, eventually supplemented by outworkers, were the preeminent units of production. Moreover, the continual renovation of the goods offered demanded a creative and high level of craftsmanship from the leather workers. By 1927, a thousand Jewish migrants were already working in this sector. Ten large morocco leather businesses in Brussels formed the core of production. However, in addition to this, several hundred small family businesses pressed, sewed, and gilded moroccan leather for the firms in Brussels, as well as for businesses in Paris. In 1928 and 1929, the peak of this industry during the interwar period, the moroccan industry provided a livelihood for approximately 1,500 migrants in 170 small and medium-sized firms (Liberman 1934 and 1939; *Rapport annuel de l'Inspection du Travail* 1927:95)

The initial economic insertion of Jewish migrants in Belgium took place in the diamond and leather trades. They were a successful endeavor and engendered a spectacular expansion of Jewish immigration into Belgium in the second half of the 1920s. The great majority of these migrants came from Poland. Thousands of Polish Jews emigrated directly from Poland to Belgium in the period between 1926 and 1931, but certainly as many Jews went first to Germany or France only to settle later in Belgium. Smaller groups of Czechoslovakian, Rumanian, Hungarian and Russian Jews also joined them. As Graph 2 on the direct emigration of Jews from Poland and Czechoslovakia clearly illustrates, the peak years, at least for legal emigration, were between 1928 and 1930.[1] But the prosperous and expanding diamond and moroccan leather industries were not able to absorb all Jewish immigrants. The boom of some half-industrial luxury industries in Brussels in the second half of the 1920s offered additional opportunities. In Brussels, the fur industry saw a sharp rise in sales in the second half of the twenties. The local furriers could barely cater to the demand and skilled workers managed to get steep wage increases. Quite a few Jewish migrants made use of this boom to offer their services as outworkers. In view of the escalating demand, these offers were thankfully accepted. The hat and leather glove industry were also short of manpower. Entrepreneurs in this sector hired qualified Italian workers as well as Jewish migrants. Jewish entrepreneurs started businesses in all these sectors. They were especially active in the production of women's hats. Jewish migrants were also able to integrate in the garment industry. Technological innovations were such that a large part of the garment sector began to be mechanized as early as the 1910s. Ready-to-wear cloth-

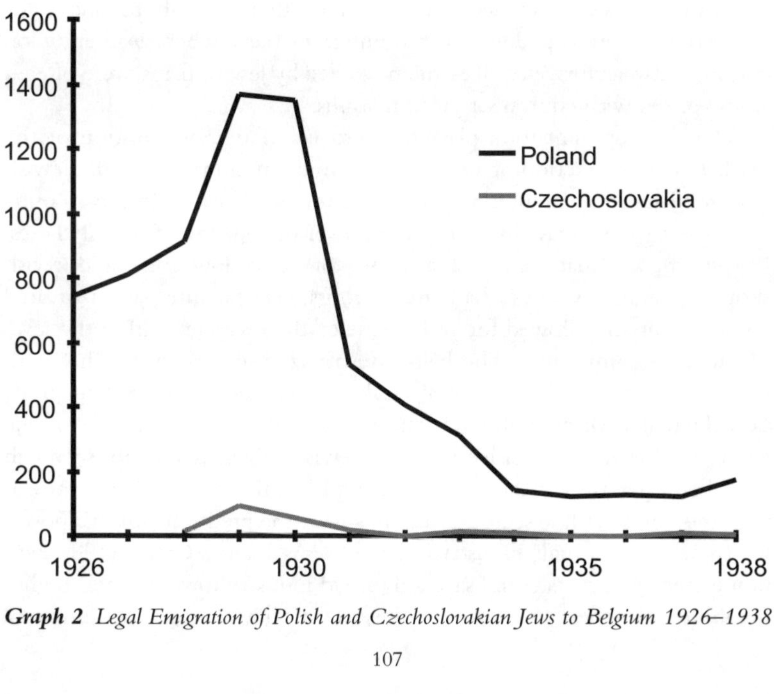

***Graph 2** Legal Emigration of Polish and Czechoslovakian Jews to Belgium 1926–1938*

ing was produced heralding the democratization of this market. It also implied a de-skilling and also feminization of the labor force, a tendency which was strengthened during the crisis of thirties. In women's clothing, mechanization was carried out much more slowly since this sector lent itself much less easily to uniformity. The seasonal nature of a part of this market was such that only small enterprises with flexible manpower could survive. The setting up of a workshop and a couple of sewing machines demanded only low investment costs. Jewish tailors established themselves first in Brussels, later also in Antwerp. Jewish migrants also ran some small furniture workshops, where the use of lower quality wood for fashionable furniture guaranteed relatively lower prices. Jewish manufacturers supplied goods for as broad a market as possible, with an emphasis on relatively inexpensive goods which demanded a limited purchasing power (diamonds were of course an exception).

There was also a notable number of Jewish migrants active in the distribution of these goods. Apart from offering goods for their own internal Jewish consumption (bakers, kosher foodstuffs, etc.), Jewish shopkeepers limited their supply to products from the Jewish artisanal sector. This was the case in Antwerp and Brussels as well in Liège and Charleroi. Even in the new industrial region of Limburg, the Jewish shopkeepers offered linens, bed-clothes, buttons, clothing, furniture, etc., mainly in small overpacked shops. Their trump cards were their language skills and the fact that they offered credit. The great majority of the Jewish migrants who were active in the distribution sector did not have their own shops, but established themselves as peddlers in the public markets, where leather, wool, cotton, knitwear, furs, etc., all of them worked by Jewish firms, were offered at low prices with equivalent profit margins.

This development took place in a process of democratization of the market. The interaction of various economic functions within the Jewish community – vertical integration – made it possible to exploit to an optimal extent the increase in purchasing power of the "lower" social classes. Despite the fact that the Jewish artisans worked for low wages and Jewish shopkeepers and vendors had small profits, vertical integration created employment and allowed for an increase of the revenues within the Jewish migrant community. The half-industrialized sectors in which Jewish migrants worked had a structural weakness. The demand for their products fluctuated sharply and was strongly dependent on the state of the economy. What was decisive for these Jewish migrants was not so much their being Jewish (or their craftsmanship) but the potential that they, as migrants, offered these sectors. Migrants were the predominant manpower for these unstable half-industrial activities. As Nancy Green (1986:246) points out: "Migrants could save a doomed industry through their higher flexibility and their lower costs. This salvation was not a conjunctural phenomenon, it was not the last gasp of a dying sector, but a structural characteristic of an industry with production methods that could not be standardized in a phase of economic development where mechanization and rationalization molded the dynamics of the economy."The traditional production methods demanded a rather large labor input and, most important, flexibility of the labor force, but only a limited fixed capital. Smaller firms which could function without many fixed costs were the optimal production units for these sectors. The structurally determined economic location of these migrants also partly answered to a number of cultural needs (not to work on Saturday, to express oneself in one's own language, etc.). These linguistic and cultural affinities, together with the recruitment network within the migrant community, carried with them an ethnic segmentation of the labor market. The specific location of this segment was, however, determined by structural factors.

In the garment industry Jewish migrants established themselves not only in the flexible market of women's clothing, but they also made a name for themselves in manufacturing characterized by intense mechanization and concentration of manpower. Ready-made trousers was the biggest branch of these industries. The production of the gabardine – the water resistant raincoat – also became a Jewish speciality. Here the Jewish migrants were present in the mechanized production technique characterized by a profound specialization of the units of production. This was also the case in the knitting industry. This industry took off strongly during the interwar period and specialized in luxury items, the so-called *bonneterie anglaise.* Because of a strong export market these enterprises could withstand economic cycles. In the above-mentioned sectors the Jewish enterprises incorporated the most modern forces of capitalism. These sectors were much less ethnically specific, as the labor force did not have to be composed of migrants. The flexibility which was the most attractive characteristic of foreign labor was not necessary here. This is especially clear in the knitting industry which employed, notwithstanding a considerable number of Jewish entrepreneurs, very few migrants. By 1930 the "Jewish" economy had expanded considerably. While until the middle of the 1920s Jewish migrants had been concentrated in the diamond and leather industry, five years later their economic pursuits had expanded to include a large number of industries (Caestecker 1993c:113ff.).

Conclusion

The ethnic businesses were a direct by-product of labor migration, their fortunes were strictly linked to the fortunes of the labor migrants. The migrants' businesses which functioned in the general economy, on the other hand, had a distinct dynamic. By the 1920s the Belgian economy was already a well-established industrial economy, which made extensive use of technological innovations and economies of scale, but opportunities for new entrepreneurs were limited. Competing with such "modern" businesses was not an easy task. The risk and cost barriers were high. Only in two cases (knitwear and men's clothing) do we see migrant entrepreneurs working in "modern" sectors. The Jewish migrant industries consisted mainly of hardly mechanized firms in sharply fluctuating markets of mostly luxury goods. The flexibility needed for these sectors had little attraction for Belgian labor and capital. The economic pursuits of the Jewish migrants in the 1920s therefore did not aim at competing with the local entrepreneurs but rather at establishing new markets or at making use of the expansion of markets, which local producers were unable or unwilling to do. What was decisive in all those endeavors of migrants was not so much an ethnic bent for entrepreneurship, but rather the opportunity structures of the local economy.

Note

1. Figures based on Polish and Czechoslovakian statistics. That the emigration registered by the Polish and Czechoslovakian authorities only partly reflected the immigration of Jewish Poles into Belgium is obvious from the estimations of the number of Polish Jews in Wallonia and Brussels (for Flanders, Antwerp, we have no such figures): three thousand in 1926, twelve thousand in 1929, and fourteen thousand the year after. At the end of 1931, it was estimated that fifteen thousand Polish Jews were residing in Wallonia and Brussels (AFAP 10,379).

Chapter 6

AT THE THRESHOLD OF CHANGE, 1929-1932

The stabilization of the franc in 1928 at an undervaluted level gave Belgian products a competitive advantage in export markets. Belgian industry made huge profits and invested heavily. Production remained limited to standardized low-value products. The investment boom between 1926 and 1929 was only directed at the old heavy and standardized-production industry. Only very few substantial qualitative improvements involving new technologies were introduced. Almost no new branches of production were developed. During the economic boom of 1929, the labor shortage was huge, while increased emigration added to Belgium's labor needs. For labor living in Belgium, working in France became, because of the exchange rate, very profitable. While the number of Belgian seasonal workers in France hardly changed in the 1920s, the number of daily commuters increased fivefold to about seventy thousand in 1929. The textile industry in the *Nord* had considerable labor needs and French employers went out of their way to attract foreign, including Belgian, workers. Buses went as deep as 50 km into Belgian territory to pick up workers. By the end of 1920s, the area from which commuters came to work in French industry had been considerably extended. Because of industry's manifest needs the administrative regulation of the insertion of Belgians into the French labor market – the need for a commuters' card – had little or no restrictive effect on migration to France (Lentacker 1974:211, 277f.; ABZ 2642bis II).

In Belgium, foreign labor was necessary to supplement the huge shortages in the labor market. Those segments of the labor market which were the least attractive were continuously short of manpower. During this period, a true immigration, en masse, occurred (Graph 21), partly induced by direct recruitment in the countries of origin. Recruitment abroad, organized and financed by employers did not offer the ultimate solution since the recruited immigrants made use of the other occupational opportunities the expanding economy offered. Recruiting foreign labor or hiring labor that had immigrated on their own initiative was only one element of the solution to the labor shortage. Given the structural need for labor in the mining industry, foreign labor also had to be convinced to stay. Employers had already planned specific disciplinary strategies targeted at foreign labor in order to stabilize it. We will see whether in this period more concrete initiatives were taken. As we have seen in Chapter 4, immigrants became much more visible as political actors as the result of the unionization drive among foreign labor, but even more so because of the presence of a very active minority of Communists among the immigrants. This new political element was in sharp contrast to previous years when immigrants were perceived as mere economic actors.

These socio-economic and political changes put the traditional alien policy under heavy pressure. In this chapter we will look at how the traditional establishment, the different factions of the state apparatus, but also the unions thought to combat the perceived threats the immigrants posed by attributing a larger regulatory function to the state. Given the absence of unemployment in 1929, as well as the political exclusion of the Socialists, the government was not likely to oppose employers' demands for foreign labor. The labor organizations had, however, a representative in the government, the Christian Democratic Minister of Labor, H. Heyman. From the mid-1920s on, the Christian Democratic labor organizations succeeded in increasing their influence among labor, especially in Flanders. While the number of Socialist unionists stagnated, the Catholic union grew steadily. Both these organizations functioned very differently. While the Christian Democratic union had a strong centralized direction, the Socialist leadership, the *Commisson syndicale (CS),* was a conglomerate of loosely organized federations which stood firm on their autonomy. Heyman could thus count on well-organized labor organizations which were on the rise.

In the middle of the period we review here, the state of the economy reversed radically. Demand abroad for Belgian products was elastic, because production remained limited to standardized low-value products. What counted was not so much the product as such – there were numerous other suppliers for those goods – but the prices. The weakness of Belgium's industrial structure became evident. The value of exports started to fall appreciably early in 1930 followed by a marked downturn in industrial activity in the summer of that year. In 1931 other industries were dragged along in this downfall. The economic downturn caused unemployment to rise which meant that the economic advantages of the intake of immigrant labor became more controversial. We will analyze whether socio-economic concerns became paramount in consideration of alien policy. Changing economic fortunes also affected the dynamic of migration as such. Aside from these "natural" forces which determined migration, we will also analyze to what extent political decisions decided the lot of the immigrants.

A Gradual Implementation of a Restrictive Immigration Policy

By the middle of 1928 the situation in the labor market had changed. The mining companies in particular, along with construction firms wanted to recruit labor beyond the borders. Notwithstanding the evident labor shortages, the Christian Democratic Minister of Labor, H. Heyman, wanted to retain control over immigration. He pointed out that he had a certain input on Italian immigration through the agreement with the Italian authorities. A similar mechanism had to be inserted in the visa policy of the Ministry of Justice. Heyman wanted to make the granting of visas to foreign labor dependent on a labor contract bearing the consent of his ministry. Foreign labor that immigrated illegally would be expelled. For those immigrants for whom no visa requirement existed, granting a residency permit would become dependent on a labor contract consented to by his department. Heyman defended the need for strict control of immigration to prevent the unemployment of national labor. In default of a new alien law, only administrative regulation could safeguard the "national" interests. The Liberal Minister of Justice, P.E. Janson, refused to follow all the suggestions of his colleague. Residency status was still granted four months following registration in Belgium. If the Sûreté had no unfavorable information on the antecedents of the alien, he automatically received an identity card. In visa policy, however, an important innovation was introduced. The input of the Ministry of Labor became institutionalized; visas could only be granted to foreign labor if they had a labor contract consented to by this department. (AAN, Ambasada RP w Berlinie, 1657)

Immigration increased considerably from 1928 onwards (Graph 21 and by nationality Graphs 24 to 27). The Minister of Labor consented to most of the labor contracts that the Minister of Justice transmitted. In 1929, 16,621 labor migrants obtained visas with the agreement of the Ministry of Labor. Heyman's demand to limit immigration to Belgium by expelling illegal immigrants was disregarded. Illegal immigrants could legalize their stay without much problem. The number of aliens expelled dropped sharply. While in 1928, 3,317 aliens were not allowed to enter the country and 2,534 aliens were expelled because of destitution, in 1929 these numbers dropped to 2,457 turned back at the border and 2,110 expelled (Graphs 14 and 15). Given the labor shortages, the intake of foreign labor was considered beneficial to the Belgian economy.

By the middle of 1929 the laisser-faire attitude of the Belgian authorities in immigration matters changed. The Minister of Justice issued a new administrative regulation to combat clandestine immigration. Aliens who had immigrated illegally, without a visa, could no longer legalize their residence in Belgium itself. They had now to pay a fine of 150 francs and had to go to the Belgian consulates in neighboring countries (Maastricht, Luxembourg,Valenciennes) for a visa. In order to obtain this visa, they had to present a passport and a labor contract approved by the Department of Labor. Aliens who immigrated legally had to register upon arrival with municipal authorities. These local authorities then had to wait for the authorization of the Sûreté before giving the immigrants an identity card. When four months had passed, the municipal authorities could no longer automatically grant an identity card, the explicit approval of the Sûreté was necessary. In the meantime, the alien's stay was covered by his visa. The authorities of the emigration countries presumed that the Belgian authorities wanted to obtain a stricter hold over labor immigration since foreign labor increasingly immigrated without passport and, for those nationalities where it was applicable, without visa. The new rules for granting visas were not designed to restrict labor migration. Granting visas was still a mere formality, and the requirement to present a labor contract approved by the Ministry of Labor was hardly ever enforced. The Ministry of Labor consented to most of the contracts anyway because of the evident labor shortages in Belgium. In fact the new regulation was only introduced by the Sûreté to combat the immigration of what they called undesirable elements. Only political "extremists" or aliens with a criminal record were singled out by the Sûreté. The procedure to force the undocumented aliens to leave Belgium and apply for a visa at a consulate abroad meant that objections to their stay in Belgium would have more chance of being followed up. Given that the French police informed their Belgian colleagues about the antecedents of those aliens who were considered undesirable in France, the Belgian authorities could, as soon as these people turned up in Belgium, take preventive action. These aliens were refused a visa or, if already in the country, expelled.

The conservative forces strongly supported this decision to crack down on undesirable aliens. The Communist penetration of the migrant communities made visible by a change in Communist strategy from 1928 onwards led to a public outcry against foreign Communists in Belgium. A virulent press campaign was waged demanding severe control over all aliens and the immediate expulsion of all undesirable aliens. Not only the departure of the Socialists from the Francqui government in November 1927, but also a change at the top of the Sûreté – the replacement of Gonne by Remy in 1927 – meant that the authorities stepped in quickly with repression. The most visible sign of this reorientation of policy was the new regulation of immigration instituted at the end of May 1929. This new policy was not especially efficient. Some nationalities did not have to apply for a visa to immigrate into Belgium, thus they could not be forced to leave the country to apply for a visa at one of the consulates of the neighboring countries. Italian immigration, in particular, was exempt from the new regulation and this notwithstanding the fact that the Italian community was the most strongly Communist-organized migrant community. The only recourse here was to expel the Italian Communists before they acquired residency status or then to make use of the complicated procedure of *expulsion*. Anyway, not only newcomers, but also politically active immigrants who had already acquired residency status, were targeted. Before November 1927 the Socialist ministers and especially E. Vandervelde had mostly successfully opposed the expulsion of immigrants for the mere fact of being Communist or professing communist ideas. Only if they disturbed the public order was expulsion acceptable for the Socialists (Council of Ministers, 16.11.1925 and 28.2.1927). Although Communist activists had been expelled before , mass expulsions now decimated the Communist organizations. While between 1925 and 1927, fifty-eight aliens were expelled by royal decree because of political reasons, this number rose to 593 between 1928 and 1930 (Graph 16). The higher visibility of the Communists within the migrant communities meant that the Sûreté had a much easier time identifying them. The Communists of foreign nationality who had organized strikes and also those who had participated in Communist demonstrations were all expelled. The Polish Communist section broke up completely. Only within the Italian and Jewish immigration could an organized Communist influence be maintained (Van Doorslaer 1996; Morelli 1983). At the same time, the new immigration regulation had to assure that the Communists could not count on new activists to continue the party work among the migrant communities (AMJ 1B6 and Klepper X; AAN, Ambasada RP w Berlinie, 2232; AFAP 11,173).

The crackdown on the Communists meant that the little progress which the Socialist union had made at the end of the 1920s in unionizing foreign labor was destroyed. The expulsions were numerous, especially in Limburg. The example of active members of the Socialist union being expelled terrorized the migrant communities. By 1931 this union had lost most of the gains it had made between 1926 and 1929 (KADOC, Broekx, 5231). In order to stop what they called the arbitrary expulsion, the Socialist put a bill before Parliament to give immigrants the possibility of appealing an expulsion decision. Due to the strong opposition of the government, the bill was never put to a vote (PHK 1929:629 and 673).

Since 1885 refugees were attributed a special status within the immigrant policy. This was a consequence of the "nationalized" expulsion policy which sent undesirable immigrants "back" to their country of origin. As this repatriation could imply extradition of political adversaries, a special procedure was instituted for refugees. All foreigners were asked upon arrival in Belgium if they were political refugees. These claims were subsequently checked by the Sûreté and a confirmation of their refugee condition protected them from expulsion to their country of origin. The unrestricted immigration to Belgium during most of the 1920s – even visa requirements were not strictly adhered to – meant that those emigrants who were forced to flee their country could find a safe haven in Belgium without too much difficulty. About eight thousand Russian "refugees" were living in Belgium by 1930. Eight hundred Armenian "refugees" who had fled Turkey in the very beginning of the 1920s after their cruel treatment at the hands of the Turkish authorities also had started a new life in Belgium. Both these groups had obtained international recognition as Nansen refugees. All other refugees in Belgium were not internationally protected. Especially Italians fleeing fascism found a refuge in Belgium. A trickle of Hungarians, Spaniards, Poles and others added to the refugee population. These refugees, mostly of distinct leftist nature, were not especially welcome in Belgium, but many of them succeeded in legalizing their residence. From the spring of 1929 onwards, refugees had increasing difficulties meeting the new formal requirement to legalize their stay. Like many other immigrants, they had immigrated without any identifying documents. While most undocumented labor migrants could easily obtain a passport from their consulate, this was not always the case for these adversaries of their countries' regimes. More importantly, many refugees had also been convicted for their political activities and a criminal record, independent of the reasons for the convictions, was enough to refuse them residence in Belgium. Information on their political activities in France was also reason to expel them. The change in the alien policy meant that many refugees were denied asylum in Belgium.

This biased policy towards refugees, just at the moment when the mines were recruiting thousands of workers in Poland and Czechoslovakia, was heavily criticized by the Socialists. Although the Socialists advocated a restrictive immigration policy, they opposed the restrictions put in place in May 1929. These restrictions were rightly seen as being targeted solely against the politically active minority among the immigrants. Also, action against undocumented aliens in Belgium was only ambiguously supported by the Socialists since the first victims of such an action would be the leftist refugees who could not legalize their residence. The Socialists advocated the extension of the definition of "refugee" to include those leftist immigrants, but the government was unwilling to do so. On the contrary, these "subversive" refugees were treated as criminals and as soon as the Sûreté could get hold of them, they were expelled.

Belgian alien policy continued to be shaped along a traditional pattern: concerns of a social nature were still largely subordinated to concerns of public order. While those with a criminal record – no matter how small the offence or how old the conviction – were expelled mercilessly, the influence of foreign labor on the national labor market was hardly an element in policy making. As the economy was in need of labor, immigrants could easily be absorbed. Informal immigration to Belgium continued in this period. Organized immigration became, however, quantitatively more important than ever before. The employers believed that only by injecting foreign labor could a balanced labor market be restored. Recruitment of labor abroad became a top priority.

A Concerted Employers' Recruitment Campaign

As mentioned in Chapter 4, on 15 November 1927 there were 16,633 foreign miners in the Belgian mine industry, 9 percent of the total labor force of this industry. By 1928, the demand for coal increased and the local supply of manpower was again supplemented with labor from abroad. This time, the boom period lasted longer; only by the second half of 1930 was the labor market in the mining industry to become less tight. By January 1931, 30,506 of the miners were foreigners (17 percent). The foreign labor force had doubled in three years. Other industrial sectors, such as construction, the quarries, and the metallurgic industry also had recourse to aliens to supplement their labor force. These aliens came from Italy, Poland, Czechoslovakia, and Yugoslavia. The share of neighboring countries within the non-Belgian labor force declined sharply and immigrants originating from Southern and Central Europe grew in number.

In the second half of 1928, a few hundred workers were recruited in Poland by the French company SGI for Belgian mines. The mining companies concerned did not evaluate this experience very favorably as a large number of these Polish workers left the mines shortly after arrival. The mines attributed their desertion to a defective selection procedure by the SGI. Recruiting Poles who had never been down a pit before coming to Belgium – the very people SGI had seemingly recruited for the Belgian mines – was considered inefficient. The regional mining associations of Limburg and Centre believed that a strict selection procedure which retained only candidates with experience in mining would diminish the number of deserters. Both associations proposed to the Polish authorities, independent of each other, to undertake the selection of Polish labor by their own representatives. These Belgian mining companies wanted not only to guarantee better recruitment, but also to keep their autonomy in relation to the Polish and Belgian authorities. The whole infrastructure of the SGI, including its transport facilities, was still deemed useful. The Polish authorities were eager to concede recruitment facilities to the Belgian employers. It would insert some competition in the recruitment of Polish labor and infringe on the monopoly of the SGI (AAD 12; ACCA; AFAP 9630).

The regional employers' organization of the Charleroi mine basin, the ACCBS, was more ambitious. They ignored the SGI and set up their own recruitment scheme. They hoped that the other mine basins would also be interested in joining this endeavor and the FEDECHAR was asked to investigate the prospect for collaboration in the field of recruiting foreign labor. An agreement between the ACCBS and the Polish authorities was easily concluded. The terms were advantageous for Poland. Not only was the SGI no partner to this agreement, but the financial arrangement was profitable for the Poles. The mines in the Charleroi basin still agreed to pay all recruitment costs including transport and in addition each mine would give a bonus – the value of a return ticket, about 300 francs – to all Poles who remained in their service for the period of one year. If a Pole broke his contract before working three hundred days, he had to pay 1.50 francs for each day he still had to work. The principle was that the employers only recouped their investment, 400 francs, after the recruits had worked for them one year. The mining companies inserted these provisions to induce the Polish migrants to loyally execute their contracts. The Polish authorities were delighted with their advantageous bargaining position. They considered that the financial sacrifices which these mines were ready to make had to be rewarded. The request of the ACCBS in January 1929 for 240 qualified and 460 unqualified miners became top priority. The superiority of Polish labor had to be underlined by this first batch of workers. The Polish authorities designated Upper Silesia – the mining region of Poland – as the area where the recruitment would take place as labor with mining experience was available only in this area. The local authorities were summoned to do all that was possible to recruit a large number of candidates with experience in mining for emigration to Belgium (BdL 181; AFAP 9630).

However, the recruitment officer of the ACCBS, Gorissen, failed to recruit the seven hundred Poles during his stay in Poland in March 1929. Of the 550 candidates presented to Gorissen only 382 were selected. The basic impediment to the recruitment campaign was its demand that candidates should have some mining experience. Due to limited unemployment among this occupational group, only a few hundred men were disposed to leave Poland. There were also other reasons for the failure of Gorissen to recruit the necessary manpower. It was stated from the very beginning that the mines of Charleroi were not able to provide adequate housing facilities to receive spouses and children of the recruited labor. France, which was competing with Belgium in the Polish labor market, did provide such facilities. In addition, France and Germany had already established a migration tradition and thus the Poles leaving for those countries did not leave for unknown territory. Belgium on the other hand had still to establish a reputation as an attractive emigration country. Gorissen was soon able to supplement the first batch of workers. The Polish labor exchange offices succeeded in assembling 960 people for the second recruitment session in April. By the first of June two thousand persons were present for the third recruitment. Gorissen selected 636 and 844 workers, respectively, for the Belgian mines. The increasing success was linked to the expansion of recruitment beyond the industrial region of Upper Silesia. Although the recruits from the Polish countryside lacked mining experience, they were eager to leave Poland for the Belgian mines as their prospects in rural Poland were slim. Gorissen's recruitment was considered highly successful by the employers (BdL 181; ACCA; AFAP 9630 and 11,173; APKielce *Urzad Woj.Kielecki* 9383 k250 and *Starostwo Chrzanow* II115).

Although it had taken some time to recruit them, the first group of Poles were indeed an exemplary batch. Of the 367 Poles who arrived in the basin of Charleroi in the course of April 1929, less than 10 percent left the mines within one month. Graph 3 illustrates the "reliable" attitude of those 367 Poles, in sharp contrast to Graph 4 which illustrates the flight of most of the 86 Italian migrants recruited at about the same time by mines in the same basin (AEL, Minerie 85 and 86). The Polish migrants generally knew what working in the mines entailed and they easily adjusted to Belgian working conditions. The Italians, like most former peasants, had

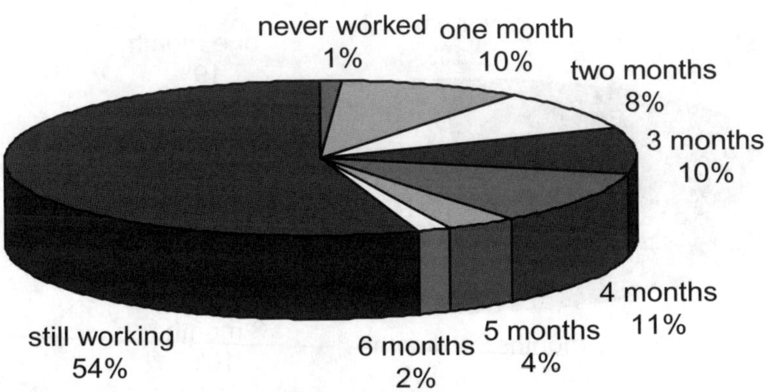

Graph 3 *Duration of employment of 367 Poles recruited in April 1929 (ACCBS, 14.10.1929)*

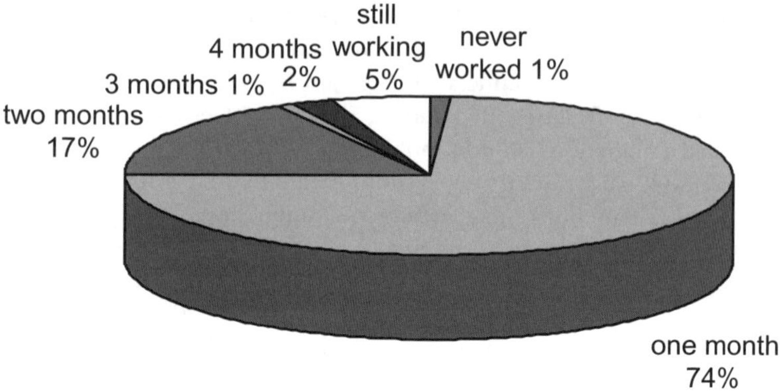

Graph 4 *Duration of employment of 95 Italians recruited between February and August 1929 (ACCBS, 14.10.1929)*

no idea what awaited them in the mines. For many of the Italians, mine work turned out to be so repulsive that they fled the mines shortly after arrival. Besides this push factor, some pull factors also have to be noted, namely other occupational opportunities and the presence of countrymen who could help these Italians to find those jobs. Nearly 75 percent of the Italians who had been recruited for the basin of Charleroi between February and July 1929 left the mines which had recruited them within one month. By two months only 10 percent of those 86 Italians were still working in the Charleroi mines. Even after five months more than 50 percent of the Poles who had been recruited in April were still in the very same mine that had recruited them.

The euphoria about the Polish recruitment was tempered a bit by the end of the summer of 1929. Graph 5 illustrates the reason why. The

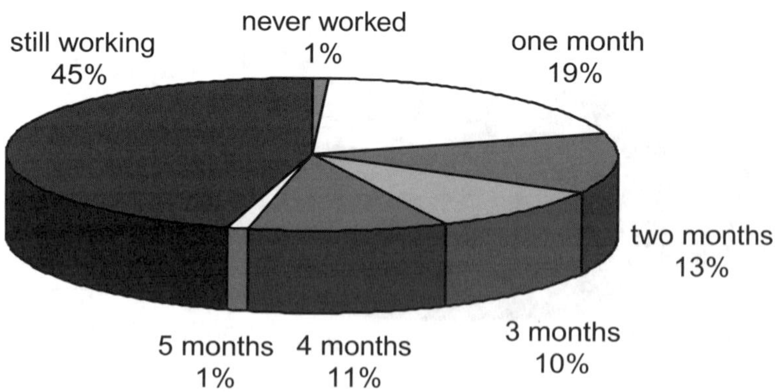

Graph 5 *Duration of employment of 769 Poles recruited in June 1929 (ACCBS, 14.10.1929)*

recruitment of June 1929, with its larger share of rurally-based migrants meant that the number of migrants who had no experience with mine work increased. During their first month, 20 percent of those 769 Poles who had arrived in July left the mine that had recruited them, but by the end of July the situation resembled the first transport. The mass exodus was over. Most of the Poles seemed to be satisfied with their lot. The employers were probably reassured; Poles remained their favorite foreign labor. Given the loyalty of Polish labor, the mining companies urged Gorissen to continue his recruitment efforts. There were, however, annoying signs. The loyalty of the Poles seemed weaker than the employers had first believed. The employers noticed an incremental increase in the number of departures, although not in alarming proportions (AEL, Minerie, 85 and 86).

In the meantime, under the aegis of the FEDECHAR, the employers' associations of the basin of Limburg, Liège, and Centre had started to coordinate their recruitment efforts. These regional mine associations realized the disadvantages of decentralized recruitment efforts. The mines were outbidding each other and a united front by the mining companies would force the emigration authorities to grant them better recruitment conditions. In June 1929 a common office for recruitment in Poland was set up (ACCA). Although still maintaining a tie to the SGI because of its transport facilities, those mines had their own recruitment agent in Poland and also agreed with the Polish authorities on establishing their own work contracts. This centralizing effort was quite successful. The mining companies signed a contract with the Polish authorities that guaranteed that the investment in recruitment of Polish labor would be recouped. The terms were much more advantageous than the ones agreed upon by the mines of the Charleroi basin. The recruiting mine only advanced the transport costs; deductions would be made from the Poles' wages during the first months until the transport costs had been covered. The bonus after one year's service was reduced from 300 francs to 150 francs, but when the one-year contract was executed, the price of a return trip was paid. Thus it became even more compelling for Polish labor to serve out the one-year contract as the workers received about 450 francs at the end of their term. The association of mining companies of Charleroi basin protested loudly when they found out about the concessions made to the other basins and their contracts were adapted to the new model. The Polish authorities in Warsaw agreed to new terms of recruitment as they thought that negotiations on a labor treaty with the Belgian authorities were about to begin. During those bilateral negotiations the whole recruitment procedure for Belgium would have to be renegotiated anyway (AFAP 9630; FEDECHAR). The Belgian authorities however, put off the negotiations on the Polish-Belgian labor treaty again and again. Throughout 1929, the Polish emigration authorities put pressure on the Belgian authorities to start negotiations on a labor treaty by threatening to withhold the emigrants so necessary for the Belgian economy. The Polish Minister of Foreign Affairs opposed this as it would damage the Polish-Belgian diplomatic relations. By 1930 even the Polish Emigration Office was opposed to a confrontational strategy as it would endanger an outlet for the increasing number of unemployed Poles (AFAP 9540).

The concerted efforts of the three basins had been fruitful and soon all basins agreed to centralize their recruitment of foreign labor. An Immigration Committee was constituted within the FEDECHAR in September 1929. It coordinated all aspects of labor recruitment abroad. One of the first things it did was cancel the contract with the SGI, their transport service was considered too expensive (UEM, II.A.1.4). Not only SGI, but also the Polish authorities soon realized that the position of the Belgian mining companies was greatly strengthened by this centralization. The negotiations between the Polish Emigration Office and the Immigration Committee of the FEDECHAR became more and more arduous (AFAP 9540). Notwithstanding the rupture with the SGI, recruitment proceeded. Between August 1929 and June 1930, 2,500 Poles were collectively recruited for the Belgian mines. Nearly all this recruitment took place in rural areas (AFAP 9630 and 10,379; UEM main d'oeuvre étrangère; APKielce, Urzad Woj. Kielecki, Praca i Opieki Spoleczny, 9205 and 9230). By 1930, support of employers for recruitment in Poland had already weakened considerably. A transport of 588 Poles for Charleroi in August 1929 had shown that Polish labor also had major defects. In fact this transport, as illustrated by Graph 6, looked very much like the arrival of Italian migrants (AEL, Minerie, 85 and 86). After one month, more than 40 percent of the recruited Poles had "deserted". That this transport was a nearly exclusive rural transport explains the striking difference – in contrast to the previous transports – in adaptation to mine work. Mostly

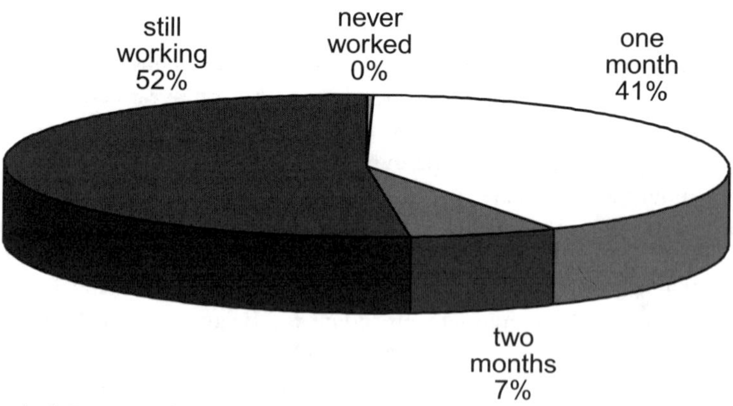

Graph 6 *Duration of employment of 588 Poles recruited in August 1929 (ACCBS, 14.10.1929)*

Poles who had never seen a mine before came with this transport and as with other peasants who had to go down into the mine for the first time, it turned out to be a horrible experience. The employers realized that the Poles were not the hoped-for immigrants.

Already in 1929 some mining companies preferred not to use the anonymous manpower delivered by mass recruitment, which only took their physical qualifications into account. They wanted to recruit the kith and kin of those Polish workers who were already in their service. They considered these personal bonds a greater assurance against desertion than a mere medical and professional selection. The Polish authorities agreed to individual recruitment under its control, with labor contracts similar to those used for collective recruitment. In 1929 one hundred workers a month came to Belgium in this way. Poles were also recruited individually from Germany where the Polish consulates continued the procedure initiated in 1926. After the defects of collective recruitment in Poland became clear and an increasing number of Polish migrants in Belgium showed an eagerness to let kith and kin join them, more mining companies applied for manpower following the individualized procedure. In the first half of 1930, about one thousand Polish workers were recruited in this manner. While certainly after June 1930, collective recruitment no longer took place in Poland, the mining companies continued to hand in demands for individually recruited Polish workers (albeit in declining numbers) until the end of 1930. Poland was no longer considered the "Land of Promise" by the mining companies, but employers still kept an eye on Poland for qualified manpower (AFAP 9630 and 10,379). Although the mining industry took the bulk of Polish labor recruitment at the turn of the decade, other industries also applied for manpower in Poland. In 1929 the Ministry of Labor agreed on recruitment contracts for 4,844 Polish migrants. At most a thousand Polish migrants were recruited in Poland for industries other than mining, mainly for the metallurgic and glass industry (AAD 12; AFAP 9630; PS 1930:209).

Poland was not the only solution to the labor shortage in Belgian industry. The very slow opening of the Polish labor market and the subsequent awareness that the rurally-based Polish migrants had the very same defects as most other migrants led employers to search for other sources of labor. In 1929, the mines used the facilities of the SGI to recruit labor in Czechoslovakia; later FEDECHAR set up an independent recruitment mission. Although the Belgian recruitment mission was largely used to recruit for the mining industry, the chemical industry also obtained manpower from Czechoslovakia in this way. The Czechoslovakian migrants in the chemical plants took on the duties shunned by local workers, jobs which were mostly very hard work or harmful to health. By the end of 1929, about three thousand workers were imported from Czechoslovakia.

By 1930 Czechoslovakia was looked upon as the country of choice by Belgian mining companies when recruiting manpower. The drawback of Czechoslovakian manpower was the absence of migrants who had experience in mining. Most of the immigrants came from the poorest region of Czechoslovakia, the province of Carpatho-Ruthenia. These emigrants had been mostly farmhands. Three advantages outweighed this defect. First, no visa was required. This diminished costs and no intervention of the Belgian authorities was necessary to import them. Secondly, the Czechoslovakian passport was only valid for Belgium; this meant that the immigrants were thwarted from leaving for France or the Netherlands to look for another job. Thirdly and most importantly, the Czechoslovakian emigrants had to pay for their trip to Belgium. The companies only had to pay the recruitment expenses (passport and medical examination) and, after the Czechoslovakian emigrant completed his one-year contract, a bonus of 200 francs (return ticket) was to be paid. In 1930 FEDECHAR recruited another two thousand workers in Czechoslovakia (AEL, Minerie, 85 and 89; BdL 306). Another country was added to the list of areas of recruitment in Central Europe: Yugoslavia. Between 1928 and 1930 a few thousand, mostly Slovenian, migrants left for Belgium. As no state-organized emigration existed, the procedure was informal, but not necessary illegal. Those who wanted to immigrate legally could obtain a passport and a visa for Belgium after the Belgian mining companies had sent them labor contracts.

Italy remained a source of labor, but it became a rather second-rate recruitment area. The main drawback of Italian migrants was their lack of mining experience. Recruitment in Italy was also expensive. Firms which recruited Italian labor had to reimburse, in quarterly installments, the cost of the trip which these workers had paid themselves. Employing Czechoslovakian immigrants could be cheaper since those immigrants received the money for the return trip only after they finished their one-year contract. The restrictive emigration policy in Italy also played a role. Due to fascist rural policies and a new demographic policy launched in 1926, emigration came to be viewed as a loss for the country. The fascist regime developed a new emigration policy based on restricting permanent emigration and promoting temporary emigration. This was combined with an increased effort to politicize the emigrant communities abroad by enrolling the emigrants in fascist organizations (Cannistraro and Rosoli 1979). Due to this new policy, the emigration of spouses and children became increasingly difficult; thus those mining companies that wanted the Italians to settle for the long term were irritated that the Italian authorities increased their grip on the emigration of Italian citizens. In 1929 Belgian industry applied for 8,849 workers from the Italian authorities, mainly for construction (PS 1930:209). A considerable number of these Italians worked as navvies on public works all over Belgium. Few Belgians were willing to live in makeshift barracks, located in remote areas away from their family. The quarries recruited some Italian stone cutters in 1929. The number of Italians in the iron and steel industry also increased considerably at the end of the 1920s. Among all the immigrants, the Italians were the most successful at making use of the diverse needs of the labor market. By the first half of the 1920s, they already had established occupational strongholds in several industries. The Italians succeeded in retaining these positions and even in expanding their presence in those industries. This plural occupational profile of Italian immigrants was partly due to organized immigration, but more important were spontaneous arrivals and occupational shifts within the Italian migrant population.

Belgium not only had a shortage of manpower, but also of female labor and in particular of domestic servants. During most of the 1920s, informal immigration had supplemented the supply of servants, but by the end of the decade recruitment for domestic servants was also organized in Central Europe. The first recruitment scheme was set up by the Polish authorities. In 1928 and 1929, 1,100 women were recruited in Poland to work as domestic servants. In 1929 a second recruitment scheme was set up by the *Ligue des Familles Nombreuses* in collaboration with the Hungarian authorities for the recruitment of Hungarian servants. This *Service du Placement des Servantes Hongroises* mediated for large families looking for maids in Hungary. In 1931 more than three hundred Hungarian maids were employed in such households (AFAP 11,736 and 10,379).

The most flexible and cheapest system for increasing the supply of labor was, of course, spontaneous immigration. Organized migration had become an important avenue for the increase of foreign labor in Belgium by the end of the 1920s, but informal immigration remained important. Because of the uncontrolled character of this migration it is difficult to assess its importance, but the metallurgic as well as the mining industry, especially in the basin of Liège, made extensive use of foreign labor arriving spontaneously, sometimes illegally, in Belgium. Not all of this immigration was that spontaneous. Some companies used advertisements or sent out agents to emigration countries to recruit manpower illegally. Those agents were sometimes employees of the firm who returned to the country of origin for a holiday. It could be a lucrative affair as a bonus per recruited worker was sometimes offered. Some professional smugglers were attracted by this offer. Hostel managers were particularly active in this field, either acting on their own behalf or with the consent of the mining companies. They urged their guests to call their relatives to join them and arranged for a smuggler to transport them across the borders. This informal immigration assured them of new guests in their hostels. In addition the hostel manager could eventually receive a bonus from the company for each worker brought into the country. Illegal immigrants also offered advantages to employers as they had a greater control over these workers and did not have to pay the cost nor carry responsibility of transportation (AAN, Ambassade RP w Berlinie, 1657). All these undocumented immigrants had little problem legalizing their stay in Belgium. Even the administrative fine of 150 francs which they had to pay to legalize their stay was generally excused. They were registered in the population register and after four months attained residency status (AFAP 11,735).

Employers' Strategies for Retaining Foreign Labor

Most mining companies realized that they no longer had a loyal Belgian workforce. The traditional Walloon miners' families had deserted and more and more Flemish workers avoided the collieries. Some employers hoped that the immigrants and their offspring would be the miners for the present and the future. To realize this ambitious desire they had first to tackle a basic problem with this new workforce. As we mentioned before, a large number of mostly rural immigrants left the mines before completing their recruitment contract. Retaining the migrants for a year had already proved to be a difficult task. The employers had to confront these migrants' fear and disgust of mining as well as their homesickness. "Carrots and sticks" were used to keep the immigrants in the mines during the term of the recruitment contract, but the employers also oscillated between incentives and repression for their long term goals. Not all employers were interested in retaining the labor they had recruited abroad for the long term. The absence of a lasting labor commitment sometimes fit the specific labor needs of those sectors of the economy which depended on a severely fluctuating demand. The metallurgic industry for example, only needed a strong and healthy workforce and loyalty was not important. A constantly rejuvenated workforce was the most adequate solution to the severely fluctuating labor needs of such firms.

The mining companies were not very satisfied with their foreign labor and they definitely had reason to complain. Notwithstanding the large scale recruitment in Poland between 1928 and 1930 for the mines in the basin of Limburg, the number of Poles in that basin still oscillated around two thousand, just as at the end of 1927. Of the more than one thousand Poles recruited in 1929 and 1930 who were entitled to a repatriation bonus if they finished their labor contract, only eleven of them applied for this bonus (AFAP 11,176). This unreliability of foreign workers covers two partially overlapping realities: occupational and geographical mobility. Occupational mobility implied "desertion" from the mines. Mere geographical mobility refers to the departure of those miners to other mines where the working or living conditions were considered better. The characteristics of the migrants' labor market behavior depended on their world views. Among the immigrants there were industrial workers with a tradition of industrial work extending across generations; on the other hand, there were also peasant workers among them, workers for whom immigration to Belgium meant the first contact with an industrial work environment.

The peasant worker, for the most part a first generation industrial worker, was a target earner whose primary motivation was to maximize temporary earnings and then return "home". Their lack of industrial skills and the need to earn as much as possible in the short term meant that they were willing to work long hours at menial jobs. During their stay abroad they wanted to spend as little as possible. They measured their income according to the standards of the country of origin. Given the wage differentials between Poland, Italy, etc., and Belgium they were mostly satisfied with the low wages of ancillary workers. They believed themselves to be making good money (Zaniewski 1942:118). These peasants saw their work in Belgium as a temporary cross to bear in order to obtain rewards in what they considered their world. Their high turnover rates illustrates their interest in short-term employment and the absence of attachment to a specific kind of work. Earning a good wage was one thing, but working conditions sometimes turned out to be unbearable for peasant workers. A considerable number of them were traumatized by what they considered appalling working conditions in the mines. The danger and discomfort of the underground environment were especially taxing for these migrants. Not the Polish miners from Upper Silesia, but the emigrants from the rural districts of Poland escaped the mines in the first weeks after their arrival (AFAP 10,379). These rurally-based workers preferred to work on farms, but work as agricultural laborers was scarce in Belgium. There were some large farms in Wallonia which needed farm hands on a seasonal basis. Since the turn of the century, Flemish small farmers had established a pattern of group emigration to do these jobs and there were not many vacancies for the immigrants. The large public works, especially the building of the Antwerp-Liège canal offered employment opportunities which were more appealing to those peasant workers. Even the wages were better than in agriculture. Additionally, the long working hours and cheap living conditions meant that savings could be accumulated. The work was not that different from what they were used to at home. So several hundred immigrants, mostly Italians, with a scattering of Yugoslavian, Czechoslovakian, and Polish mine deserters worked in 1930 on the Antwerp-Liège canal (AFAP 11,176).

Not all unskilled foreign workers should be considered peasant workers who judged their work in Belgium according to "old world" standards. Some of the unskilled foreign workers were aware of their market value.

They knew the shortage of manpower in the mining industry increased their bargaining power and they demanded higher wages. Their lack of attachment to Belgium and to any industry enabled them to be highly mobile, not merely to "improve" the nature of their work, but to maximize profits. These workers understood the principles underlying the functioning of the labor market, and with the information they gathered from colleagues and in the ethnic press, they moved in the international labor market and tried to get the most out of it. These workers shared their insight into the functioning of the labor market with the industrial workers among the migrants. The industrial workers had learned a skill, in the mines they were hewers, brattice men, or stone men, which implied a higher loyalty to the mining industry. They considered mining a secure and profitable occupation given their qualifications. Not only the Ruhr miners, but also the Polish and the few Czechoslovakian miners who had only left their countries in 1929, were distinct from their peasant countrymen who left for Belgium. The former did not flee the mining industry. If they were dissatisfied, it was not with mine work as such, but mostly with the pay they received or because of maltreatment by overseers or management. Sometimes they remained, but then they did not tolerate these "injustices". They did not refrain from striking in order to get justice. Sometimes they left the mining company that had recruited them, but they mostly remained in the mining sector. They left for another mine, a mine in which they hoped working and living conditions would be better (BdL 181; AFAP 11,173; interviews).

The Creation of Loyalty and Contentment within the Migrant Communities

Flexibility in the workplace was the first response of the mining companies to the desertion of their recruited manpower. They tried to make the adaptation process of the peasants to mine labor less abrupt. Instead of forcing them to the coal faces and to the harsh discipline of industrial labor the first day after their arrival they were sometimes first employed on the surface for a while. There was often a more lenient application of the work rules. The supervisory personnel were advised to be more sensitive towards these foreigners. To relieve the migrants' feeling that they were trapped in a mine, mining companies sometimes even agreed to their demands to be relocated to another mine. The migrants were also treated better in the hostels where they were lodged. Newspapers or books in their native tongue were put at their disposal. Ethnic food was provided for them (BdL 181). It was mostly the spouses of foreign workers prepared food for the colleagues of their husbands living in the hostels. Some mines stimulated family migration since families were considered a crucial key to the adaptation of single migrant workers. By linking the rent of company housing to the number of boarders a family took in and by providing beds and the blankets, migrant families were induced to alleviate the need for separate housing facilities for single miners. What was important in this strategy was stabilizing the single migrants by recreating a sense of home. Family migration was a strategy with a much broader scope. Mining companies provided housing and financial support (loans) to encourage migrants to have their families join them. The assumption was that workers would be less inclined to move once their families had joined them. Not only the head of the family was to be stabilized in the local mine community; the boys of these migrant families were also targeted by the employers' strategy. These boys would become the manpower of the future. In this way the employers hoped to obtain a lasting solution to their labor shortage. This strategy was quite successful. Quite a few migrants recruited at the end of the 1920s decided to send for their families to join them. The number of women and children within the migrants'colonies in the mining districts increased considerably in the beginning of the 1930s (UEM, main d'oeuvre étrangère; Interviews; ACCA 15.10.1924 and 9.7.1930; AFAP 9538 and 10,379).

Some mine companies were willing to make an even more substantial effort to stabilize migrant families in their local community, an effort which aimed at improving the work and living environment of their foreign labor in a qualitative manner. Two very different strategies were implemented, strategies which both revolved around the notion of ethnicity. The first and most widespread one was the assimilationist strategy. Its power to lead foreign labor to settle in Belgium was widely acclaimed among employers. The Limburgian mine Waterschei was the outstanding example of this assimilationist strategy. From the outset, when Waterschei initiated production in 1924, it aimed at a "flemishification" of the labor force. This mine's provision for education was limited to a Flemish school. Ethnic organizations set up by foreign labor could hardly count on support from the company, while Catholic Flemish organizations received full support. Assimilation of foreign labor into the local Flemish culture was the goal, which aimed not only at stabilizing these migrants, but also keeping them away from the Socialist movement. Catholic Flemish culture was considered a bulwark against Socialism (AFAP 10,069 and Archive Polish union, Private Papers Zdrodzyniak).

Some mines had designed a totally different strategy for building up a loyal and stable labor force. They pursued a multicultural strategy to establish ethnic communities under company control. The concept was that the mine would support pastoral care, education, and ethnic associations for the workers and their families and, in exchange, the workers and their leadership (priests, teachers, presidents of the associations) would be loyal to the company. The cooperation of Belgian secular and religious authorities, as well as those of the emigration countries, was indispensable for this strategy to succeed, but the company did not doubt their willingness to do so. The authorities of the emigration countries supported this multicultural endeavor fully, but they had different objectives than the mining companies, i.e., preserving the ethnic tradition to ensure the emigrants' return. The Belgian secular and religious authorities – to the extent that they went along with the mining company – also pursued their own objectives. The Belgian educational system, in which schooling could be subcontracted to anybody, was a special asset in the realization of the design for company-controlled ethnic communities.

Winterslag, the first mine to start production in the basin of Limburg in 1923, pursued such a multicultural strategy. Provisions were made for their Czech, Polish, and Italian workers. Ethnic organizations obtained support from mine management. Management even decided that the ethnic groups had to each have a representative on the joint board of the mine. According to mine management, the elected Socialist and the Christian Democratic unionists represented only the Belgian labor force, designated Polish and Czech representatives were to represent the foreign labor force (CNMM 12.1.1926). This multicultural strategy was also the motivation behind the promotion of some immigrants to supervisory positions. Schools for each of the different ethnic communities in Winterslag were set up (Caestecker 1991:544). The different realizations of the multicultural strategy in Winterslag should not hide the constraints under which they were implemented. The failure of Winterslag to add one more dimension – and not the least important – to its Polish colony, pastoral care, is a telling example.

In 1923 the Belgian clergy was already heavily involved in setting up a distinct religious structure for Polish migrants. Due to a shortage of Polish priests, such a structure had not yet materialized. In 1926, a Polish Catholic Mission was founded in Brussels by the Polish Primate Hlond in agreement with the Belgian Primate Mercier. Mercier's main problem was reaching the Polish migrants in the province. He urged the Polish Primate to staff his mission with more Polish priests. Limburg especially needed a priest. Mine management of Winterslag agreed to provide for the livelihood and housing of the priest. Priests, however, were in short supply in Poland and the Polish Church was not eager to provide Winterslag with one. The Belgian clergy got impatient and decided itself to provide pastoral care for the Polish migrants in Limburg. Two Flemish friars who were to get a permanent mission among the Poles in Limburg were sent to Poland for an intensive language course. This decision was not only motivated by concern over the religious integrity of the Polish migrants, it had also an assimilationist objective. The new bishop of Liège, Kerkhofs, backed the Flemish Christian Democratic movement in Limburg, which aimed at preserving the Catholic character of the new industrial basin by defending Flemish workers' material and cultural interests. The Flemish Christian Democratic movement was concerned about other ethnic communities in the mining basin which were not within its reach. This concern was exacerbated by the arrival of Polish migrants from France who became the backbone of the Socialist trade union of Limburg. The objective of the Flemish Christian Democratic movement was that Limburg remain Catholic and Flemish. A Polish priest would only inhibit quick assimilation. Flemish priests who were in sympathy with the Christian Democratic cause and knew Polish were much more instrumental to their strategy. The opposition of the Flemish community and especially the local clergy together with the refusal of the Polish Church to send more Polish priests caused the mine management of Winterslag to loose effective control over the religious dimension of its program. The Winterslag mine's plan for an insular Polish community totally reliant on the company turned out to be difficult to implement (KADOC, Broekx, 14.5.6; AAG III).

The elaborate strategy towards the ethnic groups of Winterslag was exceptional. Most of the other mines also realized that they would have to provide more than just work to obtain a loyal and lasting work performance by their foreign labor. In Wallonia all the mining companies considered the minimal necessary ethnic provision to be spiritual and moral support by a co-ethnic priest. By 1924, the mining companies were already prepared to provide financial support for Polish priests. A new preoccupation – Communist agitation – increased their efforts to pressure the Polish Church to send priests. In 1928, the rector of the Polish Mission in Belgium finally received an assistant. This Polish priest was sent to the Liège basin where Communist propaganda was considered most virulent. The Polish Mission in Belgium – now two priests – insisted that more priests were necessary; some Polish sisters would also be welcome. The rector argued that the rapid growth of the Polish community made it difficult for him and his colleague to handle it on their own. In 1929, the Polish Mission submitted its request to increase its staff with support from the mining companies in Hainaut. These companies had just started their massive recruitment in Poland. The more visible Communist influence among the migrant communities, including the Polish, caused these companies to strongly insist that Polish pastoral care be provided to their new labor force. Their strong pressure, supported by Belgian and Polish authorities alike, meant that the request was met in the end. By 1930 each basin in Wallonia had a Polish priest who was financed to a large extent by the mining companies. In Flanders, as mentioned before, Flemish friars who had learned Polish were engaged to take care of the religious needs of the Poles (AAG III; ABL, Kerkhofs, 71; ACCBS 9.12.1929).

The influence of the collieries on the institutions designed to preserve migrants' ethnic or religious identity is not to be exaggerated. These institutions (the schools, the mission and the ethnic organizations) pursued their own objectives. To conserve the national identity and to retain the faith was not what the mines necessarily had in mind when they supported these institutions financially. Control over their labor force, as well as stabilizing it and assuring future workers, was their main goal. In some instances the interests converged: docility – respect for (ecclesiastic) authority – was what some priests and mine management expected from the migrants. The Polish priests also were combating what they considered a most dangerous atheism: Communism and Socialism. In this they were also allies of the mine companies, and sometimes, in a very direct manner, even of the Belgian authorities, i.e., some priests were recruited as agents for the Sûreté to denounce Communists. We must realize too that the migrants were not mere objects. They themselves, largely because of their expected return to Poland, had asked for Polish schools, and Polish priests. However, the economic dependence of the priests on the mining companies was resented by the migrants. The migrants believed that the Polish priests' wages were deducted from their own wages. The rector of the Polish mission realized from the very beginning that this undermined the authority of the clergy, but he considered it a necessary evil. He hoped that in future the mission would become financially independent. The ethnically-based institutions also served a purpose for the migrants. They drew on their cultural cohesiveness to defend themselves. Ethnicity was a force of strength for the migrants, even if mine management sometimes tried to use it to control their labor force. It meant that Winterslag was saddled with a culturally close-knit Polish community, but in this case also a syndicalistically-minded one. Ethnic pride – part of a divide and conquer strategy of the mine company – did not succeed in deterring workers from uniting in the Socialist miners union (Interviews).

Repressive Management of Foreign Labor

By the middle of 1929 there was a growing awareness among employers in the mining sector that a refined recruitment strategy combined with providing assistance to these newcomers was not sufficient to make the foreign workers into loyal employees. New strategies had to be developed to make foreign labor into a more stable work force. Some mines had recourse to traditional means to assure the respect of labor contracts. Migrants who left the mines before their contracts were over were summoned before labor courts and compensation was asked for the losses the mines had suffered. The main problem was that it was extremely difficult to locate these absent migrants. As the number of court cases increased, the migrants became much more prudent and probably looked for jobs far away from their first employer. Another strategy was to cut down the alternatives at the migrants' disposal. The mines which had organized the immigration of labor considered it unjust that other mines could poach the newly introduced workers from them. The recruiting mines were entitled to receive some return on their investment. They had not only organized the recruitment operation, but they had also paid the transportation costs. The Regional Mine Association of the basin of Centre, which shortly after recruiting Czechoslovakian labor saw most of them leave its mines, proposed a nation-wide gentlemen's agreement among mining companies to respect the prerogatives of the recruiting mines. The proposal stipulated that during the first year after the recruitment of workers abroad, no other mine could hire those workers. This proposal aimed not only at rendering justice to the mines which invested in organized recruitment, but had strong "educational" overtones. The mines which had drafted the proposal underlined that only by enforcing a respect for the clauses of the working contract could a disciplined and loyal workforce be created. Only by the summer of 1929 when all basins were recruiting labor abroad and when all of them were confronted with an increasing number of deserters was a common agreement between the regional associations possible.

By then an experiment had already been attempted. The first mine to accept the gentlemen's agreement proposed by the employers' association of the Centre basin was Waterschei in Limburg. The mine's adherence to this proposal had already lead to the dismissal of a certain number of Czechoslovakian migrants who were still under contract in the basin of Centre in the spring of 1929. These migrants, however, refused to return to the mine which had recruited them and even decided to return to Czechoslovakia. The consternation about this unexpected turn of events caused the proposal to be much more closely scrutinized. The proposed gentlemen's agreement turned out to have major defects. Binding foreign labor to one mine was considered detrimental to the mining industry. Not only could it encourage the deserters to return to their country of origin, it was even more likely that they would offer their services outside the mining industry. In addition, forcing deserters to return to the mine they had fled would give those seeking to stir industrial ferment easy allies. This criticism caused the FEDECHAR to rewrite the proposal. The new proposal sanctioned the hiring of a foreign laborer who was still under contract of the recruitment mine, but it demanded that the new employer defray part the recruitment costs. The new proposal hence had a merely commercial aim and lost all of its disciplinary effect. By September 1929, all regional associations within the FEDECHAR had agreed to this proposal. The modalities for the execution of the agreement were quite complex. All passports of workers recruited abroad were marked by a number on the picture. If a migrant turned up at the personnel department of a mine, it had to be verified whether he was still under contract elsewhere.

This information could be found in the lists of each regional association with the names of the aliens they had recruited or in the monthly (or sometimes even weekly) lists with the names of deserters. On the basis of those lists, the amount of recruitment cost that was still to be reimbursed to the recruiting mine could be calculated (ACCA; FEDECHAR).

The mining industry wanted to extend the scope of such an agreement to other industries. The mining industry's problem of retaining their recruited foreign labor was largely the result of the alternatives which other industrial sectors, such as the iron and steel factories, the chemical plants, and construction, offered to their labor. Mining hoped to satisfy the labor needs of those industries by offering them the services of their recruitment commissions in Poland and Czechoslovakia. Those industries would then no longer poach foreign labor from the mines. Instead, they would be interested in concluding an agreement with the mining industry. Extra – sectorial agreements were even promoted at the level of the CCI, the national employers' organization. It does not seem, however, that this call had much effect. Desertion of the mine industry continued unabated. The employers looked for a means to stop this. Some employers retained the passports of "their" foreign workers to make them respect the labor contract. Opposition to this measure was, however, extremely strong. The labor migrants considered it humiliating; it lowered them to the position of mine slaves. They considered it an intolerable infringement on their dignity, an attack on their basic human rights. The protests were loud; strikes were even called. Foreign labor could count on the unconditional support of their consular authorities in these protests. Many Czechoslovakians and Poles appealed to their embassies to force the mines to hand back their passports. These embassies stated unambiguously that retaining their citizens' passports was illegal. This was an elementary principle of civil liberty, endorsed by the Belgian authorities. The mining company did not have the authority to confiscate the passports of immigrants (AFAP 11,173; UEM, main d'oeuvre étrangère). In August 1929 the Italian authorities decided to retain the passports of the Italian emigrants in Belgium. It is likely that they decided to do so because of the declining popularity of the Belgian mines for Italian labor. Italians recruited for the mines were the deserters par excellence. This measure assured that the Italian emigrants would respect the one-year contract they had signed upon departure. The employers were delighted that a legal way had been found to ensure that immigrants completed their contracts. Consular authorities were entitled to seize the passports of their citizenry abroad. The Italian authorities' decision was, however, strongly opposed by Belgian authorities. The Liberal Minister of Justice P.E. Janson stated clearly that although it was not illegal, he disapproved of this measure and contended that the Belgian authorities must grant the Italians full civil liberties even without their passports. The opposition of the Belgian authorities meant that the Italian authorities refrained from implementing the decision (AAD 1 B6 III and 33 C30/A).

Due to the relatively high number of deserters among labor recruited in Czechoslovakia, the Czechoslovakian authorities became more willing to yield some minimal control over their emigrants recruited for the Belgian mines. From October 1929 onwards, the mines, upon the arrival of an officially recruited group of Czechoslovakian labor, were able to insert a stamp in their passports which stated the regional mine association that had recruited them, their date of entry, and their work contracts' completion date. The occupational mobility of these immigrants was not limited by this formal designation on their passports. It all depended on whether a would-be employer felt bound by this contractual obligation. Also, it was unnecessary for a Czechoslovakian migrant to show his passport when he applied for a job. In fact it only required the employers to check efficiently if they – according to the gentlemen's agreement – would eventually have to reimburse some of the recruitment costs. Very shortly afterwards, the Polish authorities also conceded to this demand made by the FEDECHAR. The numerous deserters' lists which had in the meantime become a bureaucratic headache could be done away with. By 1930 all recruited labor received a stamp in their passport upon arrival in Belgium. This procedure made the process of checking if they were still bound to a recruitment contract much more efficient (AEL, Minerie, 86 and BdL 181).

The mines tried to exercise their own control over foreign labor, but soon they were forced to realize that they needed the help of outside agencies. The gentlemen's agreements with the other industries were not that successful. The mines felt they were fighting a losing battle. When it turned out that newly recruited mine workers not only left for other industries but were even recruited by firms abroad, namely for the Dutch mines, the FEDECHAR had had enough. According to the FEDECHAR this movement had been instigated by Dutch mines' agents and the government would have to protect the recruitment efforts of the national industry. It was essential to the well-being of the mining industry that the occupational mobility of these immigrants be severely curtailed at least for the term of the work contract. Otherwise the shortage in the labor market would cause serious disturbances not only to the mining industry in the near future, but also to the global economy. Just as neighboring France had done with the 1926 Law for the Protection of National Labor, the authorities had to step in to safeguard the mines against the desertion of the recruited migrants. While the Minister of Foreign Affairs, P. Hymans, stated that the government was not able to do anything, the Minister of Labor, Heyman, was more positive; he proposed to incorporate the employers' interests in a reform of the alien legislation (FEDECHAR; ARMA bD3A1) .

The First Steps Towards a New Alien Policy

The large Communist influx, which as we mentioned earlier was mainly but not exclusively confined to the Italian immigrants acted as a catalyst for setting off a new discussion on the Belgian alien policy. The authorities were very much concerned about the political activities of these Italian Communists; their skirmishes with their countrymen in the fascist organizations had even caused diplomatic protests. A reform of the alien legislation was deemed necessary.

A commission was set up under the presidency of the governor of Antwerp, Holvoet. Similar to the interdepartmental commission which discussed the Vercruysse bill during the Poullet-Vandervelde Cabinet, it consisted of representatives of three departments (Labor, Justice and Foreign Affairs). This commission discussed what changes should be brought about in the alien law to tackle the challenges caused by the increasing immigration. The Holvoet bill was drafted by the end of 1928. Although new concerns had given shape to the bill, it was in fact an elaboration of the Vercruysse bill with the Sûreté having a considerably larger input in this new bill.

The Sûreté had especially been targeted in the press campaign against the agitators. The alien administration's objective was to increase its powers over all aliens. The powers which the law of 1897 granted it were considered wholly inadequate for cracking down on subversive activities by aliens. At the end of 1925, the Sûreté had already proposed to change the alien administration by introducing a special identity card for aliens. It was meant to be a mere administrative innovation to increase the efficiency of the alien administration. By 1928 the Sûreté considered not only an increased efficiency of the alien administration, but also an enlargement of its powers necessary to keep control over the foreign population. Members of the judiciary, who were confronted in their daily practice with what they considered the inadequacies of the alien legislation expressed similar concerns.

Members of the judiciary and the Sûreté insisted that the liberal provisions of the alien law of 1897 which protected aliens against the state were to be removed. Not only denizen categories, but even residency status only disarmed the state. The law's prohibition against expelling aliens who were married to Belgians particularly weakened the power of the Sûreté as some subversive foreigners who were to be expelled intentionally married single mothers to prevent their expulsion and the authorities were then totally disarmed. The Minister of Justice and the Sûreté had to be assigned the power to remove all undesirable aliens, independent of length of residence in Belgium. The Holvoet bill heeded the demand for considerably enlarging the powers of the Minister of Justice to remove aliens. The Minister of Justice would have the authority to expel all aliens (*renvoyer*). Only two categories of aliens would still receive residency status and their expulsion would depend on a decision by the Council of Ministers (*expulser*), i.e., the *domiciliés* and aliens married to a Belgian and who had one or more children born of this marriage during their stay in Belgium or who had lived in Belgium for at least five years. The protection that residency status provided aliens would be limited to a watered-down version of those categories of aliens which, according to the alien law of 1897, were granted status of *domicilié*.[1] The virtual abolishment of residency status, which was a disposition which the Vercruysse-bill had already contained and which had aroused the opposition of the then administrator Gonne no longer met with reservations. Another demand of the Sûreté was also heeded. A loophole in alien legislation, according to the Sûreté, was the provision that only expelled aliens who returned to Belgium could be convicted for *rupture de ban*. Those who never left the country could not be punished. The Holvoet bill proposed that administrative courts would convict expelled aliens who remained in the country to prison terms of up to twelve months without the possibility of appeal.

Not only aspects of public order, but also the socio-economic dimension of the increasing immigration were under discussion. Representatives of the Minister of Labor repeated the concerns expressed by Vercruysse in 1926. Firstly, ending the unregulated employment of foreign labor was necessary in order to protect national labor and to cut government spending on unemployment benefits. Secondly, the Belgian state had to be armed against the dictates of the authorities of the countries where industry recruited labor. The Minister of Labor, H. Heyman, considered it convenient to use the impetus of the Sûreté's insistence on change to insert some articles on labor in the new bill. The Minister of Labor considered that there was no pressing need for such a regulation at that very moment, but he wanted to be ready if the economic situation deteriorated. To obtain state control over foreign labor, the Holvoet bill went beyond the Vercruysse bill by obliging employers to apply for government authorization to hire aliens. Foreign labor would hence be subject to a dual control by the public authorities. This dual control, permission and admission, would be established to ensure the watertight implementation of the new legislation. As the Vercruysse bill had already stipulated, aliens had to apply upon immigration for the authorization from the Ministry of Labor to exercise a certain profession. If the ministry gave its approval, this occupation was mentioned on their alien card. Each change of occupation and the bi-annual renewal of the card implied a new authorization from the Ministry of Labor. These provisions of the Vercruysse bill were kept intact, but in addition, control was extended to the employers of foreign labor. Prior to engaging an alien, the employer had to ask for government permission. The state would have at its disposal the means to permanently regulate not only the access of foreign labor to, but also the mobility of aliens within, the national labor market. The Holvoet bill was also drafted with the idea that the state would regulate foreign labor in a corporate spirit. The alien policy should serve the interests of labor and employers alike. This would be achieved by integrating two institutions in the functioning of the new legislation: firstly, a yet-to-be-created joint committee at the national level, with representatives of employers and labor in parity, which would advise the Minister on the implementation of the law, and secondly, the public labor exchange offices which would prepare reports on the labor market situation.

In 1926 Vercruysse had refrained from extending state control over the employers of foreign labor as it would have been considered an act of hostility towards industry. Yet only two years later the Holvoet Commission decided that the hiring practices of the employers should be regulated by the state. It was even considered one of the linchpins of the whole proposition. This control over industry was even couched in an industry-friendly discourse. According to De Voghel, head of the cabinet of the Minister of Labor, the change in the recruitment practices of the mining industry toward a more systematic and costly strategy to combat labor shortages fueled the need for more rigid state control. Strict state control over the labor market position of aliens would ensure that efforts to recruit labor abroad by those industries suffering manpower shortages would not be wasted. Other industries would no longer be able to poach these workers. De Voghel argued that only when the state wielded far-reaching powers over foreign labor could the occupational loyalty of foreign labor to those sectors which had recruited them be enforced (AAD 1B6 and 12).

That this argument was not mere rhetoric was obvious in the reception of this bill by the mining industry. The mining companies now acknowledged, in contrast to previous outright refusals of any state intervention in this domain, that this bill could serve their interests, especially as support for their efforts to stabilize their foreign manpower. The mining industry still resented state intervention in the recruitment of their manpower, but they advocated restricting the rights of other industries to employ the manpower that they had recruited abroad. This change in strategy led to a constructive, but ambiguous criticism of the Holvoet bill. The mining industry was opposed to the provision that an employer had to apply for authorization for each individual alien whom he wanted to hire. They advocated a quota system, whereby the central authorities granted a whole industry or a company a certain number of authorizations to employ aliens. Quotas would limit the bureaucratic red tape and restrict state intervention in the mining industry. FEDECHAR considered that a link to the employer was appropriate only for the term of the initial recruitment contract. Afterwards foreign labor should not be tied to a specific employer, but only confined to a certain industrial sector. Central to the view of the mining industry was the need to retain flexibility in the recruitment of aliens. Such flexibility was needed in order to make use of the services of foreign labor that arrived spontaneously at the pits. The mining companies insisted that aliens who immigrated illegally could be legalized through the mediation of the industries which were covered by the quota system. The Sûreté could weed out the undesirable elements (criminals and subversives), but the honest worker should not be punished merely for immigrating illegally in search of a job. In exchange for state support in the stabilization of the foreign labor, the mining industry was ready to politicize the national labor market, but they wanted the authorities to base their decision exclusively on economic criteria and to eschew any union influence. The mining industry blatantly refused to incorporate unions in the management of foreign labor. Trade unions and their labor exchange offices did not come into the employers' scheme of things (FEDECHAR; AHCM; BdL 181).

This criticism of the Holvoet bill by the FEDECHAR was shared by the umbrella-organization of industry, the CCI. Although the initial reaction of the CCI was one of outright refusal of any state regulation of the labor market, this changed under strong pressure from the FEDECHAR. The employers' organization of the mining industry argued that only if legislation stopped other industries from poaching foreign labor from the mines could the mines reap benefits for its recruitment abroad. The other industries, probably in particular the iron and steel industry, were warned that they would also be confronted with important labor shortages which would necessitate organized recruitment abroad. Sectors such as the building sector and the chemical industry were probably more aware of the problems involved in stabilizing labor recruited abroad as they too had called upon labor in southern and central Europe. The other industries were warned that legislation was also necessary to prevent industries in neighboring countries from pirating foreign labor from Belgian industry. By appealing not only to its own interests, but also to the interests of any industry that called upon foreign labor, the FEDECHAR could press its point. In the end, the CCI supported the principle of regulating the labor market. The amendments of the FEDECHAR to the Holvoet bill were endorsed, and especially the obstruction of any union influence in the decision making process was wholeheartedly supported by the CCI (CCI *comuniqué social* 1929: 40,48 and 61; FEDECHAR).

The government had decided in the meantime to call a commission composed of high ranking members of the judiciary to give their advice on the Holvoet bill. This Meyers Commission endorsed most of the provisions of the Holvoet bill, but disapproved of the whole section on the regulation of the labor market. The commission believed the new alien law should be limited to a police law. Economic provisions should be left out of it. They repeated the arguments against state intervention on the labor market articulated until very recently by heavy industry. The labor market should not be regulated, but be left to its natural forces. To intervene in the labor market would inhibit the smooth functioning of the economy. The opinion of the Meyers Commission was not an isolated one. Liberal ideology also had an enduring vitality in academic circles and in most of the press. While, not only the Christian Democratic Minister of Labor, H. Heyman, but also the Liberal Minister of Foreign Affairs, P. Hymans, strongly insisted that the provisions concerning foreign labor should be maintained, their pressure was to no avail. Prime Minister H. Jaspar decided in September 1929 to remove the whole section on the regulation of foreign labor from the bill (AILO E 3/7/1;AAD 1B6). The discussion on reform of the alien bill was not yet over. In the meantime the economy began to show signs of decline.

By the end of 1929, changing economic fortunes began to influence immigration policy. The Ministry of Labor in particular insisted on curbing immigration. While this ministry had been largely ignored by the Sûreté in its visa policy during 1929, this changed in 1930. Only labor contracts approved by the Minister of Labor were still accepted by the Belgian consulates abroad; this implied that immigration was only tolerated in those segments of the labor market in which there was a lack of Belgian labor. The Christian Democratic Minister of Labor, H. Heyman, wanted more influence. He strongly resented the decision of H. Jaspar, the Prime Minister, not to insert any provisions concerning foreign labor in the Holvoet bill, and he succeeded in putting the Holvoet bill again on the agenda of the Council of Ministers. On 12 December 1929 the amputated bill was discussed at the Council of Ministers. The strong insistence of the Minister of Labor, H. Heyman, supported by H. Hymans, the Minister of Foreign Affairs, brought a reopening of the discussion on the articles concerning foreign labor. The Sûreté stated that there was no need for special provisions to regulate foreign labor within the new alien law. The Minister of Justice would wield powers large enough to ensure that the presence of foreign labor was economically justified. The Council of Ministers followed this advice; no permanent control over foreign labor was to be inserted. One article was added: organized migration would depend on the authorization of the authorities, *in casus* the Minister of Justice and the Minister of Labor. Minister of Labor H. Heyman considered this an important change in the bill. He was convinced that he would be granted the power to regulate organized immigration according to the needs of the labor market. He advocated a corporate procedure, a joint advisory commission to decide about the organized intake of foreign labor. This was certainly not the idea of heavy industry, which wanted the unions left out of the whole procedure. Heavy industry was disappointed about the little reform the bill proposed; they hoped, however, to be able to exert more influence when the executive measures of the new law were drafted. The CCI hoped to insert a provision that foreign labor had to stay in the industry which had recruited them (AAD 1B6 III). On 11 July 1930 the alien bill was deposed in Parliament. In the introduction to the bill it was clearly stated that only aspects of public order inspired the change in the alien law (PBD). The bill would never become law. When the government stepped down in May 1931, the bill had not yet been brought to a vote.

In the meantime, H.Heyman demanded more input in the alien policy. He did not want to wait until the alien legislation was reformed to demand his share in the control of foreign labor. As mentioned earlier, the Ministry of Justice had obstructed the insertion of provisions to restrict the occupational liberty of foreign labor in the alien bill proposed to Parliament by stating that a regulation of foreign labor could be obtained by the powers the Ministry of Justice would wield under the new legislation. Heyman wanted the Ministry of Justice to share its powers with his Ministry. He insisted upon having a voice not only in the granting of visas, but also in control over foreign labor residing in the country. The spillover from these sectors in which a labor shortage justified an appeal to immigrants to industrial sectors in which the aliens would cause unemployment for Belgians had to be prevented. In this endeavor the Minister of Labor even targeted aliens who were not required to carry a visa upon immigration: an inscription in the population register – residency status – should only be granted if these aliens were working under a contract which was approved by the Ministry of Labor. A temporary residence permit would enable the authorities to easily dispose of immigrants if the situation in the labor market continued to deteriorate. The Sûreté, consistent with its attitude in the past, opposed this interference by the Ministry of Labor in their domain. The Sûreté repeated that on the basis of the actual legislation they had no legal ground for refusing to inscribe in the population register legally immigrated aliens who were neither a political risk nor indigent. The Administrator of the Sûreté Remy explained that he could not consider an alien destitute because he had no work contract agreed upon by the Minister of Labor but would work for an employer who did not submit the work contract to the Minister of Labor. Neither could he propose to expel an alien for disturbing public order simply because he lacked the labor authorization of the Ministry of Labor. Remy also had a more fundamental criticism, he believed the proposal of the Minister of Labor hurt the principle of liberty which was the foundation of Belgian legislation (AAD 1B6III).

This interdepartmental quibbling should not obscure the changing nature of the immigration policy in 1930. The increasing unemployment in that year also affected alien policy. Immigration was restricted and legalizing the stay of undocumented immigrants became increasingly difficult. More and more, recently immigrated workers were expelled. At the border more and more people were stopped from entering Belgium (Graphs 14 and 15). Immigration policy had, however, an extremely dual nature. While aliens who were not subject to the visa requirement could still try their luck in Belgium, their colleagues of other, less fortunate nationalities had to bear the brunt of the approaching depression. While Poles, Yugoslavians, and Hungarians found it increasingly difficult to be allowed into Belgium, there was no impediment whatsoever for Czechoslovakians and Italians (compare Graphs 25 and 27 to 24 and 26). Only undocumented aliens who agreed to work in the mines were still able to legalize their stay. The Ministry of Labor agreed with the mining companies that labor shortages were still persistent in this sector. More than a thousand aliens who had immigrated illegally to Belgium left temporarily for neighboring countries to apply there for visas at the Belgian consulates. Their labor contracts were approved by the Ministry of Labor as no Belgian miners were unemployed. In this way the immigrants could legalize their residence (AFAP 9631 and 10,379; ACCA). The unions had not been consulted in this decision and, therefore, radicalized their strategy.

The Christian Democratic union laid out its strategy in its Congress of 1930. They proposed an economic regulation of immigration identical to the one the Socialists had already proposed in 1926. A national immigration council with representatives of the labor organizations would regulate immigration in order to protect national labor. Also the unionization of foreign labor was considered essential to prevent any negative influence on the working conditions of Belgians. Although the interests of national labor were clearly a priority, both unions were wary not to alienate foreign labor. Throughout 1930 the unions insisted on stopping any further immigration. This union policy realized that restrictive measures taken against immigrants were two-edged. On the one hand, they protected national labor against the dangers of "excessive" immigration. On the other hand, they made the protection of foreign labor already in Belgium more difficult. The unions had to maneuver between these two interests. Only a halt to immigration was called for. By the end of 1930, the Christian Democratic union radicalized its policy towards foreign labor. This union deemed the interests of foreign labor secondary to those of national labor. A national immigration council composed of representatives of the labor unions, the employers' associations and of the relevant Departments should decide not only about immigration, but also about the hiring of foreigners already residing in Belgium. Labor permits, strictly limited to one profession which would be valid for only six months should be introduced. Any prolongation of the permit by the Minister of Labor should depend on the consent of the national immigration council (Arendt 1931:275ff.). The unions still had little or no influence on alien policy. The only group which succeeded in securing total protection for themselves against competition from immigration were the professionals. They succeeded by merely lobbying, without street agitation or strikes. Since the nineteenth century, Belgian universities had had a large foreign student population, mainly in the faculties of technical and commercial sciences, and some of these students stayed put to exercise their profession in Belgium. The law of 21 May 1929 made the right to exercise the professions dependent on Belgian secondary education or its equivalent as determined by a Central Board of Examiners. This law protected Belgian graduates against their colleagues of foreign nationality whose Belgian university titles were meant only for export (BS 1929).

Due to increasing unemployment among Belgian labor, the issue of foreign labor reached the Council of Ministers in October 1930. Prime Minister H. Jaspar stated bluntly that action had to be taken against foreigners who appropriated jobs from Belgian workers. As a result, from November 1930 onwards, the Sûreté refused residency status to all immigrants who had to have a visa upon entering Belgium. This enabled the Minister of Justice to autonomously decide that they had to leave the country (*renvoi*). For those nationalities whose immigration was not restricted, the traditional policy remained valid, after four months they obtained residency status (AAD 33C31). Prime Minister H. Jaspar found that the state had to be better armed against resident aliens who became unemployed. At the end of the year an immigration bill was accepted by the Council of Ministers. The previous Council of Ministers had already decided to reform the Sûreté so that it would be better able to control the increasing number of foreigners in Belgium. Additional personnel would be engaged and a separate service for foreigners would be set up. On 15 December 1930 the immigration bill of P.E. Janson was passed by Parliament (BS 1931:184ff.). The new immigration law abolished the dual nature of Belgian policy for labor migrants. All aliens who came to Belgium to engage in wage labor had to obtain the authorization of the Ministry of Justice. Authorization depended on a labor contract approved by the Ministry of Labor. For Poles, Hungarians, Germans and Yugoslavians nothing had changed, the labor migrants from countries which until then did not have to carry a visa upon immigration were now also subject to the restrictive rules.

An exception was made for French citizens, whose immigration remained unrestricted. The Belgian authorities remained conscious that the large number of Belgians working in France had to be protected against potential retaliation. In France, where the depression would only be felt later, Belgian labor was not yet worried. In 1931, 7,821 Belgians, who had not worked in France previously but had found an employer in France willing to hire them, applied successfully for commuters' cards and in July 1931 about 70,000 commuters' cards which had been granted to Belgians in previous years were renewed for another two years (PHK 1934: 9). The Belgians who migrated seasonally to the French brick works and sugar beet fields also had to satisfy the administrative requirements the French state had imposed on foreign labor. Besides some paperwork this administrative control had no influence on the migration stream. In comparison with the pre-war period, the numbers involved in seasonal migration had halved. This decline was not because the French state wanted to restrict their immigration, but because employers had found replacements through organized recruitment in Poland. Polish agrarian laborers could be controlled better by the French employers than their traditional Belgian workers. The roughly 250,000 Belgians listed in the 1931 French population census were also hardly subject to any discriminatory policy. All Belgians living in France were obliged, as were other resident foreigners, to obtain and carry an identity card. As most of these Belgians had emigrated before the First World War, they had acquired the status of permanent resident which protected them against arbitrary interventions by the French administration. Their work permits were automatically renewed. Even the few Belgians who had emigrated after 1926 were rarely restricted in their occupational choices by the French administrative controls. Given the labor needs of the French economy, the administrative restrictions were hardly enforced (Lentacker 1974:211 and 236ff.). To assure that the French state would not discriminate against any of these Belgians working in France, French citizens in Belgium had to be exempt from any discriminatory state action.

For the Dutch immigration in Belgium such arguments were not valid. The number of Dutchmen working in Belgium – about 25,000 – was about fivefold the number of Belgian workers in the Netherlands. In the 1920s the Netherlands was not an immigration country. Belgian labor migration to the Netherlands was a regional migration to the nearest employer, rather than a long distance migration. The five thousand Belgians involved mostly commuted daily to their jobs in the border regions of the Netherlands. Dutch migration to Belgium on the other hand covered longer distance. The Dutch migrants not only worked, but also resided in Belgium. The Dutch authorities hoped to restore free immigration to Belgium by concluding a labor treaty with Belgium. The Belgian authorities were, for obvious reasons, opposed to a general treaty. Only a labor treaty limited to the commuters was acceptable for Brussels. Although perspectives for a limited labor treaty were not too dim, unrestricted immigration to Belgium was a lost cause for the Dutch for the moment and after 14 March 1931 Dutch labor could even be expelled for illegal immigration (ARDH 180 and 183).

The response of the trade unions to the legislation of 15 December 1930 was ambiguous. The unions considered a law that regulated access to the national labor market an important breakthrough. They criticized, however, the manner in which immigration control was to be implemented. To abolish the unrestricted liberty of employers to recruit labor abroad was only one step, it was necessary that the trade unions also had a voice in the decision-making process. When in 1931 the mining companies in Limburg asked for the authorization to recruit skilled miners from abroad, the miners' trade unions demanded that government authorization for recruitment be preceded by a discussion in the regional joint mining commission. The Minister of Labor could then make a decision based on the advice of this commission. De Voghel, chief of the Cabinet of the Minister of Labor, accepted this proposition. The mining companies were furious, the intrusion of the trade unions in this affair was unacceptable (KS 2054; ACCA). When in the summer of 1931 some Hungarian miners were recruited with the consent of the government, but without the agreement of the unions the Christian Democratic miners' union decided to oppose all immigration until a national immigration council with representatives of the labor organizations regulated immigration. There was no need to uphold this radical stance as the authorities rarely granted authorization on immigration in the next few years (KADOC, Broekx, 512521; ACCA).

The overall restrictive immigration policy heralded by the law of 15 December 1930 did not mean that legal immigration was halted completely. First of all, immigration as such was not curtailed by this law. The entry of businessmen, tourists... from countries which did not have to carry a visa remained unrestricted. Secondly, not all immigration of labor was prohibited. In 1931 more than three thousand and in 1932 a mere two thousand immigration permits were still granted to foreign labor. Mining, agriculture, and domestic service remained, certainly until 1931, refuges for newly arrived foreigners. The situation in these segments of the labor market was still tight. Belgian laborers who had been fired in other industries were not forced to accept any job as they received unemployment benefits. This caused them to be unwilling to work in the mines or on farms, while foreign laborers could still legalize their residence by becoming miners, farm hands or servants (AAD 33C31/3; AFAP 10,379).

Another category of immigrants still tolerated in Belgium was the highly qualified manpower which Italy and France provided to the exclusive Belgian hotels at the seaside. We have already mentioned these immigrants in our overview of the late nineteenth century immigration. These hotels had preserved their elitist character of the Belle Epoque. During the 1920s these first class hotels, the so-called palaces, were only open for about 110 days a year. They had a largely foreign and very wealthy clientele and business was thriving. They had already started using more qualified Belgian personnel. Germans were no longer desirable, but Italian and French personnel trained in the hotel schools of their countries remained essential for the well functioning of these hotels. Each summer they left the exclusive hotels in Italy, Switzerland, or the French coast to head for the Belgian hotels, just as they had done at the end of the nineteenth century. The setting up of a hotel school to train Belgian personnel was considered superfluous as the palaces could only provide their personnel with seasonal employment. In some exclusive Belgian hotels in Antwerp and Brussels, aliens were hired for the whole year around. With the downward trend in the economy the clientele of these hotels stayed away and the competition for the scarce jobs was fierce. Antwerp and Brussels became attraction poles for qualified hotel personnel, traditionally a highly mobile group from all over Europe, as they hoped that the festivities to commemorate Belgium's independence a century earlier would attract a lot of tourists. The unions complained about an invasion which threatened the livelihood of their members and undermined the wage levels. There were not only complaints about the competition of immigrants in Brussels and Antwerp; in the summer of 1930, the presence of the traditional seasonal workers in the first class hotels at the seaside was also the focus of complaints. The qualified Belgian hotel personnel had hoped that they would be able to supplement their diminishing incomes with jobs at the seaside. Not only was seaside tourism also slackening off, but the opportunities for Belgians were nonexistent because the foreigners who traditionally had worked in those hotels were able to retain their jobs. In 1931, the Italian *maîtres d'hôtel* or *chefs de rang*, just as any other labor migrant, now needed the authorization of the authorities to do their habitual summer work. The hotels warned their Italian personnel who were working in the winter in Italy, France, and Switzerland that they had to apply for work permits. When the Italians arrived in Belgium in May-June 1931 for the season, not all had done so. Some of them were considered illegal immigrants. The local police ordered them to leave the country. The managers of the palaces protested that they could not do without these Italians. In the end the Sûreté tolerated all the foreigners working in these hotels for that season. The Sûreté warned that for the season of 1932 all the Italian migrants had to apply before their arrival for authorization to work. In 1932 the Sûreté permitted a few hundred Italians for the season at the Belgian seaside, notwithstanding the opposition of the unions. The Ministry of Justice considered the skills of these Italians essential for the hotels (AAD 33C34/1). While in the 1920s these migrants had attracted no public attention at all, this changed in 1930. In the following years they would get an ever increasing amount of attention.

With the rise of unemployment in most sectors, not only the unions in the hotel sector, but also in industry, changed their strategy towards foreign labor. They did not try to unionize them anymore; rather they urged employers to dismiss all foreigners before they fired Belgian labor. Most employers had no problem complying with the trade union demand. The dismissal en masse of foreign workers created a change in the occupational profile of foreign labor. Their industrial employment contracted to the mining sector. This can already be noticed in 1930 when the heterogenous occupational profile of some ethnic groups gave way to a profile largely limited to mining. In the iron and steel industry, foreign labor was dismissed en masse. In the large public works sector, the number of foreign workers diminished considerably. Unemployed Belgians replaced them. Because of their flexibility – an asset to entrepreneurs who had projects all over the country – a small number of immigrants were kept on the job. Few other sectors still attracted immigrants. The economic downturn caused agriculture, a marginal sector of the labor market notorious for its long working hours and low wages, to be able to attract more foreign labor. Domestic service also became an alternative way to earn a living for aliens who had been dismissed in industry.

In the first half of 1932, the trade unions complained that in the quarries and the mining industry the employers retained and even hired foreigners while dismissing their Belgian labor. In 1931 the unemployment problem among miners was limited to the Borinage, but by 1932 the miners in all the Walloon basins were strongly affected by the Depression. Although the proportion of foreigners in the labor force had declined considerably since 1931, Belgian miners were also fired. In any case, dismissals were only the tip of the iceberg. Partial unemployment was widespread among the miners. Belgian and foreign miners were forced to be idle half the week. That foreigners were thus also kept on the job was strongly resented by the Belgian miners. The unions felt that they had to react. The Christian Democratic miners' union demanded the immediate dismissal of all single aliens in the mines. To combat unemployment in Wallonia, this union even proposed dismissing Flemish miners. The unemployed Flemish miners could then start working in the basin of Limburg. This radical solution to the unemployment problem in the mining sector – ethnic cleansing in the Walloon mine basins – was supported by the Socialist miners' union in the Borinage. The dismissal of Flemish and foreign miners would create enough vacancies to solve the unemployment problem among the locals. The national leadership of the Socialist miners' union rejected efforts to enforce this radical solution. They considered this proposal unrealistic, even for the Borinage. They had serious doubts that the unemployed Walloon miners would agree to do the jobs foreign labor had done. They thought that even the local miners of the Borinage would not be eager to go to work in a mine other than the one they were used to, especially as the foreign labor in the Borinage worked in the most dangerous mines. They feared that the unemployed Walloon miners would prefer to remain on the dole. The Socialist miners' union was also in favor of a gradual removal of foreign labor and replacing them with unemployed Belgian miners. However, this replacement process had to take into account the willingness and ability of Belgians to replace foreign labor. The employers, in their discussions with the unions, reasoned along similar lines. In practice, however, they refused to give absolute priority to Belgian labor, as they wanted to retain the "valuable" foreign miners. This hardened the attitude of the Christian Democrats and an anti-foreigner position became more popular among the Socialists as well. Within the Socialists' ranks foreign labor was increasingly depicted as easy-to-manipulate tools of the employers, workers who accepted everything that the employers imposed.

The unions got an important ally in their insistence that priority be given to Belgian labor. In order to alleviate the unemployment problem and the expenses it caused for the Belgian treasury De Voghel, head of the cabinet of the Minister of Labor, urged the employers to fire foreign labor first. He resented the fact that the public authorities, like the unions, depended on the goodwill of the employers. The employers retained complete autonomy in their personnel policy and considered the Belgian nationality of a worker no reason to keep him on the job. The trade unions and the Ministry of Labor, on the other hand were dedicated to jettison foreign labor in order to protect Belgian labor, but both were powerless (ARMA rC22; CNMM; CMBo). The trade unions and the Ministry of Labor were confident that the dismissed aliens would return to their country of origin. This assumption was to a large extent correct. The low level of unionization among foreign labor meant that dismissal in most cases resulted in the loss of any income. Only municipal welfare – barely enough to survive – could offer some solace. Even some of the unemployed unionized aliens were reluctant to sit idly by, waiting for better times to come. Immigrants had another alternative to return to their country of origin. Now that economic changes made it difficult to find a job and declining wages made saving illusory, a lot of migrants decided to go back. Recent immigrants who had problems legalizing their residence in Belgium were the first to leave. By the end of 1930, and in the course of 1931, the number of returnees increased, especially among those who had left their families in the country of origin. In the first half of 1932 the number of returnees rose spectacularly; thousands of migrants, even families, left Belgium. The lot of the migrants who lacked the financial means to pay for their return trip was dramatic. For some, the consulates stepped in to pay for the trip, but in 1931 some consulates were already unable to handle applications for repatriation. The only help those consulates could offer was referral to the Salvation Army where the returnees received shelter and some food (AFAP 9946 and 10,379; AMSAC H1/a-1 3974). Some desperate workers left their spouses and children at the embassy as they saw no solution. Some returned to their countries on foot, hoping to earn some money for food on the way back by doing casual work or by begging. In the German border region, some were arrested and sent back to Belgium, where they were put in the vagrant colonies. The number of foreigners in these colonies increased considerably (Graph 23). After a few months – when they had earned fifty francs – the migrants were brought to the border and set free. As few of them had the necessary papers and money to cross Germany, they mostly remained in Belgium and tried to find a job. As the Belgian authorities wanted to force them to leave the country, they decided to make vagrancy more risky for aliens. Foreign vagrants were to stay three times longer in the colonies and not 50 but 150 francs had to be earned before they could be released. This money would enable them to reach another country more easily. The Belgian authorities considered return to the country of origin the best solution, hence those migrants with passports were released as soon as the paper work necessary for their return was concluded. Migrants who could not prove their nationality because of a lack of papers had great difficulties in obtaining passports, let alone the necessary transit visas. They mostly had to stay until they had earned 150 francs. An increasing number of aliens absconded from the vagrant colonies, and in July 1932 a concession was made. The Belgian authorities diminished the sum of money a foreign vagrant had to earn before he could be released from 150 to 125 francs. The authorities hoped to limit in this way the number of absconding aliens. This still implied, given the regular wage rates at the colonies, nearly half-a-year's work. Only then could these immigrants undertake the risky trip back home. As most did not have the necessary papers, the return was quite often interrupted by imprisonment and expulsion. Some of these people tried to remain in Belgium. For refugees and stateless persons return was not even an option. For them, the alternative to remaining illegally in Belgium was to live illegally in another country. Hence, a lot of them remained in Belgium to become the clientele par excellence of the Belgian vagrant colonies (AFAP 10,069; AAD 75 C 29).

Conclusion

The organized immigration of labor to Belgium increased considerably in the years 1929 and 1930. At least 25,000 immigrants arrived in Belgium, having been called explicitly by Belgian industry. Immigration organized by industry and especially by the mining companies was the innovation of this period. Until 1928, Belgian industry had hardly invested in the recruitment of manpower abroad. It also had no voice in the selection procedure. The limited output it could have had was subcontracted to the French SGI. All this changed in 1929. The industry with the largest need for additional manpower, mining, negotiated directly with the countries of emigration. As a result, these employers selected manpower according to their criteria and imported workers into Belgium at their own expense. The crucial determinant in selecting manpower was recruitment costs. Other important criteria were physical fitness and familiarity with mining. The shortage of eastern and southern European workers familiar with mining who were willing to leave for Belgium meant that the latter criterion had to be temporarily dropped. The international labor market had, however, a large oversupply of peasants. Belgian industry had to tap this labor pool. After some months of experience in recruitment, a shift away from collective recruitment to individual recruitment occurred. The urgency of the injection of manpower had slightly abated and this slower procedure suited the employers well. This hiring strategy was seen as the best guarantee for the import of a loyal and hard-working labor force. It was a relatively low-cost solution. In this period the employers won a great deal of power over the migration process to the detriment of the authorities of the emigration countries. While before 1928 the latter dictated, to a large degree, the terms of recruitment in their countries, this was much less true by the end of the decade. The Belgian mining industry and other industrial employers formed a front in 1929 and played the authorities of the emigration countries off against each other with increasing success.

The Belgian authorities hardly intervened in this process. They were under the impression, however, that they controlled immigration. They gave their consent by granting visas to the Poles and Yugoslavians who had been recruited legally; for the Italians provided by the Italian authorities, they had also their say. It was, however, heavy industry and, to a limited extent, the authorities of the emigration countries who decided who was recruited and how many were imported. Since the labor market could easily absorb all immigrants, no rigid state control was deemed appropriate. For the Belgian authorities only a slightly adjusted laisser-faire policy remained the best response to the shortage in the labor market.

From May 1929 onwards control over immigration was strengthened. Illegal immigration was no longer tolerated. The law that all aliens who needed a visa to immigrate to Belgium carried one was strictly enforced, if an alien did not, he was refused access to the country at the border. Those who slipped through could no longer legalize their residence in Belgium as had been the case in the previous years; they had to apply for a visa abroad. Political (the danger of Communist infiltration) and not socio-economic concerns decided this first departure from the laisser-faire policy. Not only criminals, but also immigrants who were or had been active in the political left were to be refused visas. This meant Belgium denied asylum to most refugees of a leftist signature. The authorities considered it inappropriate to make allowances for them. The lot of "subversive" refugees hardly stirred any consternation.

By the middle of 1929 the laisser-faire policy was criticized from an unexpected source. Heavy industry called for a more active alien policy in order to encourage labor they recruited abroad to stabilize in the mining profession. Given the considerable labor shortage in mining and other industries, all mines were forced to invest in the recruitment of labor. The labor shortage in mining, however, remained acute as a large number of immigrants left the mines shortly after their arrival. The lack of obligation that foreign labor felt towards the industry that had recruited them became a national problem of the mining industry. The mining companies refined their recruitment strategy to diminish the desertion of the newcomers and in particular to limit the financial damage this desertion entailed. The very diverse strategies the mining companies developed for increasing the loyalty of the immigrants were not very effective. Given the large occupational opportunities beyond mining and the lack of cooperation of the employers who pirated immigrants from the mines, those strategies were doomed to fail. As a result the mining companies pressured the state for greater regulation. As a rigidly controlled foreign labor system seemed to be in their interests, mining companies were willing to assign the state a greater role in the labor market. It would be the way to ensure that the investment in recruiting manpower would yield the expected return. The employers realized that only by coercion would they be able to recoup the costs of importing foreign labor.

By 1930 there was a consensus that the traditional alien policy had to change, that the state had to play a more active role in regulating international migration to Belgium. The exact manner in which this was to be done was controversial, but in contrast to some years earlier when the traditional immigration policy had only been contested by the unions and some mavericks within the administration, the principle of a reform of the alien legislation was now accepted. Heavy industry as well as the Sûreté, backed by the traditional establishment, redefined their positions towards the unions and their allies in the government to radically reshape alien policy. Since 1923, pro-labor forces had insisted on a reform which would take into account the interest of local labor. Until then an outright refusal to envisage any reform had been the answer of the traditional establishment. Industry reviewed their previous outright refusal of any change in the traditional alien policy because of the difficulty in retaining labor they had recruited abroad. By 1929 heavy industry supported the very principle of state intervention in the labor market, but the goal of this intervention and how this intervention would be decided upon was different from what the unions had in mind. The FEDECHAR and also the CCI were ready to yield some of their power over the labor market to the state, namely the decision about the number of immigrants each industry could introduce into the country. This was clearly a concession because in the 1920s the mechanism of the free labor market had hardly been touched. The Belgian state, notwithstanding visa regulations and the Italian-Belgian recruitment agreement of 1923, had remained, until then, largely absent in this domain. Heavy industry, however, strongly refuted any sharing of power with the unions.

The traditional political establishment was not convinced of the necessity of state intervention in the labor market. Reform in alien policy was deemed necessary, not to control immigrants as economic actors, but because of the alleged political danger the immigrants posed. In particular the infiltration of Communist elements was considered alarming. The Sûreté became a strong advocate of reform in alien legislation as extension of their power was considered essential to attend to the political threat these "dangerous classes" posed. This advocacy only aimed at enlarging the police powers of the state. A further extension of state power into the social domain was rejected. Among others, the members of the Meyers Commission rejected the extension of state power to the domain of immigration policy. To a large extent their view won the day. New legislation would put only organized recruitment of manpower abroad under state supervision. Heavy industry counted on using its political clout to influence the executive orders. Finally, due to parliamentary sluggishness, the whole discussion did not change anything, and the traditional alien policy remained in force. Radical reform in alien legislation would take another few years to come. Change took place, but in an incremental manner. In 1930 immigration policy received a social dimension as the Minister of Labor succeeded in grafting social concerns on the strict admission policy at the border. For the first time since the abolishment of the regulation of 1923, the Minister of Labor again got a say in the granting of visas. Only immigrants who responded to officially sanctioned shortages on the labor market were granted visas.

Given rising unemployment, the government wanted to expel all unemployed foreign labor at the end of 1930. This was, however, not executable as most of these immigrants had already acquired residency status. The realization on the part of the government that they were not able to remove these superfluous immigrants caused quick legislative action. The legislation of 15 December 1930 created the category "labor migrants" and made their immigration dependent upon an admission agreement by the Belgian authorities. Free immigration to Belgium for labor migrants belonged definitely to the past. The use of visas as a way to synchronize immigration with labor market needs was now abolished. This old procedure had considerable shortcomings: it only affected part of the immigrants and expanding it to include more nationalities would have caused serious diplomatic problems. The new means to regulate all labor migration did not distinguish by nationality and diplomatic protests were therefore not legitimized. All immigrant labor came under the special control of the Minister of Labor. The extended power the authorities wielded over immigration was not shared with the trade unions, certainly not in an institutionalized manner. The state decided autonomously at the request of the employers about the further intake of labor migrants. The change of immigration policy left the entry of domestic servants, highly qualified hotel personnel and farm hands largely unaffected. Even the mining industry with its strong union tradition continued to take in foreign labor. Undocumented foreign miners could still legalize their residence. The mining companies, to a large extent, could make their economic interests be accepted by the state as the "national" interest.

In 1932 the deterioration of the situation in the labor market caused the state to approach the unions, which asked not only for a halt to immigration, but also for the dismissal of foreign labor as needed. Since both the state and the unions were virtually powerless in the Belgian labor market, the employers could meet these demands as they wished. This dependence on the good will of the employers was not yet a matter of serious conflict as most employers disposed first of their recently recruited and unqualified foreign labor. Given the dimmer economic prospects a lot of immigrants also decided to leave Belgium. In the following chapter we will see that as the Depression continued, the immigrants who remained on the job became the focus of an escalating conflict between the state, allied with the unions, and employers.

Note

1. In the 1920s the status of *domiciliés* based on article 13 of the civil code became a status largely void of meaning. Very few aliens still applied for this status (Graph 18). It became a relic of the past. It seems that the only reason this status survived was that some exclusive private organizations required their members of non-Belgian nationality to have this status (Bekaert 1940: 231).

Chapter 7

The Xenophobic Response to the Depression, 1932-1935

The Belgian open economy, highly reliant on foreign trade, was strongly hit by the Depression and the rising protectionism in other countries. The demand for semi-finished industrial products with a low degree of added value – the non-specialized nature of Belgian production – was elastic. The decline in exports could only be limited by lowering prices to become more competitive abroad. Industry was even forced to sacrifice profit margins to retain market share (Vanthemse 1988-1989; Hogg 1986). The conservative Catholic-Liberal governments of this period followed a strict pro-business policy. They tried desperately to avoid devaluation and to stay on the gold standard after most of Belgium's trading partners had gone off the standard. The governments imposed a severe deflationary policy in order to protect the national currency and save the country's position in international trade. In June 1932, a spontaneous strike in the Borinage expanded into a general strike with insurrectional aspects. During this strike the Communist party succeeded, for the first time, in obtaining workers' support, which would only increase in the following years. The strike of the summer of 1932 was also a clear sign for the government that there was a limit to the deflationary policy. As a result, the government eased off on deflationary pressures.

Further, tentative moves to reduce government expenditure turned out to be extremely difficult politically. In particular, the increasing expenditures of the central government on unemployment benefits was a thorn in the conservative governments' side. In 1933 and 1934 benefits were drastically reduced and certain categories of laborers were declared uninsurable, but state expenditures in this field remained high (around 5 percent of the state budget). Unemployment insurance expanded considerably during the Depression and covered most industrial workers by the middle of the 1930s. As unemployment insurance was a quasi-monopoly of the unions, this trend enabled the unions to strengthen their hold over the working population. The Christian Democratic union, in particular, saw a sharp rise in union membership during the Depression. Employers argued that the unions, through their hold on unemployment insurance, could control the labor market and disrupt its "natural" functioning with the aid of state subsidies. Unemployment benefits kept wage levels artificially high, so industry was unable to reduce its wage costs in order to make its prices competitive in the world market. The employers advocated a stronger role for the state in the system of voluntary unemployment insurance. Although this system, with the crucial role of the trade unions, remained unaltered in this period, the traditional symbiosis between the government and business was kept very much intact. The Christian Democratic ministers in the Conservative cabinets had only very limited influence. They were only able to postpone certain decisions directed against their constituencies, but not to stop them (Vanthemse 1989). The Van Zeeland cabinet took power in March 1935 with important Socialist participation, and proclaimed the necessity for a more autonomous state policy, independent from business interests.

The Freeze on Immigration, a Failure

The legislation of 15 December 1930 had imposed strict conditions on all labor immigration. Other immigration (business, tourism, family reunion, etc...) remained unaffected. Between 1932 and 1935 immigration oscillated around 15,000 immigrants annually (Graph 21), a considerable decline in comparison with the previous period. After 1931 the labor market took in very few immigrants. The recruitment of female labor to work as domestic servants in private houses remained legally possible. For example the Catholic organization *Ligue des Familles nombreuses* recruited about thousand girls in Hungary from 1932 to 1935. The seasonal immigration of a few hundred qualified cooks, receptionists, and waiters, mostly Italians, for the first class hotels also continued throughout the whole period. Their French colleagues did not have to worry as the law of 15 December 1930 made an exception for citizens of France. The Dutch, however, fell under the provisions of the law. Just as any other foreign worker, Dutch workers who wanted to work in Belgium had to ask for admission from the Belgian Ministry of Labor before immigrating. Thus Dutch labor could be expelled for illegal immigration. The Belgian-Dutch agreement of 20 February 1933 stipulated in a secret provision that

Dutch labor would obtain authorization to enter Belgium without any problem. Dutch immigrants still had to apply, but authorization would be a mere formality. Labor migration from the Netherlands was no longer to be restricted. Minister of Finance H. Jaspar was strongly opposed to this agreement as it would only increase the number of unemployed and the expenses for unemployment insurance. At his insistence the ratification of the agreement was postponed. About a thousand Dutch workers immigrated to Belgium in 1933 and 1934. The Belgian authorities believed they had only aggravated unemployment in Belgium and in April 1935 suspended the liberalization introduced for the Dutch labor migrants. From that date onwards, the Dutch again fell subject to the restrictive immigration policy (ARDH 185; ARA, Jaspar, 81). Although legal immigration to Belgium in search of a job was virtually impossible, many tried their chances. In 1932 Belgian border guards refused entrance into Belgium to three times as many aliens (from 2,457 to 7,030) as in 1929. During the crisis years that followed, the border guards refused a few thousand aliens access to Belgium annually, although the number of individuals denied access never attained the heights of 1932 (Graph 14).

Those illegal immigrants who fled to Belgium in search of a safe haven became a special category. In the spring and summer of 1933, immediately after Hitler's ascendance to power, a few thousand Jews as well as a number of leftist activists fled to Belgium. The authorities were not prepared to make any allowances for them as refugees, treating them purely as any other immigrants. Since 1918 Germans had been required to request a visa before entering Belgium. Those who wanted to leave Germany for Belgium when Hitler took power had to request permission from the Belgian consulates in Germany, and the consulates were only allowed to grant visas when the central authorities felt that "Belgian" interests were being met. German citizens who had immigrated without the proper authorization were to be removed from Belgium. Orders to leave the country were handed out to these uninvited refugees from Nazi Germany. The refugees refused to return to Germany. The authorities did not impose this by force. To leave Belgium was, however, strongly pressed upon them. Many refugees left Belgium, moving on to neighboring countries such as France and the Netherlands. This policy of urging the refugees on to other countries soured diplomatic relations. France protested. By the end of 1933 Belgium had already revised its immigration policy, formulating a refugee policy.

The refugee policy consisted of a two-track policy that differentiated between two categories of refugees: the so-called refugees *stricto sensu* and the refugees *sensu lato*. The first category were political refugees and the second Jewish refugees. The refugees *stricto sensu*, a limited group of political refugees, were granted semi-official asylum. The Minister of Justice decided upon recommendations from refugee committees which immigrants were refugees *stricto sensu*. The definition of "refugee" was restrictive: only those asylum seekers whose life or freedom was endangered because of their political activities could claim asylum. Communists were excluded from this goodwill measure. By 1935 at most four hundred refugees were granted the status of refugee *stricto sensu*. The Jewish refugees were not considered refugees in the strict sense because the authorities determined that their freedom was not endangered; racist practice and legislation in Nazi Germany "only" undermined their socio-economic position. The Belgian authorities temporarily tolerated the German Jews in order to enable them to prepare to move on with the financial and organizational assistance of the Belgian Jewish community. They were strictly forbidden to engage in any economic activity. Jewish refugees with considerable financial means and/or entrepreneurial assets received their visas in the summer of 1933. These "useful" immigrants were able to immigrate on the basis of the immigration policy in force. No new provisions had to be created for them. Most of these Jewish refugees were forced to live on their savings as their visa-status forbade any economic activity. Those whose entrepreneurial assets were considered valuable to Belgium's economic recovery were granted temporary permission to work as long as they continued to live up to the government's expectations. In this way, the authorities tried to maintain control over the situation. A change in the alien law was, however, necessary to do so, because under the alien law in force these legally immigrated aliens gained full-fledged residency status after four months and controlling them would no longer be possible (Caestecker 1993c:25-33).

Since the onset of the Depression, the government had been highly irritated that it was not legally possible to expel all destitute and unemployed aliens who had acquired residency status after residing in the country for a while. The judiciary had just then endorsed the administrative practice of arbitrary expulsion of non-resident aliens. A judgement of the *Cour de Cassation* in July 1932 stated that the domicile which the Aliens Law of 1897 wanted to protect by granting residency status referred not only to a factual element, but also to a legal element, i.e., residence in conformity with the laws and regulations. This decision of the *Cour de Cassation* invalidated the decision of the same court in the Jones affair (1848) by further qualifying residency, beyond de facto domicile (*Pasicrisie Belge* 1932:232f.). Once immigrants had obtained residency status, the powers of the authorities in dealing with them remained restricted. The arrival of thousands of refugees from Nazi Germany added to the authorities awareness that a revision of the alien legislation was necessary to obtain a hold over aliens in Belgium.

As mentioned before, as of November 1930 the Sûreté had implemented a more restrictive policy. Immigrants who had to carry a visa were no longer granted an identity card after a four-month stay. The administrative practice was only to prolong their visa and thus to deny them residency status. As soon as these aliens lost their jobs, they were ordered to leave the country. The dual nature of the immigration law which was abolished, at least for labor migrants, with the legislation of 15 December 1930 had survived partly in the administrative practice. In early summer 1932, the Sûreté proposed refusing all immigrants identity cards, even those who did not have to carry a visa upon immigration. It is unclear what the result of this proposition was, but the political pressure to develop a more restrictive alien policy in face of rising unemployment and the flood of refugees from Nazi Germany in the spring of 1933 resulted in legislative action. In August 1933 the authorities took a clear-cut decision by drafting a bill introducing a new procedure for acquiring residency status. The bill quickly became law because Parliament was bypassed (BS 1933:4102 ff.). The government had full power to redress the state budget without consulting Parliament, and the bill had been presented as a change in the alien law only to improve the collection of duties from the aliens. The duties which the aliens had to pay for residing in Belgium would no longer be levied at the *arrondissement* level, but at the municipal level. The municipal authorities would not only register the immigrants, but also handle their application for an identity card, a competence which until then had belonged to the provincial authorities. The duties would not only be levied once, at the moment of the delivery of the identity card, but also every two years upon renewal of the card. As the identity card for Belgian citizens had infinite validity, this innovation implied the introduction of a new identity card for aliens with limited validity. The law not only altered the administration of the foreign population, it also revolutionized the procedure for acquiring residency status. The transitory status – aliens without residency – was now lengthened indefinitely until the Minister of Justice agreed to issue an identity card for aliens. A special document, a white card, was even introduced to cover the period in which the alien waited to obtain his identity card. When an alien entered the country legally and settled in a municipality, he had to register in the aliens' register and obtain a temporary residence permit which covered his stay for six months. The temporary residence permit could be extended a number of times and each extension lasted six months. If the Minister of Justice decided that the stay of this immigrant was no longer desirable, an order to leave the country could be issued. In the law there was no set term in which an alien should obtain an identity card. It seems the authorities considered a stay of two years the absolute minimum to be granted residency status. This law considerably enlarged the amount of leeway given to the Minister of Justice in dealing with aliens. The law did not affect aliens who had already acquired residency status in Belgium.

For them the law only meant an important financial expense every two years. For the aliens who had immigrated after 1930 and had not yet acquired residency status, their lot depended on the Ministry of Justice. In particular for the few aliens, especially wealthy German refugees, who immigrated legally after 1932, this law meant that the authorities could order them to leave Belgium at any moment. To refuse residency status over an extended period to immigrants who had to carry a visa had been the administrative practice from November 1930 onwards; in 1933 it became official policy for all aliens. They were indiscriminately placed on a long probation (AFAB 12,181).

This legislation did not stop illegal immigration. Most of the Jewish refugees who had arrived in the spring and summer of 1933 were precluded from staying in Belgium. Through the granting of a precarious residence permit and by denying them the possibility of working, the authorities forced them to move on. Most of them found a safe haven overseas, in Palestine or in South America. The authorities tried to discourage further immigration by Jewish refugees from Nazi Germany. It was clearly stated that any refugee who after the summer of 1933 immigrated to Belgium with only a tourist visa or illegally would not be granted even the time necessary to organize their ultimate emigration. This policy of discouragement did not succeed in checking the flow of refugees. In December 1934, by which point another few thousand refugees had immigrated illegally, the Belgian authorities tried again to solve the refugee problem in a repressive way. Police raids tracked the undocumented refugees and they were ordered to leave the country. They had, however, nowhere to go. Finally, these fleeing Jews were granted a temporary sanctuary to enable them to organize their emigration (Caestecker 1993c: 52ff.).

Not only refugees tried still to immigrate to Belgium. Labor migrants also continued to arrive, in particular Poles and Czechs from France. A large number of these unwanted immigrants were stopped at the border. In 1932, 7,030 aliens were stopped from entering Belgium; in 1933 the border guards registered 4,338 times that they stopped aliens from crossing the border; and in the following two years the number further declined (Graph 14). Those migrants who managed to find their way into Belgium without the necessary authorization were arrested as soon as the authorities became aware of their presence. Every year between 2,500 and 3,800 aliens were urged to leave the country (Graph 15).

Undocumented aliens of Southern European origin were brought to the French and Luxembourg borders where they could leave Belgium without any problem. Most other nationalities could not be dumped at these borders, but had to be brought to the German border. The crossing of this border was much more difficult. In keeping with the Belgian-German agreement of 1926, Central and East European expellees could not be forced over the Belgian-German border without the prior consent of the German authorities. A German transit visa was only granted if the returnees had the means to pay the train fare back to their country of origin and had passports. Unwanted immigrants of Eastern and Central European nationality were sent for a few months to the vagrant colonies before they were brought to the border, not only to deter them, but also to improve their chances for crossing the German border and returning to their country of origin. After earning 125 francs in the vagrant colony – in the meantime only few could obtain a passport and a transit visa – they were brought to Verviers where they were set free. The Belgian police advised unwanted aliens who did not have the right papers on how they could outwit the German border guards. As from 1932 onwards, the German border control became much stricter, causing an ever larger number of these expellees to be returned to Belgium. As soon as these aliens were again involved with the Belgian authorities the carousel could start all over. An example was Russian refugee André Rebrik, who left France in the beginning of 1932 because he could no longer make ends meet. He tried his luck in Belgium. Little luck awaited him there. Between 1932 and 1936 he was brought to Verviers five times and spent about one year in Merksplas with regular intervals. When he was not in Merksplas, he survived by the little help he received from the Russian refugee community. In November 1933 Minister of Justice, P.E. Janson, ordered that all destitute aliens wandering around Belgium be brought to police courts to condemn them for vagrancy and consequently to intern them in the vagrant colony. It would, according to Janson, be a sure way to convince unwanted aliens to leave the country forever. It doesn't seem this order was consistently executed (Graph 23). The reasons for this are unclear. It would have been a return to the collective sanction for foreign vagrants applied between 1892 and 1896. Probably cost factors, doubt about the efficiency of such a repressive policy, and most importantly, the changed character of the vagrant colonies which during the 1920s had become less repressive institutions made a repetition of the experiment of 1892 unfeasible. As before, only vagrants of Eastern and Central European nationality were sent to the penal colonies.

For the hard core of undocumented aliens, who insisted on staying in Belgium notwithstanding the vagrant colonies and transport to the border, the authorities had recourse to criminal sanctions. The administrative sanction of expulsion (*renvoi*) was found to be insufficient to convince them to leave Belgium. R. de Foy, the administrator of the Sûreté since August 1933, argued that in order to have efficient control over aliens, prison sentences for illegally immigrated aliens would be necessary. Only harsh repression was considered to be the solution to the problem of undocumented aliens. Illegal immigration should become a criminally triable offence. Most of those undocumented aliens were, according to de Foy, unwilling to return to their country of origin. Living conditions in Belgium, even for undocumented aliens, were still favorable in comparison to what awaited them in their country of origin. No new legislative initiatives were taken in these years as the authorities used a facility of the alien law of 1897 to punish the unwanted return of aliens. An alien who returned to Belgium after expulsion by royal decree could be imprisoned by the court for up to six months because of *rupture de ban*. Although the expulsion by royal decree of aliens who never had acquired residency status was of dubious legality, by 1935 it was the rule that every alien who was *renvoyé* twice and still dared to return was to be expelled by royal decree. A third return could then be criminally prosecuted (Graph 17). While André Rebrik, probably thanks to this refugee status, was never the victim of criminal sanctions, his colleague in misfortune, Alfred Heidler, was. This Estonian draft dodger lived unregistered in Belgium for a while and was arrested in 1930 for vagrancy. He would, in the following years, return regularly to the vagrant colony of Merksplas to be brought each time to Verviers after working some months in the colony. In 1936, after his third stay in Merksplas, the Sûreté decided that they had seen enough of him. They declared Heidler a dangerous alien, although he had never been convicted for any crime except vagrancy. He was expelled by royal decree. The result was minimal. When a few months later, he was arrested again, the court refused to condemn him for *rupture de ban*. He alleged that he never had left the country and the public prosecutor had no proof that he ever did. However, even among these undocumented immigrants who had to spent some time in jail, some remained in Belgium. Even if they wanted to return to their country of origin, most were not able to do so, at least not legally (AAD 75C20 76C21/I and 33C31; ARC 33/8).

Even if these undocumented migrants remained at large, their lot was unenviable. In 1935, according to Kopel Liberman – the most knowledgeable contemporary observer of the Jewish migrant community – there were a few hundred Jewish migrants living illegally in Belgium. These undocumented aliens were employed in the most marginal sections of the labor market which, because of their unhealthy, repulsive, and exhausting working conditions and low pay did not appeal even to other foreign labor, let alone local labor. Others were employed in more mainstream sectors, but all of them were exploited mercilessly by their employers. The administrator of the Sûreté, R. de Foy, was right in his assessment that these undocumented immigrants "preferred" to stay in Belgium rather than return to their country of origin. This statement must, however, be qualified. Among those undocumented immigrants were refugees and stateless persons for whom no return was possible. Others had left their countries of origin so long ago that they no longer had any attachment to those lands. Others did not have the means to go back. All of them endured their hard lot as undocumented aliens in hope of better times (Wiener Library London, ms.Liberman: 11f.) .

The Immigrants of the 1920s in Trouble

Actions against Criminal and "Subversive" Aliens

The repression of politically active immigrants reached its pinnacle during the Depression years. The Sûreté used to their full extent the restrictive powers which the law of 1897 granted the public authorities. During the general strike of 1932, hundreds of immigrants were expelled. The Communist organizations among the migrant communities in the basins of Wallonia were dismantled. A few months later, in January 1933, there was a raid on a meeting of the International Red Aid, which had been organized by Jewish Communists in Brussels. The raid resulted in the collective expulsion of ninety-eight Jewish migrants, Communists, and their sympathizers (Van Doorslaer 1996:95). These were only the most spectacular events; the expulsion of aliens for political reasons continued on a regular basis throughout these years. The number of migrants with residency status expelled for political reasons continued to be high: 380 in 1932 and 350 in 1933 (Graph 16). Due to the fierce repression, the Communists organized only very few immigrants during these years. Only in 1935 would it be manifest that the Communists still had a following within the migrant communities. When in October 1934, after the expulsion of fifty-two Croatian nationalists, diplomatic relations with Yugoslavia improved considerably, the Minister of Foreign Affairs, H. Jaspar, urged the Sûreté to be even more severe. Jaspar insisted that any alien who was a member of a political organization should be expelled, even if the alien did not commit any specific subversive act (AFAB, Correspondance politique Yougoslavie). Not only aliens who disturbed public order or exacerbated diplomatic relations with friendly countries, but all aliens who committed a crime, however minor, were ordered to leave the country, without regard to their length of stay in Belgium or whether they had a place to return to even (Russian "refugees" were expelled). In 1934, notwithstanding the fact that repression had strongly subdued the political activities of migrants, 260 aliens with residency status were expelled for political reasons (Graph 16). Given the commitment of the whole government to accord the Sûreté all the freedom it needed to expel "undesirable" aliens, the authorities were nevertheless hindered by the liberal alien law of 1897. The most irritating impediment to an efficient expulsion policy was that no legal action could be taken against those aliens expelled by royal decree who stayed in the country. The prosecutor had the power only to demand a prison sentence of up to six months for *rupture de ban* if he could prove that an alien expelled by royal decree had returned to Belgium. To remain in Belgium after a royal decree of expulsion was no infraction of the law. Alfred Heidler, and also numerous Communists, could in this way prevent their imprisonment.

On the first of February 1933 Minister of Justice P.E. Janson introduced a bill to change the alien law of 1897, and enable the authorities to proceed against all expelled aliens who were still in the country. The Communist, as well as the Socialist MPs, contested this bill on grounds that the Sûreté should be subject to some kind of control. The bill was defeated in Parliament (PHK 1934:1540 and 1639). This defeat was strongly resented by the government since it considered an extension of its powers to be necessary to deal with "undesirable" aliens. Another attempt to increase the efficiency of alien policy was to transfer the Sûreté from the Ministry of Justice to the Ministry of Internal Affairs. The latter department, which was responsible for public order, had the police force within its competence, and the institutional transfer would give the Sûreté a direct link with those who were to execute its orders. Due to the opposition of Socialist and Liberal MPs who feared a political police the Sûreté remained under the Minister of Justice (BS 1934:3309 and 3968). Due to the weight liberal values carried in the Belgian Parliament, the promoters of an offensive against dangerous and in particular against subversive aliens could not implement any changes in alien legislation. In nationality legislation they were more successful. The fact that a number of foreign Communists were able to protect themselves against expulsion by acquiring Belgian nationality stirred up bad feelings among the authorities. The authorities alleged that the Communists used the acquisition of Belgian nationality as part of a deliberate strategy to protect themselves against expulsion. In particular during the strike of 1932, the conservative press fulminated against the Communists of foreign origin who had acquired Belgian nationality and against whom the Sûreté stood powerless. To make an end to these abuses the authorities had to be able to revoke Belgian nationality. The legislative, but also the judicial branch of the state, took initiatives against the Communist danger. While in the 1920s the courts apparently had hardly exercised their veto power over Belgian-born aliens who opted for Belgian nationality, in the 1930s the judiciary made use of their right to turn down options for Belgian nationality by Communists. In 1931 the *Tribunal de première instance* in Antwerp turned down the option application of Israël Akkerman, a Pole born in Belgium and a militant Communist, "because he had provided insufficient evidence of his attachment to the country and the Belgian people." The option application of the Italian Communist, Jacques Grippa, was also turned down by the *Tribunal de première instance* in Liège for analogous reasons. Jaques Grippa appealed against this ruling and won; he became Belgian (Grippa 1988:26ff.). Israël Akkerman's appeal was less successful. On 9 July 1934, the Brussels Court of Appeals agreed with the *Tribunal de première instance* that membership in the PCB was a shortcoming in the duties of the Belgian citizen (Van Doorslaer 1996:169f.). The legislature was in agreement with the judicial power: being Communist and Belgian was incompatible. In 1934, notwithstanding opposition from the Socialists and Communists, a law was voted to revoke the Belgian nationality of Belgians of foreign origin who were seriously remiss in their duties as Belgian citizens (PHS 1934:1186f.; PHK 1934:1814f.). In the explanatory memorandum, the government pointed to Nazi activists and to Communists as candidates for denationalization. In order to keep the procedure, short the ruling would be made by the Court of Appeals directly (BS 1934:4242; Pabst 1964:294f.).[1]

The call for extended discretionary powers over the aliens for political reasons, disappeared when the Van Zeeland government took office. The new Minister of Justice, the Socialist E. Soudan, made much less use of the possibility of expelling "subversive" aliens; in 1935 only about a hundred aliens with residency status were expelled for political reasons. Aliens committing offenses, however minor, were still expelled. In his dealing with "subversive" immigrants, Soudan returned to the policy of the early 1920s: membership in political organizations was not forbidden; immigrants could even attend political meetings but political propaganda remained strictly forbidden. If an alien did not respect the conditions of Belgian hospitality he would be expelled (IEV, Vandervelde Correspondance, 1935). The number of aliens organized by the Communist party increased quickly. In August 1935, a few months after the repression against foreign Communists had abated, the popular front policy was adopted by the international Communist movement. This was a radical change in strategy. The Socialists were again considered partners in the struggle. A few months later the Communist unions were disbanded and all Communist immigrants had to join the Socialist unions (Morelli 1988:25; Van Doorslaer 1996:113ff.).

A Political Offensive Against the Immigrants

The economic downturn caused real hardship among the immigrants of the 1920s. It brought about a considerable change in the occupational pattern of foreign labor. The trend towards the impoverishment of the socio-professional structure at the turn of the decade intensified in the following years. Mining retained an ever larger share of foreign manpower, while domestic services nearly monopolized foreign female labor. There were, however, some exceptions. In the hotel sector, aliens remained among the most qualified and best paid personnel. This was certainly the case in the summer, but even outside the tourist season these aliens were employed in the hotels. In the quarries most of the unqualified workers of foreign nationality were fired, while qualified foreign personnel kept their jobs in this industry. In other industrial sectors, immigrants were mostly the first to be fired. The chemical and glass industries noted a spectacular fall in foreign labor: two thirds of the foreign labor was dismissed. The iron and steel industry fired its foreign labor en masse and retained only a few thousand immigrants on their payrolls. In contrast to the 1920s, most of the immigrants working in industry had been joined by their spouses and children. In construction this was not the case. Construction retained only very few of the foreign workers who had been recruited at the end of the 1920s. The contractors of large public works in particular, continued to use a number of migrants. These migrants were mostly single and of Italian or (to a much lesser extent) of Yugoslavian nationality. Agriculture still employed a small number of foreign farm hands.

Another group of migrants who had found a livelihood outside mining in the 1920s, the Jewish migrants, were also hard hit by the Depression. During the Depression, the fate of all the industries in Antwerp and Brussels where thousand of Jewish migrants had been making a living in the 1920s was very similar. The mercurial character of the demand for morocco leather bags, fur products, women's hats, and diamonds became obvious in a dramatic way. The Jewish migrants who had worked in this industry in the twenties became either outworkers or had to search for a new livelihood during the Depression. Few Jewish migrants succeeded in conquering new markets. The Jewish migrant entrepreneurs made a name for themselves in lower quality furs. They specialized in working with inexpensive rabbit fur. Until the end of the twenties rabbit skins received only a first treatment in Belgium, after which they were exported to Great Britain for the finishing work whereby they were made into felt hats. During the thirties, the Jewish entrepreneurs performed finishing work in Belgium. Survival for the immigrants in all these sectors was only possible by means of widespread self-exploitation in small, extremely flexible production units. The independent outworker, with all that this implied for the worsening of labor conditions, played an increasingly central role in this sector during the depression years. Not only the household industry, but also the vending trade offered an opening for Jewish migrants during the economic depression. The Jewish migrants living in Brussels and Antwerp flocked to the distribution part of the "Jewish" economy for an alternative livelihood. The "Jewish" economy offered, through kinship and ethnic contacts, a means of survival for these migrants. In 1935, at the nadir of the crisis, at least 2,500 Jewish migrants were peddlers. Most were Polish Jews. Nearly two thousand Polish migrants were peddling during the Depression. Along with these Poles, a few hundred Russian Jews, together with dozens of Czechoslovakian Jews, found a livelihood in this trade sector. The great majority of these Jewish peddlers had arrived in Belgium after 1926, of whom more than half entered after 1928. It was precisely those recent migrants who had been hit extremely hard by the Depression. The vending trade was their last resort. Outwork and peddling offered the Jewish migrant a means of survival during those years. The Jewish migrants did not get rich; on the contrary, most could hardly make ends meet.

Non-Jewish migrants who became unemployed were not able to make use of the economic structures of the "Jewish" economy. If no Belgian employer wanted to engage them, there was nothing left for them to do but apply for welfare or to go back to their country of origin (Caestecker 1993c:121,126ff.). Thousands of immigrants had already returned – most voluntarily, some by force – to their country of origin by 1933.The foreign population stabilized. The massive return movement in 1931 and 1932 was halted. Most aliens still in the country had decided to stay despite the economic downturn. Those who stayed in Belgium but had lost their jobs had few occupational opportunities. Women could still find jobs as domestic servants. The wives and daughters of foreign workers, as well as female refugees from Nazi Germany could earn an income, albeit minimal, in this way. The mines also continued to offer some job-opportunities (AMSAC HIII 4025). Applying for welfare was another possibility. Municipal discretion and the very low benefits meant that this was not an easy solution.

Given the persistent high rate of unemployment among Belgian workers the aliens' lasting presence became the subject of increasing agitation. The worsening economic and political atmosphere caused many migrants to find it advisable to apply for Belgian nationality. This would enable them to secure their livelihood. Others hoped, in this manner, to enjoy the full advantages of the Belgian social state. It was the only way to obtain a pension of any worth. For some of the immigrants unemployment benefits were also only obtainable in this way. Towards the end of 1931 more than two thousand requests for naturalization had to be processed. The Minister of Justice, P.E. Janson, spoke of a multitude of applicants who had shown hardly any evidence of assimilation. They had only applied for naturalization "with the wholly personal intention of enjoying the advantages of the welfare state which were reserved for Belgians." The authorities, by a tightening of the naturalization procedure, would be able to bring about lasting savings. In May 1931, Minister of Justice Janson brought forward a bill to enforce a "strict selection procedure" among aspiring Belgians (PBK). His bill called for a twenty-year period of residence for *grande naturalisation* and a period of fifteen years for ordinary naturalization. The bill was somewhat toned down in Parliament, a ten – or fifteen-year period of residence was required, respectively, for ordinary or *grande naturalisation*. The Socialist (and the Communist) MPs were the only ones to vote against this bill. This tightening of the criteria for naturalization by the law of 14 December 1932 made it impossible for thousands of immigrants who had settled in Belgium in the twenties to apply for Belgian nationality (PHVA 1931:624, PHK 1932:1350, PHS 1932:1413ff. and 1455).

Until 1933 the authorities refrained from any intervention in the personnel policy of employers. Curtailing the employers' autonomy in deciding who to hire was not deemed necessary. Foreign labor was of little concern to the government. The number of aliens was limited and, in addition, they were considered essential for the economy as they did those jobs in heavy industry which local labor shunned. Intervening in the labor market to remove foreign labor was not considered appropriate. It would not reduce unemployment among Belgians. In addition, protectionist measures on the labor market could have negative repercussions for Belgian labor working abroad. The reluctance to expel foreign labor in the first years of the Depression was thus not a matter of legal possibilities; even foreign labor who had not yet acquired residency status could stay put, at least as long as they had a job (ARA, Jaspar, 81).

While the government had no intention of curtailing the right of foreign labor to work, the fact that immigrants were entitled to receive unemployment benefits was considered unnecessarily generous. Indeed, aliens could join an unemployment fund without any restriction. Benefits equal to that of the Belgians depended on a reciprocity agreement. Belgium had reached bilateral agreements with most emigration countries. As a result most immigrants could receive full-fledged unemployment benefits. Some unlucky nationalities (e.g., the Italians, the Russians, including the refugees from Russia) received much lower unemployment relief because there was no reciprocity agreement with their country of origin. The Minister of Finance, H. Jaspar, believed that aliens should not be entitled to full-fledged unemployment benefits. He considered this generosity contrary to Belgian interests. It entailed a considerable expense to the Belgian treasury which, according to Jaspar, in no way matched the expenses of those emigration countries for Belgian citizens. The legislation of 31 May 1933 denied aliens the right to unemployment benefits. Exemptions were made for those countries with larger numbers of Belgian emigrants. French (including Algerians), Dutch, and Luxembourg citizens could still join an unemployment fund and obtain the same benefits as the Belgians (AAD 109C92). The exclusion of most foreign labor from unemployment insurance was contested by the trade unions. Refusing foreign labor benefits was not only unjust, it would also negatively influence the working conditions of Belgian labor as foreign labor would be forced to accept any work conditions in order to earn a subsistence income. The unions' protest was to no avail. The exclusion of aliens was considered the easiest way to diminish unemployment expenditures. The unions, Socialist and Christian Democratic alike, quickly felt the backlash of this measure. The mass of immigrants left the unions.

While until 1933 the trade unions insisted upon the unionization of foreign labor and not so much upon their removal, this changed in 1934. Not only the deepening depression, but also the exclusion of foreign labor from unemployment insurance and the resulting departure of the immigrants from the unions meant that the unions complained more and more about the very bad working conditions and the low wages the immigrants accepted. The unions called for government intervention. The hiring of immigrants had to be regulated, and the autonomy of the employers had to be curtailed. Another means proposed by the unions to halt the negative influence of immigrants on working conditions was to repatriate destitute immigrants. By the end of 1934 both unions advocated a gradual removal of foreign labor in order to alleviate unemployment among Belgian labor. The unions totally neglected the interests of foreign labor. L. Lazzarelli, the secretary of the Italian Socialists in exile in Belgium, expressed his disgust in private for the attitude of the Belgian comrades and wrote that in the campaign against foreign labor those most responsible were the Socialist party and trade unions (Morelli 1985:621). The xenophobic discourse of the unions doomed any campaign to unionize the immigrants to certain failure. The contradiction between the union's protectionist policy and their rarely proclaimed solidarity with foreign labor was too manifest. In the hotel sector, the unions' xenophobia was especially virulent. This reached its climax in 1934 when the Socialist and Christian Democratic unions of the hotel workers demanded that all foreign hotel personnel who had been in Belgium less than five years be dismissed and expelled. The virulent attack by the unions on the hotel sector was due to the organizations of Belgian hotel personnel independent of the union. The *Association Nationale des Employés de l'Industrie Hôtelière*, the *Centrale des Fédérations des Ouvriers de l'Industrie Hôtelière*, and *L'Union Professionele Belge (le Prévoyante) des Garçons, Restaurateurs* who agitated mainly, though not exclusively, against the aliens who took the best jobs in the hotel sector explain the exceptional attitude of the unions. Qualified Belgian hotel personnel, some of whom alleged that they had been fired in France because of nationalist reasons, demanded priority for themselves. The very vocal professional groups formulated this demand in a nationalistic discourse; it was a national shame that the hotels employed only aliens for the top functions. Belgians were certainly qualified enough to replace them. The reaction of the authorities to these complaints was limited. The Sûreté investigated some of them, looking first at the legal status of the aliens. It turned out that almost all foreign labor in the first-class hotels were long-time residents of Belgium and had acquired residency status. They were thus protected and no further action was taken. The few immigrants with only a temporary residence permit were ordered to leave the country (AAD 33C307) .

While Belgian hotel personnel had little success in protecting themselves against their competitors of foreign nationality, the medical profession assured themselves a watertight protection. As mentioned before, the law of 21 May 1929 made the right to exercise the professions dependent on a Belgian degree in secondary education or its equivalent. A Belgian university degree granted to foreigners was only meant for export. Royal decrees in 1933 and 1934 stipulated the conditions for foreign doctors, dentists, and pharmacists to be able to exercise their profession: only aliens with an exceptional scientific record or whose knowledge could be useful to the country were to be granted access to the medical professions. In other words, foreign doctors, dentists, and pharmacists, even those who had done all their studies in Belgium, were prohibited from exercising their profession in Belgium (BS 1933:786f. and 1934:3220 f.)

In the nationalistic plea of the first crisis years, all aliens were treated alike and Polish miners, leather workers, or merchants were all seen as excessive competition in a time of economic difficulties. The fact that some migrants happened to be Jews was not relevant; the agitation was directed at the general category of aliens.[2] This agitation became much more virulent, however, when the presence of aliens outside heavy industry came up for discussion. The presence of foreigners in artisanal sectors, in which many Jewish migrants were outworkers or employers, was the target of strong criticism. The hostility against this foreign intrusion was argued in the following manner: these aliens took work away not only from the Belgian workers but, as employers, they also decided over the fate of these sectors, with disastrous results. From 1930 onwards, the economic sectors in which aliens had influence declined steadily. The Jewish migrants were blamed for this deterioration. They had disrupted the market with the introduction of inexpensive goods of lesser quality. In this way they strangled these sectors. Not only did the migrants push the Belgian competitors out of the market by accepting small profit margins and starvation wages, they also did not refrain from dishonest business practices (such as tax evasion, selling of stolen goods, and disregard for social legislation). The aliens monopolized not only production, but also distribution. These sectors were conquered systematically by an actual foreign Mafia. The accusations against the migrants active in the distribution of these goods were similar to those mentioned before: Belgians were cheated out of their daily living by the dishonest practices of these immigrants. The aliens sold their goods mostly at the markets or door-to-door, a trade sector in which it was very easy to cheat.

The agitation against the foreign Mafia was limited to that of a number of professional groups, which sought protection against the severe blows they had to bear during the crisis years. Belgian merchants stated obstinately that they were powerless against the ruthless competition of the Jewish market vendors and peddlers. The agitation these circles provoked was linked with the weak structure of Belgian small trade. The market vendors and peddlers who tried to enlarge their share of the market by lower prices affected the already feeble position of Belgian retailers. The criticism by established merchants of foreign salesmen fell within the framework of an old campaign against hawking. Since the nineteenth century, shopkeepers had strongly criticized this type of trade. While the peddler, who worked in the markets, had to pay only a limited market fee and avoided any other costs, the established merchant paid heavy fiscal and rental costs. After 1930, many shopkeepers saw their revenues decrease. In search of a solution they pointed to the increasing number of peddlers. That there were many aliens among these market vendors and peddlers, but more importantly that these aliens mostly sold goods which the established merchants considered to be their monopoly, caused severe criticism. In this case it even involved products which were produced by migrants. Their profit margins were so low, not only for the market vendors and peddlers, but also for those who produced the goods that the established Belgian merchants were not able to respond to it. This ethnic connection meant that the protest by Belgian merchants coincided with that of Belgian manufacturers and even the unions. Together they petitioned for a frontal attack on the distribution channel of the Jewish economy in order to clean up the whole sector.

The agitation against the foreign peddlers was fueled in the early years of emigration from Nazi Germany by the myth of a massive invasion of German refugees. The arrival of a few thousand political militants and Jews after Hitler came to power was not looked upon with much serenity. Biased observers exaggerated this immigration to grotesque proportions. In addition they presented the motivation behind these immigrants leaving Germany in a bad light. They alleged that many failed merchants, criminals, and paupers left Nazi Germany to settle in Belgium. The authorities were notified to be on their guard; there were quite a few profiteers among the refugees from Germany. These warnings to the authorities continued in spite of the strict refugee policy. As we mentioned earlier, most Jewish refugees from Germany stayed in Belgium only for a few months, the time needed to organize their emigration. The small number of refugees who received residence permits were mostly denied participation in Belgian socio-economic life. Notwithstanding this, the Jewish refugees were perceived, already in the first half of the thirties, as a symbol in this economically motivated anti-foreigner discourse.

As we mentioned above, the economic crisis and the decision to exclude immigrants from unemployment insurance forced many Jewish migrants into trade, for the most part as market vendors or peddlers. This was not only clearly discernible in Antwerp and Brussels, but Jewish merchants also attempted to build up a Belgian clientele outside these urban agglomerations. This crisis phenomenon had obviously already begun somewhat earlier than the summer of 1933, but the exclusion from unemployment insurance in May 1933 accelerated the process. In any case, the link between the two phenomena – the arrival of Jewish refugees and the increase in Jewish peddlers – was made very quickly. The huge amount of media attention on the refugee question meant that the increase of Jewish peddlers or market vendors was immediately associated with the immigration of refugees from Nazi Germany. This confusion between refugees and migrants meant that the professional shifts of the Jewish migrants were seen as a new development with important consequences. The myth of economic threat not only from already established migrants, but also from a continuous immigration of Jews from Germany meant that the established merchants demanded protective regulations with more insistence (Caestecker 1993c:131ff.).

Few Provisions for Immigrants:

In 1933 the League of Nations took the initiative to convene a conference to establish an international status for refugees. The Nansen Office, a branch of the League, argued that the Russian "refugees" had to be exempted from the increasingly restrictive alien legislation to which immigrants were subject all over Europe. "Refugees" should be granted the same privileges as the immigrants of the most favored nationalities in order to facilitate their insertion in the host country. Also no "refugee" who was granted residence should ever be expelled. Given the absence of a country of origin which was willing to receive them, to expel "refugees" would only result in their illegal entrance to another country. This would disturb international relations and offered no lasting solution to the refugee problem. An international convention with binding recommendations would persuade the countries of asylum to follow a policy favorable to their Russian "refugees". The Belgian Minister of Foreign Affairs, P. Hymans, was on the same wavelength as the Nansen office. He agreed that something had to be done to alleviate the tragic lot of the "refugees". Aliens in Belgium were subject to increasing discrimination, and the lot of Russian "refugees" was even worse than that of most other immigrants. The impossibility of establishing a bilateral agreement with their country of origin meant that they were excluded from the advantages of reciprocity (for example, full benefit of pensions and unemployment insurance). Dozens of "refugees" were expelled each year, just like any other immigrant, mostly for minor offenses. They were "refugees" who had, however, nowhere to return. Hymans favored a generous attitude towards these "refugees". There were only a few thousand Russian "refugees" in Belgium and as they were here to stay, he argued, one had to strive for their successful integration in Belgian society. The basis for granting equal rights to aliens, reciprocity with the country of origin, was not attainable. Hymans argued that the Russian "refugees" were a case apart – unprecedented conditions had caused their flight – and totally new measures inspired by humanitarian considerations should be designed to reach out to them. Hymans proposed adhering unconditionally to the international convention proposed by the Nansen office.

This generous appeal was not appreciated very much by the other ministers. The arguments of this opposition were of a pragmatic nature. The convention could jeopardize the endeavor of the government to cut expenses. State expenditures had to remain under severe restrictions given the deflationary policy. Reaching a binding international agreement was hence not advisable. For some, assigning the Russian "refugees" the status of most favored nationality would be too generous. There were special circumstances in which the citizens of the neighboring countries were granted exceptional rights, for example in the field of unemployment insurance, and these reasons were not valid for the "refugees". The Sûreté was also not eager to grant "refugees" exceptional treatment; they insisted on retaining the possibility of expelling any alien, even "refugees". They argued that the radical decision of expelling a "refugee" would only be taken in exceptional circumstances anyway. To deprive the authorities of this ultimate sanction could endanger the stability of the regime. The most important criticism was that signing the convention would only increase unwanted immigration, because Russian refugees now residing in other countries would flood into Belgium. The Minister of Foreign Affairs retorted that the convention would only apply to "refugees" legally residing in Belgium and anyway Belgium was armed by its immigration legislation to refuse new refugees access. Although the convention was indeed only applicable to "refugees" residing legally in the country, Minister Hymans had to give in to the opposition against adhering unconditionally to the convention. The Belgian delegation to the Geneva conference got instructions not to harm Belgian interests. Belgium signed the convention, but with an important proviso. The "refugees" could not benefit from the advantages granted to the Dutch, French, and Luxembourg immigrants and expulsion of "refugees" remained possible. Although there were no tangible benefits of the convention of 1933 for the Russian "refugees", it did cause an increasing awareness among policy makers that "refugees" were an exceptional category of immigrants (AFAB 12,178). This change of mentality is to be observed in particular within the Christian Democratic trade union. This union, which sought adamantly throughout the Depression to replace foreign labor with Belgian labor, pleaded from 1934 onwards to spare the Russian "refugees". A consensus was growing that the "refugees" were to stay and that restrictive measures imposed on immigrants to make them return to their country of origin could not have the desired effect with "refugees".

While there was a growing awareness about the exceptional lot of "refugees" the expansion of repatriation policy was also an indication that the authorities took into account the bottlenecks in their restrictive policy. Following the decision to cut unemployed foreign labor from the dole in May 1933, the Minister of Justice asked the Minister of Labor for the names of the unemployed aliens whose right to receive unemployment benefits had been revoked. Rather than putting those indigent aliens on relief, they ought to be expelled. The Minister of Labor passed three hundred names to the Sûreté Publique. Fifty of those immigrants had not yet acquired residency status and were ordered to leave the country. It was legally impossible to expel the other 250. As long as these unemployed immigrants did not commit any infraction or could not be arrested for vagrancy, their expulsion was legally unjustified. An investigation was ordered to look into the means of livelihood of these 250 aliens. Those who did not have a real home or were begging in order to survive were brought before a police court and sent to a vagrant colony. After serving their sentence they were expelled by royal decree. Most of the unemployed immigrants could not be forced to leave. The administrator of the Sûreté, R. de Foy, stated clearly that it was "contrary to the Belgian judicial system to expel as a preventive measure, besides such a procedure would also damage the laws of hospitality and humanity." In addition such an expulsion would be ineffective since the majority of these unemployed aliens were not citizens of neighboring countries. The neighboring countries would refuse to accept these destitute aliens and send them back to Belgium. Only their voluntary departure was possible. To stimulate these immigrants to return to their country of origin, the Sûreté proposed to finance the repatriation of aliens who wanted to return. Since the nineteenth century repatriation had been an item on the budget of the Ministry of Justice, but the sum allotted to the repatriation of aliens in the 1920s and the first years of the 1930s (25,000 francs) was derisory and was only to be used for insane, sick, and very young aliens. The Council of Ministers asked Parliament for an additional credit of 200,000 francs for repatriation on 16 March 1934 and Parliament consented to include this sum in the Ministry of Justice's budget for 1934. This still limited budget enabled the repatriation of a few hundred aliens, in particular Poles. Although it did not cause a great change in the return movement, it was a clear and decisive change of course (AAD 109C92). Even though the return was officially voluntarily, some pressure was exerted by the communal authorities as the return of destitute immigrants alleviated their welfare budgets. Some municipalities even voluntarily contributed a third of the costs of repatriation of the clients of their welfare department. It was financially more economical to co-finance their repatriation than to continue supporting them. Employers were also asked to contribute to the financing of repatriation, but they refused to do so. Only in March 1935, when the authorities strongly pressured the mining industry to fire more of their foreign labor, were these employers willing to do so. They accepted responsibility for one third of the costs of repatriation of their former employees (Municipal Archive Genk, annual reports 1933-1935). In 1935 the repatriation budget of the Ministry of Justice remained the same (225,000 francs), but radical changes in the alien policy necessitated a request for additional credits (PBK 1935/5).

The Struggle for Foreign Labor in the Mining Sector

In the 1920s a few mines had embarked on a far-reaching multicultural strategy to turn their foreign personnel into loyal and industrious workers. Already in the first years of the economic downturn, these companies saw new constraints arise in their multicultural endeavor. Crucial in this respect were changes in the emigration policy of the countries of origin. In Poland financial support of the policy to counter the so-called "denationalization" of the emigrants was curtailed due to budgetary constraints. The state subsidy for the Polish mission in Belgium was deleted in 1932. In the same year, the three Polish schools in Hainaut were shut down. These schools were considered too expensive by the Polish Ministry of Foreign Affairs. A new discourse accompanied the tapering off of this educational network. The Polish emigrants had to acquiesce to a lasting stay abroad due to the Depression. The children of the emigrants should invest in their future in Belgium. Secondary education would open more interesting occupational opportunities for them than just mining. Upon their return to Poland, their experience as qualified workers would be of great value to the country. The provision of Polish courses, a few hours a week, together with a Polish youth movement, was considered sufficient for retaining the Polishness of the children. Some Polish schools in Limburg were closed down in 1933. The director of Winterslag forestalled this by increasing his financial support; the mine paid the salary of one of the teachers. This financial arrangement was only able to postpone the total downfall of the Polish schools for one year. The director of Winterslag was furious when, in 1934, the decision was made to close down "its" Polish school. The Polish house with its twenty-five rooms, which up to that point had housed the Polish school and was also the meeting point for

Polish social life, was shut down. From then on the Polish organizations were no longer supported by the mine (Caestecker 1991:555ff.). The Czechoslovakian authorities did not disappoint Winterslag. The Czech school remained open until the outbreak of the Second World War, and Winterslag financed it generously (AFAP 10,605; KS 210/92)

In the 1920s managers of most mining companies had already considered the implementation of an ambitious multicultural strategy unnecessary. They believed more in the power of assimilation to make foreign labor decide to stay. However, all managers of mine companies considered pastoral care for foreign labor an essential ethnic facility. In the 1930s pastoral care was still provided by Polish priests. The economic downturn, however, caused most mining companies to diminish their subsidies to the mission considerably. The material situation of the Polish clergy worsened considerably. The general refusal of the employers to continue their generous subsidies was not only the consequence of the economic downturn and the diminishing number of foreign workers, it also reflected the assimilationist strategy of most of the mining companies in Wallonia. A permanently present Polish priest was considered a hindrance to the assimilation of the Polish children (AAG II2 and 47; BdL 181). While the employers hoped for the assimilation of their foreign workers, the Belgian workers and their unions insisted upon their dismissal.

Rising unemployment in the mining sector together with a decline in real wages caused serious discontent among the miners. By May 1932 sporadic strikes broke out in the Borinage. The dismissal of some strikers and news about another five hundred redundancies in the basin caused tensions to rise. The regional miners' union called a strike, demanding stabilization of wages and the sharing of available work among local labor. The strike was a great success. All the miners walked off the job. The walkout quickly spread beyond the Borinage; all the other basins, including briefly the Limburg basin, joined the strike. Not only miners but also metal and glass workers struck. Carried away by its rank and file, the Socialist union, in agreement with some Walloon Christian Democrats, called a general strike. For a few days the strike even had insurrectional aspects, especially in the basin of Charleroi where the castle of E. Coppée, one of the leading Belgian capitalists was burned down. By the middle of July, the unions regained control over the movement. Concessions by employers in several industries, induced by the government, along with royal intervention led to the strike being called off by July 18. Only the miners' unions, due to the insistence of their rank and file, continued to strike. In September when this strike was also called off, the miners had obtained a wage increase of only one percent. The employers had agreed to redistribute work among labor by firing miners beyond the age of retirement, generalizing partial unemployment, and looking into the possibility of replacing the foreign miners with Belgians. The employers had also agreed that no sanctions would be taken against the strikers once they returned to work.

The leadership of the Socialist miners' union, which in April 1932 had still considered the replacement of the foreign labor as an unrealistic demand, dropped all its reservations during the strike and immediately joined with the Christian Democratic union to demand the removal of the foreign miners (ARMA rC22). Throughout the strike the employers had agreed to look into this problem without making any tangible concessions. The government, which had an important influence on all the settlements during this strike, did not support this trade union demand for foreign policy reasons and because of its reluctance to intervene in the personnel policy of industry. The government proposal accepted by employers and unions foresaw only a commission which would look into the redistribution of work. At least on that point the unions had hoped that they could walk away with a concession. That this was an important issue was clear from the very start of the strike. On July 4 the Socialist MP for the Borinage, L. Piérard, had clarified this demand in an open letter to the King in the Socialist newspaper *Le Peuple* in which he stated "although we are internationalists, we demand that one think first about our own jobless and breadless". In fact the strike had started in the Borinage with the slogan: "sharing of the available work among local labor."This was directed against foreign as well as Flemish labor. The platform of the miners' unions referred only to the removal of the aliens. This xenophobic demand was well received among the rank and file. During the first weeks of the strike the slogan "Down with aliens, down with immigrants in the mines" was frequently heard (AAG III1). L. Piérard's article aroused considerable controversy. The Communists denounced the Socialists: this nationalist demand was a striking example of social-fascism. Also strong opposition was voiced within the international Socialist movement. The political and syndical organizations of the Italian Socialists protested strongly. They intervened to prevent any further articles in the Socialist press against foreign labor *(Belgische Vakbeweging* 1936:256). The leaders of the Polish Socialist Trade Union (KCZZ), Zulawski and Kwapinski, also asked for clarifications. Heronimek, the representative of the KCZZ for the Polish migrants in France, left for Brussels to investigate the case. Most Belgian Socialists considered Piérard's letter a grave error. Although no rectification in *Le Peuple* followed, numerous Socialists privately expressed their disagreement with this letter. The letter was hushed up, nobody wanted to discuss it in public. The demand of the miners' union to distribute work among the locals, however, was defended. The president of the Socialist trade union, C. Mertens, explained that Belgian employers used the immigrants to put pressure on wages and working conditions. The employers, he argued, had hired a lot of miners of different nationalities in the last months, immigrants who had been expelled from France. These immigrants accepted wages lower than the ones which were traditionally agreed upon. This not only worsened working conditions, but also aggravated unemployment among Belgians. Mertens claimed that the demand of the miners' union that the employers no longer replace Belgians with immigrants was not directed against the migrants who had been living in Belgium for a long time, but only against the aliens who are being used by the companies to worsen the lot of Belgian workers . Only single migrants, especially those who had been hired recently, should leave in order to make room for unemployed Belgians. Mertens considered this demand justified and not contrary to the principle of international solidarity. The KCZZ accepted these arguments at face value, as they were useful for refuting the argument of Polish conservative forces that the Belgian comrades of the Polish Socialists were insistent on firing Polish labor. The Polish Socialist Trade Union stated that the Belgian working class was fully entitled to react against the use of unconscious forces within the emigration to worsen their working conditions *(Robotnik* 3 and 4.8.1932). Due to the international attention given to the xenophobic article of L.Piérard, such articles no longer appeared. The tone of the articles in the Socialist press changed from the second half of July onwards. Aliens were no longer singled out. Although it was still contended that the manipulation of the immigrants by the employers constituted a danger for the Belgian working class, it was the solidarity of these immigrants who were striking with their Belgian comrades that was highlighted (APCB grève de 1932).

During the more than two-month-long strike, the legally and economically vulnerable position of foreign labor was evident. These aliens, who were mostly non-unionized, received no strike pay. Legally residing immigrants could apply for welfare just like the Belgians. Success depended, however, on the discretion of the municipal authorities, who were reluctant to grant aliens any financial support. The embassies exerted considerable pressure on the municipal authorities to grant their unemployed citizens welfare. In August 1932 the Minister of the Interior even had to state clearly in a circular letter that legally residing aliens should receive welfare. If immigrants obtained support, it was usually less than that of the Belgians (APCB, grève de 1932;AFAF, Europe 1930-1940 Belgique, 223). In addition, as most aliens were living in company housing, they were much more vulnerable to direct employer pressure. The Sûreté also continued their crackdown on politically undesirable aliens. Hundreds of immigrants were expelled. During the strike about 250 members of the PCB were expelled. The expulsions went far beyond these politically organized immigrants. Any immigrant who was a bit too active in the strike was liable to be expelled *(Wiarus Polski* 15 and 19.8.1932). Eviction and expulsion, but even more so the pauperizing effect of the lasting strike, led several thousand migrants to return to their country of origin (AMSAC HIII4205; Castiau 1973:8).

After the strike there was again near full employment in the mining industry as the long period of inactivity had diminished the stocks. Only the basin of the Borinage with its expensive industrial coal was unable to re-engage all of the miners. Demand for industrial coal was slackening and strong competition in that market, which included the Limburg basin, meant that the vulnerable Borinage could not produce at full strength. A regional joint commission was established to see how the mining industry could distribute the work among the local miners. Belgian miners beyond the age of retirement and single aliens would be fired. An important condition, however, was set by the employers: the single aliens were only fired if the necessary manpower could be found among unemployed Belgians. The main argument against replacing the aliens with unemployed Belgian miners was that, as soon as the economic situation improved, the Belgians would leave those mines for the mines in which they preferred to work. Some would even leave the mining industry altogether. The rehiring practice in the Borinage was the touchstone as to how far the mining companies would accommodate the demands of organized labor. Despite the promise not to retaliate, the Belgians against whom legal proceedings were taken during the strike as well as all single aliens who had not worked during the strike, were not re-hired. The local trade unions were furious and a one-day strike was called. The mining companies gave in; all Belgians were rehired. The sanction against single aliens who had participated in the strike remained valid. The unions were in an awkward situation as they had demanded that preference should be given to Belgian labor by firing the single aliens. Hence they could not really protest the decision of the mining companies not to rehire those aliens, but when single aliens who had worked during the strike were kept on the job the unions' xenophobia was strengthened. The result of the new personnel policy was that, in December 1932, 79 percent of the foreign miners who were working before the strike in the Borinage remained in their jobs (Graph 8). The main problem with replacing the remaining foreign miners in this basin with unemployed Belgian miners was that two-thirds of the aliens were employed in the new mines at the very west of the basin. Bad communications and the unwillingness of the employers to invest in any way in the replacement of aliens with Belgians resulted in very few unemployed Belgian miners being eager to go to those mines. The Walloon miners would probably have to commute weekly to those mines and stay there six days in a hostel to return to their families for only one day a week. Tension between the trade unions and the mine directors arose in particular around the issue of acceptable wage levels. The foreign personnel in the mines in the west of the basin were paid less than their Belgian colleagues in the same mine and the mine directors insisted on pay-

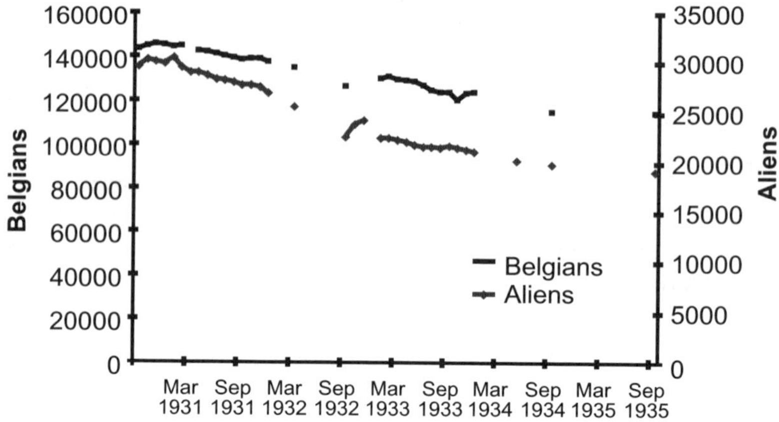

Graph 7 *Belgian and Foreign Miners in the Belgian Mining Industry, September 1930–September 1935*

ing the same low wages to the Belgians who were to replace the immigrants (ARMA rC23; AHCM; CMBo; FEDECHAR and CNMM).

In the winter of 1933 unemployment rose in the other Walloon basins. Here too the dismissal of single miners was demanded by the Socialist as well as the Christian Democratic miners' unions. The unions got strong support from the Minister of Labor, P. Van Isacker. He believed that the dismissal of foreign miners was essential for solving the unemployment problem in the mining industry. He even envisaged a state subsidy covering the transportation costs of unemployed Belgians who went to work in

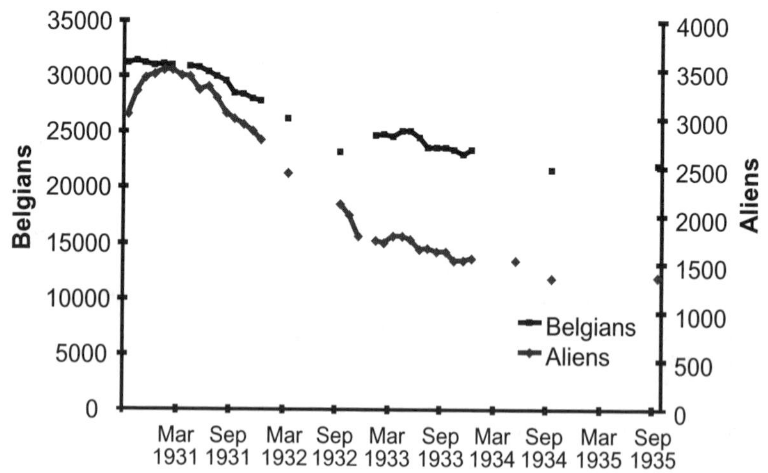

Graph 8 *Belgian and Foreign Miners in the Basin of the Borinage, September 1930–September 1935*

mines far from their hometowns. Van Isacker's motivation was twofold. The dismissal of foreign labor would diminish the unemployment of Belgians and at the same time alleviate the expenses of his department in this domain. He was under very strong pressure within the government to diminish unemployment insurance costs. To shift the burden of unemployment to the aliens was the easiest way to save some money without touching the benefits of his constituencies (PHK 1933:1161; CMBo). Van Isacker's position made the mining companies more willing to replace aliens with unemployed Belgian miners. The companies had obtained considerable economic advantages from the government and they did not want to alienate the authorities. They also realized that their cooperation was necessary to prevent more drastic measures against their foreign personnel. Van Isacker had already threatened legal measures to remove all the aliens. The employers asked for guarantees that Belgians would effectively replace the dismissed aliens. The mining companies also demanded from the government assurances that they would be authorized to recruit foreign labor when the economic situation improved (ACCBS; FEDECHAR). Especially the mining companies in the Limburg basin were anxious to retain their foreign labor as they met a structural need for qualified manpower. When the Sûreté considered repatriating unemployed aliens that were on welfare, the Limburg mining companies insisted that only those unemployed immigrants whom they considered unqualified should be repatriated. Qualified foreign miners, even if they were unemployed, were to be kept in Belgium (ACCA). The continuous pressure of the trade unions, now supported by the Minister of Labor, made a second considerable dent in foreign labor in the Borinage. As Graph 8 illustrates, between March 1933 and September 1934, another 22 percent of the aliens in the Borinage were dismissed. The amount of foreign labor also declined in the other Walloon basins.

In the second half of 1934 the mining companies were no longer willing to fire their foreign labor. They insisted that their remaining foreign workers were mostly qualified miners. A further reduction of foreign labor would aggravate unemployment among Belgians in the mining industry because Belgian ancillary personnel would have to be reduced. The main reason the employers no longer wanted to grant Belgians preferential treatment was that they wanted to secure manpower for the future. The Belgians who replaced foreign laborers would leave the mines at the first opportunity. Foreign labor was much more loyal to the mine. When the economy recovered, the aliens would remain in the mines. Mining companies not only counted on these workers in the short run, they also hoped to use the children of their foreign labor as future manpower (ARMA rC23; AHCM). The trade unions were furious and insisted upon further replacement of foreign labor. Minister of Labor Van

Isacker ordered an investigation into the feasibility of replacing the single foreign miners by unemployed Belgians in Hainaut. The report of this investigation stimulated the government to pursue this option. There were about six thousand unemployed Belgian miners and a similar number of single aliens. In order to assure replacement, transportation means had to be improved (especially between the Borinage and the basin of Charleroi), and the Belgian miners who refused to take the jobs of discharged immigrants had to be denied welfare. The report also pointed out that not only should the aliens be dismissed, but the authorities should also prevent them from receiving welfare. The dismissal of those aliens should therefore be followed by their expulsion. Retaliation against Belgians abroad also had to be prevented and international agreements had to be respected. This meant that only certain nationalities would be subject to such measures (ARMA rC23).

State Intervention in the Market, 1935

The Theunis government followed a strict deflationary policy which aimed at strengthening the competitive position of Belgian industry. At the margins of this policy, measures were taken to remedy the social consequences of the economic crisis to some extent. Only the effects on the Belgian population were taken into consideration. By pushing immigrants out of the economy, Belgians could be given more opportunity to find a decent livelihood. The first Van Zeeland government which took power on 23 March 1935 with important Socialist participation, pursued this policy. Although this cabinet broke new ground in state policy, it did not innovate in alien policy. The design of the Theunis cabinet to forcibly exclude immigrants from economic life through state intervention was not altered.

Undermining the "Jewish" Economy, the Peddlers' Law

Since the onset of the Depression Belgian retailers had asked, with increasing insistence, for protective regulations against the threat to which their businesses were exposed by the peddlers. The government yielded to their demands in 1935. With the legislation of 13 January 1935, control was established over peddlers and market vendors, and the state took over what had been an almost exclusively municipal competence. Every market vendor or peddler had to apply to the central authorities for a vendor's license. This regulation sought to guarantee greater control over the vending trade. The authorities would be able to punish the accumulation of unemployment aid and peddling more easily. Vendors who did not fulfill their fiscal obligations would also be easier to identify. In any case, the Treasury had an acute need for new revenues given the rising social subsidies as a result of unemployment benefits and the refusal of the conservative cabinet to tax industry any further. Hawking was seen not only "as an unhealthy branch of unemployment," but also as the result of "undesired immigration". Foreign peddlers were especially targeted. According to the law, aliens could only obtain a permit if they had a legal residence of at least one year in Belgium and if Belgian peddlers enjoyed the same privileges in their country of origin (the reciprocity rule). The authorities maintained complete jurisdiction over peddlers and the vendor's license of "a foreign merchant who damaged the country's economic interests" could always be revoked. In order not to place national interests in any danger, the Belgian authorities established agreements with France, the Netherlands, and Luxembourg where Belgians engaged in peddling. It became clear that the Belgian authorities were serious about the restriction of foreign peddlers when barely 10 percent of the five thousand foreign peddlers who by 1 December 1935 had applied for a license received a positive reply. The Sûreté asked for a larger repatriation budget because they presumed that about four thousand alien peddlers would now return to their country of origin.

Several embassies protested against the discriminating manner in which the peddlers' permits were granted. The Czechoslovakian authorities pointed out that peddling in their country was not restricted in any way, thus reciprocity for Belgian peddlers was no problem. The Belgian authorities had not meant reciprocity in that respect; it was not posed as an abstract principal, but as a weighing of national interests. Since there were no Belgians in the Czechoslovakian markets, the Czechoslovakian peddlers in Belgium had to look for another livelihood. The Polish consular authorities also tried to protect the livelihood of their citizens. Since in Poland peddling was forbidden, the Polish authorities did not propose a reciprocity agreement; it would in any case have stirred up very little enthusiasm. The Poles proposed economic compensation in exchange for vendor's licences for its emigrants in Belgium. Poland had always had an important surplus in its trade balance with Belgium. Negotiations on a high diplomatic level sought to remove precisely those surpluses. On 2 April 1936 a Belgian-Polish agreement was concluded to promote Belgian imports into Poland. In exchange, Belgium approved the allocation of five hundred peddlers' licences to Polish citizens. As a result, of the 1,922 applications by Polish peddlers, not five hundred but 977 were responded to positively. This generosity anticipated the new principle for the granting of vendor's licenses which was to be enacted in April 1936: a residence period of ten years implied the granting of a license. To enable the authorities to enforce the new law, peddlers and market vendors were obliged to display a badge. The Belgian merchants had to display a blue token and the foreign merchants a red one. Although quite a few aliens were refused the vendor's license and were thus denied admittance to the marketplaces, the agitation against foreign peddlers did not die down. The Belgian peddlers protested even more vociferously that their profession was inundated by aliens, along the lines that more and more red badges appeared on the marketplace. The law on peddling not only brought a number of diplomatic repercussions with it, but it also did not diminish the displeasure of the Belgian peddlers over the so-called take over of the marketplaces by the foreign peddlers (Caestecker 1993c:136ff.).

The State Regulates the Labor Market

In the first half of 1933 the authorities had decided not to intervene in the labor market. Industry could decide for itself if they needed foreign labor and those immigrants who, despite a large pool of unemployed Belgian labor, were retained in their jobs responded to structural needs. This position was partly revoked by 1934. Since the onset of the Depression the Christian Democratic Ministers of Labor, H. Heyman and even more so P. Van Isacker, had been receptive to the demands of the unions to replace foreign labor – even outside mining – with Belgian unemployed workers. Rising unemployment and the increasing state expenditures it entailed, together with the pressure of the labor unions and the Christian Democratic Ministers of Labor, led the government to re-examine state intervention in the employment of aliens. Legal constraints, the fact that most foreign labor had acquired residency status and was thus protected, forced the Minister of Labor to propose a direct intervention in the labor market to impose more restrictions on the hiring of aliens. Minister of Labor Van Isacker, developed the idea of taxing employers who employed aliens above a certain quota. This money would be used in a fund for the unemployed. This call for a labor tariff, a tax on employers who hired foreign labor, never materialized. A few months later, in December 1934, a more radical version of this protectionist principle was discussed by the cabinet. According to this proposal the state should not merely dissuade employers from hiring aliens by financial penalties, but rather impose a ceiling on the number of aliens being employed (KADOC, ACW-Nationaal, 34; ARA, de Broqueville, 696).

The CCI, the representatives of heavy industry, was strongly opposed to a quota law. They argued that foreign labor was essential to the well-functioning of Belgian industry. This employers' organization underscored the structural need for foreign labor who did mostly menial work which Belgians did not want to do. Belgians who were unemployed preferred to live on the dole rather than do this strenuous work which was, because of its unskilled nature, also poorly paid. Some foreign labor was also essential for industry because of specializations and skills which could not be found among Belgian labor. The CCI argued that using such a coercive measure against industry would not diminish, but on the contrary only create more unemployment. The CCI rejected any intervention of the state in the personnel policy of industry (ARMA rC25/2;ARA, de Broqueville, 696). This radical stance was not shared by those within the government opposed to the quota bill. The Minister of Foreign Affairs, P. Hymans, as well as F. Bovesse, the Minister of Justice, strongly opposed this proposal, but agreed that the state should acquire control over the labor market position of the immigrants. Such control was justified as it would diminish public expenditures. Hiring of foreign labor should not be left to the discretion of the employers. Both ministers proposed developing alternative modalities of state intervention, modalities without the defects of a quota law. Firstly, this bill was totally inadequate as it only allowed the dismissal of foreign labor without enabling the authorities to expel those unemployed aliens. The quota bill would only create destitute aliens who would be a burden on local welfare. The main problem was that most immigrants had already acquired residency status and expulsion because of displacing a Belgian, joblessness, or destitution was not feasible. Hymans and Bovesse deemed total control over all foreign labor necessary. Also the stay of those who had already acquired residency status should be at the discretion of the public authorities. The mainstay of their proposal was a sweeping reform of the alien legislation to curtail residency status. Secondly, the results of the quota bill would be economically counterproductive as the employers, rather than keeping their best labor, would be forced to retain those aliens who, because of bilateral conventions, were diplomatically protected. A quota procedure lacked the necessary flexibility needed for such a delicate operation (AAD 1B6II).

Two slightly different proposals to develop a more refined state action were on the table. The Liberal Minister of Justice, F. Bovesse, drew up a proposal by which an immigrant who had a temporary residence permit could only engage in wage labor if the Ministry of Labor gave its authorization. Also, if an alien wanted to change employers or the nature of his work, the consent of the Ministry of Labor was necessary. The permission to work was a dual one, a permission and an admission. The immigrant had to apply for authorization to be employed, and at the same time the employer had to receive the permission of the Ministry of Labor to hire him. In this proposal, the influence of the Holvoet bill is clearly discernable. The Liberal Minister of Foreign Affairs, P. Hymans, proposed a slightly different scheme. A dual system was proposed whereby aliens were divided between wage laborers and other aliens. The former might obtain a labor permit, the latter a residence permit. The labor permit would be granted by the Ministry of Labor to all immigrants engaged in wage labor. The Ministry of Labor would decide on the terms of this permission to stay *and* work in Belgium. For these immigrants, the right to live in Belgium would be completely dependent on the right to work. The residence permit granted by the Minister of Justice to all other immigrants would not be directly related to economic criteria. This dual scheme elaborated partly on the Royal Decree of 15 December 1930 by which a special statute for labor migrants was introduced. This proposal, which made a lasting distinction between foreign labor and other aliens, duplicated the French practice. In contrast to the proposition of the Minister of Justice, immigrants who came in as labor migrants would be expelled if they did not work or refused to do so. In the proposition of the Minister of Justice the right of stay of labor migrants was, at least formally, independent from their right to work, but their right to work depended on the right to stay.

It was Bovesse's proposal which won the day. It is highly likely that the impossibility of disposing of aliens who had acquired residency status caused the Council of Ministers to favor the proposal of the Minister of Justice. This proposal, in which the Minister of Justice continued to play a key role, enabled a smoother shift to the status of resident alien. The royal decree of 15 February 1935 stated that immigrants who had not yet obtained permanent residency (the identity card for aliens) had to apply for a labor permit. From then on every immigrant who wanted to work in Belgium had to have either an identity card for aliens or a temporary residence permit *and* a labor permit. The right to work and the right to live in Belgium were considered two distinct elements for which separate authorizations were necessary, at least in the initial period of immigration. Although the length of this initial period of immigration was not yet explicitly defined, a residence of five years was set to acquire residency status. That the administration more than doubled the period in which immigrants were dependent on administrative discretion – from two to five years – is of course significant. Another important innovation was that by this law the Ministry of Labor became institutionally integrated in alien policy. The Minister of Justice no longer took sole responsibility for control over aliens residing in Belgium. The Minister of Labor, as an equal partner in alien policy, was given responsibility for the control of the labor market position of the "recent" immigrants. Given the small number of immigrants who had not yet received residency status, the amount of leeway given to the authorities to manipulate residence and now also access in the labor market remained small. All the immigrants of the 1920s remained out of reach of this potential for a more refined state intervention in the labor market. The law of 15 February 1935 was never implemented, but it would have a strong influence on subsequent reform of the alien legislation (AAD 1B6II and 33C31).

In the meantime, notwithstanding the very diverse opposition it encountered, the quota bill became law in December 1934. Parliament was bypassed as the Theunis cabinet had obtained full power to achieve financial and economic recovery. The Council of Ministers had agreed to enact this law under the condition that an eventual implementation would take into account any diplomatic repercussions. The law gave the Minister of Labor power to restrict the employment of foreign labor in a certain region or industry (BS 1934:6501ff.). It strongly increased the authorities' power to intervene in the labor market. No immediate use of these powers was envisaged. The authorities realized that, notwithstanding the quota law, there were severe constraints on a state intervention. The problem of the expulsion of dismissed aliens, at least those with residency status, was still actual. In addition, bilateral labor treaties prevented Belgian authorities from taking any action against nationals of France and the Netherlands legally residing in Belgium. On 30 March 1935 a labor treaty with Switzerland was signed, including the Swiss among the nationalities exempt to large extent from negative discrimination by the Belgian state. The Sûreté pointed out that only by negotiating with the above-mentioned countries would the repatriation of aliens residing in Belgium and dismissed as a result of the quota law be possible. Agreements should be reached with the countries of origin in order to enable the forced repatriation of these aliens. The Minister of Foreign Affairs, P. Hymans, was rather critical of the willingness of the countries of origin to negotiate the return of their destitute emigrants. More importantly, he considered that the jobs of Swiss, Dutch, French, and Luxembourg immigrants were not to be affected by the implementation of the quota law. The labor treaties excluded any discriminatory state action against them (AAD 1B6II). It is likely that the quota law was considered rather a palliative. It was meant to placate anti-immigrant sentiments rather than to displace immigrants. The authorities counted on its dissuading power. The Minister of Labor could use his newly achieved powers as a threat against employers to stimulate them to dismiss their foreign labor on a voluntary basis. The labor unions, Socialist and Christian Democrat alike, were supportive of the quota law. Now that its Minister of Labor had achieved the power to restrict the use of foreign labor, the Christian Democratic union became much more moderate in its demands to replace foreign labor. The leadership of this union insisted that implementation of the quota law be well prepared. Humanitarian, diplomatic, and economic considerations meant that only a partial and gradual removal of foreign labor was feasible. The union argued that a flexible approach to the issue of foreign labor was necessary (KADOC, ACV, Raad and Bestuur). The replacement of immigrants with unemployed Belgian laborers was still the final aim; with the new powers their Minister of Labor had at his disposal, this also became easier to realize.

That the Christian Democratic union started to doubt whether dismissing a large number of aliens was an easy solution to the unemployment of the Belgians was especially obvious in the hotel sector. The Christian Democratic union of hotel personnel, which in 1934 had aggressively demanded, with an outspoken xenophobic discourse, the dismissal of all aliens, moderated its position in 1935 by only opposing any further immigration. The Socialist union stood firm on its position and still insisted upon the removal of all aliens who had arrived in Belgium after March

1929. No immediate use was made of the quota law. After an investigation in the hotel sector, one of the sectors where agitation against the immigrants had been fiercest, the Christian Democratic Minister of Labor, E. Rubbens, considered intervention not at all appropriate as only very few aliens were being employed in this sector. The employers' annual demand for authorization to call upon qualified labor in France, Switzerland, and Italy for the summer season was even partly agreed to. The luxurious hotels at the seaside obtained permission to call upon about hundred aliens for the season, but only for the most specialized jobs *(maître d'hôtel, chef de cuisine, chef de réception, chef de rang,* and *garçon de rang*). Not only the lack of qualified Belgian personnel but also the World Exposition in Brussels in that year, which would attract a lot of tourists to Belgium caused the Christian Democratic Minister of Labor, E. Rubbens, notwithstanding the opposition of the unions, to tolerate the seasonal immigration.

Only half a year after the enactment of the quota law would this procedure be tried out. Probably in deference to the concerns of heavy industry the conservative Theunis cabinet had not proceeded to enforce dismissal of aliens in heavy industry. A change of government radicalized the alien policy of the state. The first Van Zeeland government, which contained important Socialist participation, was less willing to blindly follow the advice of the employers. Measures to force the dismissal of foreign labor in heavy industry were now envisaged. An external factor, the tightening of the net of regulation and control around the Belgian emigrants in France in 1935 caused a radicalization in anti-immigrant sentiments in Belgium and the call for a more stringent alien policy won out.

The increasing restrictive alien policy in France and the repercussions on the Belgian community in that country radicalized not only Belgian emigration policy, but also immigration policy. During the Depression, the French authorities put a halt to most immigration, even that of Belgian labor. Between 1932 and 1935, applications for immigration by foreign labor were mostly turned down by labor exchange offices at the level of the *département.* Annually only about a thousand Belgians residing close to the border, mostly young people who had just recently reached working-age, were allowed to join Belgian commuters working in France. The Belgian border region which had been the hinterland of the industry of the Nord for more than a century saw its traditional livelihood endangered. The intervention of the French state in Belgian immigration went largely beyond stopping new immigrants. Even those Belgians who for years had been commuting to France on a daily, weekly, or seasonal basis became victims of the restrictive French alien policy. While in 1930 about a hundred thousand Belgians residing in Belgium were allowed to earn a living in France, by 1933 their number had dropped by two-thirds. The economic downturn and private business initiatives partly explain this spectacular decline, but the administrative intervention of the French state also has to be taken into account. Already in August 1932 a quota law was promulgated. French agrarian and business interests successfully opposed such an inflexible intervention in their personnel policy. In fact only very few foreign workers were laid off by employers in order not to exceed the legal ceiling set in some industries. The quota law was rather a symbolic gesture meant to placate xenophobic sentiments. Policy makers considered it too radical an instrument to be consistent with economic realities. The use of administrative powers was more apt to shift the burden of unemployment to foreign labor. Although administrative regulations were used in a flexible manner so that the French employers were not deprived of necessary labor, the interventions were disastrous for Belgian commuters. In 1933 the French authorities planned to renew only half of the commuters' cards. Due to strong Belgian protest, supported by French employers, the renewal of only 10 percent of the commuters' cards was finally refused (PHK 1933:9ff.). By the end of 1934 the French authorities, due to increasing unemployment and rightist exploitation of the immigration issue, threatened to put a ceiling of 10 percent on the share of foreigners on the labor force in the Nord. This caused great anxiety among Belgian labor in France (PHK 1935:1028f. and 1936:957; Lentacker 1974:211, 279f.).

Belgian workers residing in France were, as any foreign worker in that country, not spared the restrictive French alien policy. Early in 1935 the requirement for obtaining permanent residence permits in France and thus an automatic renewal of the work permit was increased from five to ten years. This regulation affected all Belgians who had emigrated to France in the second half of the 1920s. They became totally dependent on administrative discretion. They were prohibited from leaving the *département* where they had obtained their identity card without the approval of the prefect and each time they changed occupation they had to obtain a new work permit. The treatment of Belgians at the hands of a neighboring state was strongly resented by the authorities and the public in Belgium. The Belgian Minister of Foreign Affairs was even thinking about taking revenge against the French workers in Belgium, but although no statistics were available, it was estimated that the number of French workers would not outweigh the Belgian workers in France (AFAB 2642bis III; PHK 1934:151). This turned out not to be necessary since most of the commuters' cards were finally renewed in May 1935, and in September 1935 the new regulation concerning permanent residency status was rescinded. The work permits of Belgian immigrants in France were again automatically renewed after a period of five years residence in that country (Cross 1983:200f.). As we will see in the next chapter, the radicalization of French alien legislation had, in the meantime, stimulated the transformation of Belgian alien policy.

The Ministerial Decree of August 1935, a Failure

The passing of the quota law of December 1934 incited the mining companies to continue dismissing their foreign labor. The authorities now had a stick with which to force the mining companies to dismiss more immigrants. The employers repeated their old arguments: unemployed Belgian miners were either politically undesirable or unwilling to replace foreign labor (ACCBS). The miners' unions refuted these arguments and pushed hard to obtain further replacement of immigrants with unemployed Belgian labor (CNMM). That A. Delattre, the president of the Socialist miners' union, was nominated Minister of Labor in May 1935 put the mining companies clearly in the defensive. Delattre undertook investigations to see if foreign labor could be replaced in the quarries and the mines. Delattre hoped to be able to dismiss eight thousand immigrants, seven thousand of them miners. A draft proposal for the Council of Ministers asked for a repatriation budget of one million francs in 1935 and three million in 1936. It was argued that the savings in unemployment benefits would largely compensate for these expenditures (AAD 109C92). In the stone industry, an intervention was aborted as only few aliens were working in the quarries and their skills were considered indispensable, even by the public authorities. Delattre soon realized that even in the mining industry, the replacement of foreign labor with Belgian unemployed labor was not that easy (PHK 1935:911). As unemployment among the Belgian miners continued to rise, the trade unions more vigorously demanded the replacement of single immigrants with unemployed Belgians. The employers, however, dismissed proportionally as many Belgians as aliens and among rehired labor there were also some aliens, mostly qualified miners. The miners' unions protested strongly against this hiring, although it accounted for only a small number of people. In their view it was further proof of the arrogance of the employers. The miners' unions insisted that the only way to achieve further replacement of aliens was to implement the quota law (CNMM).

A strike in the basin of Charleroi in May 1935, which threatened to spread, led Prime Minister P. Van Zeeland to insist that the mining companies replace foreign miners with unemployed Belgians. This could, according to Van Zeeland, calm down the very tense atmosphere in the mining industry. With the backing of the whole government Socialist Minister of Labor A. Delattre decided to enforce a quota system on the employers. Unemployment among Belgian miners could be solved by firing about ten thousand immigrants. Quotas were designated for each basin. This plan, however, was considered unexecutable: certain nationalities were protected by international agreements, other immigrants had been living with their families in the country for years, and some were even married to Belgian women. As a result, after two months a more moderate plan was designed. Only 6,362 single aliens, not protected by international agreements, would have to be fired. The FEDECHAR tried to prevent this drastic measure by arguing that the mining companies were willing to dismiss those foreign miners, but only if they had guarantees that the aliens would be replaced with Belgians qualified to do the same jobs. An enforced and unselective dismissal of aliens would only disrupt the industry. The mining companies showed their willingness to cooperate by co-financing the repatriation of the "useless" among their former labor, i.e., sick and undesirable aliens. In order to find Belgians who could replace immigrants, the FEDECHAR asked the authorities to draw up of a list of all unemployed Belgian miners with their qualifications, civil status, and where they had last worked. The FEDECHAR got their way; for the moment at least Delattre took no coercive measures. A list was drawn up by the Ministry of Labor, but the FEDECHAR was not satisfied. It had to be more detailed. The Ministry of Labor sent a letter to the FEDECHAR at the end of June with a list of mines which had a too high percentage of foreign labor. The message was clear, those mines had to reduce the percentage of aliens among their labor force without delay. The FEDECHAR refused to concede to this demand and insisted that those aliens were hardly replaceable.

Delattre decided to take the issue into his own hands and on 23 August 1935 enacted a decree which declared ceilings on the employment of aliens in the Hainaut. More than three thousand foreign miners had to be fired (BS 1935:5381ff.). The Trotskyists and the numerically more important Communists protested. In a mine in the Centre basins, a one-day strike, in which most Belgian miners participated, was called to protest against the dismissal of two Poles (IEV, Vandervelde, 131). Solidarity with foreign labor was hardly an element in the resistance to the ministerial decree. More important was the attitude of the mining companies. The FEDECHAR, feeling cheated, protested strongly. Their voluntary cooperation to a gradual replacement of the foreign miners, depending on the availability of Belgians, was now "rewarded" with this coercive measure. Their protest was to no avail. The mining companies had to fire their foreign labor. A few hundred North Africans who had been working in the basin of Charleroi for more than ten years were fired, and about two hundred Poles were dismissed. In the Borinage probably few if any aliens were dismissed as the mining companies were reluctant to yield to government pressure and waited to see what the authorities would do. Two months after the ministerial decree was enacted only 417 of the 3,297 immigrants scheduled to be dismissed in Hainaut had been fired. Attempts to replace these few hundred immigrants with unemployed Belgian miners turned out to be very difficult. A second element that hindered the implementation of the ministerial decree was that the dismissed aliens could stay in Belgium and become a burden on public welfare. According to the ministerial decree the dismissed aliens could be repatriated by the Belgian authorities. The Polish and French embassies (Poles and Algerians were the primary victims of the dismissals) refused to pay for the return trip. The Sûreté applied to the mines to co-finance the repatriation of these dismissed immigrants, but the mines refused any cooperation in this field. Several hundred of the dismissed North Africans and Slavs applied to be repatriated. The Sûreté had insufficient financial means to assure the repatriation of all the applicants. However, by the time the authorities realized that they would not be able to process all the applicants and that some dismissed miners willing to return to their country of origin would have to remain in Belgium, the ministerial decree had already been revoked.

The main reason for the revocation of the decree was diplomatic. In order to show their disapproval of the measure, some mines stated on the aliens' discharge certificate that they had been fired because of the decree of 23 August. Thus, on 15 September 1935 the mines received instructions from the authorities that Russians, Italians, Swiss, Dutch and Luxembourgers were not to be fired. The French (including Algerians) were added to this list by a circular letter of 20 September. The exemption of the citizens of neighboring countries is not a surprise. It was important that diplomatic relations with France, Luxembourg, Switzerland, and the Netherlands were not be jeopardized by this measure; labor treaties also prohibited such discriminatory practices. Italians were also exempted by the Belgian-Italian trade agreement of 27 June 1935. This treaty had a secret clause in which the Belgian authorities agreed not to intervene in the right to work of 4,700 Italians who were working in the Belgians mines. This Belgian concession was given in exchange to the annual export to Italy of one million tons of coal or the production of these Italian miners (ARMA bC1b3 and rC25/2). Russian immigrants were exempted because they were protected by the international Refugee Convention of 1933. Anyway, they could not be repatriated as they had no place to go (AFAB 12,178). On October 2 Delattre semi-officially suspended the decree. The FEDECHAR was asked to continue replacing the immigrants with Belgians just as before the publication of the decree. The official character of the dismissals, however, had to be masked. The FEDECHAR refused to do so. This veto by the FEDECHAR resulted in Delattre officially revoking the decree by the end of the month (FEDECHAR; ARMA rC25/1; AHCM; AFAF, Europe 1930-1940, 224; BdL 14).

Conclusion

We previously outlined the first departure from the liberal alien policy, by 1931 restrictions had been imposed on the entry of labor migrants. Two years later entrance into Belgium became subject to permission for all immigrants. This restrictive immigration policy to protect national labor did not imply that immigration to Belgium had stopped. Only a very few foreign workers were still able to immigrate legally, more labor migrants immigrated illegally. These undocumented labor migrants were joined by several thousand refugees from Nazi Germany who also entered Belgium without authorization. All these undocumented immigrants were treated in a similar repressive manner. They were strongly urged to leave the country. The recalcitrant among them – those who had already been expelled a few times – had first to submit to a term in prison. The destitute among them from Central and Eastern Europe were to stay in a penal colony. The authorities unofficially made allowances for some of the refugees since pushing them across the border stirred conflict with neighboring countries and a return to Nazi Germany was obstinately refused by these refugees.

The sweeping reform of the alien legislation to enable the removal of all undesirable aliens, independent of their length of stay in Belgium as had been proposed by the alien bill of June 1930, was not attained. The liberal alien law of 1897 had been only slightly modified in a restrictive sense. The law of 14 August 1933 made the stay of immigrants for a longer time dependent on the Minister of Justice. Long-term control over immigrants aimed to assure that they did not depart from the original declared and officially sanctioned reason for immigration. Aliens were kept much longer under the arbitrary power of the state. The strict control over the refugees from Nazi Germany who were granted access to the country under the condition that they refrained from any economic activity was illustrative of the increasing ambitions of immigration policy.

The hiring of aliens, at least if they were residing legally in the country, remained virtually the exclusive competence of employers. Employers wanted to retain, despite high unemployment among Belgian labor, some of their foreign manpower. Not only economic, but also political factors explain this attachment. Foreign labor was not only an answer to structurally determined shortages in the labor market, but as non-Belgian and mostly non-unionized workers it constituted a potentially cheap and docile labor force. The docility of these workers was strengthened by state action. The expulsion of subversive aliens and the exclusion of aliens from unemployment insurance isolated foreign workers and made them even more dependent on the employers. Unemployment among Belgian labor and the "docility" of the immigrants caused the labor unions to demand that foreign labor be replaced by unemployed Belgians. The Socialist union, pulled along reluctantly by its rank and file, started to voice this demand during the strike of 1932. A pragmatic consideration, the difficulties of replacing foreign labor, rather than internationalism, explain this short-lived reluctance. Ideological constraints, principally due to the international affiliations of the Belgian Socialist movement turned out to be more constraints in tone, rather than in content. Solidarity with ideologically like-minded immigrants hardly played a role. The Christian Democratic union, untroubled by ideological constraints, was more radical in its demand to remove foreign labor.

State policy towards the immigrants residing and working legally in the country underwent a crucial transformation during the Depression. In the first years of the Depression the authorities were unwilling to intervene in the labor market. The government held that industry could decide for itself if it needed immigrants. If foreign labor was retained, despite a large pool of unemployed Belgian labor, this implied that it responded to structural labor needs. At the onset of the Depression, the authorities immediately added one group of immigrants, those who lost their jobs, to the category undesirable immigrants. They were considered excessive and were to be removed. The exclusion of foreign labor from unemployment insurance was a case in point. The effect of the market should not be mitigated for the immigrants; if unemployed, they would have to leave. While the Sûreté not only expelled undocumented and "subversive" aliens, and legally residing aliens lacking residency status who had become unemployed, the Sûreté remained aloof from all the other immigrants. This was partly due to legal constraints; acquiring residency status implied protection against expulsion. This protection acquired by most of the aliens in Belgium remained a bottleneck in the implementation of a brutal type of alien policy. Due to the traditional liberal values of the Belgian regime, resident aliens were granted a denizen-status which protected them against the state. Even when denizens became dependent on welfare – as long as they were not arrested as vagrants – they were not expelled. Vagrancy remained an offence and foreign vagrants were expelled. In keeping with the nineteenth-century alien policy, the limited powers which the Sûreté had at its disposal were not used to their full extent. Aliens who were of use to the employers, even if they were recent immigrants without legal protection, were not to be expelled.

The position of the conservative governments slowly shifted in this matter. The Christian Democratic Ministers of Labor, H. Heyman and even more so P. Van Isacker, pushed hard for a re-orientation of state policy. The already mentioned expansion of immigration policy was meant to enable the state to discriminate against foreign labor in the Belgian labor market. By 1934 the Sûreté had started expelling aliens who had jobs, but had not yet acquired residency status. The formal breakthrough of a restrictive state policy in the labor market occurred in December 1934 with the quota law. Only in February 1935 was the breakthrough more substantial with the institutionalized integration of the Ministry of Labor in alien policy administration. The labor market position of aliens legally residing in the country officially became a matter of concern for the authorities. The autonomy of the employers over the decision to hire foreign labor had to be curtailed. The category of undesirable aliens was expanded to include those immigrants who were perceived as displacing Belgian workers. A crucial factor in this shift of the authorities' attitude was the possible savings in unemployment insurance expenditures. Another factor was the need to placate labor to prevent economically damaging actions such as strikes or just to dampen discontent. The dependence of employers on the state in other domains, together with the strong pressure of the unions and the Christian Democratic Ministers of Labor increasingly backed by the other members of the government, resulted in the employers partly yielding to the demand for positive discrimination for national labor. Their concessions were not considered sufficient. The quota law of December 1934 was rather a symbolic support of the policy of the Minister of Labor to replace foreign labor by Belgian labor, and the conservative cabinet probably aimed more at stimulating employers to replace their foreign labor than at enforcing such replacement. The ineffective implementation of the quota law in August 1935, the first radically innovative measure in the interwar period, indicated the limits of a state-enforced collective dismissal of migrants. The diplomatic protests and the impossibility of expelling dismissed aliens were its politically determined defects, but also an economic factor – the difficulty of replacing these aliens with unemployed Belgian miners – indicated that the substitution of foreign labor by Belgian labor was not that easy to realize. The impossibility of expelling the dismissed aliens due to their residency status indicated an important constraint in implementing a radical alien policy. Those unemployed aliens who chose not to return home were entitled to claim welfare, contrary to what was perceived as the state's interests. State-enforced unemployment of aliens with denizen status could entail an increase in welfare expenditures. The authorities tried to circumvent the legal constraints of their radical alien policy by providing for the repatriation of unemployed aliens with residency status. This provision would limit welfare expenditures to aliens, but the authorities were still dependent on the willingness of these aliens to leave the country.

Not only labor migrants, but also aliens active in trade became a focus of state-intervention. In this case as well the interests of some Belgian professional groups became national interests and caused this intervention. During the Depression, due to shrinking opportunities in heavy industry, small trade and artisanal industry provided an increasing number of immigrants with a livelihood. This survival tactic aroused the ire of Belgian merchants and artisans. By evoking so-called illegal and dishonest trade practices amplified by alleged continuous immigration – the myth of an invasion from Germany – these professional groups succeeded in passing the vendor's law of 13 January 1935 which aimed at purging aliens from this trade circuit. Although much less immediate state interest was at stake in the sense of unemployment expenditures or even the danger of economically damaging actions such as strikes, these groups were able to convince the authorities to restrict access to the trade world.

The ultimate purpose of changes in alien policy was to export the social costs of the economic downturn. This was a cheap and popular form of social crisis management. The number of aliens induced to leave because of adverse market forces increased because of these political decisions. Immigrants were used as an expendable workforce which provided Belgians with a cushion against economic hardship. Aliens were thus forced to bear a disproportionate share of the cost of the Depression. Legal, diplomatic, and economic constraints meant, however, that the radical alien policy had to be rationalized in order to maximize its effects.

Notes

1. Belgian statistics register Belgian nationality revocations on the basis of the law only at the end of the 1930s. In 1938 the Courts of Appeal would revoke the nationality of six Belgians, in 1939 of nine, and in 1940 of two. A first judgement was already made, however, at the end of 1935 when the Court of Appeal of Liège revoked the Belgian nationality of four Nazi activists.
2. Although anti-semitic remarks were rare in this period, we believe that agitation against the "Jewish" economy could rely on a diffuse anti-Semitism which existed in Belgian society. To assess its influence is difficult given the limited research on attitudes towards the Jewry in Belgian society.

Chapter 8

THE "RATIONALIZATION" OF THE RADICAL ALIEN POLICY, 1936-1937

The failure of the deflationary policy of the conservative governments and an impending financial catastrophe caused business to change its strategy. Belgian trade was hindered by the overvaluation of the national currency, which continued because of the obstinate defense of the franc by the Belgian governments. In March 1935, the Socialists joined with the Catholics and the Liberals to form a new "national unity" government. This new government led by P. van Zeeland decided to implement a devaluation of 28 percent. The export-oriented industries experienced an upswing: some sectors even attained the production levels of the period before the crisis. Industries catering to the home-market, however, were unable to increase their production. Sales scarcely increased as the purchasing power of the population had been broken by years of deflationary policy. The Van Zeeland government did not have the ambition to restore the living standard of the Belgians. The reforms of Van Zeeland were not an expression of a socially progressive policy. They aimed only at a structural adaptation of institutions to the capitalist economy. The Socialists were advocating more far-reaching reforms. The traditional ruling elites successfully resisted most moves towards reform. Only an experiment with large public works was initiated. This experiment was aimed not only at reducing unemployment levels, but was also meant to fertilize the economy with an injection of purchasing power (Vanthemse 1988-1989).

Labor, however, wanted its share of the fruits of the economic recovery. In 1936 a general strike broke out spontaneously and spread rapidly. This strike marked the first formal alliance between the Socialist and the Christian Democratic labor unions on the national level. Not only the united union front, but also the attitude of the Van Zeeland government heralded a change in industrial relations. Van Zeeland called a national labor conference with employers and unions. Under government pressure, the employers agreed, in principle, to organized labor's demands: a wage hike, paid holidays, a minimum wage, legal protection for the workers' right to unionize, and a forty-hour week. Reservations were expressed only about the last demand. The forty-hour week was to be applied only in industries where the working conditions were "unhealthy" or "arduous". In the following years, in nearly all industrial sectors, joint labor management commissions were set up. The first commissions had been established in 1919-1921, but in 1921 this development came to an end. In 1935, such an institutionalized labor-employer consultation existed only in twenty-six sectors. By 1940 there were 172 joint commissions (Gerard 1991:227). The concessions made by the state, in particular, and to a lesser degree by employers during the strike of 1936 were a crucial step towards the democratic corporatist system which would only be institutionalized after the Second World War.[1]

The improvement of the economic situation also coincided with political unrest. The elections of 24 May 1936 showed a breakthrough for both extremes, the Right as well as the Left. Two parties close to fascism made significant inroads into the Catholic electorate. One new party, Rex, captured 11.5 percent of the vote, and the Flemish Nationalist Party (VNV) went from 5.9 to 7 percent. The Communists went from 2.8 to 6 percent. The success of Rex, and the VNV has to be attributed in particular to the middle class. Its politically dissident votes were the result of severe tensions afficting small business. Belgian small commerce had an extremely weak economic base. Belgium had the highest number of small merchants of any European country. It was not the large department stores which had benefited from the increasing demand in consumption of the twenties, but rather the rapidly growing number of small shopkeepers. The cooperatives, large department stores, etc. accounted for barely 8 percent of retail trade. The number of small shopkeepers continued to grow even in the crisis years, above all as a refuge from unemployment (Strikwerda 1990). The economic foundation of the overpopulated trade sector could only be strengthened by a reorganization of the sector. A comprehensive reorganization was, however, politically unrealizable and quite a few members of the middle class looked for a solution to their problems outside of traditional politics. The success of the "extremist" parties among the middle class caused the traditional parties to pay more attention to this social group. The padlock law, which was to keep the expansion of the large department stores in check, together with a better provision of credit, a broadening of a number of social laws for the self-employed, and the institutionalization of middle-class representation were attempts by the traditional parties to tie the middle class politically and economically to the regime. These measures broke with the traditional economic and political policy of the Belgian state and were among the first laborious steps in the direction of incorporating the middle class in the corporate welfare state. Above all, the padlock law was a radical break with Belgian economic policy, which had supported economic liberalism since 1830. These measures had to give small trade time to catch its breath so that small merchants could strengthen their position by means of self-regulation. This strategy paid off, the democratic regime succeeded in partly reestablishing its legitimacy.

A Liberal Immigration Policy

Political change in 1935 – the Van Zeeland government – did not end restrictions on immigration. At the border, but also in the country itself, labor immigration was not tolerated (Graphs 14 and 15). By 1936 allowances were made for a few categories of immigrants. The restriction on Dutch immigration which had been introduced in April 1935 because of growing unemployment was lifted in January 1936 when the Belgian authorities finally ratified the Belgian-Dutch agreement of 20 February 1933. That the Dutch authorities had in the meantime imposed restrictions on the hiring of foreign, including Belgian, labor was probably not alien to this exemption. A Dutch law of 16 May 1934 imposed on employers the obligation to apply for permits for their foreign workers in specified trades and industries. Only if no Dutch labor could be found to fill the vacancy was the permit granted. Initially only a few economic sectors were affected by this legislation, but their number increased quickly to cover the whole Dutch labor market by 1937. The Dutch-Belgian protocol of April 1936 guaranteed their respective immigrants an immediate labor permit (ARDH 185). Due to the economic recovery not only Dutch citizens, but other groups of aliens could immigrate to Belgium as well. Even illegal immigration was tolerated to a certain extent. The Sûreté had been forced to yield to the pressure of powerful economic interests to legalize the stay of all undocumented immigrants who were willing to work in the mines or agriculture. The Sûreté gave in very reluctantly. They argued that it would be the beginning of the end of the newly established control over immigration. In 1937 the number of immigrants who crossed the border illegally grew spectacularly. The Sûreté insisted on stopping the flood. The Minister of Justice, the Liberal V. de Laveleye, agreed that immigration had gotten totally out of control and decided that no more illegal crossings of the border could be tolerated. Expulsions would make clear to the immigrants and the employers alike that immigration regulations were being strictly enforced. These firm intentions were hardly realized. Powerful economic interests, in particular the mining companies, pressed again and again to postpone the implementation of a strict immigration policy. No bureaucratic controls were to impede the flow of immigrant labor when it was in demand. For the mining industry, informal migration was not the only source of new workers. In 1937, 8,498 foreign workers obtained official permission to immigrate to work in the Belgian mines. Not only miners, but also hotel personnel, quarry workers, farm hands, and domestic servants were being recruited officially (see below). The Sûreté, however, took precautions for the future. Strict instructions were given to the municipalities not to grant identity cards to labor migrants. The administrative transfer of aliens from the foreigners' register to the population register had to be kept to a minimum. If immigrants did not acquire residency status, it would be easier to dispose of them in the future (AAD 33C30/9-1 and 33C31).

An innovation in immigration policy in this period was that the illegal immigration of "refugees" was pardoned. This breach of the law was overlooked due to the involuntary nature of the refugees' flight. Refugees were entitled to appeal for asylum even if they had come into the country illegally. This liberalization was part of a new refugee policy which established firmly the category "refugee" in Belgium's alien policy. It was the entrance of the Socialists into the government which led to this reformulation. Until 1936 non-Communist political refugees had been eligible for a semi-official refugee status. By the royal decree of 20 February 1936, the Socialist Minister of Justice, E. Soudan, gave the refugee procedure an official character. An advisory commission was set up which would investigate whether asylum seekers were "genuine" refugees. This commission advised the Minister of Justice as to whether asylum seekers would be granted refugee status. With this provision, refugee policy lost much of its arbitrary nature. The legal recognition of the status of refugee was coupled with an enlargement of the group entitled to this status. Belgian refugee policy went beyond the international refugee regime. The latter was highly collectivist (only groups such as Russian and German refugees were considered "refugees"), while under the new Belgian refugee regime, any aliens, independent of origin, could apply for asylum. "Subversive" refugees – the Communists – who had until then been excluded from the refugee procedure, could now be granted refugee status (BS 1936:946f.). The expulsion of a German Communist refugee, Heinrich Bell, in March 1936 and his subsequent arrest by the Gestapo, caused a protest as a result of which the Communist aid organization, the Red Help, became a member of the advisory refugee commission. The German Communist refugees who had been residing illegally in Belgium since 1933 applied officially and mostly with success for asylum. The definition of refugee did not change. Only political activists whose lives or freedom were endangered were eligible for asylum, but the right to asylum was now clearly institutionalized. Asylum remained, however, a favor granted by the authorities and not a right. "Refugees" were not allowed to have a criminal record and they could still be expelled if they "misbehaved".

The few thousand Jews who fled Germany because of Nazi anti-semitism were excluded from the liberalization of the refugee policy. The Socialist Minister of Justice, E. Soudan, just as his predecessors had done, tolerated these German Jews temporarily to enable them to organize their emigration. The institutionalization of anti-semitism in Nazi Germany (the Nuremberg laws) and also, from 1935 onwards, the persecution in Germany of those who re-emigrated, brought no change in the refugee policy. The growing difficulties in finding a definite immigration country meant that the stream of Jewish refugees no longer flowed through so quickly. The Jewish committees found it increasingly difficult to carry the financial burden of sheltering these Jewish transit refugees. This, together with a temporary softening in Hitler's Jewish policy, caused the Jewish community in Belgium to show less solidarity with the refugees from Nazi Germany. Even organized Belgian Jewry called the motives of their flight suspicious; a considerable number of Jewish refugees were so-called economic refugees. The deliberate exclusion of Jews from German economic life was considered no reason to flee Germany. Also, any German refugees who had first obtained asylum in another country, even if only temporarily, were not helped. All Jewish refugees who did not have the support of the Jewish relief organizations – the majority of the arrivals in Belgium – were ordered to leave the country. The remaining Jewish refugees were only considered refugees *sensu lato* and obtained temporary residence to organize their emigration. The conservative Catholic, C. du Bus de Warneffe, who became Minister of Justice in November 1937, reversed this policy. He ordered the expulsion of all uninvited immigrants, except the refugees *stricto sensu* (the political refugees). He legitimized this tough policy, which was directed against the Jewish refugees, by referring to rising xenophobia and anti-semitism. Only by combating what he called the causes of this dangerous trend could it be nipped in the bud (Caestecker 1993c:67-73).

The Revolution in Alien Legislation, the Temporary Suppression of Residency Status

From 1933 onwards a strict immigration policy could be implemented. Advocates of a more generous attitude towards aliens residing in Belgium insisted on improving the legal status of their protégés in order to facilitate their assimilation into Belgian society. Improvements would no longer cause an increase in immigration as the authorities possessed enough power to keep unwanted immigrants out. Resident aliens should be considered equal to Belgian citizens in terms of civil and social rights. This liberal point of view had to confront powerful interests. The Sûreté advocated an enlargement of their powers to dispose of "undesirable" aliens residing in Belgium. Expulsions in particular had to become more efficient. H. Bekaert, director of the Sûreté, was the main proponent of a tougher expulsion policy. He advocated the forced repatriation of all aliens who were considered undesirable. Not only those who disturbed the public order – criminals and subversives – but also businessmen who went bankrupt should be forcibly repatriated. The "offender's" family should also be repatriated. That the family of the expelled alien could remain in the country was, according to Bekaert, one of the crucial factors which caused the expulsion policy to be totally ineffective. Bekaert insisted that an order to leave the country should apply immediately to the whole family (ARC 33/8; AAD 1B6). These contradictory options for reform of alien legislation would be decided by a very different set of concerns. It was not the wish to integrate these aliens in the national community which was the impetus for reform, and concern about public order also had little to do with the reform. Protection of national labor became the main deciding factor which brought about changes.

A New Design in Alien Policy

The Socialist Minister of Labor, A. Delattre, advocated an enlargement of the powers of the authorities to dispose of "undesirable" foreign labor in Belgium. He argued that a lot of foreign workers were settled in Belgium without the Ministry of Labor ever having given its opinion about their economic desirability. Even those aliens who in 1930 and 1931, on the basis of a labor contract, had obtained the consent of the Ministry of Labor to their immigration were no exception. These immigrants had unilaterally extended their stay beyond the term of the initial work contract and had sometimes even changed profession. Legislation to enable the authorities to keep a tight hold over those intruders in order to remove all aliens who were economically superfluous was, according to Delattre, highly desirable. Unemployed Belgians could replace those aliens. Immediately after the failure of the quota law in the mining industry, in October 1935, Delattre referred to the high number of aliens in the mining industry and the hotel sector. In these two sectors, according to Delattre, there was a high number of unemployed Belgians available to replace the numerous aliens. The Minister of Labor estimated that in total about ten thousand aliens could be removed from the labor market. In order to "eliminate" them, the state should finance their repatriation. The costs would be outweighed by the savings in unemployment expenses. Delattre changed his course very shortly afterwards; unemployment diminished considerably in the following months, certainly in the mine and hotel sectors. In both sectors it was no longer necessary to remove foreign labor, on the contrary there was even a shortage of labor in mining. Delattre now blamed foreign labor for deteriorating working conditions. They did not even respect the conditions set by law: they worked longer, in unhealthy conditions, and for lower pay than Belgian workers. He argued that this was particularly true of foreign labor employed by co-ethnic entrepreneurs. Thus, foreign entrepreneurs competed with Belgian businesses in a disloyal manner. The abuses were especially abundant in the "Jewish" economy.

The Socialist Minister of Foreign Affairs, P.H. Spaak, was also in favor of expanding the power of the authorities over all aliens in Belgium. It would enable the Belgian authorities to retaliate against those countries which expelled or dismissed Belgian emigrant workers. A reform of alien legislation in the sense of an all-encompassing control over all foreigners in Belgium would convince the authorities of those countries not to take any action against Belgian emigrants or commuters. In particular the bold decision of the French government in February 1935 to double the length of residence necessary before Belgian immigrants were able to obtain an automatic renewal of their identity card – from five to ten years – had convinced Spaak that the Belgian authorities had to wield more power over the aliens. The Van Zeeland government deemed a further reform of the alien legislation necessary not only because of those specific interests, but because there was a general sentiment among the ministers that keeping a grip over immigration to Belgium was not enough. The authorities should also be able to control the stay of aliens who were already residing in Belgium. This would not only curtail their political activities as was already foreseen by the alien law of 1897, but also restrict their economic activities. Foreign labor should not displace national labor, if only for the reason that it increased expenditures for the state. The authorities should also be able to expel destitute foreigners, independent of their length of residence in Belgium. The experience of the Depression, when destitute foreigners who had obtained residency status could not be expelled and could even live on welfare, caused a strong majority within the government to support a far-reaching reform of the alien legislation. Beyond controlling immediate immigration, the state should be able to ensure that aliens continued to serve the "national" interests.

A bill was proposed by Minister of Labor A. Delattre to the Council of Ministers on 7 December 1935. This bill was an extension of the law of 15 February 1935. Not only foreign laborers who had a temporary residence permit were to apply for a labor permit, but every alien who worked in wage labor would have to do so, independent of their length of residence in Belgium. Another crucial innovation was that not the alien himself, but his future employer, would have to apply to the Ministry of Labor for authorization to employ him. The technocrat M. Gottschalk had proposed imposing such a formality only on the employers as it would be too onerous a task for foreign labor. Delattre accepted this technical argument and changed his bill. This request of the employer would be at the same time a demand of the alien for a work permit. Permission to the employer and admission of the foreigner would be one and the same formality. The request for permission to employ an alien would have to be preliminary to the employment. The minister could, however, exempt urgent cases whereby the application for a work permit had to follow within twenty-four hours after employment. The employer would have to guarantee the repatriation of foreign labor he recruited abroad. As soon as those workers were no longer in his service, the employer would be liable for paying their return trip. Employers who hired aliens without authorization could be sentenced to a prison term of up to one month as well as a fifty – to five hundred – franc fine.

The Labor Minister could refuse any request to employ a foreigner who had been residing less than ten years in Belgium. The validity of the work permit of those "recent" immigrants would be limited with respect to the nature and the place of employment and would also be limited in time: a work permit for a "recent" immigrant, a so-called work permit B, could not extend over two years. Only if an alien who was refused a work permit could guarantee that he could live on his means would he be granted a residency permit. All the other aliens would be invited to leave the country, their repatriation financed by the Belgian state. The crucial innovation of the bill was that even aliens with an identity card – the administrative confirmation of residency status established by the royal decree of 13 August 1933 – could be expelled because of their being refused a work permit. Until then aliens who had acquired an identity card could only be expelled for disturbing public order. If an alien who was invited to leave the country because he had been refused a work permit would not do so willingly, he could be ordered to do so by royal decree. This was mentioned in the bill to make possible a penal sanction for *rupture de ban.* Since February 1935 the period of probation for immigrants had been unofficially set at five years; it was now officially extended to ten years. This doubling of the period during which foreign labor in Belgium was denied any protection against administrative discretion was due to the French decision to do the same in February 1935.

For those foreigners who had been living in Belgium for at least ten years – the privileged aliens – the employer's request for a work permit was considered a mere administrative formality. Exemptions were provided for the French who after five years residence became privileged aliens; the Dutch as mentioned before were all privileged aliens. However, the application for a work permit for a privileged alien – labor permit A – had to be renewed every two years and with each change of employer or nature of employment. The application had to be preliminary to employment, but would always receive a positive response. Although Delattre stated that a privileged alien should not be restricted in his occupational opportunities, he hoped that the preliminary permission necessary to hire a privileged alien and the biennial renewal would exert a dissuasive influence on employers' hiring policy (AAD 33C31).

De Man, the Socialist Minister of Public Works, was the only minister in the Van Zeeland government strongly opposed to this radical reform of the alien legislation. He called the whole scheme, which curtailed possibilities for immigrants to look for better paid jobs and left them at the mercy of the administration, a formidable oppressive mechanism. He argued that such legislation was not only unjust, but also economically inefficient and even inapplicable. Due to the bureaucratic burden which this legislation introduced, it would either inhibit attracting foreign labor or the law would have to be ignored. New legislation to prevent discrimination against Belgian labor abroad, argued De Man, was not necessary. The quota law could still be used in case radical action was necessary, and in order to make foreign labor respect Belgian social legislation, a few dozen labor inspectors would be sufficient, along with the expulsion of the most infamous immigrant employers (IEV, Vandervelde, 78). De Man was clearly out of tune with the protectionism which held sway within the government and also beyond it. He ignored the fact that this bill was only a step, albeit an important one, in a protectionist reform of the alien legislation.

The bill was hardly changed when it was put before Parliament. The first Van Zeeland government had obtained full power to redress the state budget. The decrees on financial affairs only had to be ratified by Parliament. This new alien bill was joined to a collection of finance-related decrees. The reports of the Commissions of Finance of Parliament did not mention that a radical change of the alien legislation was included. Parliament voted favorably without any discussion, seemingly ignorant of the bill's radical implications (BS 1936:2320ff.). That was certainly the case of the Socialist MP, M. Somerhausen, who nearly a year later was confronted with the expansion of the powers of the Belgian executive over aliens. In April 1937, in his function as a lawyer Somerhausen protested that orders to leave the country given some Polish garment workers were illegal. He argued that they had resided in Belgium since the end of the 1920s and were holders of identity cards. The Ministry of Justice retorted that these Poles, notwithstanding their long residence were, for economic reasons, liable for expulsion on the basis of the law of 31 March 1936.

Only then, to his amazement, did Somerhausen find out that he had assented to this royal decree. He was furious about the procedure the government had followed to make Parliament vote for the law. He was confident that Parliament would have never given the executive such extensive powers and that the government only was able to make the bill pass by a totally reprehensible legislative subterfuge. Parliament had ratified the law, according to Somerhausen as a result of real political fraud (ISJ Somerhausen; AAD 33C31). These objections did not change anything: refusing a work permit in 1937 to aliens who had immigrated to Belgium after 1926 implied the abolishment of their residency status.

The Ministry of Justice immediately started to attune its policy to the new legislation. The Ministry limited the registration of aliens in the population register to a bare minimum. The confusion which could be created by the expulsion of aliens with an identity card after they had been refused a work permit (or a peddler's license, see below) had to be prevented. Thus the identity card was only to be granted after ten years of residence (AAD 33C31). The executive measures of the law of 31 March 1936 weakened the provisions of the bill slightly. From August 1937 onwards the hiring of privileged aliens was no longer dependent on the preliminary authorization of the Minister of Labor. Although these aliens still had to apply for work permit A, such a permit had an unlimited validity (BS 1937:5121). The biennial renewal of work permit A was dropped to reduce the need for additional personnel to implement the new legislation. French diplomatic pressure – French citizens who had resided in Belgium for five years had considerable difficulties in being hired – probably helped to bring about this change (AAD 33C31; AFAF Europe 1918-1940, Belgique 225) . Within the Ministry of Labor, one hoped to keep the category of privileged alien as small as possible. Bolle, the director of the Service of Foreign Labor of the Ministry of Labor, proposed defining the ten years of residence for the calculation of the status of privileged alien as ten years in the Belgian labor market. He proposed that for foreign students only the years of residence after the end of their studies should count. For children of immigrants the years before age fifteen should not be calculated in the ten years necessary for obtaining the status of privileged alien. Both restrictions aimed at the extension of the inferior status of foreign labor. The Ministry of Justice could not accept this. The stay in Belgium of aliens, even in the case of students and children, had to be calculated from the moment that it was legal (AAD 333C31). Notwithstanding this reprimand, the Ministry of Labor arbitrarily extended its power beyond the legal limits by refusing to grant work permits to privileged aliens. Bolle, the director of the Service of Foreign Labor of the Ministry of Labor, explained in January 1939 that the policy regarding aliens' children did not exactly follow the terms of the law, but rather its spirit. The competent service within the Ministry of Labor tried to treat those children as new immigrants whose position on the labor market could be strictly regulated. That they should be considered privileged aliens was, according to Bolle, very delicate, because it would enable those children to seek professions of interest to Belgian nationals. Inasmuch as he could, Bolle tried to direct them to professions which were less overcrowded (PS 1939:77).

Table 4 *Survey of the different Categories of Foreign Labor in the Law of 31 March 1936 and their Dependence on the Authorities.*[2]

Labor immigrants	Their immigration depended on the granting of a work permit B by the Labor Minister for and of a temporary residence permit by the Justice Minister.
"Recent" labor immigrants	Their residence depended on the prolongation of their work permit B and of their temporary residence permit by the Ministers of Labor and Justice, respectively.
"Recent" labor immigrants with an identity card[3]	Their residence depended on the prolongation of their work permit B by the Minister of Labor.
Privileged labor immigrants[4] Denizen status	These aliens had an identity card and a work permit A (or peddler's license). Their residence was no longer at the discretion of the authorities. They could only be expelled for reasons of public order (and if they did not follow the procedure established by the law of 31 March 1936).

Given the provisions of this law, radical opposition to this legislation was not expected from industry. There had been a precedent: at the end of the 1920s, the CCI and particularly the FEDECHAR had endorsed the Holvoet bill which would have regulated the access of aliens to the labor market in a similar fashion.[5] The employers had then believed that state control over foreign labor could serve their interests by enforcing the stabilization of their foreign manpower. The employers' endorsement of the Holvoet bill has to be considered in the context of 1929 with its very tight labor market and pro-business government. The pro-business Theunis cabinet enacted the royal decree of 15 February 1935 which introduced an albeit more modest, but very similar control of foreign labor and this without opposition from industry. The situation at the beginning of 1936 was different. The labor market was still slack, although in some segments shortages could to be noted. The political situation was also different. The Van Zeeland cabinet had an important Socialist participation and the whole government aimed at more autonomous state action. The absence of employer participation in the discussions of the law of 31 March 1936 is an indication of the different way in which this government functioned. Although we lack any positive proof – the absence of protest by the mining companies is however indicative – we assume that the employers still considered state regulation of foreign labor in their interests or at least an inevitable result of the changing political configuration. Without a doubt, the employers were pleased that the participation of the unions was not institutionalized in the new policy. During the discussions on the Holvoet bill, the FEDECHAR and the CCI had strongly insisted that the unions be excluded from decision making in this field. In the second half of the 1930s the anti-union bias of the FEDECHAR and for this matter of all employers in heavy industry had not changed. The FEDECHAR also advocated the validity of work permits for the whole mining sector and not just for a specific mine. This had also been one of their amendments to the Holvoet bill. With this amendment the FEDECHAR hoped to limit state intervention in "its" labor market. Increasing the flexibility of "its" labor market was not a liberal position in favor of mobility of foreign labor within the mining sector. Rather, the mining companies, certainly in Limburg and the Borinage, wanted to curtail the miners' mobility autonomously, via their own private arrangements.

The trade unions seemed to be much less satisfied with the new legislation. However, since the beginning of the 1920s they had sought regulation of foreign labor's access to the labor market, and during the Depression that goal became even more desirable. How this control was organized by the law of March 1936 was, however, strongly criticized by the Socialist Union.[6] Unionized foreign labor, in particular, supported by the trade union groups belonging to the left of the Socialist Union, vehemently criticized the new law. The main criticism was that the law would put foreign labor at the mercy of the employers. It was the employers who had to ask for a labor permit, which made alien labor totally dependent on them. Those strongly opposed to the new legislation pointed out that respect for social legislation by foreign labor – the declared goal of the law of 31 March 1936 – could only be obtained if foreign labor felt safe in Belgium. Only if they were sure that their membership in a trade union or their participation in a strike would not jeopardize their job or even their stay in Belgium would they be ready to fight for decent working conditions. The new law only damaged the position of foreign labor and thus would only worsen the working conditions in those segments of the labor market where aliens were employed. Delattre, however, received unconditional support from some Socialist unions, e.g., the Socialist garment union was very positive about the law. The *Commission Syndicale*, the leadership of the Socialist trade union considered permanent control over all foreign labor essential and accepted the principles laid down by the new law. This union asked for two important changes to the law. Firstly, that foreign workers apply for a work permit themselves. They should not be dependent on the employer for their residence in Belgium. Secondly, and most crucial, was that not only employers and the state should regulate the immigration, but the unions should be consulted as well. That an expansion of the state's role in the labor market should occur without the union's participation was unacceptable to the unions. The trade union's proposals were to no avail. The former president of the Socialist miners' union, the then Labor Minister Delattre, did not meet the unions' demands. Employers remained responsible for demanding the work permit and the unions had no say in the decision-making process (*Belgische Vakbeweging* 1937:181f. and 209f.; and 1938:114ff.)

The new alien policy of 1936, under which aliens became free of state discretionary power only after ten years of residence was transplanted to the domain of trade, too. The reform of peddling legislation with the royal decree of 30 March 1936 made it possible to expel aliens whose application for a license to peddle was refused, but it also was a liberalization. The 1935 law on peddling had aimed at the removal from peddling of all aliens, except for those foreigners whose removal would jeopardize Belgian interests abroad. As mentioned before the "nationalization" of the peddlers' world had stirred up controversy. The new law was more liberal as it included a ten-year period of residence as the criterion for automatic approval for a license (BS 1936:2259ff.). As a result of this liberalization, not 10 percent but 50 percent of the applications of aliens received a positive response. The sharpest edges of the pre-eminently nationalistic law on peddling of January 1935 had been filed down. The new Minister of Justice, the Socialist E. Soudan, attempted to give the law concerning peddling a social dimension as well. He said that only foreign peddlers and market vendors who worsened the working conditions of their Belgian colleagues would be refused a peddler's license. For Soudan, the objective of his policy was not the "nationalization" of the peddler's world, but the improvement of the lot of the peddlers (PHK 1936:1145). This reasoning was already difficult to apply to the labor market, but to transpose it to the trade world was much more complicated, because there the mechanism of competition was much more complex. An inability to evaluate the intake of new traders led to a halt in the entry of immigrants in the vending trade. Applications of "recent" immigrants were as a rule turned down, except for those nationalities with whom a reciprocity agreement was concluded. This new restrictionist vision made a state interest of the private interests of the commercial class, which saw every new trader as a rival. The final outcome of the administration's policy became the exclusion of most "recent" immigrants. Certain nationalities, such as the Germans and the Czechoslovakians, but also the stateless, if they had not established themselves before 1927, remained banned from peddling.

For many Poles the exclusion was only temporary. By May 1936 1,145 market vendors of Polish nationality had obtained a peddling license. Of this number, 645 had probably been in Belgium for ten years and acquired their permit on the basis of the law of 31 March 1936. Five hundred of these Poles had been in Belgium for less that ten years, but obtained temporary peddler's licenses in the framework of the Belgian-Polish trade relations. The prolongation of the latter's licenses was dependent on Polish concessions in another area. The Minister of Economic Affairs, P. Van Isacker, insisted on having a corresponding concession. He was thinking about facilitating access to the Polish labor market for Belgian white-collar workers and engineers. Belgian investors in Poland had complained about the difficulties they encountered when they tried to employ Belgian personnel for their factories. For Van Isacker such a concession would justify to the public the extra peddler's licenses for Poles. The Polish authorities were asked to work out a proposal. The demand for a Polish concession remained a constant threat to the five hundred Polish traders. Notwithstanding the trade agreement of 2 April 1936, Belgian exports to Poland increased very little. The shortages in Poland's global trade balance caused the Polish authorities to institute strict controls on imports; quite a few products could no longer be imported. Between 7 December 1936 and 7 January 1937 Polish and Belgian authorities negotiated once again. Belgium walked away with a number of exclusive import concessions which sharply increased Belgian exports into Poland. The Belgian trade deficit declined. Nevertheless, complaints still rained down about Polish protectionism when the Polish Minister of Trade Roman visited Belgium in April 1937. The agreement of January 1937 was clearly not carried out to the letter. Belgium gave the Polish authorities a five-month extension before retaliating against Polish peddlers. Apparently the Polish authorities did not concede to the Belgian demands because at the end of September 1937, 327 Polish peddler's licenses were revoked. These Poles had been in Belgium for less than ten years and were issued a peddler's license in 1936 only because of the trade advantages which the Polish government had promised (AFAP 3554 and 3555).

The royal decree of 30 March 1936, which opened the peddling trade to aliens who had been in Belgium for ten years, found no favor in the eyes of Belgian merchants. The Belgian trade world had initially reacted positively to the regulation of peddling; finally the authorities had owned up to their responsibilities. The "disastrous" competition by foreign market vendors and peddlers could now be weeded out. The relaxation of the legislation was severely criticized. Hawking was for them synonymous with dishonesty and fraud. The authorities should weed out this evil by the root. This demand for a total prohibition on hawking by aliens was repeated until the end of the thirties, but in vain. The authorities did not want to diverge from the principle that ten-year's residence granted certain social rights to immigrants (Caestecker 1993:139ff.).

The new alien policy took fully into account the exceptional position of "refugees". During the Depression, it became generally accepted that refugees were a case apart. The royal decree of 20 February 1936 created the official category "refugee" within the immigration practice of the Belgian authorities. This new category also found an application in the social domain. There was some domestic pressure to grant "refugees" unconditional occupational opportunities. Their right to work should not be subordinated to the priority of national labor. As refugees they had nowhere to return, and they should be granted the possibility of earning a living in Belgium. This was a minority position; most unionists argued that refugees' access to the labor market should be dependent on vacancies in the market (*Belgische Vakbeweging* 1937:209). Only when no Belgian was available should aliens, "refugees" and economic immigrants alike, take these jobs.

That "refugees" became a privileged group of immigrants was a result largely of the international refugee regime. As mentioned before Belgium had adhered to the convention on the Russian "refugees" with reservations. Ratification of the convention had been postponed until the French agreed to sign it. In December 1936 the convention was ratified by the French Popular Front government. The Belgian government in turn put the convention before Parliament. A Socialist MP, H. Rolin, strongly criticized the Belgian reservation and called it a bad example of national egoism. His protest was not in vain, with the law of 28 July 1937 the convention was extended to Belgium in its full force (BS 1937: 5380ff.). The authorities would not expel any more Russian "refugees". In order to enable the Sûreté to sanction "refugees" if they endangered national security and public order, a provision was introduced in the law of 28 June 1937 to intern such "refugees". A Russian refugee whose refugee status was acknowledged by the Belgian authorities and who had acquired residency status in Belgium could now profit from a more favorable regime.[7]

Not only the regime of the Russian "refugees" in Belgium was influenced by international agreements; refugees from Nazi Germany also acquired some international protection. An international conference was convened in July 1936 to establish legal protection for German refugees similar to that existing for Nansen refugees. Representatives of the different frontline states (the states bordering Nazi Germany) adamantly refused to yield to even a minimal extent the power of their states to control the immigration of German refugees. In contrast to the rather definite conclusion of the Russian refugees crisis, the exodus of refugees from Nazi Germany was still going on. To yield some of their national sovereignty to a binding international agreement could have unforseen repercussions. The authorities would be defenseless if German emigration suddenly intensified.

In the final agreement, the frontline states retained complete sovereignty to decide who was a refugee protected by the agreement. The definition of a refugee from Germany adopted by the conference was not a universal definition. It was not objective criteria – the loss of protection by the German authorities – that decided who was a refugee. It was the authorities of the receiving country who decided if a refugee was eligible for refugee status. In February 1938 a new conference was convened to conclude an international convention on the status of refugees from Germany. The Convention of 10 February 1938 repeated the terms of the arrangement of 4 July 1936, but added some social provisions. "Refugees" originating from Germany were to be exempt from the legislation protecting the national labor market after three years of residence in exile. Belgium adhered to this convention, but stated that "refugees" from Germany would only be made exempt from the legislation protecting the national labor market after three years residency in Belgium. Residency was understood as acquiring residency status, i.e., inscription in the population register. Thus, "refugees" from Germany would be granted the status of privileged foreigner (labor permit A) only after five years of residence in Belgium. This restriction was introduced under pressure from the Ministry of Labor, which did not want the "refugees" to be treated more favorably than the nationals of those states with whom Belgium had reached bilateral labor agreements. The Belgian authorities made provisions in their alien legislation which spared the "refugees". All "refugees" were exempted from a strict application of the law of 31 March 1936 requiring work permits. Just as any foreign worker, every "refugee" working in somebody's service had to apply for a work permit. For "refugees", receipt of a work permit A depended on a residence of five years. Thus most Russian "refugees" received a work permit A, while recent Russian "refugees" and German "refugees" did not. Although "refugees" with less than five years residence, just as any "recent" immigrant, were only tolerated in the labor market to supplement local labor, some allowances were made for them. "Refugees" also obtained a special status in the peddlers' law of 30 March 1936; they obtained a vendors' license after not ten, but after only five years in Belgium (Caestecker 1993:80ff.).

The Uneasy Implementation of the New Policy

By 1936 Labor Minister Delattre, had lowered his ambitions regarding the new alien legislation. He no longer aimed for the removal of ten thousand aliens. He foresaw refusing work permits to only 5 percent of the eighty thousand foreign workers creating four thousand vacancies for unemployed Belgians (AML, chômage). The peddlers' legislation also aimed at the removal of a few thousand aliens: 1,700 peddlers were refused their peddlers' licenses in 1936. Therefore, about six thousand aliens who had immigrated into Belgium after 1926 were to leave the country. For repatriation purposes, one million francs had been provided in the budget of the Ministry of Justice of 1936; in 1937 half a million more was provided (PBK 1935: 93, 1937:21 and 1937:21).

The target par excellence of Delattre's policy of eliminating "unwanted" immigrants was the outworkers. They had to apply for a work permit before 15 September 1936. There were no victims among foreign labor in the diamond industry. The diamond sector was booming and all available qualified manpower, alien or not, had to be used. Between April 1936 and 23 March 1938, 2,300 work permits were granted to foreign diamond workers who had already been in Belgium for more than ten years. Moreover, another 885 work permits B were granted to aliens who had only arrived in Belgium after 1927 (PS 1939:102). Most of the foreign outworkers in other sectors were less lucky. Very soon after their application for work permits in the fall of 1936 came the verdict. Hundreds of garment workers, hatmakers, leather workers, etc. received not work permits, but orders to leave the country. Aliens who had been in Belgium for eight or nine years – the great immigration wave of the end of the 1920s – were ordered to leave the country. The Ministry of Justice ordered the police to revoke the identity cards of those aliens who had residency status. It seems that garment workers in particular were the victims of this drastic measure. This elimination policy put important economic interests in jeopardy. Large department stores and fashion houses insisted that some of these outworkers were of crucial importance for their businesses. As a result, in March 1937 some decisions were revoked. In June 1937 Delattre even decided to grant work permits to all immigrants who had been in Belgium for more than two years. Delattre justified this reversal by referring to the economic recovery which had set in by the second half of 1935 (AAD 33C31). The decline in unemployment among Belgian workers, however, was not general. While the export industries recovered, those sectors that were producing for the domestic market remained in trouble. The economic recovery can only be a partial explanation for Delattre's decision not to eliminate some unwanted aliens. Three explanations can be put forward for Delattre's leniency. First of all, it turned out that the unwanted aliens, for example the Jewish migrants in the garment industry, were not that unwanted. Their influence on the Belgian economy was a positive one. Because of their flexibility and qualifications they were of crucial importance for some economic sectors. Two additional factors were the administrative incapacity to deal with the thousands of applications and the new survival strategies of the immigrants.

Some foreign workers circumvented the new legislation by changing their professional status. They established themselves as self-employed artisans or shopkeepers, hence they no longer had to apply for a work permit. Some peddlers also did so. This was not always a calculated strategy. Unemployment among foreign labor rose in 1936 due to the mere fact that many employers were not eager to apply for work permits. Many employers fired all their foreign employees as they had ignored the exact terms of the law and did not want to run the risk of being forced to pay for their workers' repatriation. Whether it was forced upon foreign labor or a conscious decision not to be refused a work permit and thus be expelled, the consequence was that the number of small one-man businesses run by aliens rapidly increased, in commerce as well as in industry. This did not always mean that these aliens were effectively independent. Just as in the twenties, and certainly during the Depression, quite a bit of work in half-industrial sectors was subcontracted to outworkers. The number of outworkers among aliens rose sharply in the period 1936 to 1939. Graph 9 gives an overview of the commercial and industrial businesses which were run by Polish Jews in the city of Brussels in May 1939 and the dates of their establishment. It clearly illustrates the sudden appearance of Polish businesses as an important survival strategy for these aliens after 1935. The rather successful introduction of Jewish immigrants into the Belgian economic structure in the twenties by the creation of small ethnic niches was much more difficult now. The "Jewish" sectors became overcrowded and the extremely small half-industrial businesses were hardly viable economically; only by hard work and low profits were they able to survive. In the first place, the economic climate was such that new markets could not be tapped; and second, a joint effort by Jewish migrants in small and medium-sized businesses was not simple since the

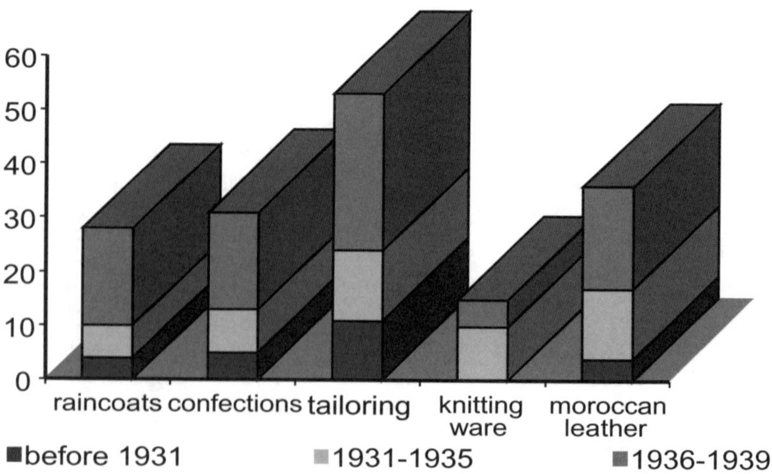

Graph 9 *Date of Establishment of Polish–Jewish Enterprises in Brussels*

employment of non-family members was dependent on the authorities' approval. The distribution of their products also became more difficult because of the vendor's license requirements. The "Jewish" economy responded in a creative manner to the attack on the distribution network. By means of sales representatives and by selling merchandise by a system of ordering, state control could be circumvented and the clientele expanded (Caestecker 1993:144ff.).

Another reason for Delattre's change of course was administrative inability to satisfy the requirements of the new legislation. Granting all foreign workers work permits was hindered considerably by a lack of personnel in the Foreign Labor Service of the Ministry of Labor. Certainly until the summer of 1937, the new service had no control whatsoever over foreign labor. By April 1937 this department had accumulated 12,000 applications for work permits which had not yet been processed. After the "amnesty" of June 1937 when all immigrants who had resided more than two years in Belgium received a work permit, the situation improved slightly. Furthermore, the department could not establish a documentation service to evaluate the demands or control the implementation of the law (AML unclassified). The judiciary could not start proceedings against foreign labor who had not yet regularized their employment. This administrative incapacity, and as we will see later, the labor shortage in mining, meant that Delattre had to warn the judiciary that to enforce the new alien policy strictly was not only impossible, but would be economically damaging, too (AAD 33C31). The administrative inadequacies of the Ministry of Labor also led to tensions with the Ministry of Justice. The Ministry of Justice had a long established tradition of handling applications for residence permits. This administration now had to take into account the decisions of the Ministry of Labor. The Sûreté was very negative about its new partner in the surveillance of aliens in Belgium. Due to the incapacity of the Foreign Labor Service to process applications, the Sûreté was forced to grant temporary residence permits to numerous labor migrants. On the other hand, immigrants sometimes received work permits from the Ministry of Labor before the Ministry of Justice had given its advice concerning their residence. Some immigrants, whom the Sûreté considered "undesirable" then tried to legalize their residence with these work permits (AAD 1B6/6-1939).

Delattre resented the limitations which economic interests, administrative inadequacy and the rush to self employment imposed on his power. He proposed to prevent foreign labor from damaging working conditions by extending his mandate. He drafted a bill to make private economic initiatives by aliens in industry or trade dependent on official authorization. The aim was not to curtail self-employment, but to ensure that foreign entrepreneurs obeyed the social legislation, paid their taxes, and did not make use of illegal trade practices. The bill provided for the expulsion of all foreign employers who did not pay their employees the minimum wage, made them work on Sundays or more than eight hours a day, etc. (AAD 33C44B/I). Although Delattre remained Minister of Labor until 1939, this bill was totally ignored in the following years, notwithstanding vehement discussions just before the onset of the Second World War on the necessity of controlling foreign entrepreneurs. Delattre's objectives could probably be attained by normal channels. The authorities had a control apparatus to enforce respect for the Belgian legislation. The labor inspection service could proceed against those entrepreneurs of Belgian and foreign nationality who violated the laws protecting labor. Tax evasion was difficult for aliens. Small businesses run by aliens, but not those directed by Belgians, were obliged to keep an up-to-date, detailed account of their affairs. Each year the Ministry of Finance also demanded from all foreign businessmen an advance on taxes due for the next fiscal year. To renew their temporary residence permit, businessmen who had not yet obtained identity cards had to present a declaration from the Ministry of Finance that they had fulfilled their fiscal obligations for the (Caestecker 1993c:168). Only in 1939 would foreign entrepreneurs become a central focus of state concern.

The Economic Recovery Needs Immigrants

The increasing demand for coal after the revival of the economy and the shortening of the working day brought in after the general strike in June 1936 caused important labor shortages in the mining industry. In order to satisfy the need for labor the mines hired aliens who had immigrated illegally. The new power constellation became visible when Delattre refused to grant those men work permits automatically. The indignation among the employers was great.

The mining companies were clearly on the defensive. When a number of mines enticed candidate-emigrants to leave for the Belgian mines, the FEDECHAR reprimanded these mines and called their action a stupid provocation. The Belgian authorities now had far-reaching competence over immigration. Only with their cooperation could immigrants be brought in. The FEDECHAR insisted to its members that only a disciplined performance by the Belgian mining industry would engender results in its negotiations with the Belgian authorities as well as with those of the emigration countries. No pretext should be given to the Belgian authorities to refuse recruitment abroad. It had to be clearly demonstrated that the need for recruiting miners abroad was a structural need and not limited to those mines where the working conditions were poor or the wages low (AHCM; ACCA; FEDECHAR).

In September 1936 the FEDECHAR submitted a request for the recruitment of four thousand miners. Delattre retorted that there were still many Belgians available. Every Belgian who applied for a job in the mines, regardless of ideological conviction, had to be accepted. Several mines refused to yield their prerogatives in recruitment totally, i.e., they still refused to hire "subversive" Belgians who, according to these employers, came to the mine, not to work, but to stir up trouble. Delattre argued, too, that the mining industry should attract unemployed Belgians from other sectors by wage increases. In order to give this approach a chance to succeed Delattre was prepared to sweeten the pill for inexperienced Belgian workers. For two months, the authorities would continue to pay out their unemployment benefits so that their limited earnings during the training period in the mine would be compensated (ARMA rC25/1). The professional instruction of the Belgian unemployed must and could solve the labor shortage in the mining industry. At that time, a centralized network of public labor-exchange offices; the National Labor Exchange Office, was being set up. Equal parity between employers and trade unions in the administration of this institution, together with an institutional link with unemployment insurance, was to assure an economically rational integration of this institution in the labor market. The new network had to make supply meet demand. The labor shortage in the mine sector put the new institution immediately to the test (Vanthemse 1989).

The mining companies rejected a national solution to their labor shortages as unrealistic. Unemployment insurance had taken away any motivation that the Belgian unemployed might have had to work in the mines. Furthermore, the demand for qualified workers could not be satisfied by the recruitment of inexperienced mine workers. Workers new to the profession could increase production only in the long run. The mining companies advocated a combined strategy, which aimed at guaranteeing production as well as clearing the way for the instruction of Belgians inexperienced in mining. The recruitment of qualified aliens would not only increase coal production, but also enable the mining companies to train Belgian unemployed labor (KADOC, Broekx, 5.2.3.1; KS, 139, 109).

The Socialist and Christian Democratic miners' unions disapproved of the recruitment of foreign labor. Their solution to the labor shortage in the mining sector was the radical revaluation of the miners' profession. Better labor conditions and higher wages, together with a training scheme for miners, would enable a rational use of the national labor reserves. The Communists agreed and joined the opposition against the recruitment of foreign labor. This protectionist standpoint was part of a fundamental shift in Communist strategy when the class-versus-class strategy was exchanged for the Popular Front strategy. The days of unreserved internationalism were over. While earlier on the Communists had only insisted upon the organization of foreign workers within the trade unions, now they also called for regulation of immigration. The recruitment of foreign manpower was portrayed as a managerial strategy to undermine the achievements of the Belgian working class. That Belgian Communist miners were kept on the dole also explains the Communist stance (PHK 1937:618ff.).

The threatened shortage of coal caused not only the FEDECHAR, but also a number of coke and steel factories to point out that the situation was beginning to become critical (ARMA bC1A10). The pressure on Delattre to give in increased, also within the government. The Minister of Economic Affairs, P. Van Isacker, and the Prime Minister, P. Van Zeeland, insisted upon a more pragmatic position (ARA bCr4dz3). Meanwhile, the unified front of the unions began to show signs of strain. The leadership of the Socialist miners' union began to regard radical opposition to recruitment as untenable. They advocated limited immigration supervised by the unions to forestall any harm to the working conditions of the Belgian miners. The Socialist unionists wanted guarantees that foreign labor was to receive the same wages as the Belgians and would be the first to be dismissed during an economic slump. If unemployed, foreign labor was to have the right to unemployment benefits. A repetition of the negative experiences of the depression years was to be avoided (AMSAB, Nauwelaerts, Executive Committee miners' union Liège). The Christian Democratic miners' union obstinately continued to stand firm on the rejection of recruitment of aliens. The Christian Democratic miners' union's aim for the long run was to expel all aliens from the mines. This union argued that Flanders was able to provide enough manpower to man the mine industry completely given the necessary instruction. In addition, national solidarity was necessary to provide the means to tangibly improve labor conditions and, in particular, wages so as to make the mine industry attractive to Belgians. The importation of foreign labor would substantially weaken the position of power in which the Belgian miners found themselves. In its negotiations with the authorities, this union denied that there was any reason to make an over-hasty decision. The shortage of manpower was limited. At first this union had proposed to "guide" aliens who were legally residing in Belgium to the mining sector regardless of the duration of their stay. This idea of a compulsory "return" of foreign labor to the mine was, however, quickly dropped. It was not consistent with a revaluation of the miners' profession, the cornerstone of the strategy to make the mine industry attractive for Belgians (CNMM; KADOC Broekx 13.2.7.5).

The short-term results of Delattre's national strategy, with the support of the unions, were extremely limited. In the second half of 1936, barely one hundred unemployed workers requested the financial support the government had promised to anyone who exchanged the unemployment offices for the mines. With some pressure the results improved somewhat.

The link established between unemployment insurance and the public labor exchanges enabled the authorities to deny the dole to those unemployed who refused a job offer. Unemployed ex-miners, under threat of withdrawing their unemployment benefits, returned to the mines (AML unclassified). In January 1937 the shortage of qualified miners became critical and the *Commission Syndicale*, the leadership of the Socialist union, gave its approval to the recruitment of foreign miners. In exchange for the renunciation of a fundamental opposition to the recruitment of foreign labor, the Socialist union was promised an immigration commission with union representation. The president of the Socialist miners' union, N. Dethier, defended this decision at the congress of the union. He exclaimed triumphantly that the employment of aliens no longer posed a threat to the labor conditions of Belgians. The immigration commission would not only be able to enforce equal labor conditions for all, but also would enable the union to adapt the employment of foreign labor continuously to the fluctuating demands of the labor market to ensure the priority of the Belgian labor force. The congress agreed to the decision of its leaders with little enthusiasm (*L'ouvrier mineur* 1937:39ff.). The recruitment of foreign labor under union control, notwithstanding the lasting opposition of the Christian Democratic union, could begin. Minister of Labor Delattre approved the recruitment of two thousand qualified foreign miners (PHK 1937:628). Delattre was also ready to legalize the stay of a number of undocumented immigrants within this quota. According to the Sûreté, this set a dangerous precedent: the mines where these laborers were employed should be obliged to repatriate them. Only in this way would the authorities be able to acquire control over immigration (AAD 33C30/9-1). Delattre warned the mining companies that this was a one-time approval; in future the letter of the law had to be respected. If the mines continued to hire undocumented immigrants, they would be forced to repatriate them at their own expense. The FEDECHAR advised its members to no longer make use of the services of undocumented aliens. The mining companies had to pay a security to cover the cost of travel to the border of the country of origin of each of the two thousand miners. This repatriation fund would ensure the return of "superfluous" foreign workers over the space of five years. The Christian Democratic miners' union as well as the Communists threatened to strike if foreign miners were brought in. Four hundred workers in Winterslag spontaneously struck in protest to the agreement of Delattre to tolerate new immigrants, but the Christian Democratic miners' union did not support the strike.

The mining companies negotiated with the Polish and the Italian authorities. The Italian authorities asked for extensive social rights for their emigrants and those negotiations were canceled. In Warsaw the authorities also advocated an improvement in the social rights of their emigrants. They urged the Belgian authorities to ratify the pension treaty of 7 November 1931 and grant Polish labor unemployment benefits. The Belgian authorities were not prepared to do this. High unemployment in Poland meant that the Polish authorities did not make an issue of this; they resignedly gave their approval to the recruitment of Polish workers. The recruitment of two thousand qualified miners posed no problem since hundreds of Poles had re-emigrated from the West and had not found a job at home. Not only the mining region of Upper Silesia, but also rural Polish regions that had supplied only unskilled manpower to the recruitment missions in the twenties now sent qualified miners to Belgium (AFAB 2652bis; AFAP 9895). The Polish miners arrived in March 1937. No strike took place. The Christian Democratic miners' union had resigned themselves to a limited import of foreign labor. The pressure of the national leadership of the Christian Democratic union not to put the economic revival in danger was most likely crucial in this decision.

The employment of these two thousand Polish miners was, however, not without difficulty. Low wages, administrative problems reuniting migrants with their families, miserable housing in the hostels, the treatment by the overseers, and lack of sufficient safety of the mines were all grounds for dissatisfaction among the Polish miners. Their discontent expressed itself in a series of collective protests. In May and June 1937, Polish immigrants went on strike in about twenty different mines. The authorities met these strikes with a restraint. In spite of the insistence of some mine directors, they rarely proceeded to expulsion. A number of "agitators" were dismissed, but the Sûreté – under pressure from the Ministry of Labor and the unions – took care that some of them were relocated to another basin. The mining companies were forced to concede partly to the demands of the Polish migrants. The FEDECHAR pointed out that quite a few problems stemmed from language difficulties, that they were merely misunderstandings. But the costs of these conflicts began to mount. Some Polish miners gave up and returned to Poland. A surveillance commission was set up to settle conflicts between the Polish miners and mine management. The workers could file their complaints with the commission, but while their complaints were under discussion they had to remain on the job. The presence of a representative from the Mine Administration and from the consulate along with a representative from mine management in this commission (interesting no representative of the trade unions was invited) meant that the interests of the Polish miners were not totally ignored. The Polish worker was able to express himself in his own language and where mine management went over the line, justice was administered to the migrant. Mostly workers without any experience in mining who were unable to cope with the work appealed to this commission. They hoped that in this way they would be able to walk away with a gratis repatriation.

If they just quit, they were afraid that they had to return at their expense. In a small number of cases where it truly seemed that the workers were not in condition, morally or physically, to continue working in the mines, they were repatriated (RABW, KS Eisden, 88).

In August 1937, as the labor shortage in mining increased, Delattre loosened his hold on recruitments entirely. The FEDECHAR received an unlimited mandate to supplement its underground workforce by means of recruitment abroad. Even unskilled hands could be recruited. This decision meant that Delattre's threat in March 1937 that illegally immigrated workers would be expelled at the expense of their employers was outdated. These aliens were now permitted immediate employment, but a work permit still had to be requested post factum. These amnesties enabled the Sûreté to eliminate subversive and criminal aliens among those who had immigrated illegally. The great demand for manpower together with the faulty administrative capacities of the Foreign Labor Service, meant that the authorities' grip on the labor market in the mines had to be loosened until 1 December 1937 when illegal immigration to work in the mines was no longer tolerated (BdL 181).

The mining industry organized the recruitment of labor mainly in Poland and Czechoslovakia. The recruitment mission had been instructed to recruit as many family members or friends of those already employed as possible. Poles and Czechoslovakians who had worked before in the Belgian mining industry and had performed well were sought after. The success of this strategy, however, depended on the stance of the emigration authorities. The recruitment mission started in Czechoslovakia, but hardly succeeded in recruiting qualified miners. Only 255 qualified miners could be recruited and 1,034 unskilled hands. The mission hoped to recruit enough qualified workers in Poland. The Polish authorities were accommodating and allowed the Belgian mission to recruit in the Wojewodztwa Poznan, Krakow, Pomorsza, the mine basin of Dabrowa, and the city of Gdynia. When the FEDECHAR was informed that a Polish mine dependent on a Belgian financial group, the Warsaw Mining Society, would close its books and five hundred miners would be out on the street the recruitment delegation immediately directed its efforts towards this group. The mine direction advised its miners to leave for Belgium since unemployment lay in the future. A few hundred miners were recruited this way. In July recruitments in Poland brought in 1,677 workers for the Belgian mining industry. On 24 July the Belgian recruitment delegation in Sosnowiec in the mine basin of Dabrowa was waylaid by candidate emigrants who contested the way in which the selection was being carried out. According to the FEDECHAR's representative in Poland, Deschamps, it was not possible to do anything in the Belgian mines with these radical workers. The candidates who had already been selected were rejected, and

Deschamps refused to continue working in the what he saw as the radical regions of Krakow and Dabrowa. Only the regions of Poznan and Pomorsza were still able to offer sound candidates. The Polish authorities could not tolerate the Belgian delegation's stipulation on where to recruit, but they were prepared to alter their permission to recruit to exclude the regions of Krakow and Dabrowa and substitute two other less "radical" areas (AFAP 9633 and 9895; FEDECHAR). At that time, the Polish workers confirmed their reputation as radicals when half of the 144 miners from the Warsaw Mining Society employed in the Limburg basin stopped working one week after their arrival and demanded to be transferred to Wallonia. These Poles were unsatisfied with labor conditions in the Limburg basin and were convinced that in Wallonia conditions were much better. The mining companies asked the Sûreté to expel them immediately. The intervention of the Socialist union was able to stop the expulsion of some of these Poles. Their transfer to Wallonia was however not conceded as it would create a precedent, something which the FEDECHAR and the Belgian authorities agreed had to be avoided at all costs. These Poles could remain in Belgium, but had to resume their work in the Limburg basin (KS, Eisden, 88; ARMA rC25/2). The Belgian mining companies had clearly had enough of the Polish "hot heads". All recruitment in Poland was stopped. The remaining thousand workers were recruited in Czechoslovakia. By the end of August 1937, all collective recruitments were put to an end. Seven thousand workers had been recruited (FEDECHAR).

Since July 1937 the FEDECHAR had already been considering shifting its recruitment strategy. The mining companies considered the results of the collective recruitments anything but successful. They argued that only personalized recruitment could supply good manpower. This type of recruitment had two objectives. On the one hand, qualified workers could be recruited who had already worked in Belgium. Their adaptation would pose fewer problems. On the other hand, individual recruitment on name could lessen the alienation that went along with migration. The authorities in Poland, Czechoslovakia, Yugoslavia and Hungary did not oppose this individual recruitment. In the following months 444 foreign workers were recruited individually by the mines (FEDECHAR; AHCM; BdL 181).

Along with these organized recruitments there was also a significant amount of uncontrolled immigration. During 1937, the stay of 1,100 aliens who had immigrated illegally to work in the mines was legalized. Therefore, taken together there was an increase of 8,498 workers in the mining sector (Rapport FEDECHAR 1938:65). The qualified miners among them posed problems similar to those of the first batch of Polish workers in March. The problems with the unskilled immigrants were of totally different nature. Their dissatisfaction was seldom or never expressed in collective protests, but that many were dissatisfied was made apparent in their search for an alternative to the mines. In Belgium, however, there were hardly any alternative employment opportunities. In France there were some opportunities in the beet harvest and also as wood-cutters. Many agricultural laborers among the new immigrants made use of the opportunity and left for France. Industry in Luxembourg also enticed some workers away from Belgium. The Belgian authorities, at the insistence of the FEDECHAR, went so far as to expel the foreign recruitment agents. The FEDECHAR also negotiated with the consular authorities to prevent desertion. The mining companies proposed that the consulates should keep the passports of the recruited workers in safekeeping until the labor contract had been completed. The consulates refused to do so. A number of mines that wanted to force the stabilization of their migrants by keeping their passports were quickly disabused of the idea. Not only the consular authorities, but also the Belgian authorities, clearly stated that this practice was illegal. Surveillance commissions were set up for all nationalities to attempt to convince workers, who in a number of cases had been sent back to the mines by the police, to complete their labor contracts. Often, if there were valid medical reasons, repatriation was financed by the security fund. If the deserter had, however, been illegally employed by another company, his repatriation had to be payed by the new employer (FEDECHAR; BdL 186). The stabilization of the new workers was a great success. As Graph 10 demonstrates, only a small segment of the recruited workers left the mines. Of the 6,954 who had been collectively recruited, 1,398 individuals left the mines in the course of 1937 (Rapport FEDECHAR 1938:65). This great success – certainly in comparison with the recruitments at the end of the twenties – was a

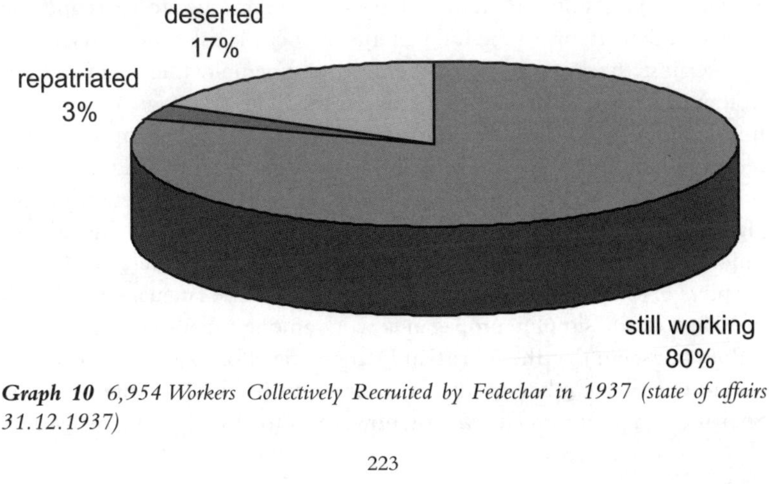

Graph 10 *6,954 Workers Collectively Recruited by Fedechar in 1937 (state of affairs 31.12.1937)*

result of the limited occupational alternatives for these migrants and of the authorities' efforts to see that they remained in the mining industry.

The organization of foreign labor became less important for the employers as the new alien legislation prohibited "recent" immigrants from leaving the mining industry. Not only the economic motivation for reaching out to foreign labor diminished, but also the political reason diminished in importance. The employers were increasingly forced by the public authorities to come to terms with the labor organizations. The state tried to convince them that the unions were to be considered partners in industrial relations. To keep the migrants away from these organizations was, therefore, not that important anymore. The heavy handed anti-union dimension in the employers' initiatives disappeared slowly.

For the trade unions, however, organizing foreign labor became a crucial task. The unions had agreed to recruitment abroad and they clearly stated that, once a worker had legally immigrated to Belgium, his interests had to be defended by the union. The Socialist union launched a national campaign to organize the Polish migrants, even a unionist permanently responsible for the Polish miners was nominated, Jeanne Pirotte (*L'ouvrier mineur* 1937:10/3). In each basin a commission was set up to look into the situation of the migrants and to see how the union could best defend their interests. The dependence of the migrants on employer's for housing, health insurance, etc. was denounced, and with the help of the Socialist party and their influence within government, the Belgian unionists tried to diminish this dependence. The immigrants' right to strike and to engage in trade union activities was vigorously defended. Expulsion of trade unionists was radically opposed. According to the Socialist miners' union, fully endorsed by the Communists, unionizing immigrants and defending their pay and working conditions was the only way to prevent employers from abusing foreign labor to worsen working conditions. The Socialist miners' union took the interests of foreign labor to heart and also defended their rights to the full benefits of social legislation. Discrimination against the immigrants in the field of unemployment and old age insurance in particular had to be overcome. The Christian Democratic union defended a similar position. Although they had opposed the recruitment, this union proclaimed that all the miners in Belgium, aliens or not, were to join their union which would defend the interests of foreign workers. The Christian Democratic as well as the Socialist miners' union set up ethnic locals for foreign labor. These locals were considered chapters of Belgian locals. An ethnic local where the language was Polish or Italian would simplify propaganda work among the immigrants. While it does not seem that the Christian Democratic effort was very successful, a considerable number of Polish miners did become members of the Socialist miners' union. It was not, however, a total success. Virtually only the recent immigrants, the ones who had been recruited in Poland in the spring and summer of 1937, joined the union. The older migrants stayed aloof. Both of the trade unions took the interests of foreign labor to heart and insisted on granting them the benefits of unemployment insurance. These pressures were to no avail. Foreign labor remained excluded from unemployment insurance. Even the Belgian-Polish agreement of 1931 on the miners' pensions was, because of financial reasons, not ratified. As the trade unions failed to adapt social legislation to their new interests, their new strategy towards foreign labor was in jeopardy.

Immigrants were also needed beyond heavy industry. Other sectors, such as the quarries, agriculture, and domestic service, which were not able to find enough Belgian labor in the 1920s because of their unattractive working conditions also obtained authorization to recruit foreign labor in 1937. For reasons similar to those in the mining industry all undocumented aliens who had been hired as agrarian labor before 27 October 1937 were allowed to legalize their stay. The hotel sector applied again for authorization to employ their highly qualified seasonal labor. These hotels insisted that they needed highly qualified personnel each season. They claimed that there were not enough qualified Belgians available and that it made no sense to train sufficient local personnel as the need was only seasonal. According to both unions, enough Belgians were willing and capable to do those jobs. The first class hotels at the seaside were given an authorization for about hundred persons in 1936, the same number they had received for the summer season of 1935. In the fall of 1936, Delattre decided to look more seriously into the matter for the next season. The National Labor Exchange Office, the state's new instrument for the regulation of the labor market was charged with this operation. By the end of March 1937, all the hotels had to make up a list of the aliens they wanted to employ and what qualifications those workers had. The National Labor Exchange Office would then look into the possibility of finding Belgians for those jobs. All Belgians, and also all aliens, residing legally in Belgium willing to do this seasonal work, had to register at the local labor exchange offices. Only after comparing the two lists would a decision be made. The employers presented lists of personnel needs with high qualification requirements. The labor exchange offices did not yet have a list of available personnel at their disposal and the unions, certain that there was no specific shortage of manpower in the hotel industry, were nevertheless unable to come up with enough qualified Belgians. The unions contested the hotels requirement for such highly skilled personnel and argued that the hotels only wanted aliens because they did not wanted to pay decent wages. Minister of Labor Delattre did not follow the advice of the unions and the hotels were authorized to hire their traditional foreign labor for the season of 1937.

Conclusion

The law of 31 March 1936 was the final step in the reform of legislation concerning foreign labor, a step prepared by the reforms of 1930 and 1935. This law remained the structure around which alien policy would revolve in the following decades. This legislation was not due to any immediate issue as the shifting motivation of Minister of Labor, A.Delattre, illustrates. He initially conceived of reforming alien legislation to eradicate unemployment among Belgians in the hotel sector and the mines as an alternative to his failed quota law. Finally, he legitimized it by the need to eliminate "dishonest" competition by foreign outworkers. The 1936 reform rationalized the exclusion aimed at by the peddlers' and the quota law by providing for the legal expulsion of economically undesirable aliens. This rationalization of the radical alien policy also had a more liberal dimension. Full occupational mobility was recovered after ten years residence in Belgium. Immigrants then also achieved permanent resident status, or in other words, denizen status. The new peddler's law was also conceived in the same spirit: it mitigated the effects of the peddler's law of January 1935 by no longer aiming at the exclusion of all foreign peddlers from this trade. The unions had been insisting on a state control over foreign labor since the beginning of the 1920s; national labor had to be protected against newcomers in the labor market. The reform of alien policy has to be seen within the broad political process of integration of labor. The influence on the alien policy of the Ministry of Labor as an equal partner with the Ministry of Justice was the institutional translation of this change within the state. The absence of an institutionalized role for the unions is an indication that corporatism was not yet a feature of Belgium's political economy. Although the state now agreed to intervene in the labor market to protect national labor, it would do this on its own terms. Except for this issue, reform was seemingly uncontroversial. Reservations were voiced concerning only the practical implementation of the reform, not its principle.

This reform was no break with the past. It elaborated on the design established in the law of 15 February 1935 enacted by the conservative Theunis cabinet, but it radicalized control over foreign labor by extending the probationary period from five years to ten and by implementing this legislation with retroactive effect. The scope of migration control had increased considerably. The doubling of the period necessary to achieve denizen status was the consequence of an external factor: the radicalization in French alien policy in February 1935. Concern to safeguard the position of Belgian nationals working in France was the immediate cause, but the desire to attune Belgian alien policy to the French one has little relevance when one considers the small size of the French workers' community in

Belgium. Imitating the restrictive French policy created a dynamic of its own. Other diplomatic considerations hardly played a role in the decision-making process of this reform. Providing for "exceptional" favorable treatment for specific nationalities was the solution to the dilemma of maintaining hold over foreign workers while meeting Belgium's interests abroad. An issue with far-reaching implications, i.e. who was to apply for a labor permit, seems to have been treated merely as a technical issue. It was decided that only employers were to apply for work permits. The opposition of the trade unions did not change anything in this respect. All previous bills and laws provided that the immigrants alone were to ask for the work permit or that both, employers and employees, were to do so. To ensure a smooth procedure, foreign labor became even more dependent on the employers. Both of these crucial changes and the way they were introduced were rooted in a total neglect of the interests of foreign labor. Labor immigrants were a negligible quantity, they were considered only extremely flexible economic actors. Labor immigrants were looked upon as a commodity to be manipulated to the benefit of the national economy. The narrow mindedness with which the interests of national labor were conceived, totally ignoring the power position of foreign workers in relation to the state as well as to the employers would, in the long run, only increase the desertion rate of the indigenous labor force from the industries where foreign labor was becoming a structural component.

An important innovation in the field of immigration policy was that the process of admitting refugees was now treated separately. During the Depression, a first unofficial step had already been made in the direction of differentiating refugees from all other immigrants. In 1936 this procedure was institutionalized. The control over the refugees' economic position was also mitigated as official allowances were made for "refugees" legally residing in the country. "Refugee" became a category fully entrenched in Belgian alien policy. The right of asylum as a liberal principle was definitely adhered to.

The retroactive validity of the legislation of 31 March 1936 which was to result in mass deportation of economically undesirable migrants – the most radical aspect of the aliens' legislation – was not implemented in the end. Administrative inadequacies, but more importantly economic interests, curtailed the considerable power the Ministry of Labor wielded over foreign labor. Foreign labor residing legally in the country was spared any restrictive intervention in its occupational pursuits. Only new immigrants were to be subject to the restrictive alien legislation. Labor recruitment became much more politicized than before. While the Belgian state was largely absent in the employer-led recruitments of the 1920s, the state now had to give its sanction to any labor recruitment. Employers had to convince the public authorities of the need to call upon labor abroad. The state sanctioned labor recruitment only reluctantly. The large pool of unemployed Belgian workers meant that strictly quantitative self-sufficiency was possible. The labor market, however, was not a homogeneous market where labor could be easily reallocated. Not only the necessary skills needed for certain jobs, but also the willingness of the unemployed workers to do them had to be taken into account.

Immigrants and employers did not attend strictly to the receiving, or for that matter the sending, country's migration policy. Despite the reform, the old informal system persisted, and undocumented aliens were still employed. Economic reasons made the authorities tolerate "illegal" immigration to those sectors with labor shortages. The Belgian state, although temporarily loosing its hold over the influx for economic and administrative reasons, was anxious to re-establish its control over foreign labor as soon as the economic conditions permitted. The policy of granting residence and work permits even to those who had immigrated illegally and at the same time demanding a security deposit from employers for all the newcomers they employed was to guarantee that if conditions changed the authorities would be able to send these immigrants back home. Legalization was an admission of failure to control entry, but demonstrated an insistence on regulation of foreign labor once it had arrived.

In the mining sector the demand to recruit abroad would cause a protracted debate over the reasons why these vital jobs could not attract local workers. A disciplined mining industry under the aegis of the FEDECHAR pushed for recruitment abroad. The unions proposed to make mining jobs more attractive by improving working conditions and pay. Not only the unions, also the Minister of Labor wanted to induce more Belgians to work in the mines. The nature of mine work and the availability of other opportunities, including the income which unemployment insurance provided, meant that the mining industry could attract very few Belgians, even among the unemployed. Short-term economic needs – in particular the dire need for coal – could not be met in this way. The union strategy to make more Belgians inclined to descend the shaft by rendering those jobs more attractive offered no immediate solution. In particular, the Christian Democratic miners' union continued to contest the economic necessity of foreign labor. They pleaded for "over-compensation" for mine work. The Socialist union was less radical. This union acknowledged that foreign labor was a structural part of Belgian mining and agreed to the recruitment of immigrants. From this perspective, organizing immigrants became a crucial task for the unions.

The need for state support for recruitment slightly diminished the amount of leeway the industries had in hiring. Belgian applicants, independent of political considerations, had to be hired before recruitments could be approved. Equal working conditions for foreign labor also had to be guaranteed. No institutional role was granted to the unions. Control over working conditions by joint commissions was promised to the unions but never materialized. These changes raised the price of immigration only slightly and thus did not force the labor deficient sectors to make hard decisions regarding alternatives to foreign labor. Who was recruited remained a prerogative of the employers. This freedom was still being used by the employers to avail themselves of a "docile" workforce, even if the economic quality of the workforce suffered from this political consideration. Emigration countries had lost much of the power they had wielded in the 1920s. As the demand for their labor supply had decreased considerably and their national economies were in difficulties, they conceded to nearly any demand made by the recruiting industries.

Notes

1. Only then did a more conciliatory faction of the employers gain momentum. Heavy industry lost influence to the advantage of transforming industry which was more eager to reach an agreement with organized labor. Organized labor then became an institutionalized partner in the bargaining process with business and the government (Luyten 1995).
2. All categories of aliens could be punished with an expulsion if they did not abide by this legislation. The first category was created by the royal decree of 15 December 1930. The category "recent" immigrants was created by the royal decree of 15 August 1933 and after two years of residence an identity card was granted. "Recent" labor migrants were added by the royal decree of 15 February 1935 and an identity card was granted after five years of residence. The third and fourth categories were created by the law of 31 March 1936. In theory, a transfer from category one to four required a residence of ten years (nationals of countries with whom Belgium had reached a labor treaty and also "refugees" five years).
3. This was a temporary category until the Ministry of Justice adjusted its practice to the law of 31 March 1936. In 1937 it covered all aliens who had obtained their identity cards between 1927 and 1933; after August 1933 it is highly likely that hardly any new identity cards were still granted.
4. Privileged immigrants could also be aliens married to a Belgian who had children born of this marriage or who had already lived in Belgium for five years. Foreigners born in Belgium and citizens of Luxembourg and the Netherlands could also be considered privileged aliens. French immigrants, including Algerians, but not other North Africans, could receive (in agreement with the French-Belgian labor treaty) the status of privileged immigrant after five years of residence in Belgium. This would be the case as well for citizens of Italy after the signing of the Belgian-Italian labor treaty of 29 September 1938.
5. The Holvoet bill foresaw a scheme similar to the French system of control of foreign labor whereby the alien card was a temporary residence permit as well as a work permit. The maximum validity of the alien card would have been two years. Granting an alien card to labor migrants would have been dependent on the admission of the alien and eventually the permission for the employer to hire him. The provisions of the Holvoet bill concerning residence had been enacted by the law of 13 August 1933. The law of 31 March 1936 enacted the provision concerning employment for labor migrants, but by a seperate administration and only dependent on a permission.

6. We did not find any criticism emanating from the Christian Democratic Union, although this union probably resented, just as in 1931, its exclusion from policy making.
7. Only a "legal" stay, defined as registration in the population register, entitled a "refugee" to this favorable regime. Newly arriving Russian "refugees", mostly fleeing Nazi Germany, retained their refugee status, but were not entitled to this refugee regime. Even when they were granted residence – a favor completely dependent on the goodwill of the Belgian authorities – they still could not profit from this regime. Only when they were registered in the population register did the refugee regime apply. Repatriation of "refugees" was, however, excluded under the principle of *non refoulement.*

Chapter 9

ALIEN POLICY IN TURMOIL, 1938–1940

With the worsening of international economic conditions, Belgium became caught up in a new recession in 1938. The sharply divided middle class had not succeeded in strengthening its economic position and received a severe blow once again. The traditional parties had shown their receptiveness to the demands of the middle class and they succeeded to reestablishing their legitimacy among this social group. The electoral score of Rex dwindled, but the VNV was able to consolidate its electoral support. The labor organizations retained political leverage through the presence in the Government of Christian Democrats and, except for the second Pierlot cabinet (18 April to 3 September 1939), also Socialists. Notwithstanding the presence of these ministers representing labor, the government returned to traditional economic policy making. The deflationary policy was resumed once again.

The Unattainable Objective: Closing the Borders

While in 1937 the Sûreté had been forced by powerful economic interests to loosen its grip on immigration by tolerating undocumented immigrants, in 1938 it could reassert its control over immigration. There was no longer a need for additional manpower and hence allowances no longer had to be made for undocumented aliens. At the border, the number of aliens refused access to the country increased by 400 percent in 1938, from 2,320 to 7,797 (Graph 14). In 1939 another 5,842 aliens were refused access to Belgium. Control over immigration was extended within the borders as well. In January 1938 the Ministry of Justice ordered the expulsion of all those who had immigrated illegally (AAD 1B6-1939). The number of aliens who were removed from within the country (*renvoyer*) nearly doubled, from 1,907 in 1937 to 3,303 the following year (Graph 15). A few immigrants still served officially sanctioned economic interests.

Tolerated Immigrants

Unemployment in these years led the authorities to believe that local labor could fill all of the needs of the labor market. The transparency of the market through the regional labor exchange offices, together with training the work force to answer specific needs, would make dependence on foreign labor obsolete. Despite impediments, three traditional groups of immigrants -farm hands, domestic servants and highly qualified hotel personnel- continued to arrive legally in Belgium. An investigation by the public labor exchange offices indicated there was a small shortage of qualified farm labor such as cowmen and year-round farm hands. For all the other categories of farm labor enough Belgians were available. Of the Polish farm hands who had been recruited in the summer of 1937, nearly all had returned to Poland by December 1938. Hard working conditions and low pay meant that very few were willing to prolong their contract. The public labor exchange offices had contacted the farmers who employed these Polish farm hands in order to provide them with Belgian labor as soon as the contracts of the Poles had expired. When, in the summer of 1939, the *Fédération Nationale des Unions Professionelles Agricoles* again applied for Polish agrarian labor, the Christian Democratic Minister of Labor, A. Delfosse, was willing to grant them a few authorizations for Polish farm hands, but only if the farmers agreed to train Belgians in the future (ALVB NBDAW). The demand to seek domestic servants abroad, mainly in Hungary and Poland was less contested. The Sûreté was opposed to the recruitment of any more Polish women, arguing that Belgium could be stuck with these women as the Polish authorities denationalized more and more of their emigrants. Importing more Poles would also add fuel to xenophobic agitation. However, the shortage of domestic servants meant that these arguments were ignored (AAD 33C30/2, AFAP 9632 and 9895). The recruitment of seasonal personnel for the first class hotels at the seaside continued in these years of high unemployment. In 1938 the National Labor Exchange Office was much better prepared for its task. The hotel sector even got a separate job placement service and special attention was paid to highly qualified Belgian hotel personnel. The trade unions were strongly opposed to any immigration of hotel personnel, but in the spring of 1938, just as in previous years, the first class hotels at the seaside received a few hundred authorizations to call upon seasonal qualified foreign labor. The Ministry of Labor agreed with the hotel managers that the Belgian unemployed were not qualified enough to work in these hotels (PS 1939:80).

The politically troubled period just before the Second World War caused an increase in forced emigration. The flow of refugees became a flood. Especially in Germany, the Nazis' total control of the state led to an expulsion en masse of Jewish refugees. To please Hitler, Mussolini followed the German example of excluding Jews from the nation. Thousand of people had to flee not only from Germany and Italy but also, with the expansion of the German Reich, from Austria, Saarland, and Sudetenland. The new dynamics of persecution of Jews in the Third Reich meant that not only young men fled the Hitler regime, but that whole families chose the path of exile. These refugees, almost without exception, had lost all their possessions before departure. To stop the illegal immigration of refugees, visas were requested from all refugee-producing countries. Personnel at the borders was increased. Thousands of refugees were refused access to Belgium. The Belgian border, however, was not impermeable; numerous refugees could slip through, mostly with the help of hired smugglers. Between the spring of 1938 and the summer of 1939 about 24,000 refugees from old and new German territory found their way into Belgium. The regulations for the refugee *stricto sensu*, the political "refugee", remained intact. "Refugees", even if they immigrated illegally, could remain in the country by petitioning for asylum. Between July 1936 and August 1939, 995 aliens petitioned for asylum; about half of them were granted refugee status. The advisory commission which investigated whether asylum seekers were "refugees" was reformed in August 1939 in order to speed up the procedure. The authorities wanted to combat the so-called abuse of the asylum procedure, they alleged that economic immigrants and even criminals used the asylum procedure to circumvent border controls. From September 1939 until the invasion by Nazi Germany in May 1940, a smaller advisory commission processed 144 asylum applications (AAD X1).

Already at the end of 1937 the Catholic Minister of Justice, du Bus de Warnaffe, had decided that no more provisions had to be made for the victims of anti-semitic persecution, the refugees *sensu lato*. J.Pholien, also a Catholic politician, succeeded de Bus de Warnaffe as Minister of Justice in May 1938. His nomination coincided with a radicalization in Nazi policies towards Jews residing in greater Germany. In the spring of 1938 thousands of Jews were brutally expelled and with the complicity of German police and military forces dumped in Belgium (Graph 11[1]). The Belgian Jewish community re-affirmed its solidarity with the Jewish refugees from the German Reich and pledged to organize their emigration overseas. They also took responsibility for the temporary reception of these Jewish expellees. In May 1938 Pholien agreed to reintroduce the provisions for refugees *sensu lato*, i.e. Jewish refugees from Germany, even if they had immigrated illegally, were again to be tolerated. During the summer no less than four thousand Jewish refugees succeeded in penetrating Belgian territory. Pholien spoke of an invasion and decided to expel all destitute male Jewish refugees arriving in the country from September onwards (AAD 37c). According to Pholien, the Jewish emigrants were merely looking for a better place to live, so no favors were to be granted to them. This decision to halt any further Jewish immigration was not radically opposed even on the left. A more restrictive immigration policy was not opposed as long as the "refugees" were not sent back to their country of persecution. Willem Vanderveken, the secretary of the Socialist refugee committee, affirmed this clearly in an article in the Socialist newspaper *Le Peuple* of 29 August, 1938 in which he stated: "Belgium has reasons to defend itself against a systematic immigration directed against the vital interests of the country. Not a few Austrians, whose departure was wanted by Hitler, have lent themselves to an expatriation deal and this with the complaisance, if not the complicity of the bosses of the Reich, and probably also of certain Belgian policemen. Such an illegal immigration will never get our support. It brings discredit on the edifice of protection which we have painstakingly constructed to the advantage of the real political refugees". In October 1938, as a consequence of this option for a more restrictive refugee policy, a few hundred Jewish refugees were treated as any other illegal immigrants and were sent back to the country they had fled. This forcible repatriation was denounced by the Jewish community which was supported by broad political circles. Pholien had to retreat. Jewish refugees were again considered refugees *sensu lato* and granted temporary residence permits to enable them to organize their emigration. Notwithstanding the increasingly bru-

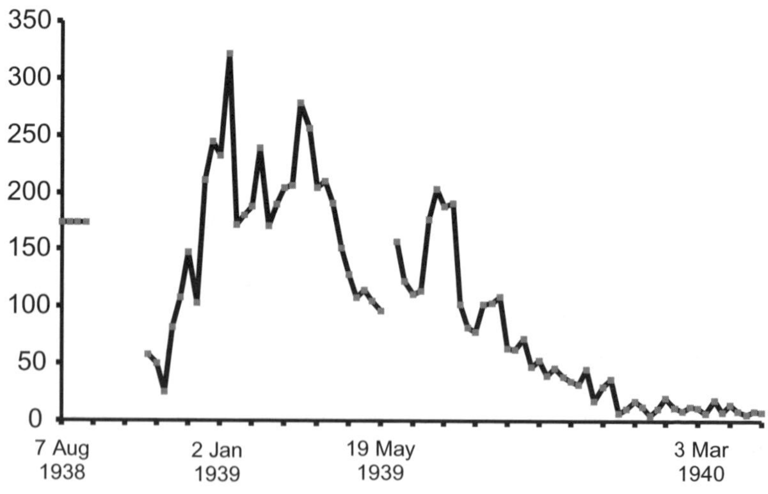

Graph 11 *Refugees Registered at the End of Each Week by the Jewish Committee, Brussels (August 1938–April 1940)*

tal state policy against the Jews in greater Germany, these victims of racist persecution continued to be denied official refugee status. The presidents of the advisory commission set up in 1936 to investigate whether asylum seekers were genuine refugees decided in January 1939 that the Minister of Justice should take into account the radicalization of anti-Jewish policy in Nazi Germany. These judges informed the minister that from October 1938 onwards – after the infamous *Reichskristallnacht* – Jewish emigrants should be recognized collectively as refugees. The distinction between refugee *stricto sensu* and *sensu lato*, in the sense of a distinction between political and racial persecution, had become meaningless. They argued that the international convention on the refugees from Germany of February 1938 obliged the Belgian authorities to recognize the Jewish emigrants as refugees as it was now obvious that they did not receive any protection from the German government. If the authorities did not want all the Jewish refugees from Nazi Germany to obtain refugee status, the task of the commission had to be changed and Belgium had to withdraw its signature from the convention. H. Bekaert, by then *administrateur-adjoint* of the Sûreté, disagreed that a radical change of course in refugee policy was necessary. He argued that the Geneva Convention gave Belgian authorities complete leeway to decide whether a refugee was eligible to apply for refugee status. Bekaert claimed that being a "refugee" was not an objectively determined category. "Refugee" was a politically constructed status which had to receive the approval of the attributing state. Although he acknowledged the collective persecution of the Jews in Germany, he stated that this was not sufficient to recognize all Jewish emigrants from Germany as refugees. "Refugees" not only had to be lacking protection from their proper state, but the national interests of the receiving state should also be unopposed to their recognition as refugees. Therefore an individual procedure was still necessary, a procedure by which "undesirable" refugees, those who "abused" the refugee status or who could not be absorbed by the receiving country could be weeded out (AAD 37C and 37C6). In practice this line of reasoning implied that the Jewish refugees were collectively excluded from the refugee procedure. The Sûreté insisted on stopping the flood and expelling all these illegal entrants. The political authorities, however, did not consider the Jewish refugees merely a problem of law and order. The illegal immigration of Jewish refugees was tolerated, but these refugees could not apply for asylum. Jewish refugees who immigrated illegally were still tolerated in order to enable them to find a definite host country. This unofficial refugee policy was based on the view of Belgium as a pivot within an international scheme of resettling refugees. In the spring and the summer of 1939 Jewish refugees continued to arrive (Graph 11). The unofficial refugee policy was questioned again and again within the government, but the authorities balked at a forcible repatriation.

The Jewish committees dutifully continued to assume responsibility for refugees who outwitted the border patrol. Complete Jewish financial responsibility for these refugees meant that their reception did not cost the Belgian treasury anything. Jewish refugees were still forbidden to engage in any economic activity. They had to live on the meager support that the Jewish aid committees distributed until their definite emigration was arranged. The limited opportunities for further emigration, together with the financial problems of the Jewish committees, signified the failure of subcontracting the reception of Jewish refugees to these private organizations. The sheer weight of numbers prevented the committee from finding sufficient resources. Certain political and social groups used the presence of these transit refugees as the focus of an increasingly virulent xenophobic agitation. In spite of this intensifying xenophobia, there was a consensus among all the traditional parties that it was not possible to send back Jewish refugees who were already in Belgium. Finally the authorities were "forced" to share the financial burden of the Jewish refugees with the aid committees. In June 1939 a budget of six million francs was allotted to the Ministry of Justice to subsidize the reception of refugees and for 1940 this was increased to eight million. Notwithstanding the outbreak of the war, Jews fleeing Nazi Germany continued to arrive. Until 13 October 1939 the stay of Jewish refugees from Nazi Germany was legalized just as it had been since the autumn of 1933 (Caestecker 1993c:180ff.).

Undocumented Aliens

An unknown number of immigrants were undocumented. These aliens were mainly labor migrants who had immigrated illegally and had been unable or unwilling to legalize their residence. Undocumented immigrants were extremely vulnerable. They had to take care to stay one step ahead of the police, or run the risk of being transported to the border. For those who had already been expelled twice, an expulsion by royal decree could follow and hence upon a third return a conviction for *rupture de ban*. The destitute, undocumented aliens from non-neighboring countries risked a forced stay in a vagrant colony. The rise in funds for repatriation enabled the Belgian authorities to settle some hard core cases. Alfred Heidler, the Estonian draft dodger who had been in Belgium since at least 1930 was in this way finally repatriated to Tallinn. By then he had been sent five times to Merksplas where he had spent, in total, about one year. In 1936 he was expelled by royal decree but never condemned for *rupture de ban* as he had never left the country (AAD). From 1938 onwards, not only at the eastern border, but also at the western border, diplomatic agreements imposed restraints on the Belgian expulsion policy. An agreement concluded with France on 21 October 1938 stipulated that Belgium could only expel unwanted third country citizens to France if these third country nationals had to pass through France to return to their country. Their nationality had to be clearly documented and for the destitute among them the Belgian authorities had to fund the transit fare (AFAB 12,181).

In the labor market, undocumented immigrants were joined by the Jewish refugees whose stay had received official authorization, but who were forbidden to work. The daily allowances which the Jewish committees granted these refugees were totally insufficient and by the spring of 1939 it became absolutely necessary for the Jewish refugees to earn some income by working. The only way they could earn a living in a legal manner was to work as domestic servants. Labor migrants and "refugees" who had not yet achieved the status of privileged aliens, but were working outside the sectors where the Ministry of Labor considered aliens had to work, were in a very vulnerable position. These immigrants and refugees without work permits were subject to severe exploitation by employers who could employ and dismiss them at will, pay them low wages, and ignore their working conditions.

After the onset of the Second World War the policy towards undocumented immigrants tightened considerably. The royal decree of 28 September 1939 made the mere fact of immigrating or staying in Belgium without the permission of the authorities a criminally triable offence which could be punished with prison terms of between eight days and one year. This royal decree not only granted the courts authority to take action against illegal aliens, the Minister of Justice was also granted the authority to expel or to intern any alien who was a threat to the national security and the national economy (BS 1939:6702ff.). The authorities deemed this enlargement of administrative and judicial power necessary for national security and public order. As mentioned before, until 13 October 1939, the stay of Jewish refugees from Nazi Germany was legalized time and again. After 13 October 1939, Jewish refugees from Nazi Germany continued to arrive (Graph 11). The Sûreté which had campaigned for years for strict control over all illegal immigration now found an ally: the military authorities. The military authorities were preoccupied with the danger of spies and considered any alien who succeeded in entering Belgian territory illegally as highly suspect and thus absolutely undesirable. The military authorities believed that they had to be expelled without any other consideration than national defense. This preoccupation with spies became paramount in immigration policy, including refugee policy. The Socialist Minister of Justice, E. Soudan, rhetorically asked in Parliament how these refugees could pass the German border and he wondered openly if they were on a mission (PHS 1939:159). From 9 December 1939 onwards, Soudan decided that all undocumented immigrants, even Jews fleeing Nazi Germany, were to be arrested and brought before the courts. Soudan did not expect very much of this decision. The experience with the law of 28 September 1939 showed, according to Soudan, that magistrates were too lenient. Indeed in 1939, of the 452 aliens brought before court because of illegal stay, only two got a prison sentence of more than two months. The judiciary considered these undocumented aliens harmless in comparison to their habitual clientele (AAD 143C-2). Anyway, even a less lenient attitude by the judiciary would not stop those fleeing Nazi Germany; for these people internment in Belgium was an improvement in comparison with their situation in Nazi Germany. Soudan, considered the only efficient policy to be the expulsion of all illegal entrants. He referred to the experiment of October 1938 when the then Minister of Justice, J. Pholien, had repatriated Jewish refugees by force. Soudan assigned this experiment a great psychological impact: not only did those repatriated refugees never return, but also the number of illegal entrants dropped spectacularly. He believed the efficiency of a radical expulsion policy was demonstrated clearly by this short-lived experiment. In addition, to expel all undocumented aliens indiscriminately had the advantage of not having to make a selection between those who were a risk to the nation and those who were not. Soudan considered that only expulsion would yield results, any other policy was doomed to fail as it would not deter those fleeing Nazi Germany. All undocumented aliens were to be expelled after serving their sentences. Due to the intervention of Prime Minister, H. Pierlot, who considered expulsion of refugees inhumane, Soudan made two exceptions: political refugees were not to be expelled and those whose existence would be in danger were not to be returned. Both of those categories were to be convicted, but after serving their sentences they were not to be expelled. Soudan stated explicitly that these exceptions were to be interpreted restrictively (AAD 37C6). The judiciary contested the decision of Soudan to arrest all illegal entrants. Some refugees who had petitioned the advisory commission for asylum before they were set free because the judiciary wanted to uphold the provisions for refugees, fully entrenched in Belgian legislation since 1936 (*Rechtskundig Weekblad* 1940:674). In most cases, however, the undocumented immigrants, including refugees, were convicted, but the judiciary sentenced them only to short prison terms. From September 1939 until May 1940, of the total number of 1,295 aliens convicted because of illegal stay, only four got a sentence of more than two months (*Statistique judiciaire* 1931-1942:56).

Soudan's career as Minister of Justice in the Pierlot cabinet did not last long. On 5 January 1940, P.E. Janson became Minister of Justice. Janson confirmed the strategy of his predecessor, but was more indulgent. He ordered that Jews fleeing Nazi Germany, except for those with a criminal record, were not to be expelled. The refugees, even if they were acquitted by the courts, were not set free. The Sûreté deemed their liberation inopportune because of national security and public order. Undocumented aliens had to stay in prison. The prisons quickly became overcrowded. As an alternative, refugees were transferred to camps, administrated like prisons (Caestecker 1993c: 262ff.). The Minister of National Defence, buttressed by the Sûreté, continued to insist that all illegal entrants were to be expelled. On 9 March 1940 the Jewish aid committees were forced once more to ask the Belgian authorities to increase their subsidies for the upkeep of Jewish refugees. Minister of Justice Janson, finally eliminated any human consideration from his immigration policy. The distinction between refugees and immigrants from the Third Reich within immigration policy was abolished. Janson decided that all German immigrants who entered Belgium illegally after 26 March were to be arrested and interned in view of their return to Germany. The invasion of Belgium by the German army on 10 May made this decision obsolete (AAD 37C1-1 and 143c-2).

Steering Migrants in the Labor Market

During this period of economic downturn the Ministry of Labor wanted to alleviate unemployment among Belgians by replacing foreign labor with unemployed Belgians. The amount of leeway retained by the authorities was, however, limited. Privileged aliens were beyond its control. For example, in the diamond industry 2,500 immigrants had acquired permanent residency permits. The Ministry of Labor only had a hold over the "recent" immigrants, those who had arrived after 1928. Rising unemployment made it increasingly difficult for diamond workers with less than ten years residence to obtain a work permit. In 1937 the policy had been very liberal: 885 such work permits had been granted. After March 1938 only 486 "recent" migrants requested a work permit B and of these only eighty-seven received a positive response. In 1938, in all the sectors together, 2,128 applications for a work permit by "recent" immigrants were refused (PS 1939:65 and 103). These applicants were supposed to leave the country. The goal of the new alien legislation was to adapt the presence of "recent" immigrants to the state of the labor market.

The administrative capability to strictly enforce the new alien legislation was, however, still lacking. The Foreign Labor Service of the Ministry of Labor could not handle all the applications in a timely manner. In the period from October 1936, when the new law came into effect, until the end of 1938, 141,163 aliens had applied for a work permit, but only 130,162 applications had been processed. The office did not catch up in 1939. In the first three months of that year, 20,059 new applications were received, and by the end of March, 14,155 of these applications had not yet been processed. The Foreign Labor Service was occupied full time with processing the applications for work permits. It had to neglect its mandate to supervise the employment of foreign labor and could not even draw up statistics on the number of foreign laborers employed by each employer. The director-general of the Ministry of Labor, H. Fuss, complained about the lack of personnel which made it impossible to implement the law. He called it a extremely deplorable situation which provoked legitimate protests not only by employers and foreign labor, but also by organizations of Belgian workers (AML, not classified). That a large number of foreign workers did not receive a timely reply to their application for a work permit caused serious problems for agencies charged with inspecting the implementation of the legislation. On the basis of quantitative information provided by the labor inspection service as illustrated by Graph 12 (*Arbeidsblad*, 1936-1940) we can conclude that infractions of the regulation concerning employment of foreign labor was an increasing percentage of the total infractions of which the labor inspection service proposed to proceed against. While in 1937 only 8 percent of complaints pertained to infractions in the employment of foreign labor, in 1938 this rose to 17 percent and even to 30 percent in 1939. These high percentages are a clear indication that the illegal employment of foreign labor became a priority of the labor inspection service from 1938 onwards. Very few legal complaints were matched by court action. While the labor inspection service wrote up 1,108 legal complaints between March 1937 and April 1940, only forty-four cases were brought before the court: thirteen of the accused were acquitted, nineteen received a suspended sentence, and only twelve legal complaints led to an effective

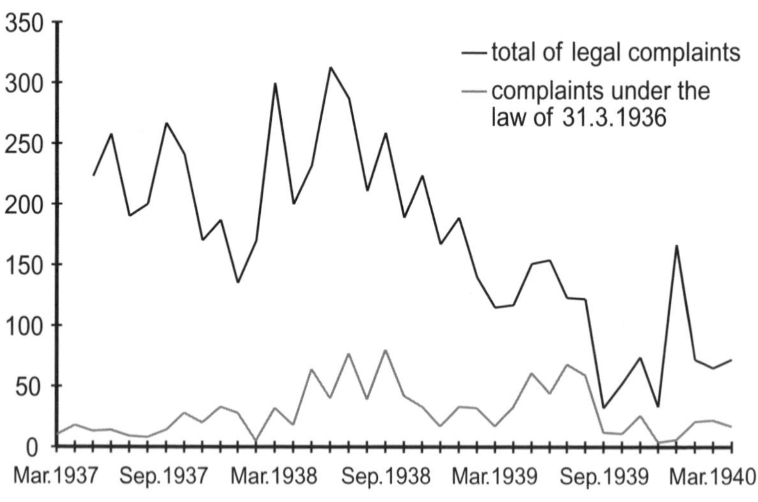

Graph 12 *Enforcement of Law of 31.3.1936 – Legal Complaints by Labor Inspection 1937–1940*

fine. No judge sentenced an illegally working alien or his employer to imprisonment (*Statistique Judiciaire* 1931-1942:71). Another problem in the enforcement of the new alien legislation was the removal of those aliens who had been refused a work permit. To what extent the surge of expulsions in this period (Graph 15) was due to the implementation of the new alien legislation is difficult to judge. The 2,128 "recent" immigrants whose applications for work permits had been turned down were probably all ordered to leave the country. At the end of 1938, the Sûreté knew of 120 foreign workers recruited for the mines in 1937 who had left the mines for another occupation. These "recent" immigrants were all ordered to leave the country (AAD 33C30/9-1). Even if the authorities decided to expel "recent" immigrants, this was not always easy to execute. In particular, Poles were difficult to repatriate. The Belgian Foreign Office complained that the Polish authorities obstructed the repatriation of the "recently" immigrated Poles on welfare. A commitment to accept these Poles was one of the compensations suggested by the Belgian authorities in exchange for an agreement on the Polish miners' pensions (AFAB 2462bis).

The policy refusing work permits to "recent" immigrants if they could be replaced by Belgians was considered insufficient by most of the unions. When in 1937 the Van Zeeland government embarked on an experiment with large public works not only to reduce unemployment, but also to stimulate the economy, the construction workers' unions were annoyed that some foreign workers -immigrants from the 1920s- were hired for public works outside the urban agglomerations. Unemployed Belgian construction workers did not consider it worthwhile to go to faraway places, while foreign labor was willing to do so. The unions insisted that the authorities should make it feasible for unemployed Belgian builders to do those jobs (*De ontvoogding* 1937:123). From 1938 onwards the agitation from within the unions against foreign labor increased considerably. The trade unions in the building sector protested against what an official of the Socialist union called "the occupation of our builders' yards" by foreign labor. Attacks on the immigrants became vehement and even overtly racist and the unions advocated the removal of all foreign labor on the building sites (*De ontvoogding* 1938:8 and 1939:3).

The unions in the hotel sector also expressed a strong xenophobic attitude at the end of the 1930s. Just as in the first half of the 1930s, some nationalistic organizations were set up around this issue. The response of the traditional labor organizations came quickly. The Christian Democratic and Socialist unions set up a defense committee to put pressure on the authorities and the employers for the absolute priority of Belgian hotel personnel. Even the Communists joined this committee. While right-wing organizations pointed to the Jewish migrants among the hotel personnel, the Communists attacked the Italian and German fascists who were working in the hotels. All the organizations involved considered it offensive that the authorities agreed with the employers that Belgian personnel were not qualified. They argued that the aliens' qualifications were not an issue here, but their flexibility, i.e., they agreed to do menial tasks and were satisfied with any salary (AAD 33C30/7).

In the garment sector the agitation against foreign labor was also virulent. The Socialist Garment Workers' Union argued that the presence of aliens, as employees or employers, had a disastrous effect on the sector. The foreign employers produced goods of lesser quality, whose low prices, made possible by the willingness of Jewish workers to accept any wage whatsoever, pushed Belgian employers out of the market. According to the union, the presence of Jews in the garment sector signified nothing other than the worsening of labor conditions and unemployment among Belgian workers, and only the removal of all Jews from the garment sector would enable improvement. In its attacks on Jews, this trade union defended an artisanal economic model, whereby quality was the only norm (*De Kleding* 1937:3,2 and 1938:4,2).

This unions' criticism went beyond the intention of the legislation of 1936 by demanding the strict adaptation of the employment of all aliens, independent of the years of residence in Belgium, to the state of the labor market. The crux of the unions' criticism was, however, directed against the so-called lax implementation of the alien legislation. The unions acknowledged that the Ministry of Labor rarely granted work permits to "recent" immigrants, but they denounced the lack of control over the employment of aliens. The state's lax enforcement of respect for the legislation was particularly denounced by the garment, leather, and diamond workers' unions, the sectors to which Jewish migrants and refugees had easy access. The Socialist Garment Workers' Union had already taken a clear stand in 1937, i.e., in order to protect labor conditions it was necessary to put a definite end to immigration, even by refugees. The protection of labor conditions for Belgians was central, all other considerations should be put aside. In the diamond sector the campaign against immigrants and refugees started only at the end of 1938 with a downturn in the diamond sector. The Christian Democratic union pushed for the removal of all foreign labor from the diamond sector. The Socialist Diamond Workers' Union considered foreign workers, who had been earning their living in the diamond industry for years, an integral part of the workforce. The Socialist union condemned the illegal employment of immigrants. The union appealed to the authorities to look for a solution to the "castaways who had clamped themselves on to our craft" (*De Diamantbewerker* 1939:4,1; PS 1939:103).

The only "safe" haven for recent immigrants was the mining industry. However, coal stocks began to pile up because of the economic downturn. The surveillance commissions for the recently recruited immigrants no longer met after March 1938. Due to the slackening of the labor market, it was no longer necessary to convince unwilling foreign labor to continue working in the mines until their contracts had been completed. "Deserters" of this sort were immediately expelled. Notwithstanding the economic downturn, most foreign labor recruited in 1937 was still needed in the mines. The mining companies wanted to retain the immigrants who performed well. They tried to impose labor contract's of a year's duration on these immigrants. Foreign workers would be bound for another year to one mine. The migrants, however, were not very eager to sign a new labor contract. Many hoped to move from the mine for which they had been recruited to a "better" mine. They hoped for a higher wage, less harsh supervisors, or better housing. The Socialist miners' union supported the immigrants' wish for mobility within the mining sector. After the completion of their recruitment contract, foreign labor in the mines was to be regarded as Belgian labor and, therefore, had to come under the customary rules of the industry, hence a labor contract of unspecified duration with termination possibilities for both parties. Labor Minister Delattre was in complete agreement with this vision. The mine employers decided, given the opposition, not to compel the stabilization of their recently acquired foreign labor by a new contract of a year's duration (BdL 186; ARMA rC15/1 and 5/2). This did not bring foreign labor in the mining industry on the same footing as their Belgian colleagues. To change mines implied that the new employer was obliged to request a new work permit, which entailed the assumption of the repatriation deposit from the former employer. This provision severely limited mobility within the mine sector of the recently recruited migrants (ARMA rC25/1).

By the spring of 1938, the economic downturn caused unemployment also in the mining industry. The Socialist miners' union organizational drive, especially among the Polish immigrants was halted in that same year. Deprived of unemployment benefits and even more insecure in their jobs than Belgians, foreign workers felt that the unions were not defending their interests. When the numerous Polish locals of the miners' union tried to organize a national conference to press their demands, the Socialist miners' union was not supportive at all (*Dziennik Ludowy*, 4.12.1937; AMSAB, Nauwelaerts, Committee 21.2.1938). By 1938 the success of the Socialist miners' union among foreign labor had evaporated. The Polish locals were even dismantled. The unions did not acknowledge that their strategy to organize the immigrants and defend their interests had failed. That the Belgian authorities continued to deny foreign workers unemployment benefits, notwithstanding strong pressure from the unions, was glossed over. The unions even imputed these developments to the countries of origin of the immigrants, which allegedly had no interest in the lot of their countrymen abroad (*L'ouvrier mineur* 1938:12, 5). In fact, refusing immigrants unemployment benefits was the most blatant expression of the subordinate role of foreign labor in the Belgian labor market. Unemployed foreign labor had to be repatriated, not financially supported.

Because of unemployment, the presence of foreign miners once again became the target of a nationalistic campaign. The Christian Democratic miners' union demanded that only those immigrants who had been in Belgium with their families for at least ten years should be kept in Belgium together with refugees and the nationals of neighboring countries. The Christian Democratic union argued that the tense international diplomatic situation meant that it was dangerous to be dependent on foreign labor for the extraction of coal. Well-paid Belgian labor should provide the necessary manpower (PHK 1938:977; PS 1939:131). The Socialist union in the Borinage joined the Christian Democrats in charges against redundant foreign workers (CNMM 28.1.1938). Although branches of the Socialist miners' union in other basins made similar proposals, this was not the official standpoint of the Socialist miners' union, which argued that the immigrants responded to a structural need for manpower; their replacement would be impossible. Moreover, it was not humane to drive these workers out after having induced them to come to Belgium in 1937. These miners were to be considered an integral part of the Belgian working class (CNMM; ARMA rC25/1).

The Socialist Minister of Labor, A. Delattre, followed a more pragmatic policy. Belgian workers had absolute priority over the "recent" foreign workers, which implied that a foreign worker had to be dismissed when an unemployed Belgian worker wanted his job. In order to force employers to give absolute preference to their Belgian workers, Delattre refused to extend the work permits of foreign workers who had been recruited in 1937. The Sûreté, however, was given a directive not to bother these aliens. This decision was aimed at increasing pressure on the mining companies. Only at the end of August 1938, when unemployment had abated,

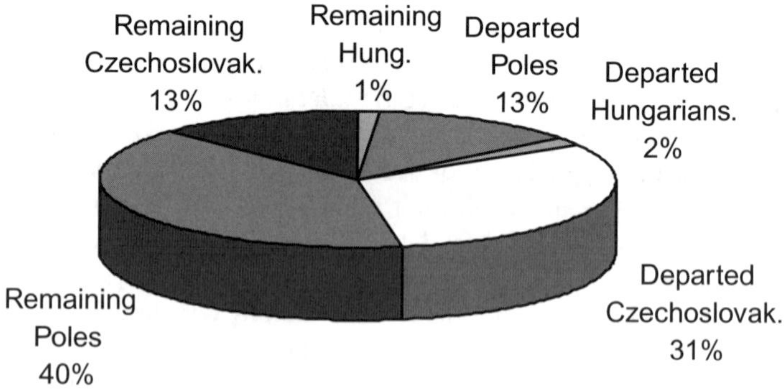

Graph 13 *7,004 Workers Collectively Recruited by Fedechar – state of affairs, 31.12.1938*

were the work permits of the recently recruited immigrants extended for another year (BdL 181; AFAP 9633; ARMA rC225/1). In the course of 1938, a significant portion of the recently recruited workers stayed put in Belgian mines. The politically troubled period (the Treaty of Munich coupled with on-going mobilization in Czechoslovakia) in the second half of 1938, however, meant that a large number of Czechoslovakians left Belgium. As Graph 13 illustrates, a large majority of the Poles, recruited in 1937, were still working in Belgium after a year and a half, while more than half of the Hungarians and two-thirds of the Czechoslovakians had left the country (rapport FEDECHAR 1938:65) .

As there was no unemployment in the mining industry in 1939, all work permits were renewed in June of that year, not for one-year as had previously been the case, but only for six months. The six-month extension brought the administrative practice of the Ministry of Labor into alignment with the Ministry of Justice which had always given the immigrants recruited in 1937 temporary residence permits -an inscription in the foreigners' register- of six months duration. With this decision, the power of the authorities over these immigrants and their employers was strengthened. At the same time, the authorities conceded registration in the population register to aliens working in the mines who had been residing in Belgium between two and ten years. This implied that these non-privileged aliens obtained an identity card valid for two years. At the same time the Ministry of Labor granted them work permits B with the same length of validity (AAD 30 33C9/1 2; AHCM). All the foreign miners, except for those recruited in 1937 were considered an integral part of the miners' population of Belgium. The immigrants who had arrived in 1937 remained subject to the discretion of the authorities; on short notice they could be dismissed and expelled.

This state power was used to adapt the presence of foreign labor strictly to the needs of the labor market. In the summer of 1939 there was unemployment among Belgian miners in the Borinage at the same time as a shortage of miners appeared in the eastern basins. As mentioned before, during the first Van Zeeland government a centralized network of public labor exchange offices was set up. By 1939 the state had at its disposal an efficient instrument for regulation of the labor market. Obliging unemployed Belgians to adapt to the needs of the labor market was seen as the solution to the tension within the market. In order to convince unemployed Belgians to work in the mines, the authorities, in agreement with the employers but not with the unions, embarked on a more muscled policy towards the Belgian unemployed. The royal decree of 2 September 1939 stipulated that a refusal to accept a job in the mines would be punished by the loss of unemployment benefits (BS 1939:6329). Employers also received a subsidy if they hired unemployed Belgians with no experience in mining. The results of this "forced" direction of unemployed Belgians to the mining sector were minimal. Notwithstanding the threat to deny unemployment benefits to those unskilled Belgians who refused work in the mines, the number of Belgian miners hardly increased. The threat itself barely materialized, largely due to the strong opposition of the Socialist union (Vanthemse 1989: 213; AEL, Colard, 70; ACCBS, AHCM and FEDECHAR 10.1939). More successful was the transfer of foreign miners. The state's total power over half of the nearly 2,000 foreign miners in the Borinage was used to force the relocation of "recent" immigrants. The Christian Democratic Minister of Labor, A. Delfosse, decided not to extend any work permits in the Borinage in order to keep the mining companies under pressure to fire aliens in order to make vacancies for unemployed Belgian miners and to stimulate the foreigners to fill the vacancies in the eastern basins (AHCM).

The onset of the Second World War caused the demand for coal to increase sharply. The neighboring countries (especially Great Britain and Germany) that exported a part of their coal to Belgium stopped doing so. They used all their coal for the war effort. Belgium also changed over to a war industry and needed more coal. The authorities hoped that increasing the number of miners would satisfy the need for more coal. The large pool of unemployed Belgians could scarcely be tapped. The Socialist miners' union was only prepared to accept the obligatory employment of unemployed Belgians in the mines, if first all those aliens who were recruited for the mines and were now working in other industries or were active in commerce would "return" to the mines (AEL, Colard, 70). The authorities conceded and concentrated on directing more aliens to the mining industry. The Socialist Minister of Labor, A. Balthazar, canceled the work permits B of about 2,500 "recently" arrived aliens who worked outside mining in the fall of 1939. Only by agreeing to work in the mining industry, could they remain in Belgium (Delbeke 1981:38; AAN, Poselstwo RP w Brukseli, 12). At the same time, all undocumented aliens could legalize their stay by entering mine work. These injections of labor did not even make up for the departure of foreign labor due to the war. The FEDECHAR called upon the Minister of Justice for measures to prevent the emigration of experienced miners and their families. The FEDECHAR proposed introducing an exit visa to prevent foreign labor from leaving. The Belgian authorities refused to do so. There was nothing illegal about the departure of the foreign miners. The government decided, however, to arrest some Poles actively recruiting for the Polish army in exile. This was legally possible on the basis of the royal decree of 28 September 1939 to impede "anti-patriotic activity" (Caestecker 1993b:241ff.; Heumos 1989:154ff.).

The Exclusion of Immigrants from Trade

When in 1936 Belgian labor obtained protection against competition from foreign labor, the organized middle class demanded a similar safeguard against aliens residing in Belgium. In 1937, due to the recruitment abroad for the mining industry, the trade sector asked insistently for such protection. The middle-class organizations feared that these foreigners would, as soon as they had some savings, leave the mines en masse to seek their livelihood in the trade or artisanal sectors. They demanded the immediate expulsion of these "temporary miners". The authorities had the power to comply with this demand by the organized middle class for only after a ten-year stay in Belgium, were immigrants granted the full-fledged right of residence -registration in the population register- which protected them against arbitrary expulsion. A broadening of alien legislation to curtail the presence of aliens in industry and trade was therefore not really necessary. The authorities were ready to use force to prevent professional mobility of the "recent" immigrants. Mining companies and middle-class organizations were requested to list all aliens who had left the mine sector with the alien police so they could be expelled. Notwithstanding the fact that the very few immigrants recruited in 1937 who found a livelihood in Belgium outside mining were all expelled, the myth of the "temporary miners" remained a recurrent theme in middle-class appeals to the authorities.

The middle-class organizations in the Limburg basin took the initiative in a virulent campaign against foreign traders. As mentioned in Chapter 5, the Eastern and Central European miners in this basin were a grateful clientele for ethnic businesses. A number of these foreign traders, but certainly not all, were of Jewish origin. In February 1938 the branch of the Flemish Nationalist Party (VNV) in Maas-Mechelen – a small town surrounded by a multi-cultural miners' community- transformed middle-class agitation by putting forward a new target: "the Jewish hucksters". From then onwards middle-class organizations targeted all non-Belgian merchants, who were all presented as Jews. This view of the "temporary miners" was applied retroactively. Established Jewish traders had, according to the Flemish Nationalists, also come to Belgium to work in the mines, but they had cheated the Belgians by setting up their own businesses. Around a rather minimal Jewish presence in Limburg, a campaign was launched on a large scale. The Flemish Nationalists who had given the initial thrust to this campaign were quickly joined by the Limburg Catholic Middle-Class Movement. To stem the rising popularity of Flemish Nationalism the Limburg Catholic Middle-Class Movement diligently attempted to outdo the Flemish Nationalists in this campaign. They called upon the authorities to put a halt to the massive establishment in the trade sector of aliens who outcompeted Belgians by dishonest business practices. The Limburg Catholic Middle-Class Movement alleged that the foremost manifestation of dishonest practices was the provision of credit which also resulted in the frequent attachment of workers' wages. The authorities had to step in not only to protect the midde class, but also the workers. These abuses were not only carried out by Jewish merchants in the mine basin, they were practiced in particular by Jewish trade representatives who offered all types of goods on order. This agitation continued for months and escalated into a protest meeting in Genk on 20 November 1938 against "the colonization of Limburg". This Limburg campaign found activities. The Belgian middle class contended with severe difficulties. In spite of the economic upturn in 1936, domestic purchasing power had not recovered. Given the weak economic basis of Belgian small commerce, these businesses could not cope with the recession of 1938. Protection was demanded. In the beginning of 1939 all over Belgium, middle-class circles began to agitate fiercely against traders of non-Belgian nationality. In the summer of 1939, even the Brussels Chamber of Commerce affiliated itself with the demand for a restrictive regulation of the commercial and industrial activities of the immigrants.

This uproar against the economic activities of Jewish migrants continued to be fueled, just as in the first half of the thirties, by the continuous stream of immigrants from Nazi Germany. This "invasion" of refugees supported the perception that Jewish immigration was a persistent menace. The reasons for Jewish emigration were made suspect. It was not a matter of their being refugees. The specific persecution of which the Jews in Germany were victims – especially the forcing of Jews out of economic life- meant that these immigrants were denied the right to the privileged label "political refugee". Perhaps they were "economically persecuted", but certainly not politically. The fact that they were not political refugees was also manifest by their apparent wealth. Not only did they have a lot of money at their disposal to hire someone to smuggle them into Belgium and even to bribe German border patrols, but they were also able to take luxurious baggage with them. Clearly, it was not a case of refugees who had left everything behind to save their skins.

The political class quickly took over the demands of the middle class. After the success of Rex in the elections of May 1936, traditional political circles clearly paid more attention to the organized middle class. The demands of these organizations to take hold of the competition they faced from aliens in Belgium received immediate approval in the political world. That the complaints about dishonest competition were not always well-founded was not an issue for the politicians. The Catholic Party was especially eager to do something about these middle-class demands. In the long run, the party wanted regulation of the retail trade to protect the middle class. In the short run, the vending trade and trade by aliens especially had to be restrained. In the first half of the 1930s, a number of small racist groups, with little success, had agitated about the refugee and migrant issues. But after 1937 racism received quite a large following. The movement around the paper *Volksverwering*, published from January 1937 onwards, focused on this theme. The central purpose of this movement, based mainly in Antwerp, was to combat the presence of Jews in Belgium. The virulent anti- Semitism of these groups was supplemented by broader political formations. The Antwerp city council elections in October 1938 clearly illustrated this change in climate. The important Jewish community in the city, a center of attraction for many refugees, together with the ties which the Jewish community had with the Socialist mayor of Antwerp, Camille Huysmans, meant that various political parties hoped to use the Jewish theme to their advantage. Election slogans blatantly stated this. Rex proposed," Belgium for Belgians! Down with Jewish overcrowding!" The Flemish National VNV was even clearer; its election meetings were decked out with banners proclaiming, " Away with the Jews". The Catholic party did not let itself be outbid. An election leaflet from October 1938 did not refrain from using the Jewish issue to criticize their political opponents: the Socialists "who made our town into a refuge of all different strange rabble who despise the born Antwerpian".

These elections let loose the floodgates. Racism penetrated the political scene. The sense of reserve still valid in the first half of the thirties, was thrown overboard from 1938 on. The changing vocabulary is indicative. When one talked about the influence of Jewish migrants in trade and industry one did not speak about aliens anymore, but about Jews. The refugees were not spared; their negative influence on the economic sphere was underlined by the political class. Concerns about the presence of Jewish migrants became a national preoccupation. Anti-Jewish agitation was not only fed by the economic activity of the immigrants; the mere fact that these aliens were different added fuel to the fire. The multi-cultural society which was a visual reality for many Belgians in the big cities, obviously could not be coped with easily. It was considered an expression of the failure of the national community to assimilate new elements. Belgium was a small country with eight million inhabitants and to incorporate these immigrants, who were totally foreign to the local culture, a long incubation period would be necessary. The Catholic politician, J. Pholien, as Minister of Justice expressed this xenophobic vision in the highest political echelons of the country in 1938. He stated that Belgium had already taken in too many aliens and in particular, too many foreign Jews. The Belgian community could not assimilate these masses. This "otherness" of the Jewish immigrants found its expression, according to these circles, also in their political activity.

A Jewish characteristic which had been deeply underlined throughout the whole interwar period within xenophobic discourse was its revolutionary extremism. At the end of the thirties, a component of Communist thinking of that time, anti-Fascism, was denounced in particular. Within the tense international climate of the thirties, this political dimension had a mobilizing force which was not to be underestimated. The Belgian neutrality policy and the appeasement policy of the other democratic states in Europe were motivated by the hope of safeguarding the peace. That this took place at the expense of the Sudetenland in September 1938 was considered unfortunate, but peace was of the utmost importance. Within this search for a peaceful association with Nazi Germany, the totalitarianism of the regime and the anti-Semitism that went along with it, was minimalized. By their mere presence, the Jewish refugees warned of the imminent danger of war and a section of the Jewish community actively strengthened this warning. Jewish anti-Fascist agitation attempted to thwart the trust that the democracies gave to Nazi Germany. For that reason the supporters of the neutrality policy in Belgium portrayed the Jews as warmongers. According to them, the Jewish refugees wanted only revenge. National interest was best served by neutrality; Belgians had to live together with their neighbors on a peaceful footing, not only for the sake of peace, but for economic well-being also. The boycott of Nazi Germany launched by a section of the Jewish community, was - according to these "nationalists"- a typical expression of Jewish policy, which only thought about the interests of the Jewish community and ignored Belgian interests. The evocation of the political, economic and cultural threat, allegedly posed by Jewish immigration was a vehicle used by middle-class organizations in their pleas for restricting the access of aliens to independent economic pursuits.

The pressure on the authorities increased. Within the administration there was a strong current for a restrictive stand. The head of the Sûreté, R. de Foy, and also the second in command in the Sûreté, H. Bekaert, shared completely the argument of the middle class. The authorities were ready to take action against the "abuses", but the economic consequences of the curtailment of market initiative by foreign businessmen had first to be evaluated. On 15 September 1939 the authorities decided to organize an actual census of aliens in Belgium and their economic pursuits. This survey, supplemented by investigations by municipal councils was intended to enable the authorities to gain a true picture of the aliens' economic activities and to punish those who had "abused" the permission to immigrate. In particular, the authorities targeted those aliens who had circumvented the legislation on work permits by setting up their own businesses. The ground rules of the offensive against "the abuses" had already been laid down. The preoccupation of the authorities was very different from the one that motivated A.Delattre when he had made up his bill to control foreign employers in December 1937. His bill aimed at ensuring that foreign entrepreneurs respected fiscal and social legislation. The entrepreneurial activities of aliens as such had not been contested. In 1939, the authorities felt very differently about the commercial and industrial activities of the immigrants. The government embraced the much repeated accusation of middle-class circles that many immigrants had left the mines – the sector for which they had been granted their immigration permits – for the commercial or artisanal sectors.

With the Law of 16 November 1939 professional permits were introduced for aliens who were active in industrial or trade activities. The protection of the economic life of the nation was the purpose of this law. Although the self-employed activity of aliens was evaluated extremely cautiously, it clearly pointed out abuses, fraud, difficulties which were paired with the industrial and commercial activities of immigrants. Regulation of the economic activity of aliens forced itself to the fore. Aliens who had legally resided in Belgium for five years, as well as Russian and German "refugees" would receive a professional permit without any problem. Their professional activities would, however, remain under constant state supervision. The obligatory renewal of this permit every two years, together with the duty to resubmit their request with every modification of professional activity, stood as guarantor of this. If these aliens went beyond the bounds of these specifications or the more general regulations, or went bankrupt, or were convicted or "transgressed the customs of the commercial and industrial activity of nationals" the professional permit could be revoked. Revocation could be paired with a simple administrative decision of expulsion. The powers which the state wielded over aliens was extended by this provision. Now even long-established immigrants could be expelled for economic reasons by an administrative decision. For immigrants who had been in Belgium less than five years the administration would investigate the usefulness of their future business.[2] Towards the end of 1939, the government added to its attempt to curtail the activities of foreign merchants or artisans further restrictions in peddling. In 1936 P. Van Isacker, then Minister of Economic Affairs, had tried to limit the range of products offered by peddlers. He was successful only to a limited degree. G. Sap, who became Minister of Economic Affairs in April 1939, was more successful and outlawed the sales of cloth, hats, shoes, leather, furs and skins in the markets (Caestecker 1993:149ff and 258ff.; AAD 33c44B/1).

Conclusion

In contrast to the first half of the 1930s, the reaction of the authorities to increasing unemployment in the late 1930s was immediately translated into a very restrictive immigration policy. The increasing importance of the interests of national labor in the functioning of the state and the instruments the state had acquired to control (foreign) labor explain the immediate reaction to the changing economic fortunes. After a few months, however, the decision to clamp down on unauthorized immigration was already being challenged by the influx of refugees from the German Reich. Although the Sûreté would have certainly liked to stop the immigration of these unwanted guests, it turned out to be politically too sensitive to do so. Most refugees who succeeded in outwitting the border patrols were allowed to stay, at least temporarily, even though they had come uninvited and served no economic needs. This tolerance was not a part of the official refugee policy, which was derived from the refugee law of 20 February 1936 and the international refugee regime to which Belgium had adhered. Although the authorities paid lip service to the idea of providing arrangements within alien policy for refugees, most refugees were denied refugee status by the authorities. To define who was a "refugee" was a prerogative of the state and it decided not according to an objective assessment of persecution, but according to national interests. It was considered inopportune to grant Jewish refugees official refugee-status as they would acquire certain rights of settlement and access to the labor market in this manner. Notwithstanding this power of definition, the authorities took into account the objective reality of these immigrants for whom return was no option. After the short-lived experiment of "extradition" in October 1938, repatriating refugees became politically inconceivable. Liberal and/or humanitarian values imposed restrictions on the radical alien policy. Refugees, even if they were denied official acknowledgment of their status, turned out to be an impediment to the implementation of a restrictive immigration policy.

The new powers the state wielded over aliens could be utilized more effectively in the labor market. The state dramatically changed the manner in which immigrants could become integrated in the economy. The authorities consciously manipulated "recently" immigrated labor according to the vagaries of the labor market. Even within the mining sector they pursued a crude policy of directing foreign manpower to gaps in the labor market. When there were no shortages in the labor market to be filled, these "recently" immigrated laborers had to be repatriated. The central preoccupation of the authorities was to achieve full employment of Belgian workers. This became the paramount national interest. In the first half of the 1930s, although foreign labor had born a disproportionate share of the social costs of the Depression due to discriminatory dismissal practices, employers retained considerable autonomy in their personnel policy. In mining, the employers' freedom to prefer foreign labor above Belgian labor because of the former's "docility", "cheapness", or even skills and stability had been strongly contested by unions and the state alike during the Depression, albeit without either the state or the unions having, at least until 1935, any direct influence on the companies' hiring policies. In other industries and certainly in agriculture, employers' freedom in this respect had not even been contested. In the late 1930s, however, the state was able to impose "nationalization" of the labor force even outside the segments of the labor market where labor was organized. The preferential treatment of Belgian labor was now imperative everywhere. The state had the power to assure that the immigrants were the first victims of an economic downturn. Export of unemployment was now institutionalized. This manpower policy of the state was based on short-term considerations; in fact it was a contract-labor system supervised and enforced by the state. This short-term state policy conflicted with the medium- and long-term manpower policies of employers, especially in the mining industry. The outbreak of the war and the resulting labor shortages in the mining industry caused the conflict to be subdued.

The short-term policy to demand priority for Belgian labor with each slight increase in unemployment, which had characterized both unions during the 1920s and the Depression, was now official state policy. Only the Christian Democratic union pushed for a radical implementation of this policy. The Socialist union tried to combine a restrictive immigration policy with a strategy of solidarity with those immigrants whose arrival was officially sanctioned. During an economic downturn, however, defending the immigrants' interests was difficult, as their interests conflicted radically with the basic assumptions of the new alien policy, which was designed to accommodate national labor's interests. So, only if the unions challenged the crudest aspect of the state's manpower policy could the unions be considered by the immigrants as defending their interests. At the end of the 1930s, the unions, including the Socialist one, stuck to the old paradigm to defend only the interests of national labor. This strategy alienated the immigrants from the unions and undermined the unions' strength on the shopfloor in those industries where immigrants had become a structural part of the labor force.

The state's ambitions to master immigration not only at, but also within Belgium's borders, were put in jeopardy by the difficulty of enforcing the new legislation. This was mainly due to the sudden upsurge in the influx of refugees, people desperate enough to defy any immigration legislation and circumvent its enforcement agencies in order to flee persecution. An internal factor hindering enforcement of the new legislation -the importance of which is difficult to judge- was the administrative capabilities of the state. After enacting the alien legislation of 1936, the administrative apparatus was scarcely equipped to grant, renew, or revoke the labor permits of all immigrants. The straightjacket into which all "recent" immigrants were officially forced by the new legislation did not take into account either the reality of immigration or the ability of the state apparatus to enforce strict observance.

The discrepancy between declared policy and reality fed the political movement against the aliens. It gave the myth of the "temporary miner" more credibility and cast an aspersion on all aliens, independent of their length of residence in Belgium. A fertile ground for anti-foreigner agitation was the ambiguous refugee policy which, by denying Jewish refugees the prerogative of refugee status, delegitimized the presence of these Jewish refugees in Belgium. These elements were cunningly used by the middle-class to promote their own interests. The economic and international political crisis at the end of the 1930s was an ideal climate for a xenophobic discourse. It was a discourse which united phenomena that had little or nothing to do with each other into an one-dimensional national threat, in which the self-employed Jewish migrant was presented as the main culprit. These migrants, many of whom had immigrated in the twenties or even earlier, were accused of illegal immigration or of deliberately violating immigration regulations. The legislation on immigration in the thirties, which had put a definitive end to free immigration, was transposed on the past. It was presented as if all aliens in Belgium had only been admitted to work in the mines. Continuous immigration, first in 1937 with the recruitment for the mine sector and then in 1938 and 1939 with the stream of refugees from Nazi Germany, activated the demand for the regulation of the entrepreneurial activities of the immigrants. A regulation was called absolutely necessary not only to punish aliens' dishonesty, since they had allegedly left the mines soon after their officially sanctioned immigration, but also to prevent these unscrupulous characters from competing with Belgian businesses. The specific political mobilization and institutional integration of the middle class provided for the translation of this xenophobic preoccupation to the political world. While the "nationalization" of the labor market and the regulation of labor migration were developed via tripartite negotiations (employers organizations, unions, and the state), the middle class tried to secure the "nationalization" of artisanal and commercial activities by street agitation and political dissidence. Legislation was demanded to restrict all entrepreneurial activities of aliens without taking into account the length of residence of immigrants in Belgium. This elimination of, or at least control over, competition by aliens demanded a radical break with the liberal principles of the Belgian state's economic policy. While in 1936 traditional *laisser-faire* values were already overriden in the labor market and the marginal section of retail trade, this was extended in 1939 to the general economy in order to defend the national interests. The introduction of professional permits was radical since it denied all self-employed aliens denizen status. The denizen status which protected long-established aliens against arbitary expulsion was part of the 1936 legislation on foreign labor and peddlers, but in 1939 it was denied to self-employed aliens.

This provision was the only extension in the state's power brought about by the law of 16 November 1939. Without this provision, the introduction of professional permits could either be seen as a symbolic concession to middle-class demands or as an administrative rationalization of the alien policy. By the latter, we mean the introduction of total administrative control of the economically active alien population in Belgium by imposing government authorization to earn a living not only on those engaged in wage labor but also on all self-employed aliens. Without the provision enabling revocation of professional permits of long-established immigrants *and* their expulsion, the law would be only a symbolic concession, as the authorities already wielded total power over most "recent" immigrants. Since "recent" immigrants were not granted denizen (i.e., privileged alien) status an administrative decision was sufficient to expel them. A regulation restricting their entrepreneurial activities was, therefore, unnecessary. The law of 16 November 1939, however, went beyond this, by putting self-employed aliens on probation until they became Belgians. It implied the demise of denizen-status.[3] New "national" interests, i.e., the private interests of the middle class, had again increased the power the state wielded over aliens.

Notes

1. These figures refer to the number of people (not families) who were registered by the Brussels committee for Jewish refugees (AAD 37C6). This committee was the most important aid committee, but there was also a Jewish committee in Antwerp which supported a large number of Jewish refugees. Therefore, this graph shows only the dynamic in illegal immigration of Jewish refugees, not the absolute numbers. The figures of August 1938 refer to the weekly average for that month.
2. The executive measures of this law were ready to be published by May 1940. Due to the German invasion they were only published after the war, in 1945 (Caestecker 1992:172).
3. In retrospect, more crucial for the abolishment of denizen status was the royal decree of 28 September 1939, a war measure which enabled the authorities to expel or intern any alien who was a threat to the national economy or security. This law was part of the policy which targeted immigrants primordial as political actors. We have ignored to a large extent that part of alien policy which singled out immigrants as political actors in Chapters 8 and 9, because with the law of 31 March 1936 the policy which targeted immigrants as economic actors -the focus of our research- had its own logic, separate from that policy which dealt with immigrants as political actors. Before 1936 these policies were closely intertwined. In addition, there is also a heuristic reason: in the archival material we consulted concerning the political activities of immigrants for this period there is little information concerning the period after 1936, Morelli and Van Doorslaer are also much less documented for this period. The law of 28 September 1939 which did away with any residence right for aliens was only meant to be valid for the circumstances of the war. After the war it was, however, extended several times until 1952.

General Conclusions

When we compare Belgium's alien population in 1910 to its alien population before the Second World War it becomes evident that an important change has occurred. First of all, the alien population had risen from 254,000 to 340,000 people by 1938. It is not the mere growth in the alien population that is striking; the number of aliens was already on the increase during the nineteenth century. The innovation is rather the change in composition of that population brought about in the interwar period. While in 1910, 88.8 percent of all aliens were nationals of neighboring countries, in 1938 this dropped to 51 percent. What is more, the occupational profile of the immigrants from non-neighboring countries dramatically changed the economic position of aliens in Belgium. The nationals of neighboring countries in interwar Belgium still had no specific occupational profile; in this they repeated the characteristics of the alien population in the nineteenth century. For this reason the distribution of the active aliens among the three economic sectors had not radically changed. Only the secondary sector gained some importance.

The gain of industry, the secondary sector is only to be attributed to the new immigrants, those of the non-neighboring countries. They have a distinct occupational profile. The large numbers of Italians, Poles, etc., performed the menial, poorly paid, and often dangerous jobs. In 1939, 39 percent of the Italians, 59 percent of the Yugoslavians, 58 percent of the

Table 5 *Distribution of Economically Active aliens, 1910 and 1939*

	agriculture	*industry*	*services*
1910	6	41	53
1939	3	56	41

Poles, and 78 percent of the Czechoslovakians were working in the mines. The remaining percentages were to be found in construction and the metallurgy industry. This picture of the livelihood of these immigrants stresses the underprivileged, marginal position of aliens on the Belgian labor market, a condition which will remain dominant in the second half of the twentieth century.

A central question of this book is how this shift in occupational pattern came about. A shortage of manpower in specific segments of the labor market occurred due to a lack of social disposition of national manpower. That Belgian labor "deserted" heavy industry reflects a social and cultural dynamic to improve one's position. This ambition is to be noticed among the traditional workers' population of Wallonia in the last quarter of the nineteenth century. Industrial labor's dissatisfaction with its lot was also translated into political mobilization. This, in turn, was one of the main forces in the creation of the incipient welfare state, which increased the ability of the indigenous labor force to resist pure market forces. It also caused the traditional establishment to protect peasant workers from total proletarianization by offering cheap transport from the countryside to the industrial basins and the cities. These politically-determined benefits expanded the choices available to peasants in danger of proletarization and enabled them to adjust, in a flexible manner, to industrial society. Even the domestic periphery underwent transformations which made its population no longer suitable for filling the labor demands of Belgian heavy industry. Only by attracting foreign labor was heavy industry able to have a dependent and loyal manpower at its disposal. In the interwar period, at least fifty thousand workers were directly recruited abroad by labor-hungry industries. The mining industry took the lion's share in this organized recruitment effort. Informal migration, partly induced by this recruitment, added to the workforce. The exact importance of this "spontaneous" immigration is difficult to evaluate, but its quantitative importance is certainly not to be neglected. Organized immigration had only a minimal share (10 percent) in the total migration to Belgium. A part of the informal migration was directed to small firms that produced for widely fluctuating markets. These firms with a foreign labor force were managed by co-ethnics. Belgian producers were unwilling to serve these unreliable markets. Immigrants greased the gears of the economy. Foreign labor became a structural element of the Belgian production system. Immigration compensated for the inadequacies – from an economic point of view – of the Belgian work force. Heavy industry in particular became fundamentally dependent on immigrants, even during economic downturns.

This study demonstrates that immigration to Belgium was not a haphazard result of "push" and "pull" factors. It was not only the spontaneous response of a labor surplus in peripheral regions to the needs of the labor market in core regions which explains immigration into Belgium. Migration was, to a large extent, the result of deliberate policy decisions. The archetype of migration created by political decisions is of course refugee movements, but economically-induced migration has also an important political dimension. Labor recruitment in particular became a strongly politicized endeavor. In 1911 the recruitment of Poles for the mining companies was hardly politicized. The employers contacted a semi-private emigration organization which recruited labor for them. The migration of these Poles was tolerated by Belgian and Austrian authorities alike. In 1937, the employers, in agreement with the Belgian state and the authorities of the emigration countries, decided who was to be recruited, for what kind of jobs, under which conditions, where the recruitment would take place, and under whose supervision. We have analyzed the decision-making process in several recruitment campaigns. While about half a million people immigrated to Belgium in the interwar period (Graph 21) the focus on the organization of the immigration of fifty-thousand workers can seem to be exaggerated. For our political focus, however, the politics of organized migration reveal the interests at stake and the strategies implemented by the different interests groups to achieve their goals. In addition this organized migration generated spontaneous migration as news spread about opportunities in Belgium and migration was facilitated by establishing links between emigration regions and Belgium.

Socio-economic factors and the political decisions to stimulate migration to Belgium alone do not account for the specific location of foreign labor in the Belgian labor market. Political decisions during the 1930s, which were meant to make foreign labor dependent on market forces in extremis, carry a weight, the exact importance of which is difficult to evaluate. Immigrants were refused access to the newly created refuges, such as pensions and unemployment benefits. Foreign labor was forced, in contrast to Belgian labor who had succeeded to emancipating itself from the market, to remain an extremely flexible industrial labor force responding to pure market forces. In addition, in order to secure foreign labor to compensate for "deficiencies" in Belgian labor, political decisions were taken to confine immigrants, in the long run, to segments in the industrial labor market which were characterized by onerous work, low pay, and bad working conditions. The changing logic of alien policy therefore has to be scrutinized to understand why these decisions were taken and what the consequences were for the immigrants.

The Creation of the Alien

For most of the nineteenth century the concept of alien was nebulous. Membership of the state was hardly codified and formalized. The Belgian state did not know exactly who its members were. There was also no need for a clear delineation between Belgian and alien as nationality – the direct relationship between state and citizen – had no importance for the majority of the population in a time when the state was hardly present. Social rights were scarce and political rights were limited to a happy few. The state also imposed hardly any duties. Social and political changes caused the scope of state action to expand vastly. In the wake of this increasing intervention by the state, social reality became "nationalized". The vertical tie between citizen and state was thrust upon society to identify the bearer of the duties and rights to which the expanding state had given rise. The legal reality of citizenship became a social reality by the end of the century. The distinction between Belgian and alien became clear-cut and its significance increased. Alien policy had an increasingly important impact on the daily life of those inhabitants of Belgium who were not citizens.

Also in the neighboring countries, the expansion of the role of the state during the nineteenth century implied an intrusion upon social life whereby the state defined a new social distinction: alien versus national. As a case in point, in 1889 the Dutch population census registered the nationality of the inhabitants of the Netherlands for the first time. Much earlier in France and Germany, nationality became an element used by statisticians to structure social reality. The introduction of male universal suffrage in 1848 in France and in 1870 in the German Empire certainly played a role in this process, although it only acquired real significance in the last quarter of the nineteenth century. Because little research has been done on the state-led aspects of the nationalization of European society, it is difficult to pinpoint the other elements in this process. In the first half of the nineteenth century, one's nationality had little or no influence on daily life. Politicians and even jurists were unaware of the exact provisions of nationality legislation (Noiriel 1988:73; Fahrmeier 1997:723). This changed in the second half of the century. For Germany it is highly likely that the Prussian state's strong interventionist policy, including in the social domain, meant that the state imposed its criteria of membership on social reality early. Numerous other German states, which from 1870 onwards were part of the German Empire, also grafted this new distinction of alien versus national on social reality, either due to Prussian instigation or on their own initiative. This is most clearly discernable in the German treaties on deportation of undesirable aliens, culminating in the Gotha treaty of 1851 which delineated nationals from aliens in the German states (Fahrmeier 1997:734ff.; Brubaker 1992:68ff.). In France at the turn of the century, being French began to entitle a person to benefits in daily life which were denied to aliens. The positive actions of the French state – the very slow process of the creation of a French welfare state – were directed only to French labor (Noiriel 1991:63-92). Aliens who had obtained the status of denizen (*domicilié*) lost most of their prerogatives; to recover them they had to become Frenchmen (Lescoeur 1899:137). In all these countries the need for a clear-cut distinction between aliens and nationals caused a radical reform in nationality legislation in accordance with the view the elites had of their nation. France was the first to make this reform in 1889, the Netherlands followed in 1892, Belgium in 1909, and finally Germany in 1913 (Heijs 1995; Brubaker 1992:85-137).

Changing Categories of Alien Policy

The most salient change occurring in Belgian alien policy during the period under scrutiny is the changing tension between desirable and undesirable immigrants. The subtitle of this book, which refers to the creation of guest workers and illegal aliens, evokes this conspicuous change. The guest worker became the desirable, even sought after, immigrant, and the illegal immigrant became the undesirable one. The distinction basically refers to immigrants as economic actors. Immigrants as human beings are not only economic actors, but also political actors. They not only evoke economic concerns, affecting the labor market and the global economy, but also concerns in the field of national identity and the functioning of the political system. The category of guest worker addresses this political dimension: Guest workers should not be politically active.

Already in the nineteenth century, aliens were targeted as political actors. In the first half of the century this was due to the weak position of Belgium in the diplomatic arena. After 1860 and until the end of the period envisaged, the alien as a subversive agent becomes a target of state repression. It is, however, striking that notwithstanding the political turbulence of the period between 1880 and 1914 and rising immigration, there was no discernable upsurge at the end of the century in the targeting of aliens as political actors. The authorities also did not call for extended powers over aliens. After the First World War, and certainly from the second half of the 1920s onwards, combating the subversive alien became paramount. The traditional elites accused aliens of threatening law and order. At every Council of Ministers meeting, a number of subversive aliens who had acquired residency status were ordered expelled. Legislative action to enlarge the amount of leeway the authorities had in dealing with these undesirable political actors was strongly urged and in the field of nationality law this even made it possible to revoke the Belgian nationality of subversive Belgians of foreign origin.

The alien as economic actor had hardly existed in nineteenth-century politics. It was not a matter of concern to the authorities if an alien did the work an unemployed Belgian was willing to do or if an entrepreneur of foreign nationality residing in Belgium outdid a local producer. The twentieth-century national interest in this domain had changed fundamentally. The radical alien policy had to assure that nationals were not harmed by the introduction of economic actors from abroad. This implied a restrictive control over their access to self-employment and preventing immigrants from displacing Belgian labor in the labor market.

The radical alien policy transformed the desirable immigrant from the self-supporting alien to the guest worker. This central category in the radical alien policy was not to pursue any independent economic activity. The work (s)he was allotted was also defined: it was work the indigenous population shied away from. Upon entry the guest worker was channeled into those segments of the market which had a structural labor shortage. (s)he was confined, in the long run, to these unappealing jobs. In 1939 this implied that the male immigrant had to become a miner, and the female immigrant could only be a domestic servant. Refusing to work in these segments of the labor market within the first ten years after immigration implied expulsion. Beyond work, the guest worker did not exist. The guest worker had to be rotated in and out of the Belgian labor market as necessary. An unemployed guest worker was a contradiction in terms; a guest worker living on the dole or welfare was inconceivable. The status of guest worker was only a temporary status; it was only a category of immigration policy. The guest worker after ten (eventually five) years of residence became a privileged alien. The privileged alien achieved permanent residency status; in this sense they acquired denizen status. In 1939 the self-employed immigrant was denied the status of privileged alien; self-employed aliens remained under total discretion of the executive power until they became Belgian. They could be expelled, among other things, if they "transgressed the customs of the commercial and industrial activity of the nationals".

The legal status of privileged alien cannot be equated to the status of *domicilié* for most of the nineteenth century or the residency status which immigrants could acquire until 1936, the two previous denizen status. The status of privileged alien permitted immigrants – similar to the previous denizen status – to remain indefinitely in the country. They could only be expelled in exceptional cases and in this sense they were almost equal to Belgians. Denizen status implied more; it was a status which permitted aliens to participate in social and economic life on the same terms as nationals. That implied full access to the labor market, business, social welfare, education all on equal terms with nationals. This full assimilation was certainly true for the *domiciliés*, and to a large extent also, de facto, for aliens with residency status.[1] The limited social citizenship of the nineteenth century was not denied to these denizens. The increasing intervention of the state in social reality after the First World War meant that social citizenship expanded as the benefits were differentiated between the basic provision of welfare and the "luxury" of social insurance. In the 1920s most denizens (aliens with residency status) were excluded from the newly created provisions of social insurance, but welfare remained accessible to them. Aliens could get access to these social insurance provisions, not by virtue of their denizen status, but by virtue of being a national of a state which had concluded an agreement with Belgium. In the 1920s there was no stringent opposition to including foreign labor in bilateral agreements on social security schemes. In the 1930s, however, there was an overtly discriminatory policy to exclude them. Interests similar to those which gave rise to guest-worker status explain this reversal of policy. By 1931, although the labor-market position of the alien with residency status was exempt from state-control, this settled alien remained severely handicapped in comparison to Belgian workers as (s)he continued to be refused access to most of the provisions of the social state. (S)he could, as such, not participate in social and economic life on the same terms as Belgian citizens. In this they repeated the characteristics of the "pure" guest worker. The guest worker did not exist as a category in nineteenth-century alien policy. Foreign labor in the nineteenth century was made up of workers who were not considered distinct from their indigenous colleagues. No special legislation was developed to confine them to specific segments of the labor market or for that matter to keep them away from independent economic pursuits. In the nineteenth century, however, an unemployed foreign worker was, at least in principle, also inconceivable. If an alien residing in Belgium lost his source of income due to economic misfortune, an accident, or sickness, he was not entitled to public welfare. A destitute alien could be obliged, independent of the length of his stay in Belgium, to leave. This brutal legal provision hardly corresponded with the reality of alien policy, which put resident aliens on a par with citizens.

The radical alien policy transformed the undesirable immigrant from the destitute to the undocumented alien. The undesirability of the nineteenth-century immigrant was not caused by administrative regulation, but by the market. The undesirable alien of the nineteenth century was the destitute immigrant, a social category rather than an administrative category. In the daily practice of alien policy, if an administrative category played a role, it was an attenuating one in the sense that expulsion was mostly limited to those who had just arrived or had not yet been registered. The need for registration was established very early on in Belgium. From 1846 onwards all inhabitants of Belgium – Belgians and aliens alike – were obliged to declare their presence at the commune where they were residing. This registration was, however, largely a formality. There was hardly any risk involved in declaring one's presence to the authorities, on the contrary. In the twentieth century the character of undesirability changed. Politics rather than economics now defined the undesirable alien. Due to administrative regulation of the admittance of aliens to the economy, the twentieth-century undesirable alien was not by definition without a source of income. What income (s)he had, however, was illicit; it had not been obtained with the necessary approval of the public authorities. The undesirable immigrant became the undocumented worker.

As the nineteenth-century alien could always be expelled for being destitute, independent of the length of his stay in Belgium, we call the nineteenth-century alien policy brutal. We call its historical successor in the twentieth-century a radical alien policy. The harshness of the radical alien policy can not be overlooked by the dehumanization of the "recent" immigrants to a one-dimensional economic actor. Only after a long period of residence did the state yield its absolute power over the immigrants. We call it radical because the implementation of this elaborate design demanded the far-reaching and refined intervention of the state. The prerequisites for a smooth functioning of this radical alien policy were not only a sophisticated registration of the length of residence of the guest workers, but also strict control over the economic insertion of these immigrants, even to the extent that the labor market position of immigrants was followed up meticulously. The total exclusion of all other entrants was also required. The radical alien policy created the guest-worker system which became a general feature of Western European alien policy.

The alien policy of the nineteenth century was brutal in its design, but not in its reality. By the end of the nineteenth century this, the at least formally brutal alien policy evolved into a liberal alien policy due to legislative changes and the attitude of the judiciary. We call it liberal as most immigrants, irrespective of social class, were granted denizen status after a short period of residence. At the same time the impact of this attenuated policy on the foreign population in Belgium increased. In the neighboring countries the latter evolution can be observed as well. In nineteenth-century France, Germany and the Netherlands the social significance of nationality also increased and the distinction between national and alien would brand social reality in the twentieth century deeply.

The Political Process Through Which the Guest Worker was Created

Our analysis indicates that the creation of the guest worker was a complex process in which very different interest groups had a stake. Because of the two different set of concerns alien policy evokes – aliens as political and as economic actors – the political process is not easy to disentangle. The bills being proposed, laws being accepted, and policies being implemented created alliances which cut across the classical ideological alignments of left and right. Very divergent and sometimes conflictual strategies led to the radicalization of alien policy. In the following paragraphs we will repeat some of our main findings on the interests behind the radical alien policy. We will first examine the domestic political scene, followed by an analysis of what influence international politics had on the transformation of Belgian alien policy.

Domestic Politics: From Parliamentarism to Corporatism

The alien law of 1835, its prolongations, and the final statute law of 1897 as well as the liberalization of nationality legislation were voted on in Parliament after long debates, as was any other important piece of nineteenth-century legislation . The will of the electorate – a restricted elite – decided the outcome of the discussions. The way in which the radical alien policy came about in the 1930s reflects a new political process which was very different from policy-making in a nineteenth-century liberal parliamentary polity. In the interwar period, not the passing will of the electorate through their representatives in Parliament, but the logic of issues and of the underlying social cleavages were the major determinant of political alignments. The continuing brokerage of interests no longer took place in Parliament, but in offices of organized interest-groups and ministries. Power was displaced from elected representatives to the major organized forces of society. Parliament as a source of effective power was definitely weakened. The legislative process tended to register rather than to shape the results of bargaining between different political actors, as was spectacularly illustrated by the manner in which the reform of March 1936 was pushed through Parliament. As most Belgian governments in the 1930s had obtained full power, such a humiliation of Parliament was in most instances not necessary. The MPs could just be bypassed. The Belgian Parliament had hardly any influence on the decision making process. It was rather the executive power, mostly in direct consultation with the interest groups involved, that made the decisions.

The political and social realignment in the interwar period is crucial to an understanding of this change in the policy process. The social basis of the political community was enlarged by including labor and the middle classes. This process started in the 1890s, got its formal breakthrough after the First World War and accelerated in 1935. The incorporation of the interests of labor and the middle classes within the Belgian polity brought about not only a different functioning of the state, but also an extension of its power. The enlargement of the national political community led to a redefinition of national interests. In order to attend to the interests of labor and the middle classes, the state had to intervene in a different and more crucial manner in more areas. The dividing line separating state from society and economy was moved to the detriment of the latter's autonomy. In this way the state conquered an important new domain with the radical alien policy. To control aliens as economic actors became a state function. The radical alien policy was one of the many expressions of the manner in which the regime was adapted and renovated in order to stabilize and extend its viability. The new alien policy did not emerge automatically out of the new political and social realignment. In the beginning of the 1920s, when this realignment occurred in its most dramatic expression, alien policy had not yet changed its objectives. This would only take place more than a decade later. This belated adaptation of the alien policy can be attributed to the power the traditional elites and especially business interests were able to retain in the Belgian polity of the 1920s. The traditional elites had succeeded in reconsolidating the social order within a few years after the First World War. New institutional arrangements were created and in many domains the distribution of power had altered fundamentally, but in the field of alien policy a simple return to the nineteenth-century pattern had been possible. In the second half of the 1930s, capitalist restructuring and institutional renovation by the state was pursued with exceptional vigor. Alien policy also had to be adapted to twentieth-century politics. Although by 1940 there was as yet no institutionalized integration of labor in alien policy formation, the interests of organized labor were no longer simply disregarded.[2] To identify the national interest on the issue of immigration became the state's responsibility, but as employer and labor interests were not identical this turned out to be a trying decision.

The transformation of alien policy implied a different balancing of interests. The radical alien policy was beneficial to all Belgian participants, but some interest groups won more than others. The employers, whose interests during the nineteenth century were the "national" interests, lost power. They could no longer autonomously decide whether to have recourse to immigrants as a way of availing themselves of a more tractable, skilled, diligent, or cheaper workforce than the national labor market offered. The state not only decided on the number of foreign workers that industry would attract, but also regulated the conditions under which these aliens would work. Within these constraints, the employers' interests were still considered "national" interests. The radical alien policy was also beneficial to the employers whose labor needs were officially agreed upon. That state intervention in international migration could be of benefit was recognized by heavy industry, when by the end of the 1920s the mining industry, followed by the CCI, demanded a change in alien legislation. Crucial for the shift in policy of heavy industry was the fact that the labor pools, which up to that point had been easily available, became exhausted. Belgian heavy industry was forced to invest in recruitment in faraway labor markets in order to attract enough labor. The recruiting employers pressured the state to ensure that no other employer could pirate these workers, procured at great cost, by restricting foreign labor's access to the national labor market. The radical alien policy guaranteed labor-hungry industries a sure return on their investment in recruited manpower by confining those workers to certain segments of the labor market. In the long run it guaranteed these industries foreign labor, without these employers having to compete for these workers with industries with better working conditions.

The constraints imposed on employers were due to the incorporation within the state of the interests of national labor as defended by the unions. The unions, identifying with national economic interests, considered the recruitment of foreign labor as unavoidable, but sought priority-hiring for Belgians. The unions wanted to lessen eventual unemployment among national labor by using foreign labor as a cushion against economic hardship. The fact that in this way they placed a whole category of workers in a legally inferior position was considered a necessary disadvantage. This position was Janus-faced since, in this way, immigrants were kept from organizing and fighting for better working conditions. Since foreign labor was extremely vulnerable to pressure by the state and by employers, they had an inhibiting influence on the power of the unions on the shopfloor.

The integration of national labor in the social and political system and the interests of some fraction of the employers were not the only factors leading towards the formulation of the radical alien policy. The middle classes were also, in particular in the second half of the 1930s, to be integrated in the regime. Leaders of the extremely fragmented middle classes demanded that the state also regard their private interests as the "national" interest. The introduction of the vendors' license and, in particular, the professional permit indicates that the interest of the artisanal and commercial classes in the exclusion of aliens from competition also became accepted as "national" interests. The state intervened not only in the labor market, but also in the national economy to align international migration to private interests. The development of the radical alien policy has to be credited to a diverse collection of social groups with very divergent and sometimes conflicting strategies.

The radical alien policy was not only developed by grafting private interests on the state, it also represented new state-interests. The incipient social state which represented the enlargement of the social basis of the regime caused expenses for the state treasury. Among others, full employment for indigenous labor became an objective of state policy due to the state subsidies to unemployment benefits for national labor. The expulsion of "superfluous" aliens saved the authorities from soaring welfare expenditures due to rising unemployment. Immigrants as political actors also caused pressures on the state to increase its power over aliens. In particular, the Sûreté and traditional elites considered an extension of state powers over aliens necessary to attend to the threat of subversive actions by migrants. Due to parliamentary sluggishness (1930) or even opposition (1934), little extension of state power to combat subversive aliens was obtained. The authorities were not totally stymied; they used to its constitutional limits the leeway which the alien law of 1897 granted the executive power. Numerous aliens, even some who had been residing in Belgium for a long time were expelled because of their political activities. We consider this repressive stance an expression of the nostalgia among traditional elites for the deferential and stable bourgeois order of nineteenth-century Belgium. The stability and status they dreamed about was now threatened by mass politics. That they had not yet digested this democratization of society was expressed in the treatment they inflicted upon politically active aliens. This treatment was reminiscent of the reaction of the Belgian state to the first expressions of the emancipation of the industrial labor class in the second half of the nineteenth century. As workers were recognized as full-fledged citizens after the First World War, a simple restoration of this nineteenth-century relation between state and subjects was beyond reach. However, only national labor profited from this change. For foreign labor, a return to the nineteenth-century police state was to a large extent possible.

Given the very diverse pressures to increase state power over aliens, it is no surprise that aliens were confined to a precarious legal status by 1939. All newcomers arriving in Belgium remained completely at the mercy of the arbitrary power of the state for a long time. State power had to ensure that immigrants would not only be subservient industrial workers, but also be unable to become political actors. By the end of the 1930s, the brutal nineteenth-century alien policy which enabled the state to expel settled aliens was restored. The possibility of expelling settled migrants was reintroduced as a principle for all aliens in 1933, and more specifically in 1936 for labor migrants during their first ten years of residence and in 1939 for self-employed migrants until their naturalization.[3] In contrast to the nineteenth century this had a clear-cut influence on social reality as the state made ample use of its newly granted powers.

Immigrants were clearly the losers in this transformation of alien policy, this was due to their exclusion from the decision-making process. Therefore, we do not write 'the making' of the guest worker, but 'the creation' of the guest worker. The different constituent members of the new Belgian polity succeeded in presenting their private interests as state interests which were incorporated in the transformed alien policy. Corporatism, in the words of C. Maier (1975:7), meant "the growth of private power and the twilight of sovereignty". The hold that private interests had over the state led to the disregard of proper state interests.

That the sovereign power of the state lost ground is illustrated by the state's lack of interest in making inhabitants of foreign origin into loyal inhabitants of their new country. We can interpret the decision not to extend the probationary period beyond ten years as a concern that some foreign workers would remain in the country as permanent residents, and that, after the probationary period, their integration into the national community should not be hindered. The decision, in 1939, to undermine the permanent residency status of those privileged aliens who requested a professional permit indicates that this long-term interest was of little interest to the policy makers. The state hardly envisaged a need to develop devices to integrate aliens. On the contrary, aliens became subject to an ever-deteriorating legal status. The sharpened exclusion of immigrants challenged the capacity to integrate newcomers. This absence of a political will to provide for channels of integration is confirmed to a large extent by the changes in nationality law. In contrast to the end of the nineteenth century when various legal reforms were introduced to provide for easier access to Belgian nationality, during the 1930s some provisions of nationality law were changed in a manner detrimental to the interests of the immigrants. In 1931, the period of residence required to qualify for naturalization proceedings was doubled, from five to ten years. The need for integration of newcomers into Belgian society was no issue.[4] This aspect of the radical alien policy was short-sighted. That the political authorities lacked vision is illuminated by juxtaposing the state policy to the efforts by employers and even the unions to integrate the foreign labor. Numerous employers, in the mining industry in particular, realized that their foreign labor responded to structural labor needs and developed a policy to encourage their settlement. These companies actively pursued the reuniting of migrants' families and some mines even developed an ambitious multicultural program. In 1937, the Socialist miners union, faced with the inevitability of foreign labor in the industry, also opted for the incorporation of immigrant labor within its ranks by providing ethnic locals and by defending, to a limited extent, the immigrants' interests. The state remained aloof.

Besides the private interests of each of the different groups involved, the precarious balance between the state's interests and the individual's interest, which is so important in liberal polity, was clearly tipped to the side of the state by the radicalization of alien policy. The radical alien policy introduced overtly discriminatory rules directed against aliens residing in the country and implied a roll-back of their civil and social status. Although Belgium became an immigration country, even immigrants who had become an integral part of the society were set apart. They became a category with an inferior legal status, and due to changes in nationality legislation, it became more difficult for them to escape this condition.

Liberal values definitely lost ground as the individual of foreign nationality was confronted with an increasing powerful state.

International Politics: Migrants as Citizens of States on the Periphery of the World System

The aliens' exclusion from political and social power meant that their interests were not taken into account. The only protection of which they could avail themselves was their membership in another state within an interdependent world. The limited weight of supplier states' diplomatic protection on Belgian alien policy is an indication of the exploitation of the periphery by core countries. The lot of most aliens was hardly attenuated by Belgium's political and economic interests abroad. Due to the expansion of the dominant core regions of European capitalism, labor migrants traveled increasing distances from the dependent periphery of this economic system to supplement the Belgian industrial labor force. In addition, the division of the German and the Austrian-Hungarian Empires into a multitude of nation-states after the First World War caused most immigrants to be citizens of diplomatically and economically weak nations; nations which had no leverage on Belgium's politics. State power does not directly correlate with economic power. The example of the Italian state, which successfully negotiated the conditions of migration to Belgium in the early twenties, is an example of this, but as more suppliers presented themselves the power position of the Italian state was eroded. The Dutch state, also a supplier of manpower, retained its power position during most of the 1930s. The ambiguous policy towards Dutch migrants in the 1930s illustrates diplomatic constraints on alien policy. The preferential policy towards French migrants in Belgium points to another interest shaping Belgian alien policy. The policy towards French immigrants meant to divert any exclusionary action against the large number of Belgians working in France. So not only internal political and economic conditions, but also diplomatic considerations, put constraints on the degradation of citizens from Belgium's neighboring countries to guest worker status.

The Creation of the Guest Worker in the Neighboring Countries

During the nineteenth century, state action in regulating migration in France, the Netherlands and Germany was similar to Belgium's. The central aim of alien policy was to prevent aliens from disturbing public order. Aliens who commited a crime as well as those who had no "honest" means of making a living, including beggars and vagrants, could be removed. Disturbing the public order had also a political connotation; subversive aliens had to be expelled. What subversive meant was, of course, subject to change. Prussia and later the German Empire were probably the least liberal in this respect. In Prussia, aliens had been closely supervised since the early nineteenth century. Taking part in a strike was sufficient provocation to be conveyed to the border (Kulczycki, 1994:62). In 1885 about 40,000 immigrants, mostly Poles and Jews of Austro-Hungarian and Russian nationality, some of which were even long-time residents, were expelled from Prussia. This radical decision is to be attributed to the political strategy of Prussia to create a German people. This mass expulsion did not aim at the regulation of the labor market, but at protecting a nation which was perceived as being threatened by Polish nationalism. Poles (and Jews) were considered subversive immigrants, therefore security risks. These specific susceptibilities of Germany's national identity had to be balanced with the growing economic need for immigrants, especially on the agrarian estates in Prussia's east. From 1890 onwards, Poles were only allowed to immigrate as single temporary laborers and they were not allowed to be employed in industry in the Prussia's western provinces, in public works, or in trade. Every year foreign Poles were required to leave German territory before December 20 and were forbidden to return before February 1. These restrictions in the occupational and geographic mobility of Polish workers of Austro-Hungarian and Russian nationality were politically motivated. Not only the entry, but also the mobility of all other immigrants, whether Dutch, Belgian, Italian, or Ruthenian remained unrestricted. In addition, indigenous workers had no legal advantages over these foreign workers on the German labor market and the freedom of the employers to recruit foreign labor, or for that matter the freedom of most foreigners to immigrate to Germany was not touched upon. Immigrants who were only perceived as economic actors were hardly the object of state interest. The fear of a Polish campaign to "resurrect" their own state or any mere threat to the Germanization of the Prussian Poles was the main motivation of the Prussian Government. German alien policy was innovative for nineteenth-century Europe as it introduced institutionalized discrimination against some foreign labor. In 1909, the Prussian state introduced a new qualitative step: the control of all foreign labor. Alien policy aimed at disciplining foreign labor by diminishing their turnover. All foreign workers had to carry an *Inlandslegitimationskarte* which tied them to their employer. A foreign worker breaking his contract had to leave the country. This new alien policy took only industrial and agrarian interests into account and was an expression of the high level of organization of German society and the central role of the state. A polity in which labor interests were hardly represented (Bade 1987 and 1980).

German alien policy, in its intervention into migration crossing its borders, was exceptional for Europe at that time. During the nineteeth-century German alien policy was also exceptional in the sense that no provisions at all were made for settled aliens. A denizen status did not exist in the authoritarian German Empire. Aliens, independant of social status or length of residence, were always eligible for summary expulsion (Olshausen 1904:71, 103ff.; Wertheimer 1987:52f.). In liberal regimes such as Belgium, France, and the Netherlands aliens could acquire protection against arbitrary state power. French legislation (on which Belgian legislation was largely based) provided that aliens could ask for the status of *domicilié* which put them on a par with Frenchmen (Lescoeur 1899:135ff.; Lentacker 1974:231). Resident aliens – a status acquired after staying for a year in France – could only be expelled by the Minister of the Interior, while non-resident aliens could be expelled by the prefects (Martini 1909:96). In the Dutch alien legislation of 1849, aliens who could prove their means of existence acquired a protective status from the local authorities. They could only be ordered to leave the country by royal decree, or in case of destitution, by a decision of the judiciary. In these liberal regimes, a protected status was attributed to well-to-do immigrants to a large extent. The granting of any protected status was explicitly refused to prostitutes and musicians, but the extent to which labor migrants were protected against arbitrary expulsion through this means is still an open question. Some categories of especially deserving aliens (those married to nationals, born in the country, etc.) were, as a rule, indiscriminately entitled to such a status (Leenders 1993:86, 122; Feblowicz and Latour 1938:413).

The fact that there was no automatic protection against expulsion on the grounds of lasting residence in the host country does not imply that settled aliens were summarily expelled for whatever minor reason. In this age of little political centralization, long-time residents were considered part of the local population, even if they kept their foreign nationality. Competition by aliens in the labor market or in the national economy was considered a wholly private affair, not an issue for the state. This changed when the state increased its intervention by the end of the nineteenth century. The distinction of alien and national gained real significance in social life; a shift of the dividing line separating the state from society and economy. In 1888 in France and in 1918 in the Netherlands, it became mandatory for all aliens to register at the municipality in which they resided (Leenders 1993:170; Noriel 1988:88). In France the presence of aliens in the labor market became a public issue. From 1893 onwards, all foreigners arriving in France to look for a job had to declare themselves at the commune, which in its turn had to notify the central authorities of their arrival and also of each change of residence of these labor migrants. This measure was designed by Parliament as a hidden protectionist measure. The declaration of residence or arrival entailed a payment. For the MPs, this payment was the crux of the new legislation, control over the aliens was seen mainly as a means of receiving an income tax, a variant on tariffs. The assumption was that this "tax" would assure that preference would be given to French workers (Noiriel 1988:88). On the eve of the First World War the two camps, France and Germany, had taken the first steps towards a radicalized alien policy which would be a combination of the social protectionism of the French and the economic dirigisme of Germany. Belgium and the Netherlands had only laid the foundations for the radical alien policy by grafting the distinction between citizens and aliens onto social reality. Belgium had, however, a clear-cut advantage in terms of administrative experience with population control. Central registration of aliens was introduced shortly after Belgian independence and was constantly updated by the local authorities. The geographical mobility not only of aliens, but also of nationals, was monitored from very early on. Since 1846 all inhabitants, aliens and Belgians alike, had to notify the communal authorities of their whereabouts. After the First World War, this even meant that all inhabitants had to carry an identity card. In this manner Belgium had even a more developed control capacity than Germany, a control capacity which was strongly constrained by the liberal values which its polity embodied.

Immediately after the First World War, France and Germany, the two forerunners in the radicalization of alien policy, structurally embedded the control of migrants as economic actors. This discriminatory practice of the German Empire was reformulated in the Weimar Republic by integrating organized labor in the regulation of migration. The immediate post war turmoil made business more conciliatory to organized labor. The German state became a corporate state in which the unions had an institutionalized role. The state monopolized the recruitment of foreign workers and a system of yearly work-permits was introduced for all foreign workers. This permit was only granted to an employer if the public exchange offices, in which employers and labor were equally represented, had confirmed that there was no equivalent national labor available for the job. High unemployment in Germany meant that few authorizations were granted and those few were mainly for seasonal labor in agriculture (Bade 1987:78ff.).

In France the radicalization of alien policy had been dependent on a different alliance of interest-groups; the role of the employers was much more important. During the war, the French state had recruited foreign labor to satisfy the needs of the war economy. These imported workers were controlled by the state through a system of identity cards in order to ensure an optimal allocation of labor. At the end of hostilities the employers, especially those in heavy industry and capitalist agriculture, did not return to their prewar commitment to a free labor market. Due to declining labor reserves because of war casualties, a low fertility level, and the ability of French peasants to resist proletarization, the importation of labor had become an absolute necessity. Employers pressed the French state to become a partner of industry in manipulating the flow of foreign labor. The labor-exporting states, Italy in particular, monopolized recruitment and imposed the conditions on which their citizens could emigrate to work abroad. Only the French state could counter these demands through diplomatic negotiations. Treaties were concluded with Italy, Poland, Czechoslovakia, etc., to ensure an abundant labor supply for French industry and agriculture. Heavy industry and capitalist agriculture also embraced state intervention to ensure the confinement of the foreign workers they recruited to their segments of the labor market.

The French state imposed the restriction to a certain economic sector on foreign labor through the obligation to carry an identity card. By the terms of the *loi sur la répression du débauchage* (1926) employers were made liable for the "illegal" employment of aliens. Not only were employers punished if they hired aliens that were not entitled to work, but hiring foreign labor whose recruitment contract had not yet expired was also prohibited. The new law had to exact solidarity from all employers with the industries that had invested into recruiting manpower abroad (Niklewski 1930: 130f.). French organized labor also insisted on regulating migration, but rather in order to assure priority to national labor. Its influence on the new regulatory mechanism in France was weak. Even the Popular Front did not change this state of affairs. State officials together with business decided about the influx of foreign labor and their integration on the labor market. The fluctuating administrative regulation of foreign labor reveals the state's aims regarding foreign labor during the Depression. In 1935, geographical and occupational restrictions were inflicted on foreign labor. The identity card only became valid for one department and a renewal of the card was necessary for each change of job. These measures made it easier to use foreign labor as a cushion against economic hardship. During the Popular Front the geographical restriction was revoked. In 1938 the geographical restriction was reintroduced for those immigrants with less than ten years residence. In the 1930s, aliens undertaking independent economic activity also became subject to state-control. The political empowerment of the middle classes led them to call upon the state to protect them from local competitors of foreign nationality. In 1934, artisans were required to apply for authorization to exercise their profession. From 1935 onwards peddlers also had to obtain a licence. In June 1938 all independent economic activity by aliens became subject to state authorization. Also employers' liability was extended. Employers were made legally responsible for hiring aliens only in the departments and the professions that were mentioned on workers' identity cards. With this decision to regulate the hiring practices of employers, France came close to the manner of regulation in Weimar Germany to which, by then, Belgium also had adhered (Cross 1983 and Ponty 1988).

In the Netherlands, rather an emigration than an immigration country, the radical alien policy was rather late to arrive. Immediately after the First World War, due to the deteriorating international climate, border control was reinstated and visa requirements were reintroduced. Crucial to this decision was a perceived need to prevent subversive aliens from entering the country. By the middle of the decade, the nineteenth-century pattern of migration control was reinstated in the Netherlands. Italian ice cream vendors and terrazzo workers, German domestic servants together with some German and East European miners for the Limburg coalfields, were the only immigration to be noted until the Depression of the 1930s. The radicalization of alien policy in Germany, which by 1930 had also been initiated in Belgium, had clear-cut repercussions on Dutch emigrants, but the Dutch government refused to be drawn into legislation of its own. The interests of Dutch workers abroad and the strong opposition of Dutch industry to state intervention on the labor market meant that only border control was strengthened. After the arrival of refugees from Nazi Germany, the authorities imposed the first restrictions on foreign labor. By January 1935, aliens' access to the labor market was restricted in specific trades and industries; two years later, all wage-labor by aliens was dependent on official permission granted to the employers and granted only if no Dutch labor could be found to fill the vacancy. In practice, most aliens already working in the Netherlands were allowed to continue, but access to the labor market for newcomers became extremely difficult. The increasing political power of the middle classes also allowed them to obtain protection against local competition from foreigners. In 1937 aliens undertaking independent economic activity became the subject of state control (Moore et al. 1998:75ff.).

The Western European continental countries gradually introduced the radical alien policy. Germany was the first country to do so. France joined the Germans by an incremental process of ever more restrictive measures between 1893 and 1938. In the meantime, during the Depression of the 1930s, first Belgium and shortly afterwards the Netherlands also installed their guest worker system by eroding liberal provisions in their alien legislation and by making any economic activity by immigrants dependent on a public authorization. The radical alien policy intended to make all immigrants into a reserve army of workers who operated as a buffer against economic fluctuations. Certain manpower needs were to be met, while at the same time various costs, in particular the cost of periodical unemployment, were to be externalized. The liberal regimes were, however, constrained institutionally and ideologically in their treatment of resident aliens. That guest workers would become resident aliens and be accredited with rights could, by the liberal nature of these regimes, not be avoided. Within the radical alien policy, long-term residents continued to be granted exemptions from arbitrary state power. This protected status was derived from a discretionary administrative practice which was challenged less and less by the judiciary. Rights bestowed on resident aliens largely became favors granted by the state and that grant was postponed for ever longer periods. Alien policy became more an immigration and less an immigrant policy. In Belgium during the 1930s, the period in which immigrants were under the arbitrary power of the state immigration policy was prolonged from four months to ten years. A similar evolution can be noticed in neighboring countries. The nineteenth-century liberal provisions for resident aliens were also dismantled in these countries. In France the legal protection granted to settled aliens by the legal status of *domicilié* was abolished; the denizen status in the Netherlands fell largely into disuse (Lucassen 1990:114, 160ff.). In France, according to administrative practice in the 1920s, aliens were granted an automatic renewal of their identity card after five year's residence and were, in this way, largely exempt from administrative discretion. In 1935 the length of residence necessary to be granted such protection was prolonged from five to ten years. In May 1938 the period of residence was extended even further, to fifteen years (Ponty 1988:294; Cross 1983). After the First World War, protective measures for settled aliens were introduced in Germany as liberal values were part of the Weimar ideology. Immigrants who had been employed in the country at least five years were exempt by the *Befreiungsschein* from the restrictive work-permit system (Volkmann 1926: 31). In 1932, provisions for settled aliens in Germany were even entered in the statute books. Exemption from arbitrary state powers was to a large extent conceded to all aliens with more than ten years residence (Dohse 1981:107ff.). These liberal provisions were, however, eroded by regulations on the immigration of labor. In Weimar Germany, farm hands were recruited in Poland, but they were forced to leave Germany before winter. In this way, the practice of the *Kaiserreich* was duplicated, due to the nature of the labor shortages but also to prevent these aliens from acquiring any rights in Germany (Elsner and Lehmann 1988:134ff.). Nazism did away with any liberalism in Germany's alien legislation.

One can wonder if the similarities among alien policies in the different European states are ones of form only. Radical alien policy entailed the organization of, or a mere control over, immigration, together with monitoring and channeling foreign labor on the national labor market. Implementation met with constraints of a very varied nature. Administrative, economic, diplomatic, and ideological factors played a role. The adaptation of immigration to the ambitions of the policy makers was not an easy task. One can also wonder to what extent radical alien policy influenced the dynamics of migration. Guest workers had to be a reserve army of workers who operated as a buffer against economic fluctuations.

The market makes migrants serve such a function. Foreign labor had already served as a buffer in the nineteenth century (and in the 1920s): a reduction in immigration after each economic downturn and an increase in return migration as a spontaneous process in reaction to declining economic opportunities. Nineteenth-century alien policy had already added to this natural migration dynamic by expelling destitute immigrants. Formally, it aimed at expelling destitute aliens, but in practice mainly if not only new arrivals seemed to have been victims of this police measure. With the radical alien policy, enforcing this buffer function on settled aliens became official policy. The state was to be guarantor that immigrants responded adequately and immediately to changes in the labor market. The alien policy tried to influence the dynamic of migration by enforcing the quick response of immigrants, even to local and temporary changes on the labor market or the economy. The litmus test for the influence of alien policy on social reality is expulsion policy. Only an analysis of the implementation of the radical alien policy can provide us with an answer to the uniqueness of each country's historical experiences with the regulation of migration.

The Creation of Refugees

The authorities resolve to master immigration according to "national" interests resulted in the guest-worker system, which purported to align immigration with labor needs. It was a political settlement aimed at a rational solution to the tensions raised by immigration within the Belgian polity. The guest-worker system as a rational alien policy quickly proved to be a myth. The straightjacket into which all immigrants were forced immediately ripped open. Another category through which immigrants were able to enter and reside in Belgium, that of refugee, was an offspring of the guest-worker system. Refugees came to be treated as a category of immigrants deserving special assistance. It was a constant in Belgian history to provide arrangements for "refugees" with every restriction introduced in the immigration policy. In the first half of the nineteenth century and again in 1885 and in 1933 allowances were made for "refugees". Humanitarian values and ideological considerations together with considerations of efficiency were paramount in this decision to make exception for refugees. Within the radical alien policy the provisions of 1933 were extended and institutionalized in 1936. Not only was refugee policy codified in that year, it also went beyond nineteenth-century practice. As alien policy extended its hold over immigrants, the discrimination which aliens residing in Belgium were increasingly subjected to, had to be, to some degree, relaxed when applied to "refugees". It was accepted that "refugees" were here to stay and that they did not have the alternative, as did all other immigrants, of returning to their country of origin. Belgium amended its radical alien policy not only to prevent "refugees" from being returned to the country of persecution, but preferential measures were also included in favor of the insertion of "refugees" into Belgian society. The liberalization of the treatment of "refugees" was not a unilateral Belgian decision; it has to be seen within a newly established international refugee regime. This international refugee regime made for the durable settlement in the first country of asylum of those refugees to whom the international community catered. Thus, an influx of "refugees" in Belgium following the establishment of a liberal refugee policy was not to be feared.

The advantages granted to "refugees" as an exceptional category of immigrants meant that refugee status was only selectively attributed. The main criteria was that their immigration had to be caused by political, not economic forces. The interpretation of politically-induced migration was, however, restrictive. Only political activists whose life or freedom had been threatened were eligible for refugee status. This traditional concept of refugee – the political refugee – did not take into account new forms of persecution. Therefore, the Jewish exodus from Germany due to the collective persecution of Jews by the Nazi regime, officially, was not considered a refugee movement. Even after the spring of 1938, Jewish refugees were still denied refugee status, although the distinction in terms of state violence between the refugee *stricto sensu* and *sensu lato,* between those who were politically and racially persecuted had become meaningless. Not even all political activists were eligible for refugee status. Those who had to flee because of political activities which were considered subversive in Belgium were mostly excluded from eligibility (for example refugees who had been active in the Paris Commune in 1871, Socialists before the First World war and Communists between 1929 and 1936). "Refugee" was a politically constructed concept. To define who was a "refugee" was a prerogative of the state, and it decided not only according to an objective reality, but also according to national interests.

Also in neighboring countries with a liberal regime, special arrangements were provided for refugees. Concomitant with the abolishment of the choice of border for expellees at the end of the nineteenth century, France forbade the expulsion of "refugees" while the Netherlands retained the choice of exit point for "refugees" among the expellees (Martini 1909:137; Leenders 1993: 105 and 112). These two distinct strategies remained characteristic for both countries. France continued to grant an informal status to "refugees" until 1936 when France joined the international refugee regime and introduced a formal refugee status, an evolution on which the very similar Belgian refugee policy, at least in the 1930s, partly depended. The Netherlands refused to accord a special status to those fleeing persecution because of their political beliefs and, in the 1930s, did not adhere to the international refugee regime. In the Netherlands until 1935, political "refugees" were merely offered a choice of exit points at deportation, which meant they were expelled to Belgium. After 1935, due to Belgian complaints, subversive political "refugees" were interned. The French and Belgian authorities expelled politically active aliens who had been forced to leave their country of origin, but the refugee quality of these expellees was mostly unacknowledged. The Dutch authorities, on the other hand, were conscious that they were deporting refugees; even the mere fact of being a political refugee could make someone liable for expulsion. Although the Dutch authorities were much more anxious about political elements engaging in subversive acts than the French and Belgian authorities, the direct handing over of political refugees to the authorities of the state of persecution was considered politically unacceptable in all three countries. Repatriating political activists, even those who were considered subversive aliens, was contrary to the liberal tradition of asylum (Moore et al. 1998).

With the introduction of the radical alien policy, refugee policy was extended beyond immigration policy. In the 1920s Weimar Germany already provided special provisions for Russian refugees within its guest-worker system (Dodenhoeft 1993:15). In the 1930s special provisions were made for "refugees" in France, similar to those in Belgium (Caron 1998). States bordering Belgium also defined "refugee" to suit national interests. This is to be noticed in the case of Jewish refugees in the 1930s in particular. Jews fleeing Nazi Germany to the Netherlands and France, even after the spring of 1938, were not considered deserving of a privileged status. While from the second half of 1938 onwards, the decision makers in France and the Netherlands clearly stated their intention to expel Jewish refugees, after the `disastrous experiment' of October 1938 this option was considered politically impossible to pursue in Belgium. The extent to which the Dutch and French actually implemented a policy of forcible repatriation remains unclear. According to the French and Dutch authorities, however, Jewish refugees were not refugees. In this way, their flight was totally delegitimized and they could be repatriated. The Belgian political authorities, on the other hand, acknowledged the reality of the persecution of Jews in Nazi Germany and in this way continued, notwithstanding the arrival en masse of Jewish refugees, to adhere to liberal and/or humanitarian values.

The Creation of Illegal Aliens

The ultimate touchstone for the influence of alien policy on social reality is the ability to make undesirable aliens leave. As closing the border was an unattainable objective, strict enforcement of alien policy had to be obtained by stringent internal immigration control, i.e., apprehending and expelling unwanted aliens. The issue at stake was not the prevention of unauthorized immigration, the stay of aliens who had immigrated illegally was, when they responded to officially sanctioned labor needs, legalized again and again. Only those illegally immigrated aliens who did not fulfill the (fluctuating) residence requirements set by the executive power were to be removed. The radical alien policy made them into undocumented aliens, but this was only a bureaucratic decision. To what degree this entailed a cutting off of any means of livelihood in Belgium or even physical removal of these immigrants depended on enforcement of the new legislation. Expulsion was a troublesome affair, due mainly to the resistance of the aliens themselves. Numerous undesirable aliens did refuse to leave the country voluntarily, and even if they were escorted to the border by the police, they returned. Until September 1939, the unauthorized stay of aliens in Belgium was, as such, not a criminally triable offence. Expulsion of undesirable aliens was merely an administrative decision; their return could not be sanctioned by a prison sentence. They could only be subject to another administrative decision of expulsion. Until September 1939, a legal sanction was only possible for two kinds of unwanted immigration. Firstly, vagrancy (and begging) was an offence for the whole period, and offenders, whether they were Belgian or not, could be imprisoned. In the last decade of the nineteenth century, the use of this legislation even took the form of a collective sanction against the unwanted immigration of poor aliens. The police courts exercised sweeping exclusionary powers with respect to (foreign) vagrants. This repressive immigration policy was, however, short-lived (1892 to 1896) and would not be repeated. The financial costs and bureaucratic burden of such a tough immigration policy turned out to be too high, certainly as the return in declining undesirable immigration was deemed unsatisfactory. From the second half of the 1920s onwards, vagrants from Eastern and Central Europe, i.e., those who had to pass through Germany on their way "home" were confined for a few months in one of the penal colonies. This was partly aimed at dissuading them from remaining in Belgium, but the main motivation behind their arrest was to provide them with some money and eventually the necessary papers to enable them to leave Belgium and return to their country of origin. Secondly, imprisonment could follow upon the return of an alien expelled by royal decree. Aliens who acquired residency status could be expelled by royal decree for disturbing the public order and if these dangerous aliens returned they could be sentenced to a maximum of six-months imprisonment because of *rupture de ban*.

Outside the two above-mentioned cases, no sanction was available against unwanted immigration. For the most part, only administrative decisions – *renvoi* – were taken against unwanted immigrants. These expelled aliens, if they still had the means could return to Belgium without running any risk, except of another expulsion. Sometimes numerous expulsions could not convince an alien not to return to Belgium. This stubbornness stymied the policy makers, and the Sûreté in particular looked for means to enlarge its administrative power over aliens. It was felt that only repression could convince these recalcitrant aliens to finally stay away from Belgium. Since 1878, undesirable aliens, who, after several administrative decisions of expulsion still returned to Belgium were, notwithstanding the fact that they never had acquired residency status and that they had never been convicted of any serious infraction of the law, also considered dangerous aliens and expelled by royal decree (*expulser*). The argument was that only by making unauthorized stay in Belgium much more perilous would these undesirable aliens be dissuaded from returning to Belgium. While in the last quarter of the nineteenth century only the most notorious of these inoffensive, but stubbornly returning, unwanted aliens were singled out for an expulsion by royal decree, this decision to arm the executive authorities against the return of expellees became a collective sanction for all returnees by 1935. All unwanted aliens who did not leave Belgium were considered dangerous aliens. Tolerance of undocumented aliens dropped spectacularly in this half century, not in correlation with any actual increase in danger to society. Rather political pressure and an ambition for total control explain this momentum. The hope which the administration put in the criminal prosecution of these aliens was only partly met by the courts. The courts hardly ever meted out severe sentences. The judiciary considered these undocumented aliens much less of a danger than its habitual clientele. The judiciary was more responsive than the executive branch of the state to the notion of equal treatment for all, including undocumented aliens.

The nineteenth-century susceptibilities in expulsion policy, granting free border choice to expellees and preventing disguised extradition, disappeared after the First World War. The nationalization of society and the establishment of liberal, parliamentary regimes at Belgium's borders, at least until 1933, can explain this change. This does not mean that liberal values no longer played a role in the treatment of undocumented aliens. That Parliament refused to give its approbation to bills which would give the executive more power to repress undocumented aliens is an indication of the weight liberal values still carried in the Belgian polity. According to the proponents of a tougher immigration policy only a big stick would diminish unwanted immigration. Seen from within – in particular by the Sûreté overwhelmed by a seemingly chaotic migration to Belgium – immigration control was singularly imperfect. The Sûreté strongly advocated a more repressive policy against undocumented aliens, but only got satisfaction at the onset of the Second World War. From September 1939 onwards prison terms of up to one year could be inflicted upon aliens for the mere fact of being undocumented. The judiciary which was now granted greater repressive power to deal with undocumented aliens, continued to use its power moderately. The courts still counterbalanced the pressure from the executive to repress crudely aliens immigrating or residing in an unauthorized manner in the country.

Undocumented immigrants presented an interesting hiring option for certain employers. The increasing state regulation of the economy meant that there was a growing economic advantage attached to illegal immigration from the point of view of the employers. Indeed, a side effect of the radical alien policy was to provide manpower for an informal labor market. In this informal labor market, state regulation was circumvented and the advantages obtained by doing so grew with the increasing interference of the state in the terms of engagement of labor. Undocumented aliens became the manpower par excellence for this unregulated labor market. Not only immigrants who immigrated illegally, but also those who had migrated legally but were not satisfied with the position on the labor market allocated to them by the Belgian state or who had been denied access to the labor market altogether provided the informal market with a labor force. Undocumented workers were a cheap, elastic, and docile workforce as they were totally dependent on the employer and had to accept the job whatever the terms, due to their lack of legal status. In the final years of the 1930s, the presence of undocumented aliens on the labor market seems to have been out of the authorities' control. To a large extent this was the result of ambiguity in the immigration policy, i.e., the toleration of the illegal immigration of Jewish refugees from Germany. For the unions, providing the informal labor market with manpower was clearly an adverse effect of the radicalization of the alien policy since undocumented aliens could undermine officially sanctioned working conditions.

Within the parameters of the radical alien policy, the undocumented alien had to be combated, combat which was very costly and which did not offer a clear-cut victory. The problem was not only that immigrants were not willing to leave, but sometimes were not capable of leaving. This was not only the case for refugees. The nationalization of expulsion procedures since the end of the nineteenth century caused a hindrance to the removal of undesirable aliens who did not originate from a country adjacent to Belgium. As more and more citizens of non-neighboring countries arrived in Belgium, and, in particular, from Eastern and Southern Europe, diplomatic barriers to effective expulsion rose. From the end of the nineteenth century onwards, an efficient removal practice for Eastern Europeans depended on the agreement of the German authorities, procedure with high costs in terms of the aliens' upkeep, a long bureaucratic process and eventually their transport. The result was not always satisfactory as some aliens could not (or were not willing to) prove their nationality and, therefore, could not obtain a passport. In the second half of the 1930s, a partial solution to the financial problem was found by calling upon employers to co-finance the repatriation of undesirable aliens. For every worker the employers recruited abroad, they had to pay a security deposit to the value of the cost for travel to the border of the worker's country of origin. As soon as this immigrant no longer filled an officially sanctioned labor need, he had to be repatriated at the expense of this fund. The motivation was not to humanize the expulsion procedure, but to rationalize the new alien policy. It was cheaper to repatriate "superfluous" foreign labor than to keep it in the country.

The bottlenecks in removing unwanted aliens were similar in the neighboring countries (Caestecker 1998:91ff.). In contrast to Belgium, the neighboring countries during the interwar period were less willing to accept this state of affairs. The starting position was alike; the nineteenth-century alien legislation in the three Western European liberal regimes provided similar means to punish non-compliance with an expulsion order. In France the law of 1849 provided for prison terms of up to six months for *rupture de ban*, very similar to the Belgian (1835/1897) and the Dutch (1848) provisions during the nineteenth century. This sanction was only for those aliens who had been forced to leave after residing in the country. Unwanted non-resident aliens expelled (*refouler*) summarily could upon return only be expelled once more. During the interwar period the Dutch and certainly the French authorities designed a tougher alien policy. In 1918 the Dutch authorities had already enacted legislation which enabled the executive power to intern dangerous aliens. The Dutch government wanted these powers in order to combat the infiltration of subversive aliens in their country. Foreign Communists in particular were, during the interwar period, interned in civil prisons, but also in camps especially set-up in Harderwijk (1920-21), Honswijk (1935), etc. Liberal elements in Parliament, notwithstanding the opposition of the government, succeeded in providing aliens some protection by enabling them to appeal in court a decision to intern them (Leenders 1993:173ff.). In France after the First World War new legislative measures were also enacted. Illegal residence, i.e., lack of an identity card, became liable to punishment with a prison term of one to six months. In France a more active policy to combat illegal entrants and returnees started at the darkest hour of the depression, in 1935. The nearly century-old provision for non-compliance with an expulsion order as stipulated by the alien law of 1849 was raised to a minimum of six months and a maximum of two years. By May 1938, foreigners who lacked visas or identity cards (undocumented aliens) became subject to automatic prison sentences of one month to one year and failure to comply with an expulsion order *(rupture de ban*) would result in an even harsher prison sentence of up to three years. While previously the police had brought illegal aliens to court only at the behest of the *prefecture* or the Interior Minister, the intervention of higher authorities was no longer necessary and all illegal aliens had to be brought before the courts. Combating illegal immigration – including Jews fleeing Nazi Germany – had become a priority for the French government and only punitive police measures were felt to be a solution. Even the role of the judiciary, which before 1938 had used its power moderately, was curtailed. Judges were not allowed to take extenuating circumstances into account (Feblowicz and Lamour 1937:101; Caron 1999). The efficiency of this harsh French policy was minimal, certainly in light of the huge resources mobilized in the effort.

This stepping-up of the repression of undocumented aliens with several legislative initiatives in France (and to a lesser extent the Netherlands) was very different from the Belgian situation. Although Belgium also stepped-up repression of unwanted immigration, this was done on the basis of the nineteenth-century legislation until the outbreak of the Second World War. That the Belgian government did not obtain any new powers is an indication of the weight liberal values carried in the Belgian polity, although mere inertia played a role too. Well-informed observers pointed out that the Belgian system of reprimanding undocumented aliens was less harsh than the French one. In particular the stateless and refugees, those for whom return was no option, found more comprehension in Belgium than anywhere else (Philonenko 1937:703ff.).

One can wonder, certainly seeing that fewer resources were being mobilized, if the efficiency of Belgian expulsion policy was not much higher than those of the neighboring countries. The question is whether that mattered for the policy-makers as these repressive measures were designed primarily to assuage public opinion. The authorities wanted to be perceived as pursuing an activist policy. However, and certainly if the objective reality of migration is not taken into account (for example that Jews were highly motivated to flee Nazi-Germany) the return this investment in repression yields can even be negative. The political pressure to halt immigration can create a momentum of its own, even further afield from the objective reality of migration, A momentum increasing in relation to the impressions created by the imperfect repression of unwanted immigration. To adapt public policy to such an irrational drive creates not only considerable hardship on those involved, but is also highly inefficient.

After this overview of the creation of the three categories within West European alien policy in the twentieth century, we succinctly summarize this transformation of alien policy and present some of the challenges it gave rise to. In the nineteenth century, although alien legislation had some brutal provisions, settled aliens were mostly treated on a par with nationals. Limited administrative capacities and, most importantly, the irrelevance of nationality in social life meant that alien policy had little impact. Alien policy, however, acquired an increasing influence at the end of the nineteenth century as immigration policy was definitely tightened and nationality became an all-pervasive point of identification concomitant with the increasing role of the state in society. In the nineteenth-century liberal regimes, this restrictionist drive was attenuated by favorable legal provisions for settled aliens and refugees. The status of resident alien lost much of its importance between the end of the nineteenth century and the 1930s. In those four decades liberal alien policy crumbled. Although immigrants increasingly performed work essential to the functioning of the economic system, they were denied some of the most basic rights citizens enjoyed. The democratization of formal politics and the transformation of the nineteenth-century state into a welfare state was concomitant with the state becoming more of a nation state, hardly catering to the needs of the aliens residing in the country. Only citizens became bearers of the duties and rights to which the expanding state gave rise. While the state was evolving into a welfare state for all its citizens, it was becoming a police state for immigrants. This dialectical process forced immigrants, political as well as economic actors, into nineteenth-century enclaves. Notwithstanding the democratization of Western European society immigrants were doomed to be guest workers. The executive power in liberal regimes remained constrained by liberal values and/or humanitarism partly enforced by the judiciary. The objective situation of those immigrants who could not become guest workers was, due to those restraining forces, taken into account. This was particularly beneficial to refugees, but also illegal aliens could in this way be treated more considerately than by mere use of repression. That liberal values and/or humanitarism constrained the executive power to repress undocumented aliens was more obvious in Belgium than in the neighboring countries.

The three categories of the new alien policy – guest worker, refugee, and illegal alien – were complex and ambiguous categories. While citizenship is a neat category, simple and straightforward, defining persons as refugees or guest workers was done following imprecise criteria. The sociological reality of a person's situation was but one element, economic and political considerations decided to a large extent which classification a person would fall into. This lack of explicit and unambiguous criteria in radical alien policy was instrumental to the national interests as defined by the state. Alien policy was not a rigidly functioning system, it was extremely flexible, to the advantage of national interests.

Crucial for the understanding of the dynamic in alien policy is the degree to which alien policy went beyond mere rhetoric, i.e., to what extent the state mobilized resources to master immigration. Even in those cases where the state invested heavily to control migration, the authorities could not realize their ambitions to their full extent. Politics seem unable to totally control such a complex social process as migration. Certainly as long as the economic attraction of (illegal) immigration was left untouched, it was a losing battle. Since the social foundations of immigration, i.e., employer-based migration networks, and the motivation for migration (refugee movements in particular were difficult to master) were hardly taken into account in the setting of policy goals their failure is no surprise. Failure is, however, relative. Effectiveness should not be measured against some unrealistic ideal of total control, but rather against the potential pressure at the border.

That this radicalization of alien policy occurred in a democratic era when the working classes gained citizenship and attendant social rights was, on the one hand, logical, but, on the other hand it undermined democratization. It was logical because denying rights to non-citizens meant substantial advantages in terms of savings and economic flexibility. On the other hand, it not only compromised humanitarian and liberal values, but also had an inhibiting influence on further democratization of society. The unions were especially quick to come to this realization, since the radical alien policy undermined their strength. The inferior status forced upon foreign labor also implied that the state had undermined its ability to make loyal citizens out of newcomers. To what extent the radical alien policy influenced international migration to Western Europe – the stated intent – is still unclear, but for the democratic standard of Western European society this alien policy certainly mattered.

Beyond the scope of this research is the slow demise of the radical alien policy during the second half of the twentieth century. The radical alien policy quickly lost some of its flexibility. Increasing international interdependence and the influence of supra-national regimes (most spectacularly for refugees), the upsurge of humanitarian and/or liberal values, resistance by the aliens' themselves, are, among other factors, most likely the main factors explaining the departure from the radical alien policy in the decades which followed. This process of inclusion of resident aliens whereby rights became based on residence, rather than on nationality, while at the same time all undocumented aliens became targeted for an ever more repressive policy, is a topic for another book.

Notes

1. During the whole period covered, immigrants, independent of their residency status, could be expelled for vagrancy or applying for welfare. Apparently this state power had not been made use of since the end of the nineteenth century. The regulation of welfare was liberalized in 1891 which necessitated only a short stay in one municipality to acquire a *domicile de secours*. A cumbersome procedure for expelling aliens on welfare made the use

of this power even less likely. The accessibility to local organized welfare for aliens implied that destitute immigrants settled in Belgium were less prone to vagrancy. It is surprising that the provision which enabled the state to expel aliens who were dependent on municipal welfare was never recalled in the 1930s.

2. The procedure for balancing interests and resolving conflicts over alien policy was fundamentally transformed only after the Second World War. In 1946, not withstanding the opposition of FEDECHAR – an indication of the shifting balance of power within the Belgian polity-a truly corporate agency was established to regulate migration in which labor had a say. Only then was organized labor integrated into alien policy through a bargaining system supervised by the state (Martens 1975; FEDECHAR).
3. The Law of September 28, 1939, which did away with the status of resident (or privileged) alien, was only valid during war-time.
4. It is remarkable that the provisions for claiming nationality were not touched upon after 1922. That this corresponded to a need for integration of Belgian-born aliens was, however, never articulated and the nationality law of 1932 did not provide, in contrast to nineteenth century changes in nationality law, an amnesty for those Belgian-born aliens who had neglected to claim Belgian nationality by a declaration of indigenousness at the age of majority.

Appendices

Appendix 1: Migration, Expulsion, Judicial and Nationality Statistics

Graphs 24-27 register statistics of legal migration to Belgium. It is generally argued that the receiving countries migration statistics are to be preferred to those of the sending country. The Belgian figures refer to all those persons who declared their arrival to the municipal authorities and were recorded in the population register (from 1933 onwards those registered in the foreigners' register were not included in the foreigners' register). The figures were published first in *the Exposé de la situation du Royaume* and later in the *Annuaires statistiques*. For the first decade (1841-1850), only the average number was published; later, yearly figures were at our disposal. The Belgian statistics are conceptually aligned with the notion of immigration in that they count the number of people actually entering the country. Until 1932 the basic criteria of the Belgian immigration statistics was not nationality, but the country where the immigrant had his last place of residence. From 1884 onwards a distinction is made between those immigrants born in Belgium and those born abroad. The percentage of immigrants born in Belgium within the total number of immigrants oscillated around 25 percent in the thirty years before the First World War. All those born abroad, Belgians and aliens alike, immigrating to Belgium were counted together. Until 1932 these statistics were still very much relics of the nineteenth century. From 1884 onwards, we only took the data on the immigrants born abroad, so as to exclude "returning" Belgians born in Belgium. In this way we also exclude the aliens born in Belgium who "returned" to Belgium. The figures of immigrants born abroad include also those born abroad, who on the basis of *jus sanguinis* were Belgians. An important disadvantage of the Belgium immigration statistics is that, until 1927, the number of specific countries mentioned was extremely limited, which meant that the greatest number of immigrants in the 1920s was to be found among the category "other countries in Europe". Poland and Yugoslavia were only included as separate categories in 1927 and in 1933 Czechoslovakia was added.

Data from the sending country are considered less reliable than those of the immigration country as they are based on the movement, or more often the anticipated movement, of people leaving their native country. Indeed the figures on emigration to Belgium are based on the passports issued to citizens of the emigration countries. We had at our disposal data from Poland, Czechoslovakia, Yugoslavia, and Italy (*Statystyka Pracy*, 1925–1938; *Un secolo di emigrazione italiana* 1978:371 and 351; *Zpravy Statniho Uradu Statistického Republiky Ceskoslovenské*, 1929-1940; *Annuaire Statistique Royaume de Yougoslavie*). These figures only deal with temporary labor migration or definitive emigrants; those leaving for tourism, business trips, or study are not included. There may be a discrepancy between the true number of emigrants and those actually recorded in the statistics of the sending country. Issuing a passport does not imply an effective emigration, it only indicates an intention to leave. Effective emigration data, at least those registered at border control point is to be found in the Czechoslovakian statistics from 1926 onwards. In general, Belgian data show slightly higher numbers than those of the emigration countries. This difference can be due to non-citizens who left emigration countries for Belgium and who were incorporated in the Belgian statistics and not in those from Italy, Yugoslavia, Poland, and Czechoslovakia. Probably more important is illegal emigration, that is emigrants leaving their country without notifying their authorities, but who, upon arrival, registered in Belgium. The emigrants who only immigrated to Belgium after residing in another immigration country are not listed in either of these statistics. A large number of Polish, Italian, Czechoslovakian, and Yugoslavian immigrants resided first in Germany or France before coming to Belgium. They were registered in the Belgian statistics as coming from France and Germany. We did not use these figures as they provide little information about labor migration. Here we are dealing much more with general population exchanges. The data on emigration from Belgium are not used as they were deemed unreliable by Belgian statistical authorities. Also the data on professional qualifications of emigrants are of little use, since the majority of the emigrants were cataloged under non-defined professions and as because it is unclear if these data refer to the profession of these emigrants in the country of emigration or to the profession they exercised in their country of origin.

A second source of data on immigration to Belgium is the number of files opened by the central aliens registration office of the Sûreté. The local authorities had to notify the central authorities in Brussels, i.e. the Sûreté, of every alien arriving in Belgium and a file was opened on him/her by this office. How the numbering of files at the central registration office progressed was based on a sample of foreigners arriving in Belgium between 1840 and 1940. The amount of files opened on new arrivals give us an indication of immigration, although they are also a function of administrative centralization. As time progressed the central authorities seem to be better informed about the number of aliens in the country as is indicated by the decreasing time lag between the date of registration with the municipal authorities and the date of opening a file at the central aliens registration office. In contrast to the first set of immigration figures, aliens who had never registered with the municipal authorities but were reported directly to the central authorities, for example foreign vagrants caught by the police, were also included in these figures. An increase in the number of vagrants as well as an increase in action against vagrancy can result in higher figures by the alien police. Thus the figures of the Sûreté are a function of immigration as well as immigration policy. On the other hand, the figures of the alien police underestimate immigration because firstly, in contrast to the immigration statistics which count individuals declaring their arrival to the municipal authorities, these figures refer to cases, either individuals or families who came to the attention of the central authorities. Secondly, an alien who resided in Belgium and then left for a considerable period of time will be counted as an immigrant for the immigration statistics, at the moment he returns, but he will not be counted in the figures of the alien police because a file had already been opened on him/her. From 1899 onwards the alien police published data on the number of new entrants yearly, distinguishing between nationalities and, until 1930, also between vagrants and resident aliens (*Statistique Judiciaire de la Belgique*, 1892-1940). The figures on new entrants as published by the alien police are always lower than the number of new files opened at the Sûreté. This is surprising as a possible explanation points to the contrary. Newly arriving aliens could be given an old number which was no longer in use, as for example, when a returnee at first did not declare that he had been registered in the country before or when the documents of a spouse, for whom a file was opened, were transferred to the file of the head of household. This seems, however, to be much more the practice in the nineteenth century, and after 1930 done away with. The two sets of figures – the number of files opened and the published data on the number of new entrants – differed only slightly in the period 1899-1913, except for 1909 to 1911 which showed 15, 36, and 30 percent differences. This striking discrepancy can be due to the "discovery" of aliens who had been residing for a long time in Belgium who then claimed Belgian nationality. Although a foreigner's file was opened on each of them it is possible that they were not calculated as new immigrants. The differences between the two sets of data increased considerably after the First World War for unclarified reasons. In any case putting together the different data collated by the Sûreté on the immigration of aliens with those on aliens registered by the municipal authorities, as in Graph 21, illustrates a trend in the dynamic of migration into Belgium.

A third set of figures, graphs 19 and 20, are those on naturalization and claims of Belgian nationality, the latter only available from 1871 onwards *(Exposé administrative de la situation du Royaume; Annuaire Statistique de la Belgique)*. Those who claimed Belgian nationality after age 22 on the basis of the diverse amnesties declared at the end of the nineteenth and the beginning of the twentieth century are not counted in these figures. Those older than 22 who claimed Belgian nationality between 1919 and 1923 and between 1926 and 1929 are included in these figures as the statistics did not account for them separately. We have no separate figures on those who claimed Belgian nationality at age 18 after 1912. In the period 1910 to 1912, most Belgian-born aliens who claimed Belgian nationality did that at age 18.

Another set of figures are those on the aliens interned in the vagrant colonies (ARMJ 650 and 651; RABW, Merksplas, jaarverslagen 1919-1934; AAD 75C20 and 10C; *Statistique Judiciaire* 1899-1930).This data, which records the number of internees at the end of each year (Graph 23), also includes would-be aliens, i.e., Belgians who pretended to be of foreign nationality in order not to be imprisoned or to be set free earlier. A fifth set of figures are those concerning expulsions (*Statistique Judiciaire* 1892-1940, PHK 1868: 206/10f. and *Exposé de la situation du Royaume 1861-1900*, more detailed in AAD 10C). For aliens expelled by royal decree (the dangerous aliens) graph 16 gives a detailed account of those expelled for political reasons and of the category created in 1883, i.e. expelled for disturbing the public order without being condemned and without political reason (recidivist vagrants, pimps, gamblers, prostitutes). The residual category is those expelled because of a previous conviction in Belgium or abroad. The figures on the expulsions of non-resident aliens in the country (*renvoyer*) and on migrants refused entry (*refouler*) refer to the number of expulsions, not to the number of aliens. The expulsion of non-resident aliens is detailed in Graph 15 for those brought to the border because of destitution or after a conviction for vagrancy or begging (and thus previously, but not necessarily, interned). For the long nineteenth century, the residual category contains the very few who were expelled for political reasons and for destitution but who received an order to leave the country instead of being brought to the border. More important within this residual category of the nineteenth century are those aliens disturbing public order in a non-political sense (mainly pimps, prostitutes, gamblers) and in particular those convicted for crimes and misdemeanors other than vagrancy. In the 1930s the proportion of aliens disturbing public order in a non-political sense within the residual category rises (mainly due to the insertion of undocumented aliens in this category), as well as those expelled for political reasons. A last set of figures are those on *rupture de ban* (Graph 17) which refer to the annual number of convictions, except for the years 1885 to 1896 when the figures refer to the five-year average (*Administration de la Justice Criminelle et Civile* and *Statistique Judiciaire*).

APPENDIX 2: GRAPHS

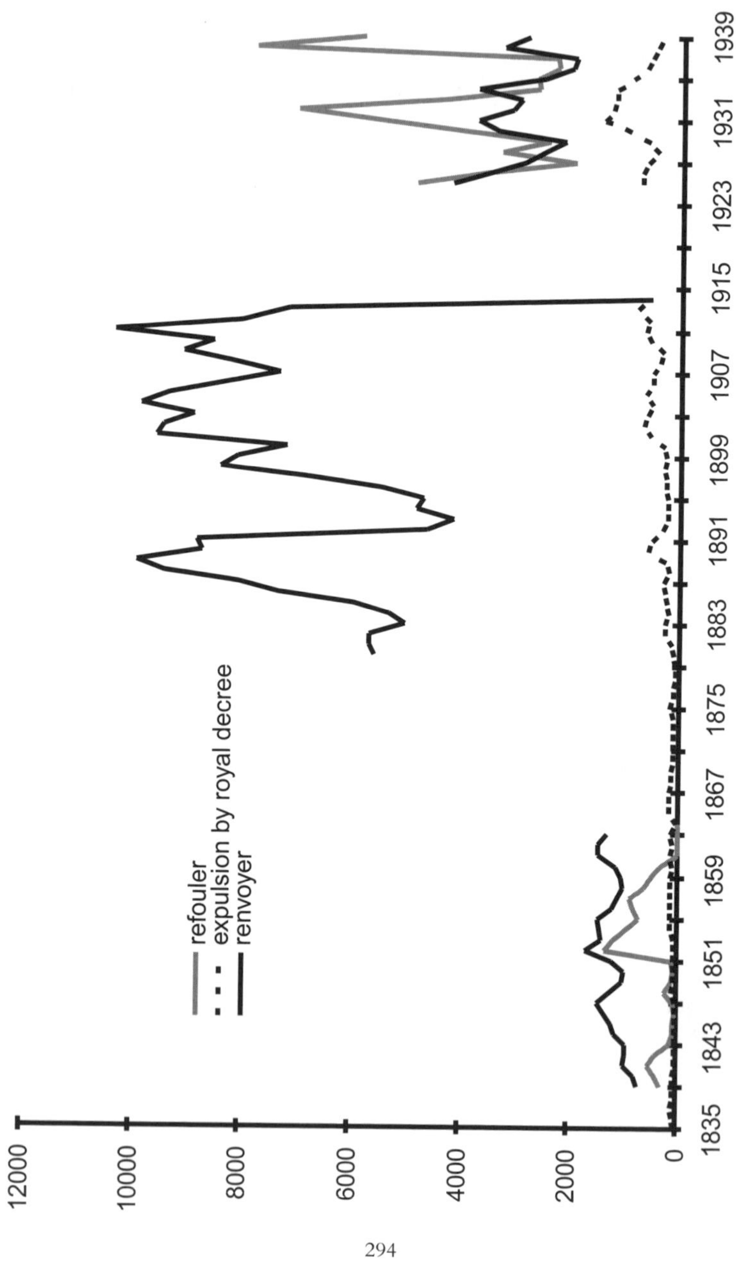

Graph 14 *Aliens Not Allowed to Enter or Removed from Belgium, 1839–1939*

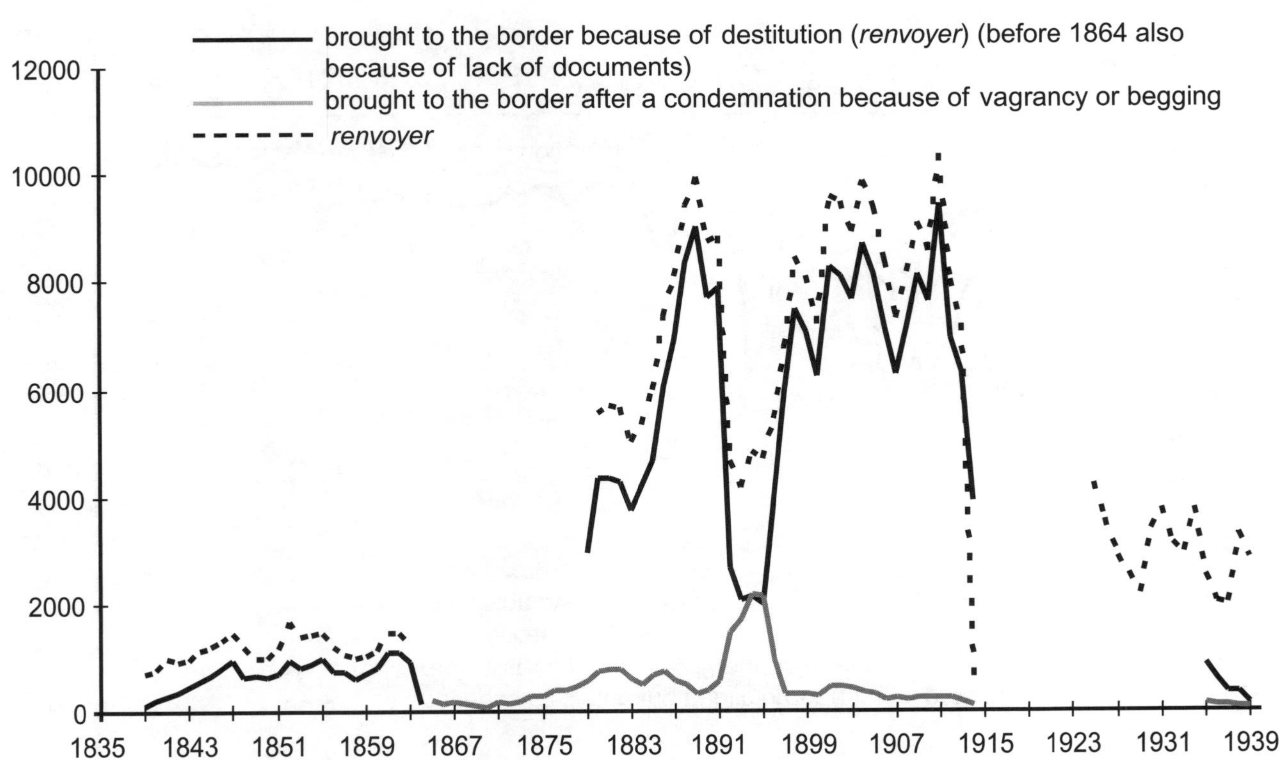

Graph 15 *Non-resident Aliens Expelled* (renvoyer), *1837–1939*

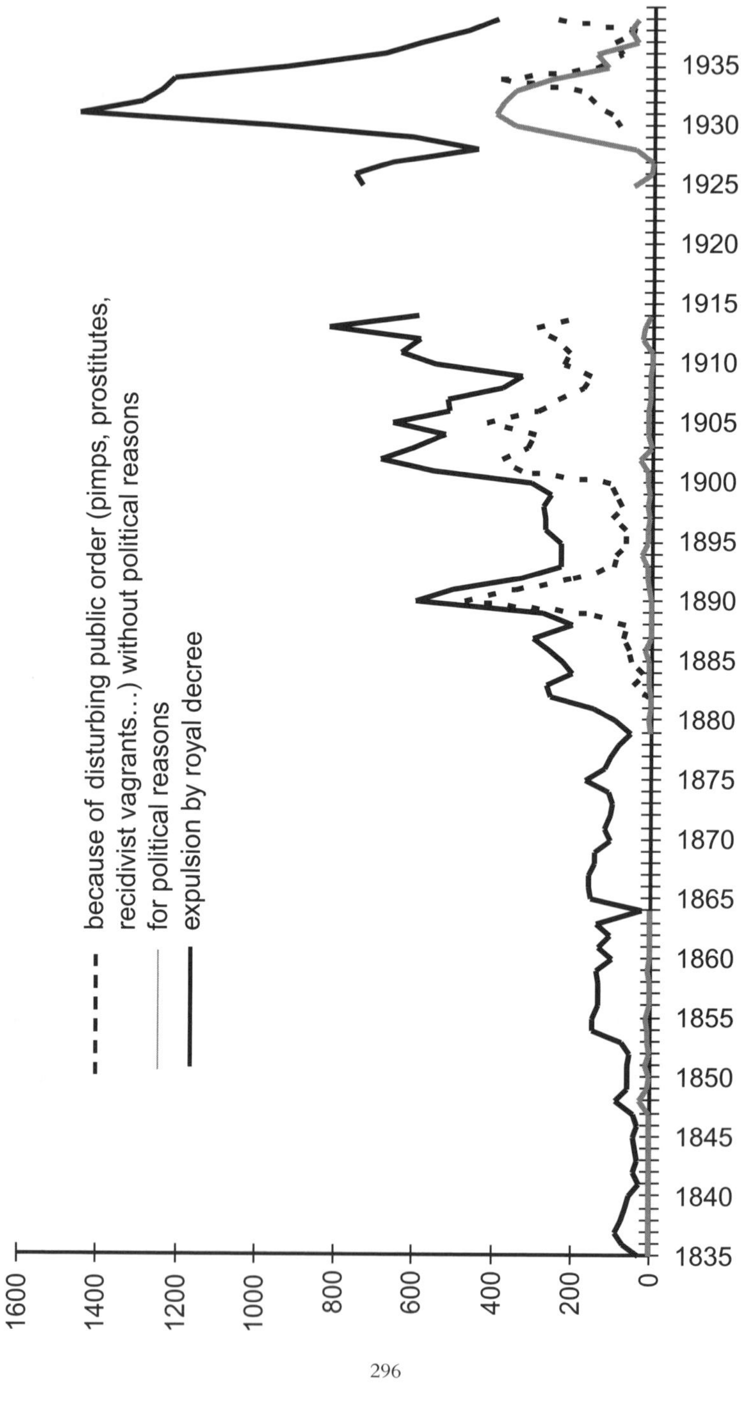

Graph 16 *Aliens Expelled by Royal Decree, 1835–1939*

Graph 17 *Aliens Condemned in Belgium for* Rupture de Ban, *1868–1940*

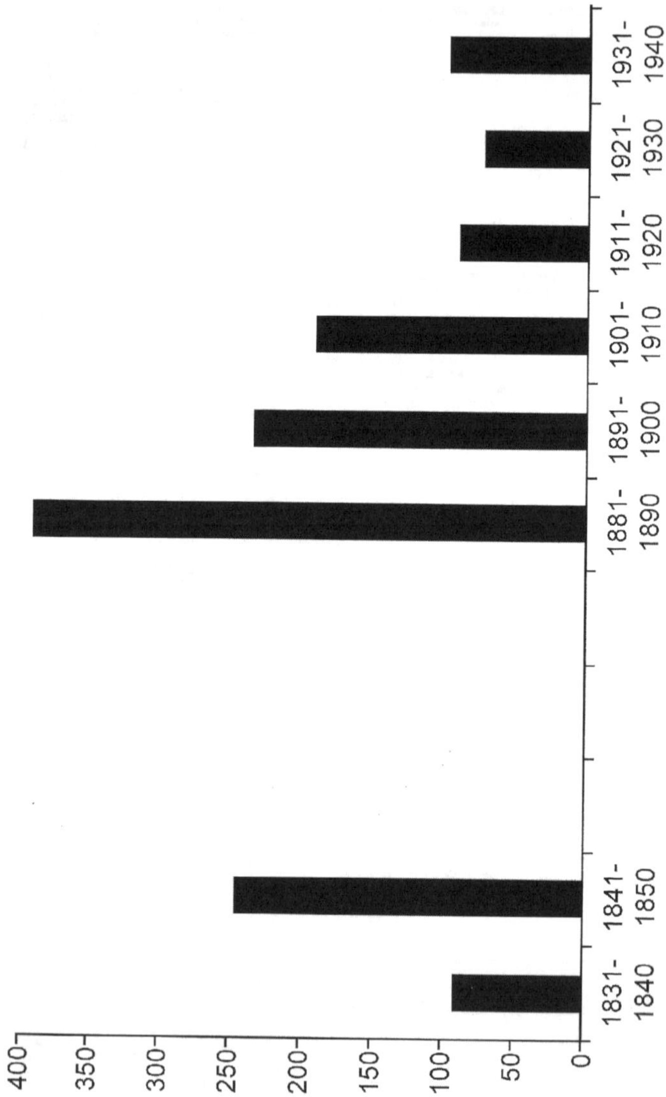

Graph 18 *Status of Domiciliés, 1831–1940*

Graph 19 *Naturalization in Belgium, 1831–1940*

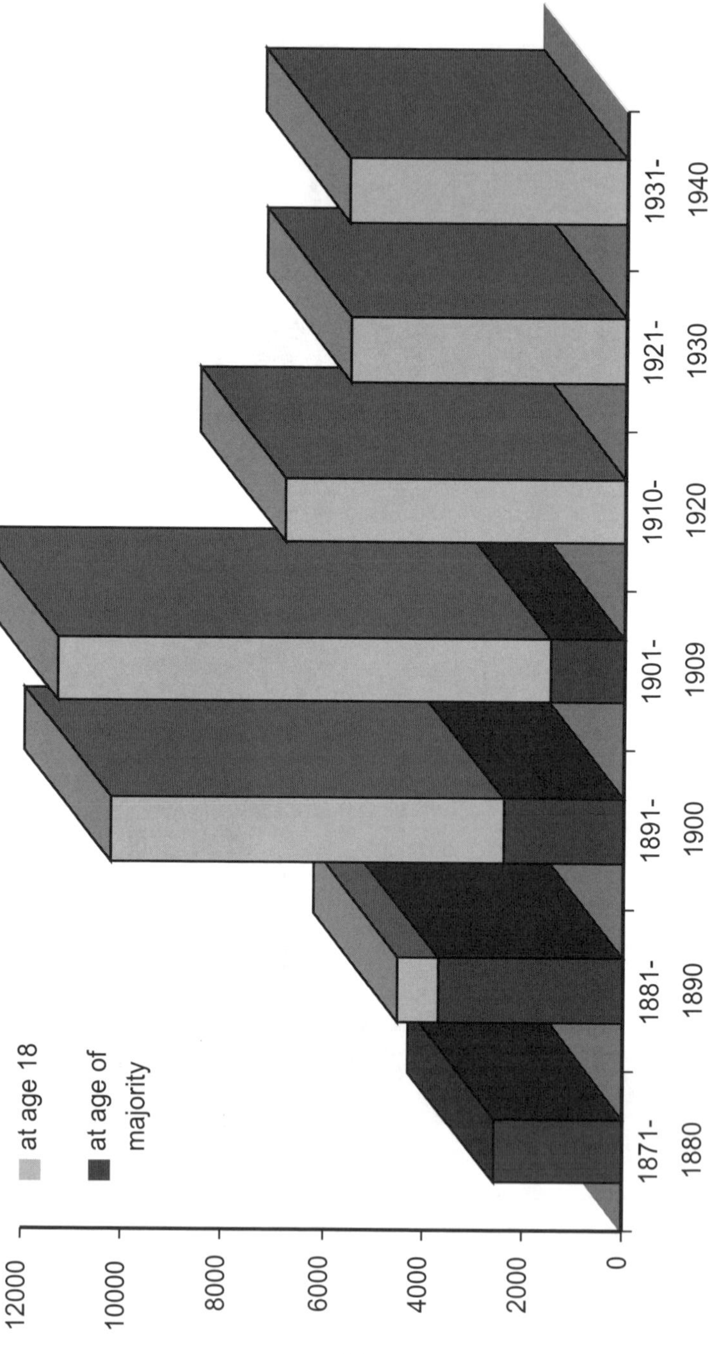

Graph 20 *Claiming Belgian Nationality by Aliens Declaring Birth in Belgium, 1871–1940*

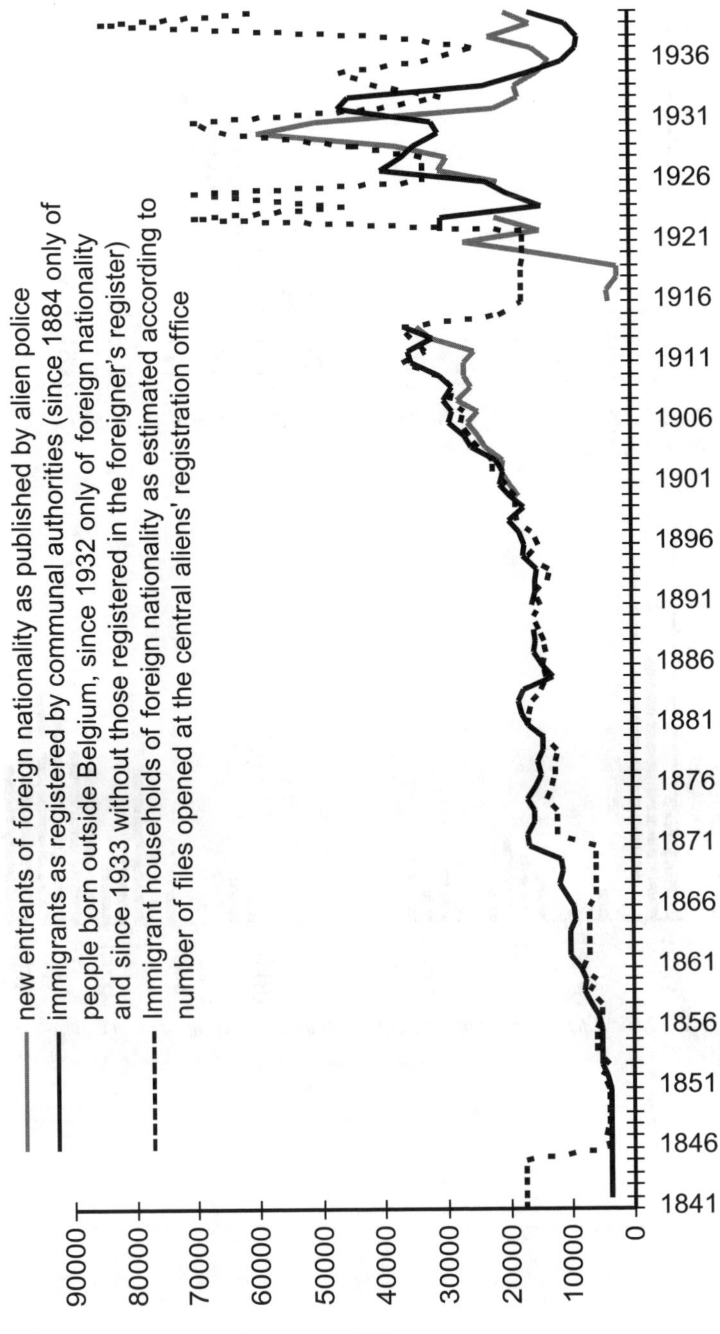

Graph 21 *Immigration into Belgium, 1840–1939*

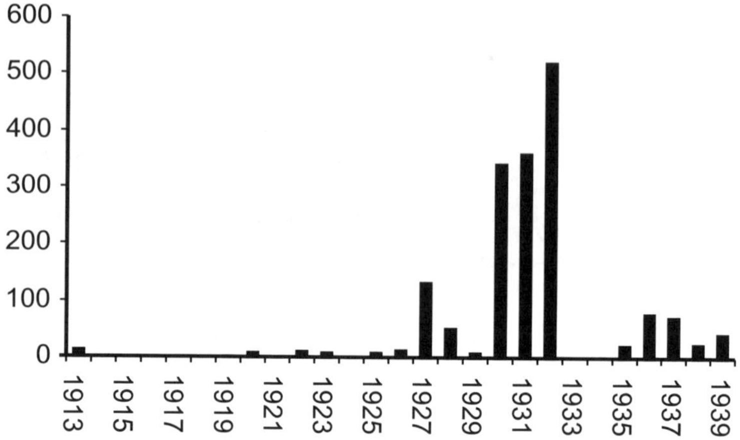

Graph 22 *Male Aliens Brought to the Border from the Belgian Vagrants' Colony at Merksplas, 1913–1939*

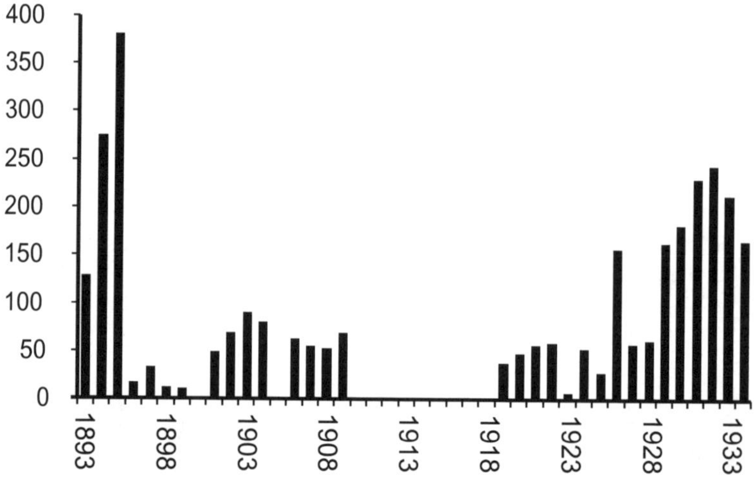

Graph 23 *Male Aliens Interned in the Belgian Vagrants' Colony at Merksplas at year end, 1893–1934*

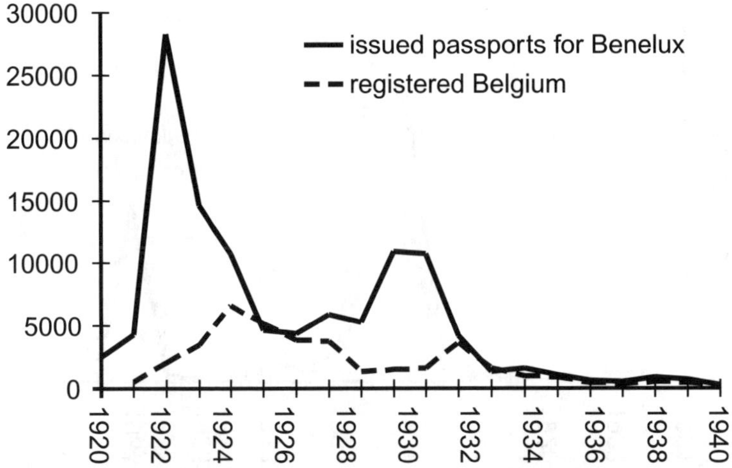

Graph 24 *Legal Migration of Italian Citizens to Belgium, 1920–1939*

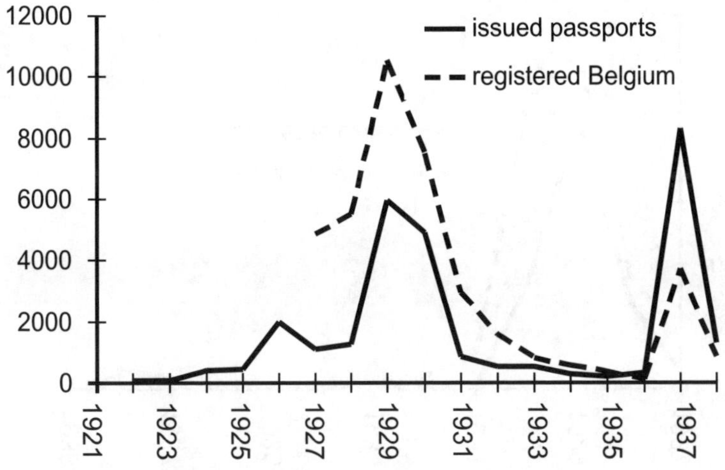

Graph 25 *Legal Migration of Polish Citizens to Belgium, 1922–1939*

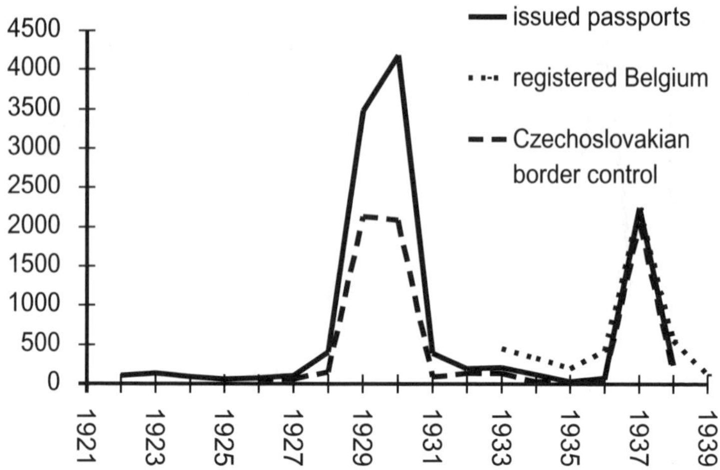

Graph 26 *Legal Migration of Czechoslovakian Citizens to Belgium, 1922–1939*

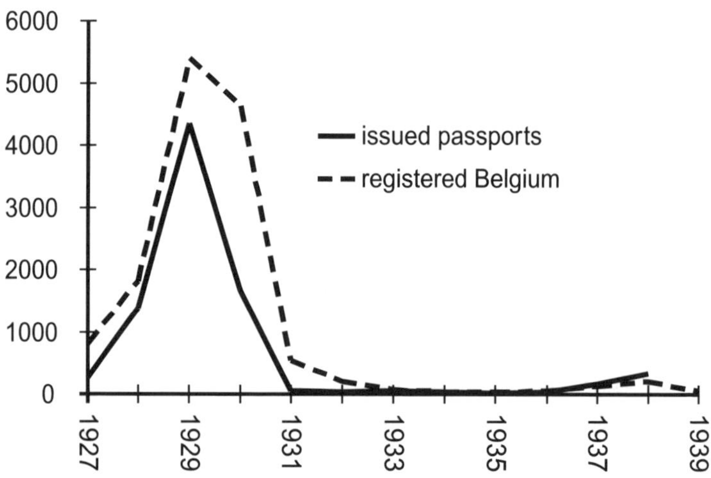

Graph 27 *Legal Migration of Yugoslavian Citizens to Belgium, 1927–1939*

Appendix 3: List of Main Archival Sources

1. Belgium

Archive Archbishopric, Mechelen
Papers Mercier, Dessain and Van Roey

Archive Aliens' Department at the Ministry of interiors, Aliens Department Brussels
General files

Archive Bishopric Liège
Papers Rutten and Kerkhofs

Private Papers Zdrodzyniak, Genk
Archive Polish Union

Archives de l'Etat, Liège
Mine Administration
Archives of Industrial Firms

Archives de l'Etat, Saint Hubert
Mine Administration
Judiciary Archives
Archives of Industrial Firms

Archive Foreign Affairs Belgium, Brussels
Political Correspondance during interwar period: Poland, Czechoslovakia, France, Italy, Yougoslavia
Labor, Refugee and Emigrant Affairs

Archive of the Mining Industry of the Borinage, Mons
Association Houillière du Couchant de Mons
Charbonnage d'Hensies-Pommeroeul

Archive Liberaal Vakverbond België, Ghent
Archive on Unemployment Insurance in the 1930s

Archive Ministry of Labor, Brussels
Non classified Archive on Foreign Labor

Archive and Museum of the Socialist Labor Movement, Ghent
Papers Anseele, Bondas, Nauwelaerts, Massin
Metallurgic workers' and Garment workers' Union
Executive Committee and National Council POB

Archive National Miners'Union, Brussels
Reunions of the Socialist Miners'Trade Union of the Borinage
Reunions of the Socialist Miners'Trade Union of Belgium

Archive Red Cross, Brussels
Aid to Indigent Foreigners (cassier 33, colis sec.8)

Archive Belgian Communist Party, Brussels
Microfilms Institute Marxism-Leninism Moscow

Algemeen Rijksarchief, Brussels
Administration of the Mining Industry
Ministry of Justice, Aliens' Department, General Files
Papers de Broqueville, Frère Orban, Coppée, P. Huysmans, M.H.Jaspar, H.Jaspar, Poullet, Theunis, H.Velghe

Archive Bois du Luc, Bois du Luc
335: Reunions of ACCBS
181 and 306: Reunions Fédération des Charbonnages Belges

Archive FEDECHAR, Brussels
Main-d'Oeuvre Etrangère
Statistics
Reunions Fédération des Charbonnages Belges

Institute Emile Vandervelde, Brussels
Papers Emile and Jeanne-Emile Vandervelde

Institute for the Study of Belgian Jewry, Brussels
Non classified archive on pre-war Belgian Jewry
Transcripts of Interviews

Katholiek Archief en Documentatiecentrum, Louvain
Papers Broekx, G.Crean, Van Buggenhout
National Council ACV

Municipal Archives Genk, Charleroi, Chapelle-lez-Herlaimont, Antwerp, Brussels, Quaregnon

Rijksarchief Beveren Waas, Beveren Waas
Archive of ACCA
Archives of Mining Firms
Archive Rijksweldadigheidskolonie Merksplas

2. Other Countries in Western Europe

Algemeen Rijksarchief, The Hague
Ministerie van Sociale Zaken, onderafdeling Arbeidsbemiddeling van de Rijksdienst der Werkloosheidsverzekering en Arbeidsbemiddeling 1916-1940: 180-187

Archive Foreign Affairs France, Paris
Europe 1930-1940 Belgique

Archives Nationales, Paris
Ministère de l'Intérieur (F7).

Archive International Labor Organization, Geneva
A48-52, A80, A120 A520, A1374, A2207, A2211-2214

Archive of the United Nations Organization, Geneva
Minutes of the International and Inter-governmental Conference for the Adoptation of a Convention/Statute for Refugees Coming from Germany (1936-1938)
Files related to refugees in Belgium

Archive Foreign Affairs Germany, Bonn
R1501, 8273, 70433

Hauptstaatsarchiv, Düsseldorf
Regierung Aachen 22891, 22938, 23084, 23104 23423
Regierung Düsseldorf 42783

Geheimes Staatsarchiv Preussischer Kulturbesitz, Berlin
Bestand I.HA Rep.77 Innenministerium

3. Eastern Europe

Archivum Archidiecezja Gnieznienska, Gniezno
Zespo Prymasa Polski, 111, Akte Protektora Wychodztwa Belgia Generalna

Archiwum Akt Nowych, Warsaw
Archive Foreign Affairs Poland

Archiwum Panstwowe Kielce, Poznan and Krakow
Archives of the districts

Hungarian National Archives, Budapest
K85, Brüsszeli Követseg, 12t

Statni ustredni archiv, Prague
Archive Ministry of Social Affairs (MSP)

4.United States

YIVO, New York
Papers David Trocki

American Jewish Joint Distribution Committee, New York
Archives 1933-1940

Bibiliography

Ageron Charles-Robert. (1981). Emigration et politique: L'étoile Nord-Africaine et le Parti du Peuple Algérien. *Cahiers de la Méditerranée*, 273–297.

Arendt E.P. (1931). *De syndicale aktie*. Brussels: ACV.

Bade K.J. (1980). Massenwanderung und Arbeitsmarkt im deutschen Nordosten von 1880 bis zum Ersten Weltkrieg. *Archiv für Sozialgeschichte*, 20, 265–323.

Bade Klaus J. (1984). *Auswanderer-Wanderarbeiter-Gastarbeiter: Bevölkerung, Arbeitsmarkt und Wanderung in Deutschland seit der Mitte des 19.Jahrhunderts: Referate und Diskussionsbeiträge des internationalen Wissenschaftlichten Symposiums*. Ostfildern: Scripta Mercaturae.

Bade Klaus J. (1987). Labour, Migration and the State: Germany form the Late 19th Century to the Onset of the Great Depression. In Bade Klaus J. (Ed.), *Population. Labour and Migration in 19th- and 20th-Century Germany* (pp. 59–86). Leamington Spa: Berg.

Bade Klaus J. (1992). *Deutsche in Ausland-Fremde in Deutschland: Migration in Geschichte und Gegenwart*.Munich: Beck.

Bade Klaus J. (1994). *Ausländer-Aussiedler-Asyl: Eine Bestandsaufnahme*. Munich: Beck.

Balace F. (1987). La droite belge et l'aide à Franco. *BTNG*, XVIII, 3–4, 505–690.

Bartier John. (1981). La police politique de Napoléon III et la Belgique. *Libéralisme et socialisme au XIXe siècle*. Brussels: éditions de l'ULB, 413–429.

Baudhuin F. (1946). *Histoire économique de la Belgique (1914–1939)*. Brussels: Bruylant.

Bekaert H. (1934). L'expulsion des étrangers et le délit de rupture de ban. *Revue du Droit Pénal et de Criminologie et Archives Internationales de Médecine légale*. Leuven: *XIV, 1–3*, 1– 26, 103–136, 225–249.

Bekaert H. (1934b). Uitzetting van vreemdelingen. *Rechtskundig Weekblad, III, 17*, 1–2.

Bekaert H. (1940). *Le statut des étrangers en Belgique*. Brussels:Larcier.

Benamrane Djilali (1983). *L'émigration algérienne en France: passé, présent et devenir*. Alger: Société Nationale d'édition et de diffusion.

Biddaer P. (1898). *Formulaire des actes des administrations communales et des établissements publics subordonnés à la commune* (Vol. II, pp. 567–569). Brussels: Bruylant.

Billiet Germain (1987). Over de exploitatie van het Splendid Hotel (1908–1914). *De Plate, XVI, 5–8,* 136–147.

Bovenkerk Frank and Ruland Loes (1991). Artisan Entrepreneurs: Two Centuries of Italian Immigration to the Netherlands. *International Migration Review, XXVI, 3,* 927–939.

Bovenkerke F. (1983). *Italiaans ijs, de wonderbaarlijke historie van de Italiaanse ijsbereiders in Nederland.* Boom: Meppel.

Brubaker Rogers (1992). *Citizenship and nationhood in France and Germany.* Cambridge (US): Harvard University Press.

Bruwier Marinette (1981). L'industrie avant la révolution industrielle: une protoindustrialisation. *L'industrie en Belgique. Deux siècles d'évolution 1780–1980.* Brussels: Snoeck-Ducaju , 13–24.

Caestecker Frank (1991). Le Multiculturalisme de la Belgique. Une analyse de la politique de scolarisation des enfants polonais en Belgique, 1923–1940. *BTNG,* XXI, 3–4, 535–573.

Caestecker Frank (1992). *Vluchtelingenbeleid in de naoorlogse periode.* Brussels: VUB Press.

Caestecker Frank (1993). Europese historici ontdekken migranten. Europese en Amerikaanse migrantenonderzoek: sociale geschiedenis met twee snelheden? In Delsé E., Witte E. en R.Lestdaghe (Ed.), *Denken over migranten* (pp. 53–73.). Brussels: VUB Press.

Caestecker Frank (1993b). Poolse migranten uit België in het Poolse leger in ballingschap, 10.1939–5.1940. *Bijdragen en Mededelingen betreffende de Geschiedenis van de Tweede Wereldoorlog,* 233–255.

Caestecker Frank (1993c). *Ongewenste gasten, joodse vluchtelingen en migranten in de dertiger jaren.* Brussels: VUB Press.

Caestecker Frank (1993d). L'Italie à l'avant-garde de la politisation du phénomème migratoire: les recrutements de main d'oeuvre italienne pour les mines belges, 1922–1924. In Dumoulin M. et H. Van Der Wee (Ed.), *Hommes, cultures et capitaux dans les relations italo-belges aux XIXe et XX siècles.* (pp. 43–52). Brussels-Rome: Institut Historique Belge de Rome.

Caestecker Frank (1994). Alien Policy in Belgium, 1830–1940. The Creation of Guest Workers, Refugees and Illegal Immigrants. *Unpublished dissertation,* European University Institute.

Caestecker Frank (1997). Vakbonden en etnische minderheden, een ambigue verhouding. Immigratie in de Belgische mijnbekkens, 1900–1940. *Brood en Rozen,* II,1, 51–63.

Caestecker Frank (1997b). In het kielzog van de Natiestaat. De Politiek van Nationaliteitsverwerving, -verlies en -toekenning in België, 1830–1909. *BTNG,* XXVII, 1997, 3–4, 323–349.

Caestecker Frank (1998a). The Changing Modalities of Regulation in International Migration within Continental Europe, 1870–1940. In Böcker Anita, Kees Groenendijk, Tetty Havinga and Paul Minderhoud (Ed.), *Regulation of Migration: International experiences.* (pp.73–98). Amsterdam: Spinhuis.

Caestecker Frank (1998b). Vervanging of verdringing van de buitenlandse mijnwerkers in Limburg. De emancipatie van de Limburgse mijnwerkers (1920–1940). *Limburg-Het Oude Land van Loon*,77, 309–326.

Caestecker Frank (1999). Migratiecontrole in Europa gedurende de 19de eeuw, een schets. In Art J. en François L. (Ed.) *Docendo Discimus. Liber amicorum Romain Van Eenoo* (pp.241–255). Ghent: Academia Press.

Caestecker Frank (2000). De geschiedenis van grensoverschrijdende migraties uit en in Vlaanderen, weinig grensverleggend onderzoek. In Vranken J., C. Timmerman en K. Van der Heyden (Ed.) *Komende generaties. Wat weten we (niet) over allochtonen in Vlaanderen?* Louvain: Acco.

Caestecker Frank and Van Doorslaer Rudy. (1988). Poolse vrijwilligers uit België in de internationale brigaden. *BTNG*, XVII, 215–241.

Cannistraro Philip and Rosoli Gianfausto. (1979). Fascist Emigration Policy in the 1920s: an Interpretive Framework. *International Migration Review*, XIII, 4.

Caron Vicki (1999). *Uneasy Asylum: France and the Jewish Refugee Crisis, 1933–1942*. Stanford: Cambridge University Press.

Castiau Claude (1973). *Pastorale et intégration, Eléments pour une histoire religieuse de l'immigration italienne en Belgique*. Roma: l'Université pontificiale gregorienne, faculté d'histoire ecclésiatique (unpublished).

Chatelain Abel (1977). *Les Migrants Temporaires en France de 1800 à 1914*. Villeneuve-d'Ascq: Publications de l'Université de Lille III.

Chlepner B.S. (1972). *Cent ans d'histoire sociale en Belgique*. Brussels: Editions de l'ULB.

Craeybeckx J. (1973–1974). De agrarische depressie van het einde der 19de eeuw en de politieke strijd van de boeren. *BTNG, 1–2 and 1–2*, 190–230 and 181–226.

Cross Gary (1983). *Immigrant Workers in Industrial France: The making of a new laboring class*. Philadelphia: Temple University Press.

Cuvelier F. (1939). *Technique de l'arbitraire ou le statut des étrangers en Belgique*. Brussels: Larcier.

Dabrowski S. (1927). *Spoldzielcza Belgia (wrazenia z wycieczka)*. Warsaw.

De Belder J. (1981). Stad en platteland: inleiding tot de problematiek. *Taal en sociale integratie*. Brussels: 169–182.

De Boeck Ch. (1927). L'expulsion et les difficultés internationales qu'en soulève la pratique. *Recueil des cours de l'Académie de droit internatonial*, III, 447–647.

De Brabander G. (1983). *Regionale structuur en werkgelegenheid: een economische en geografische studie over de Belgische lange termijn ontwikkeling*. Brussels.

Delbeke Ann (1981). *De "Auslands-organisation der NSDAP" in België (1932–1944)* Louvain: KUL (unpublished).

Delrée Henri. (1981). Main d'oeuvre étrangère en 1876. Extrait du rapport sur la situation de l'industrie minérals et métallurgique dans la Province de Liège pendant l'année 1876 par M.Jules Van scherpenzeelthim. *Bulletin de la Société Le Vieux – Liège , 213*, 57-58.

Deneckere Gita. (1997). *Sire, het volk mort: sociaal protest in België, 1831–1918*. Antwerp: Hadewych.

De Schaepdrijver Sophie. (1990). *Elites for the capital. Foreign Migration to mid-ninteenth-century Brussels*. Amsterdam: Thesis Publishers.

Destatte Philippe. (1991). L'émigration russe antitsariste en Belgique. *Socialisme*, 226, 273–278.

Devreese Daisy E. (1990). Belgium. In Vanderlinden Marcel/ Jürgen Rojahn (Ed.), *The Formation of Labour Movements 1870–1914. An international perspective* (pp. 25–56). Leiden: E.J.Brill.

De Wever Bruno. (1995). *Greep naar de Macht. Het VNV, 1933–1945.* Tielt-Ghent: Lannoo- Perspectief.

Dodenhof Bettina. (1993). *"Laßt mich nach Rußland heim" Russische Emigranten in Deutschland von 1918 bis 1945.* Frankfurt: Peter Lang.

Dohse K. (1981). *Ausländische Arbeiter und bürgerlichen Staat. Genese und Funktion vom staatlicher Ausländerpolitik und Ausländerrecht: vom Kaiserreich bis zur Bundesrepublik Deutschland.* Köningstein: Hain.

Dupont-Bouchat M.S. (1986). Stratégies du maintien de l'ordre en Belgique et en France au XIXe siècle: la doctrine de la défense sociale. In Heyen E.V. (Ed.), *Historische Soziologie der Rechtswissenschaft* (pp. 79–105). Frankfurt/Main: Klostermann.

Edgar. (1899). *Recueil général des lois commentées, arrêtés, circulaires, instructions sur la police des étrangers et la répression du vagabondage et de la mendicité.* Tournais:Van Gheluwe.

Elsner Lothar and Lehmann Joachim. (1988). Ausländische Arbeiter unter dem deutschen Imperialismus, 1900 bis 1985. Berlin: Dietz Verlag.

Fahrmeier Andreas K. (1997). Nineteenth-Century German Citizenships: a Reconsideration. *The Historical Journal*, XL, 3, 721–752.

Feblowicz S. et Lamour P. (1937). *Le status juridique des étrangers en France. Traité pratique.* Paris: Librairie science et litterature.

Foutre G. (1985) Een onderzoek naar de werking van het Belgische politionele apparaat 1830–1848. Genth: University of Ghent, contemporary history (unpublished).

Garfinkels Betty. (1974). *Belgique, terre d'accueil. Problème du réfugié 1933/1940.* Brussels:Labor.

Garsou Jules. (1938). La Belgique, La Suisse et les réfugiés. *Archives diplomatiques et consulaires, 3/2*, 55–59.

Gerard Emmanuel. (1985). *De katholieke partij in crisis.* Louvain: Kritak.

Gerard E. (1991). Ontplooiing van de christelijke arbeidersbeweging (1904–1921). In Gerard Emmanuel (Ed.), *De christelijke arbeidersbeweging in België* (pp. 114–243). Louvain: Universitaire Pers.

Godding P. (1970). L'expulsion des étrangers en droit belge-Aperçu historique (1830–1952). *Annales de Droit de Louvain, XXX*, 301–329.

Gotovitch José (1996). La peur du rouge dans les dossiers de la justice belge. la signification du procès de 1923. In Gotovitch J. et P. Dewit (Ed.), *La Peur du Rouge* (pp. 87–116). Brussels: Editions de l'université.

Green Nancy (1986). Immigrant Labor in the Garment Industries in New York and Paris, variations on a structure. *Comparative Social Research.* Greenwich/London: JAI Press, *9*, 231–246.

Grippa Jacques (1988). *Chronique vecue d'une epoque 1930–1947.* Antwerpen: EPO.

Gubin Eliane et Lefèvre Patrick (1985). Obligation scolaire et société en Belgique au XIXe siècle. *BTFG, 63–64*, 324–376 and 731–782.

Guillaume L. (1935). Le vagabondage international. *Le Service Social, 7–8.*

Hallot A. (1900). *De la situation légale des étrangers en Belgique.* Brussels: Bruylant.

Hammar T. (1990). *Democracy and the Nation-State.* Aldershot: Avebury Press.

Heijs Eric (1995). *Van Vreemdeling tot Nederlander. De verlening van het Nederlandschap aan vreemdelingen 1813–1992.* Amsterdam: Het Spinhuis.

Herder (1913). Wanderarmenwesen an der deutsch-belgischen und an der deutsch-holländischen Landesgrenze. *Caritas,* XIX, 13–14, 13–17 and 79–83.

Heumos Peter. (1989). *Die Emigration aus der Tschechoslowakei nach Westeuropa und dem Nahen Oosten 1938–1945.* München: R.Oldenbourg.

Heyrman Peter. (s.d.). *Voor eigen winkel. Honderd jaar middenstand in middenstandsbeweging in Oost-Vlaanderen.* Ghent: Vanmelle.

Higginson John. (1989). *A Working Class in the Making. Belgian Colonial Labor Policy, Private Enterprise, and the African Mineworker, 1907–1951.* Madison: University of Wisconsin Press.

Hogg Robin L. (1986). *Structural rigidities and policy inertia in interwar-Belgium.* Brussels: Koninklijke Academie voor Wetenschappen, Letteren en Schone Kunsten van België.

Houzié de l'Aulnoit A. (1885). Les Ouvriers belges à Lille. Etude sur les conditions d'admissibilité des indigents étrangers aux secours public. Lille: Danel.

Jacquemyns G. (1928). *Histoire de la crise économique de Flandres (1845–1850).* Brussels:.

Janowska Halina. (1981). *Emigracja zarobkowa z Polski, 1918–1939.* Warsaw: Panstw. Wydawn. Nauk.

Jaumain S. et Gaiardo L. (1988). "Aide-toi et le gouvernement t'aidera" - les réponses de l'état à la crise de la petite bourgeoisie (1880–1914). *BTNG,* XIX, 3–4, 417–471.

Jaumain Serge (1985). Un métier oublié: le colporteur dans la Belgique du XIXe siècle. *BTNG,* XVI, 307–356.

Johnston Robert H. (1988). *New Mecca, New Babylon. Paris and the Russian Exiles, 1920–1945.* Kingston-Montreal: McGill-Queen's University Press.

Joris L. (1940). Wetgeving op de vreemdelingen. Grondwettelijke princiepen en rechtsevolutie. *Rechtskundig weekblad,* IX, 19, col.674–679.

Keunings L. (1980). Geheime politie en politieke politie in België van 1830 tot 1914. *Panopticon,* IX:2, 128–158.

Kleßmann Christoph (1978). *Polnische Bergarbeiter in Ruhrgebiet 1870–1945. Soziale Integration und nationale Subkultur einer Minderheit in der deutschen Industrieges ellschaft.* Göttingen: Vandenhoeck & Ruprecht.

Kleßmann Christoph (1986). Comparative immigrant history: Polish workers in the Ruhr area and the north of France. *Journal of Social History, 20,* 335–353.

Kulczycki John J. (1994). *The Foreign Worker and the German Labor Movement. Xenophobia and Solidarity in the Coal fields of the Ruhr, 1871–1914.* Berg: Oxford.

Kurgan G. and E.Spelkens. (1976). *Two Studies on Emigration Through Antwerp to the New World.* Brussels: Center for American Studies.

Kurgan-Van Hentenryk Ginette und Puissant Jean (1989). Die Industriellen Beziehungen im belgischen Kohlenbergbau seit dem Ende des 19. Jahrhunderts. In G.D.Feldman/ K.Tenfelde (Ed.), *Arbeiter, Unternehmer und*

Staat im Bergbau. Industrielle Beziehungen im internationalen Vergleich (pp. 220–255). Munich: C.H.Beck.

Leboutte René (1987). Au carrefour des transitions: fécondité, niveau de vie et culture populaire. *Annales de Démographie Historique*, 175–212.

Leboutte René (1988a). *Reconversions de la main-d'oeuvre et transition démographique. Les bassins industriels en aval de Liège XVIIe–XXe siècles.* Paris: les Belles Lettres.

Leboutte René (1988). *Le livret d'ouvrier dans la province de Liège.* Liège: Musée de la vie wallone.

Leën W. (1937). *Het verrichten van arbeid door vreemdelingen.* Antwerp: De Sikkel.

Leenders Marij (1993). *Ongenode gasten. Het vluchtelingenbeleid in Nederland, 1815–1938.* Hilversum:Verloren.

Lentacker Firmin (1974). *La frontière franco-belge: Etude geographique des effets d'une frontière.* Lille: Morel et Corduant.

Lescoeur. (1899). *La condition légale des étrangers et particulièrement des Allemands en France.* New York: Elwert.

Liberman Kopel. (1934). *La maroquinerie.* Brussels: Comité pour la défense des droits des juifs.

Liberman K. (1935). *L'industrie et le commerce diamantaires.* Antwerp: Duchatel.

Liberman Kopel. (1939). *La maroquinerie et les industries connexes.* Brussels: Conseil des Associations Juives.

Lis C. (1986). *Social change and the labouring poor. Antwerp, 1770–1860.* New Haven:Yale University Press.

Lucassen L. (1990). *En men noemde hen zigeuners. De Geschiedenis van Kaldarasch, Ursari, Lowara en Sinti in Nederland, 1750–1944.* Amsterdam: Stichting Historische Reeks.

Luyten D. (1995). *Sociaal-economisch overleg in België sedert 1918.* Brussels:VUB PRESS.

Maga T. (1985). *America, France and the European refugee problem (1933–1947).* New York: Gerland Publ.

Mahaim E. (1910). *Les abonnements d'ouvriers.* Brussels.

Mahaim E. (1911). Les ouvriers mineurs abonnés au chemin de fer en Belgique. *Annales des Mines de Belgique, 16,* 67–116.

Maier Charles S. (1975). *Recasting Bourgeois Europe. Stabilization in France, Germany and Italy in the Decade after World War I.* Princeton: Princeton University Press

Marrus Michael R. (1985). *The Unwanted: European Refugees in the Twentieth Century.* New York: Oxford University Press.

Marshall T.H. and Bottomore T. (1992). *Citizenship and Social Class.* London: Pluto Press.

Martens A. (1975). *Les immigrés, flux et reflux d'une main-d'oeuvre d'appoint.* Louvain:Vie Ouvrière.

Martini A. (1909). *L'expulsion des étrangers.* Paris: Sirey.

Meeuwissen E. (1981). Les dépôts de mendicité au tribunal de l'histoire. *Annales de la Société belge d'Histoire des Hôpitaux , 19,* 47–67.

Melnyk M. (1951). *Les ouvriers étrangers en Belgique.* Louvain: Université catholique de Louvain-école des sciences économiques.

Michielsen A. (1953). *De syndicale beweging in het diamantbedrijf.* Antwerp: Ontwikkeling.

Mokyr Joel. (1976). *Industrialization in the Low Countries, 1795–1850.* New Haven and London: Yale University Press.

Moore Bob et al. (1998). Refugees Policies in Western European States in the 1930s. A Comparative Analysis. *IMIS Beiträge*, 7, 55–103.

Moore Bob. (1986). *Refugees from nazi Germany in the Netherlands, 1933–1940.* Dordrecht/Boston/Lancaster: Nijhofff.

Morelli A. (1979). L'immigration et les prêtres italiens en Belgique. *Revue de l'Institut de Sociologie*, 239–249.

Morelli A. (1983). Le mouvement ouvrier belge et l'émigration italienne, du début du 20ième siècle à 1940. in *Gli italiani fuori d'Italia.* Milan: Franco Angeli.

Morelli A. (1985). *Fascisme et antifascisme dans l'immigration italienne en Belgique (1922–1940*). Brussels: ULB (unpublished dissertation)..

Neuville Jean. (1976). La condition ouvrière au XIXe siècle. Brussels: Vie Ouvrière.

Niklewski. (1930). *La réglementation de l'immigration des travailleurs polonais en France.* Nancy: Grondville.

Noiriel G. (1984). *Longwy: Immigrés et prolétaires 1880–1980.* Paris: Presses universitaires de France.

Noiriel Gérard (1986). *Les ouvriers dans la société française, XIXe–XXe siécles.* Paris: Seuil.

Noiriel Gerard (1988). *Le creuset français. Histoire de l'immigration XIX–XX siècles.* Paris: Seuil.

Noiriel Gérard (1988b). Du "patronage" au "paternalism": la restructuration des formes de domination de la main-d'oeuvre ouvrière dans l'industrie métallurgique française. *Le mouvement social, 144*, 17–35.

Noiriel Gérard (1991). *La Tyrannie du National. Le droit d'asile en Europe 1793–1993.* Paris: Calmann-Lévy.

Nouschi André (1984). Esquisse d'une histoire de l'immigration maghrébine. In Morsy Magali (Ed.), *Les Nord-Africains en France* (pp.39–49). Paris: Seuil.

Olshausen. (1904). *Die Fürsorge für Ausländer in Deutschland* (Vol. Schriften des Deutsche Verein für Armenzorg und Wohlfahrt). Leipzig: Duncker und Humboldt.

Ostuni M.R. (1973). Momenti dela "Constrastata vita" del Commissariato Generale dell'Emigrazione (1901–1927). *Gli Italiani fuori d'Italia.* Milan: Franco Angeli, 101–118.

Pabst Klaus (1964). Eupen-Malmedy in den belgische Regierungs- und Parteienpolitik, 1914–1940. *Zeitschrift des Aachener Geschichtsvereins*, 76, 206–315.

Payne Howard C. (1966). *Police State of Bonaparte 1851–1860.* Seattle: University Press Washington.

Philonenko M. (1937). Expulsion des Heimatlos, jurisprudence et pratique administrative. *Journal des droit international*, LXIV, 699–707.

Piore M. (1979). *Birds of Passage and Promised Lands: Long-Distance Migrants and industrial Societies.* Cambridge (Mass.): Cambridge University Press.

Ponty Janine. (1988). *Polonais méconnus. Histoire des travailleurs immigrés en France dans l entre-deux-guerres.* Paris: Publications de la Sorbonne.

Porter B. (1979). *The Refugee Question in Mid-Victorian Politics.* Cambridge: Cambridge University Press.

Raeff Marc. (1990). *Russia Abroad. A Cultural History of the Russian Emigration, 1919–1939.* New York-Oxford: Oxford University Press.

Reiter Herbert. (1992). *Politisches Asyl im 19 Jahrhundert.* Berlin: Duncker und Humbolt.

Ronin V. (1993). *Antwerpen en zijn "Russen". Onderdanen van de tsaar, 1814–1914.* Ghent: Stichting Mens en Kultuur.

Ronin V.(1992). Russen in België 1815–1861. In Waegemans E. (Ed.) *Het land van de blauwe vogel. Russen in België.* (pp. 23–61). Antwerp: Dedalus.

Sabel Charles. (1982). *Work and Politics: The Division of Labor in Industry.* Cambridge: Cambridge University Press.

Saint-Ferreol A. (1870). *Les proscrits français en Belgique, ou la Belgique contemporaine vue à travers l'exil.* (2 Vol.) Brussels: Muquardt.

Schepens L. (1973). Van Vlaskuster tot Franschman. Bijdrage tot de geschiedenis van de West-Vlaamse plattelandsbevolking in de negentiende eeuw. Brugge: Provinciebestuur West-Vlaanderen.

Schreiber J-Ph. (1995). *Politique et religion: Le Consistoire central israélite de Belgique ou XIXe siècle.* Brussels: Editions de l'ULB.

Schreiber J.-Ph. (1996). *L'immigration juive en Belgique du moyen age à la première guerre mondiale.* Brussels: Editions de l'ULB.

Soignie J. (1858). *Des Belges et des étrangers en deux parties. Distinction des Belges et des étrangers ou des moyens d'obtenir, de perdre et de recouvrer la qualité de Belge. Exposé analytique du droit des étrangers en Belgique.* Liège: Verhoven.

Soignie J. (1873). *Traité de la nationalité des individus d'après la loi belge.* Mons: Manceau.

Steinert Johannes-Dieter (1995). *Migration und Politik: Westdeutschland-Europa-Übersee 1945–1961.* Osnabrück: Secolo Verlag.

Stengers Jean (1976). Emigration et immigration en Belgique au XIX et au XXe siècles. *Koninklijke Academie voor overzeese wetenschappen. Klasse voor morele en politieke wetenschappen, XLVI.*

Stengers Jean (1992). L'immigration de 1830 à 1914: données chiffrées. In Morelli A. (Ed.), *Histoire des étrangers et de l'immigration en Belgique* (pp. 91–104). Brussels: EVO.

Stora Benjamin. (1985). Avant la deuxième génération: le militantisme algérien en France (1926–1954). *Revue Européenne des Migrations Internationales, 1, 2,* 69–93.

Strikwerda Carl. (1990). Corporatism and the Lower Middle Classes: Interwar Belgium. In Koshar Rudy (Ed.), *Splintered classes, politics and the lower middle class in interwar Europe* (pp. 211–239). New York/London: Holmes and Meier.

Strikwerda Carl. (1991). Interest-group politics and the international economy: mass politics and big business corporations in the Liège coal basin, 1870–1914. *Journal of Social History, XXV, 2,* 277–307.

Strikwerda Carl (1989). France and the Belgian Immigration of the Nineteenth Century. In Guerin-Gonzales C and Strikwerda C (Ed.), *The Politics of Immigrant Workers* (pp. 101–132). New York: Holmes and Meier.

Swierenga Robert P. (1993). The Delayed Transition from Folk to Labor Migration, the Netherlands 1880–1920. *International Migration Review*, 406–424.

Van Damme D. (1990). Onderstandswoonst, sedentarisering en stad-platteland-tegenstellingen. Evolutie en betekenis van de wetgeving op de onderstandswoonst in België (einde achttiende tot einde negentiende eeuw). *BTNG, XXI, 1–2*, 483–534.

Vandersteene L en Schiepers P. (1994–1995). Natievorming, nationalisme en vreemdelingen. Beeldvorming rond vreemdelingen en Belgen in de Kamerdiscussie over de eerste Belgische vreemdelingenwet. *BTNG*, XXV, 1–2, 31–78.

Vandervelde E. (1903). *L'exode rural et le retour aux champs*. Paris: Alcan.

Van Doorslaer Rudy (1996). *Kinderen van het getto. Joodse revolutionairen in België (1925–1940)*. Antwerp: Hadewijch.

Van Mighem U. (1882). *Notice sur la police des étrangers pour la rapport des droits et des devoirs des administrations communales et des mesures préventives et coercitives dont les étrangers peuvent être l'objet en Belgique*. Brussels: Vandenbrouck.

Vanhaute Eric (1994). De meest moordende van alle industrieën. De huisnijverheid in België omstreeks 1900. *Tijdschrift voor sociale geschiedenis*, XX, 4, pp.461–483.

Vanhaute Eric (1993). *Heiboeren. Arbeid, inkomen en bevolking in de Antwerpse Kempen*. Brussels: VUB Press.

Van Molle L. (1990). *Ieder voor Allen. De Belgische Boerenbond*. Louvain: Universitaire Pers.

Vanthemse Guy (1978). De val van de regering Poullet-Vandervelde, een "samenzwering van bankiers"? *BTNG*, 165–211.

Vanthemse Guy (1982). De mislukking van de vernieuwde economische politiek in België voor WO II: de OREC van 1935 tot 1938. *BTNG, 2–3*, 339–389.

Vanthemse Guy (1985). De oorsprong van de werkloosheidsverzekering in België: vakbondskassen en gemeentelijke fondsen (1890–1914). *Tijdschrift voor Sociale Geschiedenis*, XI, 130–164.

Vanthemse Guy (1987). De economische actie van de Belgische Staat tijdens de crisis van de jaren 1930. *Res Publica*, XXIX, 2, 127–151.

Vanthemse G. (1988–1989). De fysionomie van de werkloosheid in België tijdens de jaren 30. *BTNG*, XIX, 3–4, 269–344 and XX, 1–2, 1–106.

Vanthemse Guy (1989). *De werkloosheid in België 1929–1940*. Antwerp: EPO.

Van Velthoven Harry (1988). De parlementaire positie van de christen-democratie 1894–1914. *Arbeid in veelvoud. Een huldeboek aangeboden aan Prof. J. Craeybeckx en E. Scholliers* (pp.225–231). Brussels: VUB Press.

Verbruggen P. (1995). Le Mouvement mutualiste en Belgique. In Dreyfus H. and Gibau B.(Ed.) *Mutualité de tous les pays. Un passé riche d'avenir* (pp.71–85). Paris: Mutualité Française.

Verhelst J. (1977). *Het archief in Hongarije en de archieven over de Hongaars-Belgische betrekkingen*. Brussels: Algemeen Rijksarchief.

Vints Luc (1989). *P.J. Broekx en de christelijke arbeidersbeweging in Limburg, 1881–1968*. Louvain: Universitaire Pers.

Volkmann Hans-Erich (1966). *Die Russische Emigration in Deutschland, 1919–1929*. Würzburg: Holzner.

Wertheimer Jack (1987). *Unwelcome Strangers. East European Jews in Imperial Germay.* New York: Oxford University Press.

Witte Els, Craeybeckx Jan en Meyen Alain (1990). *Politieke Geschiedenis van België van 1830 tot heden.* Brussels:VUB Press.

Wouters Hubert (1963). *Documenten betreffende de geschiedenis van de Arbeidersbeweging (1831–53)* (3 Vol.). Louvain-Paris: Nauwelaerts.

Zaniewski R. (1942). *L'influence du milieu physique en éducation. Enquête socio-pédagogique sur les écoliers polonais émigrés en Belgique.* Louvain: KUL (unpublished dissertation)

Zolberg Artistide. (1974). The Making of Flemings and Walloons: Belgium 1830–1914. *Journal of Interdisciplinary History, 5,* 179–235.

Zolberg Artistide. (1978). Belgium. In Grew Raymond (Ed.), *Crises of Political Development in Europe and the United States* (pp. 99–138). Princeton: Princeton University Press.

Zolberg A. (1981). International Migrations in Political Perspective. In Kritz M.M., C.B. Keeley and S.M. Tomasi (Ed.), *Global Trends in Migration: Theory and Research on International Population Movements* (pp. 3–27). New York: Center for Migration Studies.

Zolberg A. (1990). Reforming the Back Door: The Immigration Reform and Control act of 1986 in Historical Perspective. In Yans-McLaughlin (Ed.), *Immigration Reconsidered. History, Sociology and Politics* (pp. 315–339). New York: Oxford University Press.

List of Abbreviations

AAB	Archive Archbishopric
AAD	Archive Aliens' Department
AAG	Archivum Archidiecezja Gnieznienska
AAN	Archiwum Akt Nowych
ABL	Archive Bishopric Liège
ACC	Association Charbonnière du Centre
ACCA	Association Charbonnière de la Campine
ACCBS	Association Charbonnière de Charleroi et de la Basse Sambre
ACL	Association Charbonnière de Liège
ACV	Algemeen Christelijk Vakverbond (=CSC)
ADB	Antwerpse Diamantbewerkersbond
AEL	Archives de l'Etat à Liège
AESH	Archives de l'Etat à Saint Hubert
AFAB	Archive Foreign Affairs Belgium
AFAF	Archive Foreign Affairs France
AFAG	Archive Foreign Affairs Germany
AFAP	Archive Foreign Affairs Poland
AHCM	Association Houillière du Couchant de Mons.
AILO	Archive International Labor Organization
ALVB	Archive Liberaal Vakverbond België
AML	Archive Ministry of Labor
AMSAB	Archive and Museum of the Socialist Labor Movement
AMSAC	Archive Czechoslovakian Ministry of Social Affairs
ANMC	Archief Nationale Mijnwerkerscentrale
ANMI	Archives Nationales, Ministère de l'Intérieur (F7)
AP	Archiwum Panstwowe

APCB	Archive Belgian Communist Party (Microfilms Institute Marxism-Leninism Moscow)
ARA	Algemeen Rijksarchief, Brussels
ARC	Archive Red Cross
ARDH	Algemeen Rijksarchief, The Hague
ARMA	Algemeen Rijksarchief, Brussels Administration of the Mining Industry
ARMJ	Algemeen Rijksarchief, Brussels Ministry of Justice, Aliens' Department, General Files
AUNO	Archive of the United Nations Organization, Geneva
BdL	Archive Ecomusée, Bois du Luc
BS	*Belgisch Staatsblad*
BTFG	*Belgisch Tijdschrift voor Filologie en Geschiedenis*
BTNG	*Belgisch Tijdschrift voor Nieuwste Geschiedenis*
BWP	Belgische Werklieden Partij (=POB)
CAAVAA	Comité d'aide et d'assistance aux victimes de l'Antisémitisme en Allemagne
CCI	Comité Central Industriel
CGE	Commissariato Generale dell'Emigrazione
CMB	Socialist Union of Metal workers of Belgium
CMBe	Socialist Miners'Union of Belgium
CMBo	Socialist Miners'Union of the Borinage
CNMM	Commission nationale mixte des mines
CS	Commission Syndicale
CSC	Confédération des Syndicats Chrétiens
FEDECHAR	Fédération des Associations Charbonnières de Belgique
HstAD	Hauptstaatsarchiv, Düsseldorf
HNA	Hungarian National Archives, Budapest
IEV	Institute Emile Vandervelde, Brussels
ILO	International Labor Organization, Geneva
ISJ	Institute for the Study of Belgian Jewry, Brussels
JDC	Jewish Joint Distribution Committee, New York
KADOC	Katholiek Archief en Documentatiecentrum, Leuven
KCZZ	Komisja Centralna Związkow Zawodowych
KS	Federation of the Mining Industry of Limburg
KUL	Katholieke Universiteit Leuven
PCB	Parti Communiste Belge
PHK	*Parlementaire Handelingen Kamer*
PHS	*Parlementaire Handelingen Senaat*
PBK	*Parlementaire Bescheiden Kamer*
PBS	*Parlementaire Bescheiden Senaat*
PHVA	*Parlementaire Vragen en Antwoorden*
POB	Parti Ouvrier Belge

PS	*Le Progrès Social*
PUPP	Panstwowy Urzad Posrednictwo Pracy
RABW	Rijksarchief Beveren Waas
SGI	Société Générale d'Immigration
SK	Syndikale Kommissie (=CS)
UE	Urząd Emigracyjny
UEM	Université de l'Etat de Mons, Archive of the Mining Industry of the Borinage, Charbonnage d'Hensies-Pommeroeul
ULB	Université Libre de Bruxelles
VUB	Vrije Universiteit Brussel
YIVO	Yiddisher Visnshaftlekher Institut, New York

Glossary of Legal Terms

Dangerous aliens: see *expulser*

Domicilié: a legal status based on article 13 of the civil code, which permitted aliens to remain indefinitely in Belgium. These *domiciliés* were authorized by the king to establish their main residence in Belgium after a request on their own initiative.

Expulsion: an administrative decision. In the Belgian judicial practice "to expel" was expressed in three different ways: *expulser, renvoyer* and *refouler*.

Expulser: the expulsion of aliens with residency status, i.e. an expulsion by royal decree. Since aliens with residency status were to be expelled only in exceptional cases these aliens had to be dangerous to the public order (subversive and criminal aliens). To return after an *expulsion* was an offence (*délit*), i.e., *rupture de ban d'expulsion*.

Privileged aliens: a legal status created by the law of 31 March 1936 which exempted aliens from occupational restrictions through the system of work permits and peddlers' licenses.

Recent immigrants: tolerated aliens whose stay was totally dependent upon administrative discretion. The central authorities could arbitrarily expel them *(renvoyer)*. These aliens with a temporary residence permit had not yet acquired residency status. After the enactment of the law of 31 March 1936, recent immigrants were those resident aliens who had not yet obtained the status of privileged alien.

Resident aliens: Aliens with residency status whose expulsion was only possible by royal decree *(expulser)*. In the alien law of 1835/1897 there were no legal provisions concerning the granting of this status. The central authorities made the granting of residency status dependent upon formally approved domicile. This was contested by the judiciary in the Jones affair. The court decided that the alien law of 1835 did not qualify the type of domicile needed for residency status, and therefore, de facto domicile had to be taken into consideration. In administrative practice, however, residency status remained largely dependent upon formally approved domicile. From 1846 onwards, the administrative confirmation of this formally approved domicile was inscription in the population register. From 1933 onwards, such domicile was confirmed by the granting of an identity card. After the law of 31 March 1936 came into effect aliens also had to have the status of privileged alien.

Refouler: refusal of entry at the border.

Renvoyer: the expulsion of aliens with temporary residence. To return to Belgium, after a *renvoi* was not a criminally triable offence, but only a misdemeanor (*infraction/overtreding*) which could only be punished by an administrative sanction.

Rupture de ban d'expulsion, here referred to as *rupture de ban*: conviction by a court for returning to Belgium after departure because of an expulsion by royal decree. Only if an alien had been expelled by royal decree, was a return to the country considered an infraction of the law. Convicting an alien merely for disobeying an expulsion order was not possible. The prosecutor had to prove that the alien had left the country. No legal action could be taken against those expelled aliens who stayed in the country. A conviction for *rupture de ban* carried a prison sentence from fifteen days to six months.

Index